JOHN PRINCE
1796-1870

John Prince was a lawyer, farmer, military officer, politician, judge, and entrepreneur. Born at Hereford, England, in 1796, he emigrated to Upper Canada in 1833 because he was ashamed of his ne'er-do-well father. His interest in farming took him to Sandwich where he became involved in the many careers open to him.

An unhappy and volatile man, he was constantly at odds with himself, his family, and his associates. As colonel of the Third Essex Regiment, he was sometimes unpredictable in his actions and on one occasion, during the Upper Canada Rebellion, unjustifiably violent–ordering the summary execution of five prisoners after the Battle of Windsor.

As a politician, despite his haughty and melancholic nature and his erratic individualism, he held the loyalty of his constituents, representing Essex in the House of Assembly from 1836 to 1854 and the Western District in the Legislative Council from 1856 to 1860.

In 1860, after a lifetime spent in politics, farming, railroading and mining speculations, and canal schemes, he obtained a long-sought judgeship in the new District of Algoma. Leaving his wife and children behind, he went off to his 'New Siberia,' where he continued his restless struggle to escape 'the importunities of mankind,' and where his long, tragic life ended in 1870.

Entries from Prince's diary, excerpts from newspaper accounts, and letters give a vivid picture of the politics and life of his time. In his Introduction, R. Alan Douglas emphasizes the contribution made by the discovery of the diary to our perception of the people, places, and events of mid-nineteenth century North America.

(Ontario Series of the Champlain Society, 11)

R. ALAN DOUGLAS is curator of the Hiram Walker Historical Museum in Windsor, Ontario

John Prince (1796–1870). From a miniature, about 1830

Prince family

ONTARIO SERIES
XI

JOHN PRINCE
1796-1870

A Collection of Documents

Edited with an Introduction by
R. Alan Douglas

THE CHAMPLAIN SOCIETY
IN CO-OPERATION WITH
THE GOVERNMENT OF ONTARIO
UNIVERSITY OF TORONTO PRESS
TORONTO BUFFALO LONDON
1980

© *The Champlain Society 1980*

Reprinted in paperback 2015

ISBN 978-0-8020-2378-0 (cloth)

ISBN 978-1-4426-3127-4 (paper)

Canadian Cataloguing in Publication Data

Prince, John, 1796–1870.
  John Prince 1796–1870

(Publications of the Champlain Society : Ontario series ; 11 ISSN 0078-5091)
Bibliography: p.
Includes index.
ISBN 978-0-8020-2378-0 (bound)   ISBN 978-1-4426-3127-4 (pbk.)

1. Prince, John, 1796–1870. 2. Statesmen–Ontario–Biography. 3. Ontario–Politics and government–1791–1841 – Sources.* 4. Ontario – Politics and government – 1841–1867 – Sources.* I. Douglas, R. Alan. II. Title. III. Series: Champlain Society. Publications of the Champlain Society : Ontario series ; 11.

FC3071.1.P74A3   971.3'02'0924   C80-094303-1
F1058.P74A3

This volume has been prepared
and published in co-operation
with the Government of Ontario
and made possible through a
grant from the Ontario
Heritage Foundation,
Ministry of Culture and
Recreation

FOREWORD

JOHN PRINCE was undoubtedly one of the most colourful individuals to reside in Upper Canada during the half century that preceded Confederation. His eventful career as an attorney, politician, soldier, entrepreneur, and jurist caused him to become a legend in his own lifetime both in Essex County, where he resided at Sandwich from his arrival in 1833 until 1860, and in Sault Ste Marie where he spent the last ten years of his life as Judge of the Algoma District. As Colonel of the Third Essex Militia he participated, with characteristic flamboyance, in repelling Patriot raids from the United States following the Rebellion of 1837. A member of the Legislative Assembly from 1836 to 1854 and the Legislative Council from 1856 to 1860, he was constantly in the midst of the hurly-burly of Upper Canadian politics. In the legislature his independence and erratic individualism soon earned him the reputation of a political maverick. Business interests and entrepreneurial instincts attracted him to railway and banking ventures as early as the 1830s. Individualist and eccentric though he was, John Prince was still very much a man of his age.

In the documents which Alan Douglas has assembled for this volume, Prince emerges as a rather tragic figure perpetually at war with the world around him. Hitherto, relatively accessible sources such as Prince's correspondence with political figures and public officials, and newspaper editorials and reports of his speeches conveyed only a baffling impression of his erratic political gyrations, his dour outlook and, occasionally, his wit. The discovery of his diary in 1963, however, shed new light on the man and his struggle. The result is presented in detail for the first time in this volume. It is indeed fortunate that Prince was a faithful diarist throughout his career and that his personal and vivid reactions to many of the people, places, and events of mid-nineteenth century British North America have been preserved.

His extraordinary diary, encompassing a third of a century, was the generous gift of Mrs Alan C. Prince to the Hiram Walker Historical Museum in Windsor. To ensure the widest possible access to researchers, it was subsequently deposited in the Archives of Ontario and a microfiche copy will be made available at the Museum.

It is particularly appropriate that Alan Douglas, whose personal interest in Prince led to the discovery of the diary, should be the editor of this volume. On behalf of the Government and people of Ontario, I wish to thank Mr Douglas for the hours of research and effort he has spent to make the interesting and colourful life and times of John Prince better known.

The Ontario Series is produced through the co-operation of the Government of Ontario and the Champlain Society which has been publishing historical documentary studies for more than seventy years. The society selects and guides the editors of each volume, while the costs of preparation and publication are defrayed by the Government of Ontario and the Ontario Heritage Foundation. The volume editor's task is to assemble a selection of documents that will illuminate his subject as fully as possible and to write an introduction that will enable the reader to understand and appreciate the significance of the documents.

This volume, the eleventh in the series, is the first to be concerned with the career of an individual rather than with a specific subject, or the historical development of a region or community. In future, some volumes will continue to deal with regional themes while others will be devoted to specific subjects and individuals. Three volumes in preparation are concerned with the Rebellion of 1837, the Upper Ottawa Valley, and the Bank of Upper Canada.

Queen's Park　　　　　　　　　　　　　　　　　　　WILLIAM G. DAVIS
Toronto　　　　　　　　　　　　　　　　　　　　　　*Premier of Ontario*
17 March 1980

PREFACE

JOHN PRINCE was still, a century after his death in 1870, the enigmatic figure that he had been in life. The mythology that had grown up around his memory in southwestern Ontario identified him as the product of an illegal marriage between George IV and Maria Anne Fitzherbert. Prince, it was said, had been given a fortune and quietly exiled to Sandwich, where he acted the role of the prince that he really was by peremptorily shooting prisoners at the Battle of Windsor and by pursuing a violently erratic political career. So regally autocratic was the Prince of legend that, to get rid of him, his exasperated colleagues in public life eventually gave him a judgeship at Sault Ste Marie. The possibility that Prince's own secretiveness had encouraged such speculation, that the facts might be far more compelling than the fiction, was widely overlooked.

My interest in John Prince began in 1961, when William G. Ormsby, who was then instructing in a training course at the Public Archives of Canada, assigned to me the exercise of locating all the entries for Prince in the Archives' many finding aids. In 1962, a chance meeting in Detroit led to a friendship with the late J. Mercer Quarry, of Windsor, who subsequently recounted an anecdote of having, decades before, seen Alan Charles Prince, John Prince's great-grandson, reading what looked like old notebooks. A telephone call to Alan Prince's widow, Florence, then living in Detroit, confirmed the exciting possibility that much of John Prince's diary had survived the years and was in her possession. Her personal loan of several volumes to me (which led to a paper on the Battle of Windsor, read to the Ontario Historical Society in 1969) became a gift of all of them to the Hiram Walker Historical Museum, Windsor, in 1970.

Since Prince's diary carries much of the narrative burden of this biography, a brief physical description might be useful. Diary volumes survive for 1826 and 1832, and for 1836 through 1868 – that for 1836 beginning on 5 January, and the one for 1868 extending to 4 January 1869. The first three are small in format, and the entries are necessarily concise. Conversely, those for 1862 through 1866 are of nearly legal size, permitting much longer entries. The larger volumes originally consisted of month-by-month bundles of separate sheets, fastened at their upper left corners, and Prince filled them up somewhat like end-bound stenographers' notebooks. Difficulties occurred when the bundles were later assembled and bound by their long edges: first, every other page was made to appear inverted, and second, the order of the bundles was disturbed. July and August 1864 are missing altogether. Still, we are left with a run covering 12,723 days in the eventful life of a fascinating individual.

Lost diaries – particularly those that would have shed light on the move to Canada – and a lack of references in any of the surviving volumes to relatives on the paternal side, led to the suspicion that something was indeed amiss. Moreover, there was an apparent change in Prince's outlook some time between 1832 and 1836. The word 'lowspirited' entered his vocabulary during that interval, and it occurred hundreds of times thereafter.

Prince's English background had to be reconstructed by roundabout means. Diary references to the death of his mother ultimately proved to be the agency through which the context of his formative years was discovered. They suggested a search for obituary notices in the Hereford newspapers which, after several other approaches had failed, not only identified both his parents, but also located his boyhood home and revealed his father's occupation. Other allusions in the diary to English people and places were followed up, as were statements in Prince's autobiography, published in 1867 in William Notman and Fennings Taylor's *Portraits of British Americans*. Assessment records, law lists, parish registers, directories, maps, and newspapers found in record offices and libraries in Hereford, Gloucester, Cheltenham, and London all yielded useful material.

Selecting and editing documents to point up biographical values posed special problems. However absorbing a study of John Prince's inner world might be, it was decided at the outset that emphasis in a Champlain Society publication should be placed on his role in the public affairs of Canada. Although this criterion, together with space limitations, meant that a mass of material had to be set aside – less than three per cent of the diary is published here – much of a private nature seeped through nonetheless. It was considered that, because of their high biographical content, diary entries selected for publication should not be subjected to internal editing. Therefore they have been given in their entirety, except for marginal notes. (These notes, when retained, have been set off in double parentheses.) Correspondence has been more freely edited, and newspaper editorials and reports of speeches have been, in some cases, drastically abbreviated. An attempt has been made to identify the dozens of peripheral figures whose names appear in often cryptic, passing references, but, regrettably, only partial success can be claimed.

Although in general the sources of documents have been given in full, the following abbreviations have been adopted to avoid unnecessary and tiresome repetition:

For AO, read Archives of Ontario.
For CPD, read *Canada Parliamentary Debates* (Canadian Library Association Microfilming Project).
For MTCL, read Metropolitan Toronto Central Library.
For Nish, read Elizabeth Nish (ed.), *Debates of the Legislative Assembly of United Canada*.
For PAC, read Public Archives of Canada.

In the Introduction, documents published in this volume are cited, by number, in square brackets. Original spelling, punctuation, and capitalization have been retained throughout the Documents section. It will be understood, however, that in many cases the decision as to whether a given letter was intended as a capital, or was merely written large, was subjective and arbitrary.

To be consistent, all Latin phrases, no matter how simple, have been translated. However, a reading knowledge of French has been assumed.

It is a particular pleasure for a museologist, unaccustomed to the techniques and lacking the expertise of the historian, to acknowledge the help of all those who assisted with this project. A grant in 1974 from the Canada Council (now the Social Sciences and Humanities Research Council of Canada) enabled me to journey to England, where three weeks' work provided a far better understanding of John Prince than would have been possible otherwise. Archival repositories whose staffs were always helpful included the Public Archives of Canada and the Archives of Ontario, and in England, the County Record Office, Gloucester, the Record Office, Hereford, and the Public Record Office and Somerset House, both in London. Canadian public libraries, among them those at Hamilton, Sault Ste Marie, Toronto, and Windsor, provided much valuable assistance. Other help came from the university and law libraries of Toronto and Windsor. In England, the Central Library, Cheltenham, the Gloucester City Library, the Hereford Library, the library of Gray's Inn, London, and the Westminster City Libraries all made important contributions. The files of the Dictionary of Canadian Biography also provided needed information about a number of obscure figures.

Those whose personal interest was always encouraging were nearly all unknown to each other. The list includes, but is by no means confined to, David J. Brock, Dennis Carter-Edwards, T.E. Durham, Robert M. Fuller, Francis and Lois MacNamara, and Gladys McNeice. Daphne Hubbard, in the Record Office, Hereford, and Nancy Pringle, local history librarian at Cheltenham, each went well beyond the call of duty to see that I received the help I needed, even after my return to Canada. The same William G. Ormsby who first interested me in John Prince in 1961 conceived the idea for this volume and devoted many hours to correcting and suggesting revisions to the manuscript. To these and to many others – among them the Prince family, whose generosity, understanding, and interest were of fundamental importance – I am deeply grateful.

Finally, it should be added that despite the assistance acknowledged above, and although every effort has been made to avoid overstatement, to label speculation as such, and to base assertions of fact on demonstrable proof, I concede the inevitability of error. All inaccuracies are mine alone.

R. ALAN DOUGLAS

CONTENTS

Foreword to the Ontario Series
   by the Honourable William G. Davis,
   Premier of Ontario vii

Preface ix

Introduction xix

Documents 3

Bibliography 209

Index 215

ILLUSTRATIONS

Frontispiece
John Prince (1796–1870). From a miniature, about 1830
Between pages xvi–xvii
Jersey Villa, Prince's residence in Cheltenham, Gloucestershire, 1826–33
The Park Farm buildings. Pencil drawing in the Prince Family Papers
The Park Farm homestead, *ca* 1835, photographed about 1910; demolished 1966
'Rough View of Sandwich, W.D., U.C. Taken from Spring Wells Michigan Territory, U.S. August 13th 1833.' Pencil drawing attributed to W.R. Wood
Sketch map of Sandwich, 1835, by John A. Wilkinson
Niagara and Detroit Rivers Railroad stock certificate
With these pistols Prince and W.R. Wood fought the duel recorded in Prince's diary on 11 February 1839
Prince's diary account of the Battle of Windsor, 4 December 1838
The Essex Peninsula in Prince's day. Detail from a map attributed to Sir Richard Bonnycastle, *ca* 1845–47
Sault Ste Marie in 1855
John Prince, *ca* 1866 [Photo: William Notman. McCord Museum, Montreal]
Belle Vue Lodge, Prince's residence at Sault Ste Marie, 1861–70
Lord Brougham, Prince's assailant in the House of Lords in 1839. Engraving, with Prince's vindictive comments added following the subject's death in 1868

Jersey Villa, Prince's residence in Cheltenham, Gloucestershire, 1826–33

ABOVE 'Rough View of Sandwich, W.D., U.C.
Taken from Spring Wells Michigan Territory, U.S. August 13th 1833.'
Pencil drawing attributed to W.R. Wood.
Prince's brewery is the large building at the left, near the windmill.

Hiram Walker Historical Museum

OPPOSITE TOP The Park Farm buildings.
Pencil drawing in the Prince Family Papers

Hiram Walker Historical Museum / Archives of Ontario

OPPOSITE The Park Farm Homestead, *ca* 1835,
photographed about 1910; demolished 1966

Hiram Walker Historical Museum

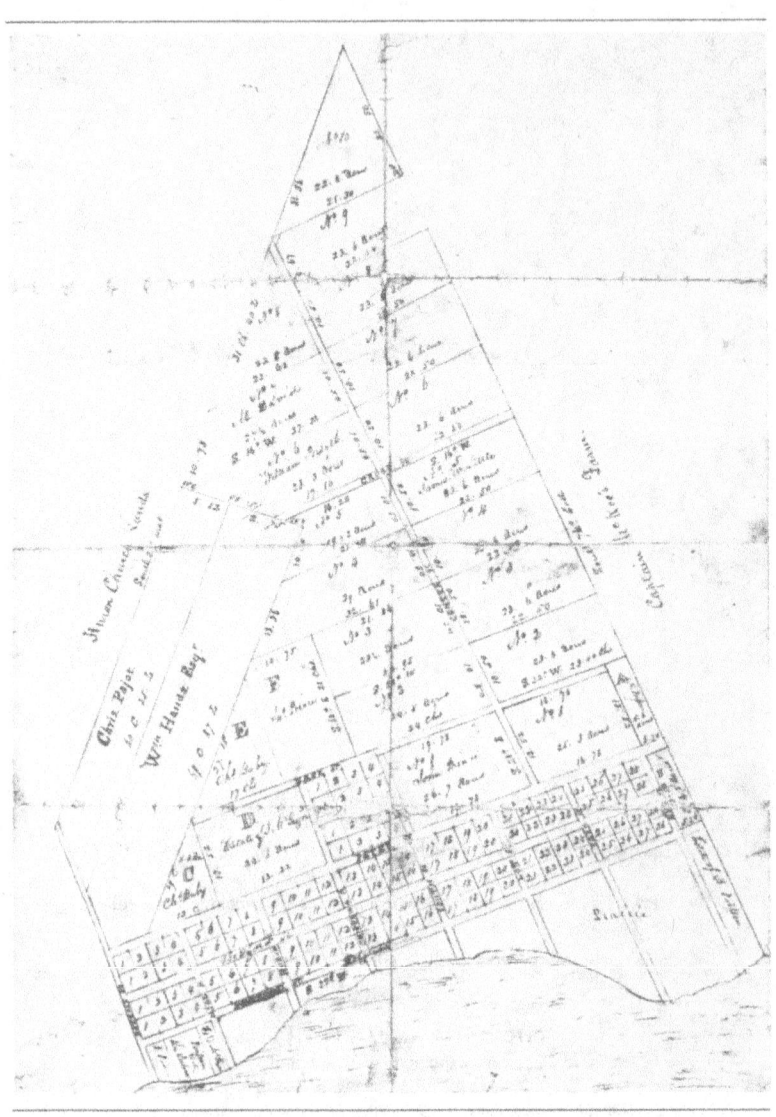

Sketch map of Sandwich, 1835, by John A. Wilkinson.
At this time Prince was acquiring the lots that became The Park Farm,
ultimately encompassing about 200 acres in the rear of the town.
The house and farm buildings were on Park Lot 2,
left of Centre Street (present Prince Road).

Hiram Walker Historical Museum / Archives of Ontario

Niagara and Detroit Rivers Railroad stock certificate

Jasperson Family Papers,
Hiram Walker Historical Museum / Archives of Ontario

With these pistols
Prince and W.R. Wood fought the duel
recorded in Prince's diary on 11 February 1839.
See document 91.

Pistols: Prince family.
Diary: Hiram Walker Historical Museum /
Archives of Ontario

OPPOSITE Prince's diary account of
the Battle of Windsor, 4 December 1838.
See Document 78.

Hiram Walker Historical Museum / Archives of Ontario

The Essex Peninsula in Prince's day.
Detail from a map attributed to Sir Richard Bonnycastle, *ca* 1845-47

Photostat in Hiram Walker Historical Museum

SAUT de Ste MARIE
CANADA WEST

Sault Ste Marie in 1855.
Notes added later include one locating Prince on Lot 4,
First Concession, on the point of land
opposite a group of islands

Public Archives of Canada

John Prince, ca 1866

Photo: William Notman. McCord Museum, Montreal

Belle Vue Lodge,
Prince's residence at Sault Ste Marie, 1861–70

Hiram Walker Historical Museum

Lord Brougham,
Prince's assailant in the House of Lords in 1839.
Engraving with Prince's vindictive comments added
following the subject's death in 1868

Fort Malden National Historic Park

JOHN PRINCE
1796–1870

INTRODUCTION

JOHN PRINCE was born at Hereford, England, on 12 March 1796, the eldest son of Richard Prince, a grain dealer and miller at the Lugg Bridge Mills, about two miles northeast of the town. His father's love of turning a pound wherever it might be found had exposed the family to at least one bankruptcy by 1803. At the height of his career the resilient Richard was said to have been worth £140,000–150,000, but his taste for sharp practice and tax evasion led to frequent trouble. Another bankruptcy overtook him in 1815, and although he continued to operate the Lugg Bridge Mills he lost ownership of them. In 1818 Richard Prince was to be found piously serving as an overseer of the poor among the parishioners of Lugwardine – even while he was renting a property near the mills called Shelwich Court, which contained hidden rooms for the production of malt for sale to a select clientele, tax free.

Apparently using money inherited from his paternal grandfather, John Prince had commenced his study of the law in 1815. In 1821 he began to practise as an attorney at Westerham, in Kent, where in 1823 he was the senior partner of Thomas Holmes Bosworth. On 17 June of that year he was married, at St George's Bloomsbury, London, to Mary Ann Millington, and thereupon embarked on a new practice at Cheltenham, Gloucestershire. It appears that the ambitious young Prince selected Cheltenham because of the numbers of wealthy potential clients who at that time were moving there to take the waters at its celebrated mineral baths. At Cheltenham he became the junior partner of Joseph Cooper Straford, and there, on 18 April 1824, his first son, William Stratton, was born. It was also in 1824 that John Prince's father pleaded guilty to making malt illegally and was fined £1,000.

On 4 August 1825, the firm of Straford and Prince defended William Fitzhardinge Berkeley in an assault case; this was the first known instance of Prince's acting for that important Whig family.

John Prince flourished at Cheltenham, and so did his family. On 17 November 1825, a second son, Albert, was born. By 1826 Prince had moved out of the earlier rented space in Cambray and into new offices at No. 5, The Colonnade. The family residence was now Jersey Villa, in Hewlett Road, commanding a splendid view of Cleeve Hill northeast of Cheltenham.

On 17 February 1826, at Westminster, another trial of Richard Prince led to an even larger fine, more than £1,100, and John borrowed £1,200 to pay the fine on his father's behalf. His own financial position was such that within the month he had paid off £900 of the principal plus all the interest to date, and he expected to discharge the balance from the proceeds of the harvest at Jersey Villa.

It would seem that the potential threat to the law firm's respectability was too great, however, and by the end of March the partnership of Straford and Prince was no more. Clearly it would not do for Prince's clients to know too much about his father. When, in September, Richard turned up in Cheltenham, after returning from a sojourn in France, John discreetly put him up at the Plough Inn, apparently to prevent his being seen around Jersey Villa.

Later that fall Prince moved to offices in Vincent House, opposite his former quarters in The Colonnade, where it seems that his energies found an outlet in the overzealous pursuit of any who were so unwise as to oppose the interests of his clients. In 1828 he was fined for the malicious prosecution of a bankrupt.

Arabella Delancy, Prince's only daughter, was born on 9 April 1829, and by that time Prince felt the need for an estate, not only for his growing family (a third son, Charles, had been born 10 July 1827), but also appropriate to the station of one of Cheltenham's most-sought-after lawyers, the founder of the firm of Prince and Kell. He was strongly attracted to an estate called Westwood, about four miles northeast of Jersey Villa, which he added to his holdings in 1830.

In London meanwhile, an insolvent debtor named Prince, then technically in the custody of the Fleet Prison, had figured in a tavern brawl, over whether five or seven brandies and water had been consumed.[1]

It was with the intention of relinquishing his solicitorship and becoming a barrister that John Prince joined Gray's Inn on 7 November 1831, although it appears that he was not actually called to the bar. He headed the firm of Prince, Kell and Howard in 1832, and in the election of that year he identified himself with the Whig interest by actively canvassing on behalf of two candidates, Tracey in Tewkesbury and Berkeley in Cheltenham.

On 19 February 1833, Richard Prince was convicted of illegally operating a soap factory in Bethnal Green, London; his stock was seized and a mitigated fine of £125 was levied, which he could not, and his exasperated son evidently would not, pay. Richard was therefore committed to the House of Correction, Coldbath Fields.

1 The hearing took place on 17 June 1829, Prince's sixth wedding anniversary. While the prisoner's first name was not reported in the London *Times* story published the next day, an allusion to events of 1829 in John Prince's diary of 18 June 1864 leaves little doubt that the subject was in fact his father.

John Prince might well have concluded that his father posed a threat both to his reputation and to his finances. Perceiving himself as the white sheep of the family, he had tried to return his father to the fold, but he had failed. Now he decided to emigrate, and quite possibly his decision reflected a conscious, or unconscious, desire to escape from the perpetual embarrassment of his father.

John Prince passionately loved hunting, and early in 1833 the famous hunter Dr William ('Tiger') Dunlop, who had contributed stories of Canada to *Blackwood's Magazine*, and who knew at first hand the comparative joys of the chase in India and in Canada, was in London and full of tales that Prince wanted to hear.[2] Upper Canada it would be, where a man of capital could start over, where game was plentiful, and where, at a suitable distance, one could still be British.

After a last late-spring vacation visit to Tor Bay on the Channel coast, Prince and his family departed hastily for Canada. He left a cousin, Thomas Webb, in charge of his substantial resources, the fruits of just ten years' practice at Cheltenham that were in large part to maintain him in style for the rest of his life. Henry, a fourth son, was born on 29 August 1833, and on 5 September John Prince purchased property on the bank of the Detroit River just above the town of Sandwich, in the Western District of Upper Canada.

It is likely that Lieutenant Governor Sir John Colborne's policy of encouraging immigrants of substance to locate in areas where they would serve as bulwarks against American influence played a part in Prince's choice of Sandwich, then one of the remotest outposts of British civilization. Probably there was also a psychological factor. By abandoning his father, Prince had violated the gentleman's code of respectability. He was a man with a secret, and he began to exhibit severe behavioural symptoms that plagued him for the remainder of his days: deep, almost unrelieved gloom, self-blame, a chronic desire to avoid routine and to seek refuge through escape. There were frequent suicidal wishes, and occasional episodes when he found himself physically unable even to leave his room to face the world.

Almost immediately on his arrival in Sandwich, Prince inserted an anonymous advertisement in the newspaper, seeking to invest in the milling trade.[3] It was not easy for a gentleman of substance to remain in obscurity in the Western District, however. Late that November

---

[2] W.H. Graham, in *The Tiger of Canada West* (Toronto and Vancouver, 1962), pp. 116–18, places Dunlop in London and Edinburgh at this time, lending credibility to the undocumented assertion in Robina and Kathleen Macfarlane Lizars' *In the Days of the Canada Company* (Toronto, 1896), p. 235, that Prince met Dunlop in the London offices of the Canada Company.

[3] Patrick Shirreff, a visitor to Sandwich in October 1833, in *A Tour Through North America* (Edinburgh, 1835), p. 213, identifies the newspaper advertiser signing himself 'A.B.' as a recently arrived capitalist.

sufficient notice of his presence had been taken that he was named to the panel of magistrates for the Western District.

The major characteristics of John Prince's complex personality had emerged by the time of his father's ignominious death in debtors' prison on 1 January 1834. He had inherited the attractive and persuasive manner that had enabled his father to cajole his way through life, even at Coldbath Fields. John Prince was one to whom people naturally gravitated in time of trouble, but his contempt for his father became, on the one hand, scorn for those who turned to him for help, and on the other, disdain for those who did not. He was genuinely devout, but his gift of a splendid communion service and tablecloth to the English Church[4] at Sandwich in July 1834 could have been in some measure an atonement. He was not known thereafter for unusual generosity towards the church, or for freedom from bigotry, although in his lifetime he was on friendly terms with dozens of clergymen of various persuasions.

Prince was haughty and aloof, and yet he rapidly established himself as a leading citizen in the community of his choice. His extensive land holdings in the Western District, acquired for the most part in 1834 and 1835, included a number of park lots encompassing about 200 acres in the rear of the town, which he dubbed The Park Farm.[5] There he built a regency cottage with its back turned to the road and, by extension, to the world. For commercial purposes he built a wharf on his lot near the foot of Detroit Street where, instead of the mill he had planned, he established a brewery [3]. In April 1835 he acquired an interest in a ferry connecting Detroit with the Canadian shore above Sandwich, near a hamlet that was shortly to become Windsor. The Princes – John, Mary Ann, William, Albert, Charles, Arabella, Henry, and little George, born on 22 September that year – and their long-time servants, William Stevens and his wife Susan, had found a new Westwood.

Still, it was obvious to those around him that the morose John Prince was not like other men. A dispute over a case involving a pair of accused juvenile horse thieves, Russell and Orin Stanborough, led to an exchange of published insults between Magistrate Prince and Judge Charles Eliot [1–4], with appropriate classical quotations. Prince's personal attack on Eliot had a precedent in the malicious prosecution of which he had been convicted in 1828, and his later life offered examples of similar excess. Eliot's assessment of his opponent as a man whose

---

4 St John's, Sandwich, was not formally named until some years later. From its inception it was simply called the English Church to distinguish it from the French Church (Assumption Church).

5 The name Park Farm occurs frequently in England, and so cannot with certainty be said to allude to the park lots at Sandwich. The property is not known to have taken its name from any previous owner named Park.

generous feelings were minimal – Prince's declarations to the contrary – was remarkably accurate.

The death of the infant George Prince on 17 February 1836 was one of a series of unhappy events in his father's life that was closely followed by a change in direction. This time Prince's new course took him into politics. In May he attended meetings in Sandwich where he supported Lieutenant Governor Sir Francis Bond Head in his clash with the Upper Canadian Reformers. He had met Head in Toronto, and shared his view that responsible government was impossible in a colony. The Executive Council's function could only be to advise the lieutenant governor. The Council could not be made responsible for his actions, because the ultimate authority for governing Upper Canada rested with the British government, and the lieutenant governor was required to act on instructions received from London.

It was not long before Prince found himself standing in the election of 1836 [5]. Heading the poll with 42% of the vote [6–11], he must have regarded his first election victory, and the humiliating defeat of one of his opponents in particular, Charles Eliot, with double satisfaction.

Prince's apparent longing for the life of a recluse was contradicted by his entrepreneurial spirit. Transportation links with the outside world were essential to prosperity, and Prince soon became involved in a project for a railroad to take the products of the Western District to eastern markets, one that would also interest Americans by providing a shortcut between Michigan and New York. The Niagara and Detroit Rivers Rail Road Company was incorporated on 20 April 1836. When the company met at the courthouse in Sandwich on 1 June, Prince took the chair, and by September he had become its president [12].

For the rest of his life Prince saw leadership as a burden, thrust on his unwilling shoulders by those who crowded around him. It was such an onerous duty that on 16 October he confided to his diary: 'House full. Positively distracted with company. Worried to death. I occasionally wish for death.'

John Prince's political career was erratic. Even before the new parliament met, he was involved in the choosing of the speaker [13, 14]. When the session began he introduced legislation [15] and participated actively in the debates as a government supporter [15, 16]. His support, however, was tempered by an often-repeated assertion that English attorneys deserved special consideration [17]. His inherent respect for both law and religion was revealed by his attitude towards the long-standing clergy reserves question. Education might well merit support from a part of the proceeds from the sale of the reserves, he thought, but they had been created to support the Protestant clergy, and that was how they would have to remain [18–21]. Although he did identify himself as a Reformer on 24 November 1836, his words were enigmatically dropped into a speech supporting a handsome salary increase for the attorney general. Still, it would not be accurate to say that his only consistency was inconsistency; throughout his parliamentary career he sought to advance local and personal interests.

The philosophy that what was right for John Prince was right was clearly evident in 1837, the year of his most effective political contribution. Having succeeded early in January in forming a shaky alliance between his Niagara and Detroit Rivers railroad and the London and Gore line, he supported the Great Western's plan to connect Hamilton with the new settlement of Port Sarnia. In exchange for concessions he withdrew his objection to a grant of £200,000 to finance the railway [22, 26], and he continued to promote his own line [37, 39].

Banking was another of the subjects of concern to John Prince during that busy year [23–25]. A Western District bank, he thought, would stimulate economic activity in his own locality, and at the provincial level a British American bank would end the monopoly of the Bank of Upper Canada. When the 'Panic of 1837' caused a run on the banks, he stood, unsuccessfully, with Head and a few Tories, in opposing the banks' suspension of specie payments [42]. Provision for 'alien' (i.e., American) settlers to hold land, albeit with restrictions [33, 40, 42], was another need felt particularly close to the border in the Western District. A bridge [36] and a lighthouse at the mouth of the Thames, a ferry to Detroit from Prince's wharf, and a game bill [41] all involved some degree of Prince's personal interest as well.

He was also engaged in disputes with Solicitor General Hagerman over English lawyers' privileges in Upper Canada [17, 27–29]. In a disorderly debate on the question of the rectories which Sir John Colborne, just before his recall, had established to benefit Anglican parishes, Prince declared that Hagerman had displayed 'a most unparalleled stock of assurance and most unwarrantable IMPUDENCE' [31–32]. More charitably, he supported the registrar of the Court of Chancery [30], who had refused to answer questions of a committee of the House, on the ground that doing so would usurp the privilege of the head of government. He even shook hands, on Good Friday, with his old antagonist Charles Eliot. Soon Eliot resigned the chairmanship of the Western District Court of Quarter Sessions, and Prince replaced him [38]. His interest in parliamentary reform was demonstrated when he introduced and carried a bill to terminate the practice of dissolving the Legislature and holding a new election on the death of the sovereign [15, 34, 35].

The well-read Prince was already familiar with the writings of Frederick Marryat when that author, then touring America, visited the Detroit frontier in the summer of 1837. The two seem not to have impressed each other [43], however, and Marryat failed even to mention Prince when his travels were published.

At The Park Farm that August Prince conferred with the Indian chief Thomas Splitlog and others concerning the sale of the Huron Reserve, between Sandwich and Amherstburg, which was subsequently opened to settlement [44] as Anderdon Township. This was the first Indian surrender to which Prince was a party; there would be others, late in his career.

In a speech on 9 January Prince had characterized William Lyon Mackenzie as an enemy to the province and its government, concealed under the specious and captivating name of patriotism. During the spring and summer Mackenzie became the leader of an increasingly radical group bent on rebellion, from which the more moderate Reformers uneasily withdrew. Deteriorating economic conditions accentuated the difficulties of farmers and labourers, and increased the number of those willing to follow Mackenzie in open revolt. In December the rebellion became a reality, and the Detroit frontier, which had been uneasy since June [39], was alerted to a possible invasion by Americans who sympathized with Mackenzie and his followers [45-49].

As a lieutenant colonel of militia, under the command of Colonel William Elliott, Prince was present early in 1838 at the schooner *Anne* incident [50, 53, 54], and the battles of Fighting Island [57, 58] and Pelee Island [59, 60]. As a spokesman for the magistrates of the Western District, he was also in communication with the American authorities [51, 52, 55, 56] in an effort to have them enforce the neutrality laws. The *Anne* affair was a bungled attempt by a handful of idealists to lob a few shots into Amherstburg and Fort Malden, and thus cause embarrassment to the government and the garrison. This was expected somehow to lead to republicanism in Upper Canada. Instead, the Patriots succeeded in running their commandeered schooner aground. The Battle of Fighting Island appears to have been part of a co-ordinated attack on the western frontier, involving a simultaneous landing on Pelee Island. The cause suffered a setback, however, when word of the Patriots' triumphant occupation of Pelee failed to reach the mainland for a week. The Battle of Pelee Island was one more in the Patriots' string of dreary defeats.

Prince's ability to take either side of an issue, as suited the interests of his constituents, was evident in the weeks following his fortuitous capture of the Patriots Sutherland and Spencer, whom he encountered alone, afoot, and nearly unarmed, on the ice at the mouth of the Detroit

River [61, 62]. During the trials of various schooner *Anne* prisoners [63, 64], Prince became exercised over the lack of compensation for witnesses who, although supporters of the prisoners, were his constituents nonetheless [65, 66]. No doubt such gestures contributed to his enormous popularity among the sons of Essex, who besieged him so energetically at his home that early in May 1838 he published a notice requiring those seeking his advice to do so by letter.

The pressure on Prince was prodigious. The commencement of his railroad [67] was soon followed by the news that he had been gazetted colonel of the Third Essex Militia. On 20 May his son Septimus Rudyerd was born, and preparations were under way for the proceedings against the Pelee Island prisoners [68]. A dispute over whether they could be tried locally, as common criminals, or whether they must be treated as prisoners of war [69, 70], coincided with the illness and near death of his dear Mary Ann. Even during her delirium Prince was calling up the men of the townships of Colchester, Gosfield, and Mersea for service in the Third Essex. The unilateral action of the magistrates in closing the border to small craft [71] was only partially effective in relieving Patriot pressure, and an attack on Sandwich was still expected every night.[6]

Prince was formally admitted that August to the practice of law in Upper Canada [72, 73]. (Actually he was made a barrister by act of Parliament, rather than by the Law Society.) A scant two weeks later a newspaper notice appeared, expressing his professional relationship with the inhabitants of the Western District more pointedly than heretofore: he would give no more free legal advice.

In a world that seemed to be made up entirely of clients, constituents, and Patriots, peace of mind was not easily come by. On 28 October he called out his regiment, but even as late as 15 November he was complaining that the response remained poor. The threats of attack and the all-night patrols persisted [74, 75], and Prince's overexertion was noted in his friend Henry Rudyerd's diary. On 28 November he was left in command at Sandwich [76]. Exhausted and dosing himself with quinine, on 1 December he reported once again to the authorities at Detroit [77] in an attempt to head off an attack.

The most fateful episode of John Prince's long life occurred on the morning of Tuesday, 4 December 1838 [78]. His orders to execute five prisoners taken at Windsor were a defiant response to American officials, whose attempts to stop Patriot activity had been ineffective, and also to the Patriots themselves, whose antimonarchical cause and piratical methods he detested. His action was also aimed at the judicial

---

6 In time of trouble local convenience tends to override the diplomatic niceties on the Detroit frontier. Rioting in 1967 in Detroit again led to the closing of the border by local agreement, without waiting for higher consultation.

authorities in Upper Canada, who had allowed the Pelee Island prisoners to go untried for so many months.

Even so, had Prince actually fired the shots himself, the matter might have been handled with some degree of finesse. As it was, his orders were carried out by others, prominent among whom was his quartermaster, Charles Anderson, who staged the executions with bloodthirsty glee, at widely separated points, for the benefit of the greatest number of onlookers [85, 93].

For the next day or so Prince was so exhausted and in such poor health that specific events during the attack at Windsor became blurred in his memory, and he reported only four executions instead of the five that had actually taken place. The old fire had returned, however, by 10 December when he wrote to Colonel Richard Bullock, 'I lament that I was prevented by some whimpering Gentlemen here from having Every Mother's Son of the murderers who were taken Prisoners Shot on the Spot.'

That was what Prince wanted the world to believe, but he knew that he was in serious difficulty. The lieutenant governor's displeasure [79] was no surprise, and on 14 December Prince reprimanded Quartermaster Anderson [80], presumably for his handling of the executions.

Prince's dramatic action was immensely popular with the residents of the Western District, and the garrison at Fort Malden gave him a dinner on 26 December. But he informed Bullock, '*I* am in high odour among the Miscrea[n]ts – They offer $800 *in specie* for yr. humble Servant dead or alive.' As the year ended John Prince was living in fear of vengeance by the Patriots [81].

Meanwhile many of his friends had also ventured to speak out against him [82], but any uneasiness about Sir George Arthur's reaction was dispelled on 11 January in 'a very long and Satisfactory interview' [83]. By the next day he was equating the several whimpering gentlemen of his acquaintance with the Patriots themselves, whom he had vowed to crush [84].

Unfortunately they did not know they had been crushed, and by 14 January 1839, an account printed by a Detroit newspaper had mysteriously appeared [85], employing for the first time the phrase 'Battle of Windsor.' It made repeated use of language from Prince's own post-battle dispatch to Colonel Airey: 'Of the Brigands and Pirates, twenty-one were killed – besides four who were brought in just at the close, and immediately after the engagement, all of whom I ordered to be shot on the spot, and which was done accordingly.' It was clear that the ill-defined disapproval of Prince's action was becoming organized [86, 87].

The anonymous article was known to have had thirteen contributors, and Prince set himself the task of dealing with those he could identify, one by one [88–91]. After putting a ball into W.R. Wood's jaw he was arrested by a fellow magistrate (who was one of the co-authors) and bound to keep the peace for six months.

A court of enquiry was convened on 18 February [92], and sat until 27 February, when Prince testified [93]. The enthusiastic reaction of the House of Assembly to Prince's entrance on March 11 [94] anticipated the verdict [95]. Prince rapidly became a new hero of Upper Canada that spring and summer, the recipient of public banquets and congratulatory addresses wherever he went.

Lord Durham's *Report* recommending responsible government and the union of Upper and Lower Canada diverted attention from the Windsor affair, and Prince no doubt welcomed the opportunity [96] to change the subject. On 22 and 23 March he spoke on union in the House, on 26 March he introduced a bill to reinvest the clergy reserves in the crown, and on 3 April he carried a resolution for an additional tax on the ratepayers of the Western District, whose treasury was then in a sorry condition.

Prince had become so popular throughout the province that his name was deemed an asset to almost any list of candidates. The electors of Simcoe County sought him as their representative at a dinner on 16 April; possibly they shared his lack of confidence in the Executive Council [97]. His rebellion losses bill [98, 99], however, was intended chiefly for the relief of his own constituents in Essex.

Despite the adulation that greeted Prince throughout Upper Canada generally, in the Western District he had some distance to go to escape the consequences of his high-handed measure. On 14 May he was looking for a residence for his family and himself, west of Toronto, towards the Humber. His Sandwich mail was to be addressed to his servant William Stevens, at Detroit. By early June he had taken steps to discourage intruders from lurking about The Park Farm [101]. Still, there was real admiration for him in Sandwich. For example, on 11 June the soldiers of the 85th Regiment drew his carriage to a testimonial dinner in Mears's orchard.

Careers had been injured by the Windsor episode. Prince sustained minimal damage, but others were not so fortunate. William Elliott lost his command of the Second Essex Militia, and Charles Eliot lost his judgeship of the Western District Court. Eliot had been elected chairman of the Quarter Sessions in April during Prince's absence in Toronto, but on 9 July 'the gallant Col.' (as the *Western Herald* had taken to calling him) had little trouble in deposing him [102].

Meanwhile Prince's notoriety had reached England, where the debate in the House of Lords [100] occupied three days. On Sunday, 14 July, a French version of the exchange between Lord Brougham and Lord Normanby was circulated at the door of the Church of Our Lady of the Assumption, near Sandwich – but so divided were the world's opinions that the newspaper reporting this fact also carried a story about Prince's townsmen in Hereford preparing to send him a handsome gift.

Possibly the thought of the debate in the House of Lords being published in the Western District depressed Prince, for he used the key word 'lowspirited' to describe his state of mind in his diary entry of 12 July. Yankee insults, he said, caused him to hang down his head as an Englishman. The day the French version of the debate was circulated, he blamed the episode on 'the infamous Conduct of the still more infamous *Whig Government* at home.'

By mid August Prince had nearly extricated himself from his difficulty, when Sir George Arthur personally reprimanded his tormentors [103]. The matter was finally resolved, as completely as it ever would be, with a reconciliation on 21 September [104], and by 21 October Prince was taking on new local duties as a boundary line commissioner.

It was a time of endings and beginnings. On 27 December Mary Prince, his mother, died, apparently in indigent circumstances, in a house in St Owen Street, Hereford; and on 31 December Prince met British North America's new governor general, Charles Poulett Thomson, to whom he took an instant liking [105].

There was a quality of loneliness in Prince's visits to the House in the opening days of 1840 [106, 107], when he found himself outnumbered and opposed in his views on the clergy reserves and the union of the provinces. An Anglican and an Englishman to the core, he could not accept Governor Thomson's plan to solve the vexed problem of the clergy reserves by permitting all denominations to share in the proceeds of their sale. Nor could he face with equanimity the prospect of a provincial union, which he saw as a threat not only to British institutions in Canada, but to the very connection of Canada to Britain. He was so profoundly disturbed by these questions that this might have contributed to his growing prejudice against Canada [108].

On 21 January 1840, a resolution which Prince had introduced, to grant £50,000 for payment of rebellion losses in Upper Canada, was carried [109]. Soon he was opposing the government he had generally supported since 1836 [110]. A new election for a united province of Canada was in the air, and possibly he perceived the need to establish his independence in the minds of the electorate. For whatever reasons, the freeholders of both Essex (14 February and 10 March [112]) and Kent (25 and 29 February, and 1 March) eagerly sought his candidacy, as had Simcoe County previously, and the Sandwich *Western Herald* came out strongly in his support [111]. He chose Essex, and the campaign began [113].

The news of his mother's death combined with the pressures of electioneering to darken Prince's outlook even more than usual [114]. Still, the leisurely campaign went smoothly enough for the first few months of 1840 [115–117], until he ventured into the territory of his opponent, Francis Caldwell [118]. Being on the defensive [119] was a new experience for Prince, but, nonetheless, his scornful reaction towards his electors [120] and political life generally [121] was in keeping with his personality. In some things John Prince was predictable after all.

Early in 1841 two of Prince's old antagonists, William Elliott and Charles Baby, became identified as allies of Caldwell and the authors of a variety of schemes designed to embarrass Prince [122, 123]. Elliott, a fellow boundary commissioner of Prince's, went so far in February as to have the accounts of the commission falsified in order to 'expose' an overcharge in Prince's name.

Nevertheless, Prince was elected as the member for Essex in the first Parliament of the province of Canada [124–128]. His satisfaction was enhanced by the safe delivery of his last son, Octavius, on 14 April. When Parliament opened on 14 June [129], Prince, perhaps mindful of the French Canadians in his constituency, joined the Upper and Lower Canadian Reformers in supporting Augustin Cuvillier as speaker [130]. Indeed, two days later he sought out and socialized with French-Canadian members.

In an enigmatic speech on 23 June [131] Prince explained, in self-pitying terms, why he could be expected to oppose Lord Sydenham and Canadian union, but pronounced himself a supporter nonetheless. He supported union, he said, 'as the independent Member for the County of Essex – as a Member entirely independent of the Executive – as a Member uninfluenced by the Executive, either directly or indirectly – as a Member who has never been offered place or power, at the hands of the Executive, or been lead [*sic*] to believe that any such offer will be ever made to him.' However contradictory it might seem, the independent John Prince now supported union. Possibly his support of Sydenham's union had some bearing on Prince's professional future [136, 142, 143].

Charles Baby's sudden friendliness [132], after an enmity dating from the Battle of Windsor, was perhaps related to Prince's equally sudden solicitude for Patriot exiles [133, 134]. Be that as it may, Prince's apparent change produced an immediate [135] and almost entirely negative [141, 144] reaction in the press. An expression of support did come from the faithful of Essex [140], but those who signed it included Prince's fellow boundary commissioner John A. Wilkinson, Charles Baby's uncle Jean Baptiste, and Robert Mercer, whom Prince had whipped after the Battle of Windsor. Prince's softening towards Patriots might have reflected a new empathy towards Americans generally [137].

By opposing the secret ballot [138, 139], the physically aggressive Prince aligned himself with the advocates of muscular democracy. He, of course, felt an affinity with respectable, but misunderstood, English lawyers fleeing to Canada in search of new beginnings. Early in July 1841 he persuaded his colleagues to permit one of that description, Robert John Turner, to practise in chancery. It also seems possible that his introduction on 2 August of a bill abolishing imprisonment for debt had its motivation in his personal background.

Leaving Kingston on 6 September (cheered on his way by some hon. French-Canadian members), Prince arrived home to face considerable hostility in Sandwich, thanks to editorials opposing his inconsistency and his support of amnesty for Patriots which had been appearing in the *Western Herald*. Though he first suspected that the author of those editorials was Charles Wiggins, he soon discovered they had been written by Henry Grant. Prince thought he saw his opportunity for revenge in a trial held on 12 October [145]. The verbal excesses for which he was so well equipped led to a denial of his allegations [146], a libel action [147], and a much-delayed verdict that gave him satisfaction only in principle [149] – but principle having been upheld at whatever cost, a grudging reconciliation took place [150].

Prince quoted the Anglican Litany in tendering his resignation from the command of the Third Essex at the close of 1841 [148]. Ironically he had not yet been relieved of responsibility when a new Patriot scare struck the frontier in June and early July 1842. For a time it appeared that the unhappy warrior would be celebrating American Independence Day in his old fashion, but fortunately the alert proved to be groundless.

Attorney General Draper had confirmed on 25 August 1841 that Prince was to be made a queen's counsel, and the commission was dated three days later. The *Western Herald*'s ambivalent reaction was illustrated in its issue of 8 September which carried two items on the same page, one praising this 'trifling reward for his useful public services' and the other condemning his 'reckless shiftings and turnings' in the name of 'Christian principles.' It was not until 1843, after Prince had rejoined the panel of magistrates of the Western District [151], that Draper's successor, Robert Baldwin, offered him the western circuit [152], which he eagerly accepted [153]. Prince's correspondence with Baldwin began in a friendly tone, but rapidly progressed through confidentiality [154] to sycophancy [156].

Early in November 1841 Prince had approached Draper and others about the judgeship of the Western District. Although he was disgusted with the Canadian legal fraternity in general [155], the urge to lead was such that after waiting two years he energetically pursued the appointment with Baldwin [159].

Prince's lack of conviction concerning the plan to move the seat of government to Montreal [157, 160] was probably similar to his reaction to a proposal that had arisen in September 1842 to remove the district seat from Sandwich to Chatham. This was an issue of direct concern to his constituents, although it was worth no more than a postscript in his letter to Baldwin. Perhaps a greater personal concern was his game law bill [158]. The resignation of the Baldwin-LaFontaine government [161] caused a crisis that forced Sir Charles Metcalfe, the governor, to carry on without a ministry. This brought forth another denunciation of Prince's expediency from a Metcalfe supporter [162].

The year 1844 began with Prince in command of his constituency, receiving an address [163], engineering a political meeting at Sandwich [164], and reporting on it with evident satisfaction to Robert Baldwin [165]. The offer of the commissionership of bankruptcy for the Western District [166] must have seemed vindication (even if it was not the judgeship he had wanted) of what he considered to be his scrupulous adherence to principle in all things. Still, he was a man with a past, and such a nostalgic occasion as his birthday, 12 March, brought forth a private cry of anguish: 'Alas, the day I Ever left my native Land to set my foot upon the Soil of this horrid, horrid Land! But I deserve all my losses, miseries, & troubles, & even ten times more!'

Perhaps it was that moment of bitter regret and self-accusation that triggered the turmoil that followed. Within the week he was in correspondence with Charles Eliot about the judgeship of the Western District – a position that Eliot had held since 1833 and that some later maintained had been Prince's real ambition when he accepted the commissionership of bankruptcy on 20 March. If that had been his goal, Draper's offer of the Sandwich and London circuit [167] must have seemed a jewel of equal value, with the added advantage that it involved travel. He accepted it the next day, and then wrote Eliot about the judgeship, presumably to relinquish it.

It was part of the contradiction of John Prince that his attempts to remove himself from public affairs tended only to embroil him more and more deeply; it was another that to a man of such rigid moralistic persuasion, surface appearance mattered a great deal. Prince's resignation from the command of the Third Essex Militia had never been accepted, and so it was still as colonel of the regiment that he addressed Adjutant General of Militia Richard Bullock [168] in an attempt to ingratiate himself with the governor general. Just eighteen days later, however, in a letter to Robert Baldwin, the Reform-minded Prince was praising Baldwin and condemning Metcalfe for his appointment, after much delay, of a Conservative administration. 'The Governor General's Policy is really to me quite unintelligible,' he wrote. 'I wonder if he means to meet Parliament with his present Council! If he does, in the name of Heaven where did he gather Laurels as that Statesman for which the world has given him Credit?'

Prince's intended resignation from politics [169] might well have combined his contradictions – part withdrawal, part appearance of withdrawal. By early 1844, in southwestern Essex a body of Reform support for Prince and Baldwin had developed around Rowland Wingfield, Jean Baptiste Laliberté, and others [163]. The choice of an heir apparent seems to have been discussed with Laliberté, with whom Prince corresponded about the middle of June, and whom Prince soon introduced to Louis Hippolyte LaFontaine [170].

The news that their idol was not to run saddened the men of Essex, 356 of whom petitioned Prince to reconsider [171], and on 7 October he relented [172]. This reversal caught other candidates in the field, notably Rowland Wingfield and another friend of Prince, Robert Lachlan. Their angry reaction [173–175] caused him to reverse his position and withdraw once again on 9 October. In a well-intended display of impartiality he addressed similar letters to that effect to the Reform-minded Wingfield and the Tory Lachlan [176, 177]. Soon the Sandwich *Western Express* was screaming 'Shameful Exposé' and alleging that Prince had come out in identical terms of support for both candidates [178]. An aroused Prince forthwith demanded refutations of both charges, and reversed himself once more to enter the contest again [179]. The next day, 14 October, he resigned his bankruptcy commissionership [180], and on 16 October, with both Lachlan and Wingfield still in the running, the formal nomination took place [181]. W.D. Baby, Prince's one-time law partner and now his campaign manager, dined with him on 19 October and, as well they might in the circumstances, they had 'a dish of politics.' As the polling proceeded it became clear that Prince was far in the lead [182, 183], and on 29 October the election of 1844 ended with the declaration that John Prince had won in Essex.

The year was drawing to a close, but it was still the season for ironic reversals. Pierre Hector Morin of Sandwich proposed the 'Gallant Colonel' as speaker of the Legislative Assembly [184], maintaining that Prince, representing the constituency that he did, was almost a French Canadian himself. On 28 November, however, Prince nominated A.N. Morin, who *was* a French Canadian, for the post, but he was defeated by Sir Allan MacNab [185]. Prince at this time supported bilingualism – he had been consulted about a proposed bilingual newspaper for Amherstburg the previous April – but this attitude, like so many others, would change.

On 5 December Prince found himself 'much embarrassed' over an amendment to the speech from the throne that had been moved by Robert Baldwin the day before, and on the following day he sent a letter from his sickbed informing Baldwin of his change of allegiance [186]. John Prince was now an independent. He remained active in the House [187], but his shift had doubtless cost him considerable political strength. Moreover, the genuineness of his conversion was highly questionable in the mind of Sir Charles Metcalfe [188].

Prince failed to carry his bill for the preservation of wildfowl in February 1845, when an amendment prohibiting hunting on the Sabbath cost him the support he needed, in particular among French-Canadian members from Canada East [189]. The member for Dundas, who was of Indian ancestry, wondered if his brother, the Great Chief from the country toward the setting of the sun, was afraid that wildlife could be threatened by hunting alone, and suggested that deforestation and agriculture were the real culprits. As to the Sabbath, it was that other Indian, Moses, who had taught that the Great Spirit had made the beasts, birds, and fishes so that his children could kill and eat them whenever they were hungry. Shortly Prince introduced a Sabbath profanation bill [190], including a prohibition of Sunday hunting, applying to the united province of Canada generally. When he saw extensive opposition in Canada East, he speedily replaced it with one pertaining only to Canada West [191], thus assuring passage of both the Sabbath and the game bills [194, 195] (albeit with appropriate comment in the debate as to the special problems of his own constituents).

Sir Charles Metcalfe seems to have been persuaded of the sincerity of Prince's latest change of heart by his moving of a congratulatory address on Sir Charles's becoming a baron [191, 192], and by 20 March 1845 had warmed to him considerably [196].

Prince's return to Sandwich after the London assizes [197] was, as usual, a triumph [198], and the conclusion of the Sandwich assizes provided an opportunity to settle the matter of the Western District judgeship [199]. Alexander Chewett had taken over the related bankruptcy commissionership after Prince's resignation, and Prince had arranged matters about the judgeship itself in Montreal earlier that spring [193].

The events of 1844 and the early part of 1845 attested to a waning of interest on Prince's part in political life. It was time for a change, and his restless mind soon turned to business concerns. A revival of Prince's railroading activity, dormant since the disturbances of 1837 and 1838, and a new interest in the mineral resources on the north shores of Lake Huron and Lake Superior [200] occupied much of his attention during the summer months of 1845. He did, however, take time on 20 July, in a letter to the commissioner of crown lands, to pronounce himself a supporter of Sandwich's claims to be the district town, as opposed to those of Chatham, in more positive terms than previously [157].

On 12 December a minor event took place that was to have a fundamental effect on the rest of Prince's life. It seems that for the several months previous, to alleviate his sufferings, Alexander Chewett had been taking to the bottle, leaving Mrs Chewett despondent. John Prince saw it as his duty to console the wife of a legal colleague by visiting her. There was no suggestion of any impropriety, but that was not how Mary Ann Prince viewed the matter [202, 203]. Prince's promise not to repeat the episode was broken on 6 March 1846, when he again 'Called & sat an hour or two with Mrs. Chewett'; the next day he confessed to his diary, 'I did very very wrong.' Perhaps it was as well that on 9 March he departed for Montreal to attend the second session of Parliament.

Prince's domestic crises had been followed by much public activity in the past, so it is not surprising that he participated so energetically in the debates, particularly those of 20 March [204–207]. Regardless of his studied nonconformity, he did betray in at least one respect that he was a product of the Victorian age when he asserted [206] that it was an obligation to exploit mineral resources to the fullest possible extent.

An evening with Metcalfe's successor, Lord Cathcart [208], established the right atmosphere for Prince to pursue his mining interests a few days later [209, 212]. Meanwhile his bill to extend the incorporation of the Niagara and Detroit Rivers Railroad Company had run into difficulty [210, 211]. It was seen, however inconsistently, on one hand as of little benefit to Canada, and on another as a threat to the Great Western. He was particularly incensed at Malcolm Cameron, the Reform member for Lanark, who in 1845 had sat on a select committee to consider reviving the Great Western, in which Cameron had an interest.

Prince's contribution to the debate of 23 March [207] might possibly have been prompted by trouble at home; so too might a letter volunteering his military services which he wrote on 24 March, and clarified on 4 April [213].

When the private correspondence between William Henry Draper and René Edouard Caron was published, it was revealed that Draper had been attempting to woo French-Canadian support for his ministry, and to promote Caron as an alternative leader to LaFontaine. In the ensuing debate in the Assembly on 7 April, Prince supported Draper's efforts and was critical of LaFontaine and other French-Canadian leaders. By rejecting attempts to conciliate French Canadians on British constitutional principles, he asserted, their leaders had been guilty of base ingratitude, and this was particularly true of LaFontaine [214]. Similarly, on 9 April he turned on the local leadership in his own constituency in a debate on the district councils [215, 216]. Although he was quickly reconciled with one of his opponents in that debate, Malcolm Cameron [221], in at least one respect he was proved to be right. On 2 February 1847 the Western District clerk, John Cowan, absconded, and Prince advanced Cowan's son as a replacement [227].

The twin diversions of railroading [218] and mining [217, 219, 220] occupied much of Prince's mind and energy as his marriage deteriorated. He made mining speeches and attended mining meetings, and in his legal capacity he used his contacts in July 1846 to see to a patent for a rock-drilling device. By 28 July the new British North American Mining Company, of which Prince was a director, required the services of Mr Townsend of Notre Dame Street in Montreal, probably for a corporate seal [223].

Meanwhile, promises to the contrary, at Sandwich Prince had not been neglecting the Chewetts. On 11 June he had occasion to visit the good judge on patent business. It was not long before this led to a confrontation with Mary Ann [222, 224], although her list of suspects had earlier (on 21 January) been extended to include, in Prince's words, 'The Ritchies & other Nonsense which she has got into her head.' Then there was an exchange about 'that Mrs. Johnson' on 6 October, at which time Prince declared his and Mary Ann's lives to be 'Miserable & wretched beyond all description'; later, for consolation, he 'Called on Mrs. Chewett.' By 5 November the prospects for a happy marriage, and life itself, seemed to have disappeared [225]. Still, suicide was not an acceptable alternative because it was un-Christian [226]. The best he could hope for was an accidental death.

The theme through 1847 was similar. The world might be askew, as in militia affairs [228], but Prince could not concern himself with petty annoyances. On 10 May he 'had a long, & serious, & violent discourse with Mary Ann about various matters.' The next day, now nearly ready to kill himself, he had to conceal his agony at a public dinner in Chatham

[230, 231], where he spoke in support of the separation of Kent from Essex and its erection as a separate district.

Prince's anti-government stance [231–234, 236–239] was viewed with suspicion by the Toronto *Globe* [235] which, possibly reflecting the sentiments of Baldwin [229], sought to promote the Reformer Malcolm Cameron as his replacement. Since his vote meant a great deal in a nearly evenly divided House, Prince appears to have been enjoying his position as an independent. He was, in fact, in consultation with the 'English' Liberal Thomas Aylwin of Quebec [234, 236], who was a potential leader of a new ministry.

Prince's success on 25 June [240], when he carried his railroad bill and his Western District division bill, attested to his new political strength, and it was the same with his mining bill [241, 242], which received its third reading and final passage on 27 July. Suddenly all things had become possible, including a meeting concerning the absorption of the Niagara and Detroit Rivers by the Great Western on 9 July. A final arrangement on 11 July [243] provided for GWR stock as compensation to the directors of the then-defunct N & DRR (whose demise seems to have come as a shock to some [260]).

For all his activity, however, it was characteristic of Prince that there were days when he found himself 'the slave of melancholy broodings & forebodings,' and he sequestered himself in his room [244].

By 1846 a good deal of interest in the mineral resources of the north shores of the upper Great Lakes had been aroused and, like many of his associates, Prince was caught up in the excitement. His mining location of about ten square miles, southwest of Thunder Bay, was the subject of a speech in the summer of 1847 [242].[7] A month later his skill as a negotiator was demonstrated when he was able to resolve a dispute between two directors of the Bruce Mines, James Cuthbertson and Arthur Rankin, and then bring about the absorption of the Bruce Mines by the Montreal Mining Company [245–247]. In recognition of his service to the company, Rankin made Prince a gift of stock, but after reflecting overnight, Prince decided to pay for the stock instead of accepting it as a gift. The settlement was all the more remarkable considering that two years earlier, Rankin had been prosecuted by Prince on a charge of libel, apparently for vehemently objecting to a list of magistrates [201]. At the same time Prince was advancing the interests of the British North American Mining Company, which was one more in a bewildering array of mining enterprises in which he was involved.

7 A silver vein on Prince's location was worked, but not during his lifetime.

Even as Prince's mining affairs were being resolved, his restless mind was turning in a new direction. A fishery at Rondeau, in Kent County on Lake Erie [248], would occupy his attention for the next while [251], and would eventually become yet another disappointment.

The election of 1847–48 (1847 in Essex) was among the least eventful episodes in the eventful life of John Prince. On 13 December he was solicited and agreed to stand [249], and on Christmas Eve he was elected by acclamation [250].

Prince lost no time in taking the Toronto *Church* to task for its failure, by omitting an asterisk, to indicate in its report of the election results that he had been unopposed [252]. In the process he (no doubt inadvertently) used the phrase 'a Country such as this Canada is.' The words were picked up in a response in the Hamilton *Spectator* [253] and flung back in Prince's reply [254]. It was not long before 'this Canada,' like 'and it was done accordingly,' became a catch phrase. Henceforth Prince consistently used 'this Canada' to emphasize his contempt for his adopted country.

During the campaign Prince departed from the course he had steered (somewhere between the Tories and the Reformers) in the parliamentary session recently ended. In Kent he let it be known that, in a contest between Camerons, the Tory John Hillyard would have his vote, not the Reformer Malcolm [255]. By late February he was firmly in the Tory government camp, advancing MacNab as speaker [256]. Perhaps it was his new political alignment that secured to him the presidency for 1848 of the British North American Mining Company [257], but whereas in the previous parliament he had held a position of real strength, an independent in a House nearly evenly divided, in 1848 he found himself, as a Conservative supporter, heavily outnumbered. His legislative performance suffered in consequence, although he did bring in a bill to incorporate the Huron Copper Bay Company on 1 March, two days before the ministry was defeated [258].

It was the nimble John Prince – to whom party affiliation meant so little, who noted (as others had before him) that one could equate English Whigs and Canadian Tories [259] – who was ridiculed by the Reformer Malcolm Cameron, now representing Kent, in an open letter to Robert Baldwin, published 8 February. Cameron would introduce a new university bill and Prince could occupy the proposed chair of humbug. In a speech on 16 March [261] Prince criticized the new, Reform, LaFontaine-Baldwin government for its apparent inability to carry on the business of the country, and, his tongue thrust firmly into his cheek, vigorously defended his good friend John Barleycorn. Two days later, in a demonstration that business and political interests were not necessarily the same, he alone opposed the seating of Francis Hincks [262], whose mining bill he had supported [241].

In the Kent election the returning officer, Prince's friend George Wade Foott, had questioned Malcolm Cameron's qualification as a candidate, and in the face of an overwhelming vote had declared the Tory John Hillyard Cameron elected. The election was contested in the House, where the Reformer was seated on 2 March 1848. Foott, exposed to potential humiliation, was defended by Prince.

A nearly identical circumstance occurred in the Oxford election. There the returning officer, John George Vansittart, declared the Tory Peter Carroll elected over the Reformer Francis Hincks. Prince's defending of the returning officer in the Oxford election [263] led to a memorable clash on 22 March [264] with George Brown, who replied in kind, and in support of Malcolm Cameron in Kent, in the columns of his newspaper [265]. Brown devoted many a column inch (for example in his issue of 12 April) to cataloguing the shortcomings of 'one of the most lamentable examples of perverted talent to be found in any country,' than whom there was 'not a more despised, contemptible loafer in her Majesty's dominions,' a poor creature so far gone 'that he has to get strong over-proof spirits smuggled into the House for his own use.' It might be that Malcolm Cameron's eventual acclamation in Kent was achieved in part through the independent Prince's own activity, as a critic of the Tory administration he professed to support [266]. Prince's fondness for alcohol had been brought to the public's attention in the process, and a libel action against George Brown would follow.

Yet another quarrel with Mary Ann took place on 26 April; this time, however, there was no reconciliation until 18 September [267]. A week later Prince bought his wife a team of horses and a carriage, and on 11 October, when he was sick, she treated him kindly. On Christmas Eve, however, he sat with Mrs Chewett again, and Mary Ann was incensed once more. As 1848 departed Prince was again 'perfectly wretched,' declaring that his life was 'absolutely wearisome' to him at the end of 'the most miserable, unhappy, and unprosperous of all the miserable years' he had lived. On 6 January 1849, however, he made up with Mary Ann once more.

In Montreal early in the new year Prince was again elected to the directorate of the British North American Mining Company, and the convivial visit to Dolly's Chop House that followed [271] was one of the few occasions when he experienced anything resembling amusement in Canada.

At the opening of the second session Prince introduced into the House the subject of his libel action against George Brown. He attacked the new, Reform administration of LaFontaine and Baldwin, ranging over a variety of subjects including Malcolm Cameron, the diversion of the crown business to others (actually Prince had refused it the previous May), and even the use of French in the speech from the throne – a reversal of his earlier pronouncements so dramatic that it seems doubtful that he knew, or particularly cared, what he was saying [268]. In a speech on 8 February [269] Prince kept up his attack on Brown, who had sided with Hincks against the returning officer, Vansittart, in the contested Oxford election. He had faint praise for Vansittart, however, and the equivocation he displayed on the subject was typical of his erratic thinking.

The Vansittart case ended on 13 February, and the members turned to the Lower Canadian rebellion losses bill. Joining forces with Sir Allan MacNab and the Upper Canadian High Tories, Prince opposed it, however implausibly asserting that the people of Canada West, whose land had been invaded, who had not rebelled, would be asked to contribute towards the losses of the people of Canada East, where the rebellion had taken place [270, 273, 274, 276]. Prince now thought the Canadas ought never to have been united [273], and in pressing this view he heaped more scorn on French, the language of many of his own electors [276]. However, the man who could turn William Lyon Mackenzie out of the Parliamentary Library [275] was a hero in Essex, and Prince's return to Sandwich late in March was, as usual, a celebration.

Prince's dramatic ejection of Mackenzie must have been as pleasurable to him as his victory over another of his antagonists, George Brown, in a libel action [277, 278]. In Parliament he continued playing his customary independent role, speaking against a fellow opposition member, Henry Sherwood [279], during a seat-of-government debate, and within the week he condemned the ministry for the high salaries enjoyed by the Executive Council [280].

Parliament was prorogued on 30 May [281]. As local political activity engaged Prince's attention, he spent 21 July writing replies to his enemies in both languages, although not four months previously he had ridiculed the use of French in the Assembly [276]. It was the same John Prince who, as a compelling orator in February [272], apparently enjoyed the attentions of tremendous crowds, but was so reclusive on many other occasions that on 31 August, for example, he recorded that the house at The Park Farm 'gradually became *filled with people!* so that I became almost deranged & rushed *frantic* to my room where I lay till Morning.' He spent that summer and fall demolishing the 'Rads' [282, 283], to the delight of his constituents and local rebellion-loss claimants. (Still only grudgingly conceding that there had been a rebellion in Upper

Canada, he was careful to call them 'claimants for Rebellion & Invasion claims'.) In December his electors presented him with a silver claret jug and a gold watch.

Occasionally Prince's relentless pursuit of evildoers led him into his own circle, and he showed no more restraint there than elsewhere. In January 1850 he challenged the election of William Duperon Baby, his former law partner and campaign manager, as reeve of Sandwich Township [284, 286]. Baby, who had held elected office since 1846, completed his term, but his political career ended at that point.

On 17 February 1850 Prince began to draft the long letter to Arthur Rankin that came to be known as his 'Independence Manifesto' [287, 288]. That document, although overtly political in nature, was probably, in its central thrust – a plea for national independence – an extension of Prince's bitterly evolved personal philosophy.

In the Independence Manifesto Prince pointedly paraphrased Proverbs xxiv, 15 ('He that is surety for a stranger shall smart for it'), possibly referring to his father. Ironically, he had ignored this precept as recently as 30 January, when he guaranteed the honesty of County Treasurer George Bullock [285]. Perhaps he did so on the tenuous ground that Bullock was also proprietor of the Amherstburg hotel where the Masonic Lodge, which Prince had recently joined, held its meetings. He should have known better, for the previous summer W.R. Wood, deputy treasurer until 1848, had absconded to the United States when a shortage had been discovered in his account.

Prince, who had so often been misunderstood and unappreciated before, or who thought he had, must have known that his pronouncement would open up whole new worlds of misunderstanding for him. That he knew he had placed his position as a queen's counsel in jeopardy was clear by 30 March [289]. He anticipated the inevitable by resigning on 9 April, although his resignation seems to have crossed in the mail with his dismissal [290, 291, 302].

The Assembly declined by a massive majority (57–7) to hear his petition for independence, leaving Prince to splutter [292] and hurl criticism, first at the ministry [293], then at both sides of the House [294]. He must have known that independence from Britain would be confused with annexation to the United States [295], and that he had no chance whatever of succeeding. This was classic Prince, indulging in activity for its own sake. In the same vein, the attacker of French-Canadian linguistic rights in the House was soon defending the land rights of the seigneurs against those members who were of a mind to abolish the 'feudal' system in Lower Canada [296].

For a time in the summer of 1850 Prince thought he saw an opportunity to revive his railroad. Conservative leader A.N. MacNab, to whom the Great Western was dear, was an opposition member; if, therefore, an independent such as Prince were to give the government side something with which to set back such an opposition member, perhaps the Niagara and Detroit Rivers line could be revived. On 21 June Prince carried a railroad resolution against MacNab, and on 12 July his second Niagara and Detroit Rivers Railroad bill was reported from the Standing Committee on Railroads and Telegraph Lines. The brief dream ended the next day, however [297], and Prince's capitulation was epitomized when he accompanied MacNab to the theatre on 14 August.

It might not have surprised anyone but Prince that William Lyon Mackenzie could be polite to the author of the Independence Manifesto [299]. However, the feeling was not reciprocated [301], not even when Prince presented the petition of John Montgomery, whom he characterized as the guiltless dupe of others [300].

In a public life dominated by dislike of Canada [298], in which real accomplishment tended to be of limited importance [303] and appearance counted for much [304], one of the few genuinely gracious gestures occurred on 30 June 1851, when Prince spoke on the occasion of Robert Baldwin's resignation from the House [305]. Soon he was his old self, however, on 7 July calling the venal press of Canada a parcel of jackasses.

As the third parliament drew to a close Prince, still resenting the revoking of his appointment as a queen's counsel, declared himself in favour of abolishing the title [307] (although he represented the crown again at the assizes that fall). He also revealed that he was coming to regard the Great Western Railroad more favourably, although he was not yet ready to give it his full support [308]. Having at first declined a suggestion that he offer himself once more as a candidate for Essex [306], on 12 September Prince relented [309]. His apparent reluctance seems to have been linked with the discovery that Arthur Rankin had abandoned his High Conservatism and was running as a Radical [310]. He would be a powerful rival for the affections of the southwestern part of the province.

The ordeal of compaigning began on 15 November [311–313]. But Prince found time for a trip to Chatham on 3 December, where the opportunity to attack one of the candidates in Kent, George Brown, was not to be passed by. When a French Canadian, Francis Caron, was nominated to oppose him in Essex, it was evident that Prince's gyrations in Parliament had cost him some support in the heavily French-Canadian northwest of the county [314]. However, he had lost none of the old magnetism in the more Anglo-Saxon south, the area from which his militia battalion had been raised [315], and victory was assured [316, 317].

Arthur Rankin's change of political persuasion [310] in the autumn of 1851 earned him a lecture from Prince early in 1852 [318]. It was the beginning of a hostility that was to last fifteen years – yet Rankin and Prince did have their similarities. In the 1840s Rankin had exhibited Indians in England as curiosities of nature. Both men regarded non-whites simply as natural resources, to be used as required. One did not have to associate with them, however, and Prince for one was prepared to spend money acquiring land in order to avoid them [319].

The hamlet of Windsor had sprung up in the 1830s around the ferry landing above Sandwich, in the expectation of a rail connection with the east, and in 1852 all the dreams of riches were about to be fulfilled. Soon, with John Prince's guidance, the railroad would arrive. The insignia on the rolling stock would be GWR, not N & DRR, however, and the terminus would be Windsor, not Sandwich [320, 321]. This decision sent Sandwich into a decline from which it never recovered, but at the time the important thing was that the Detroit frontier would at last be linked effectively with the east.

Since the rebellion losses debate of 1849 Prince's stance had been, if not pro-Tory, at least anti-Reform. By the autumn of 1852, however, he was again changing his political position. That fall in the Assembly Prince declared himself to be a supporter of temperance [322], ridiculed Mackenzie (over the latter's proposal to establish courts of conciliation or arbitration) [323], and seconded a motion of Mackenzie's the next day [324]. He was also critical of Englishmen who hunted and fished in Lower Canada on Sunday [325], even though he had previously insisted that it was not a desecration for his French-Canadian constituents to follow their practice of fishing in the Detroit River on Sunday. Once again he insisted that, although he was in favour of independence, he did not support annexation [326]. Perhaps it was the Tories' rigid insistence on maintaining the British connection that propelled Prince once again towards the Reformers. The realization that the Reform alliance led by Hincks and Morin was firmly in power also influenced his outlook. He supported Hincks on the secularization of the clergy reserves [327] and on railroad matters, even at the risk of alienating MacNab [329, 330], and he succeeded in moving an adjournment from November to 14 February 1853 [328, 332].

The loyal opposition at this time included George Brown and William Lyon Mackenzie who, when they were not opposing the ministry, were wont to oppose each other. Prince, to complete the isosceles triangle, wasted no love on either [331, 333].

Early in 1853 Prince reported on the north country to a committee of the House [334]. He praised the remote country north of Lake Superior, and he called attention to the need for courts – which, of course, would require the services of just such as himself. Seen in its context, this report is significant. On 3 January, Prince had leased property near Rondeau, on Lake Erie, and on 11 January this lamentation appeared in his diary: 'Mrs. Prince sets her face agst The Rond Eau, & has sealed my Ruin!' Once again, a frustrated John Prince wanted to be on the move.

If he was not a Reformer at heart, at least Prince looked enough like one to satisfy the editor of the *Canada Advertiser* [335]. To succeed as a private member in carrying a bill, for example his measure to legalize the poisoning of wolves in Upper Canada [336], he needed the support of a majority in the House. (As it happened, this bill, like many others of Prince's devising, seems to have evaporated at about the time of first reading.) Support of fellow members' private bills, in return for their support of his own offerings, cast Prince in what was, for him, the unexpected role of sustaining the cause of charity, and Lower Canadian charity at that [337]. In fact, he found himself supporting the granting of twice the sum that had originally been requested.

The wooing of the government side, also, was implicit in a great deal of the independent Prince's parliamentary activity in 1853 [338–340]. On 1 March he defended Mr Speaker J.S. Macdonald and members of the Executive Council against what he considered to be improper observations, in the Toronto *United Empire*, on their appearance and deportment in the House. It was the same, contradictory appearing Prince, however, who on 24 March declared himself to be fond of society [341], and on 26 April poured out his scorn for Canadians and their manners [342].

Presumably the '*Plebs Canadiensis*' did not include certain Hurons, Prince's clients, who were the proprietors of the Huron Church Reserve between Detroit Street and the Huron Church Line, just above Sandwich (long since known as Mears's Orchard). The Reserve was in the process of being secularized and formally thrown open to settlement, and once again Charles Baby, the political ally of Arthur Rankin, had the role of villain [343], as a would-be buyer of the Indians' rights in their negotiations with the white occupants. Whether Prince knew it or not, the scene was being set for another confrontation, not only with Baby, but also with Rankin.

Through the summer of 1853 Prince pursued his independent path, approving here and finding fault there [344], threatening Mackenzie after the latter called him, with some justice, a deserter from MacNab's Conservative camp [345], saying what Americans wanted to hear on the subject of annexation [346], and in company with his friends on both sides of the House, pressing forward with railroad matters [347].

It was on 17 January 1854 that the Great Western was finally opened to Windsor. After the ceremonies Prince crossed over to Detroit to speak at a dinner at the depot attended by more than 2,500 people [350].

Prince visited Sault Ste Marie in the autumn of 1853, and it was characteristic of his restless personality that he assessed its potential as a future home. He found it wanting [348]. It was just as characteristic that on 2 October of that year he applied for the judgeship of the county of Lambton, which had just been separated from Essex. If he had been pressed for an explanation, Prince would, of course, have blamed impending financial disaster at the hands of his rapacious family in general, and Mary Ann in particular [349]. 'Ruin! Ruin!! at this curs't place, & yet I can't coax or *drag* the family from it! *What madness*! but they are resolved on *my* ruin' he wrote on 11 February 1854. Certainly Prince's declared financial worth, in terms of ready cash at least, seems to have been modest for one who lived in style [351].

Prince resumed his duties as a magistrate on 17 February, and in April as a queen's counsel [352], but peace of mind and security of pocketbook were as far away as ever. On 13 May he recorded: 'In the Evening I took a slow & Melancholy stroll thro' the woods of The Park Farm (where I have laid out £6000 & upwards & have spent 20 years of the prime of my life in making it a farm – to my Ruin!!). So depressed are my spirits at times, & so excited at other times, at my *disappointments* & losses in this horrid & detestable Country, that I believe I shall *go mad, or shoot myself.* God Almighty *preserve me*!' On 26 May he applied (unsuccessfully) for the post of superintendent general of Indian affairs; an interview with Attorney General Ross on 13 June [353] presumably dealt with that other iron in another fire, the judgeship of Lambton County.

During the short second session of Parliament in 1854 Prince, despite his complaints [354], acted generally as a Reformer, a government supporter. It was a most unstable government, however. With a substantial opposition both to its right and to its left, it was doomed to a quick death. Prince barely had time to express his views on land policy (perhaps originating in his local experience with Charles Baby in the Huron Church Reserve matter [354, 355]) when the ministry was defeated on 20 June.

John Prince did not run in the election of 1854. By 11 July it had been decided that Albert would stand for Essex in his father's place. Colonel Prince would volunteer for service in the Crimea [356].

Meanwhile there was still election business to occupy his mind. He supported Malcolm Cameron and opposed George Brown in Lambton [357], and supported Albert Prince against Arthur Rankin in Essex [358]. Ironically, both were defeated [359–361]. In Essex, Albert's loss to Rankin, helped it was suspected by the deputy sheriff, Denis Moynahan [362], entrenched an enmity towards Rankin that had begun nearly two years before.

Prince's unpredictability was no doubt related to the number of options he had at any given time. During the election of 1854 he found himself in what, even for him, was an unusual position of flexibility. He had applied for a judgeship in Lambton, he had applied to be superintendent general of Indian affairs, and he had volunteered for the Crimea. Less than a year before, he had visited Sault Ste Marie and had rejected it as a future home. Now, with his son's defeat, on 23 August he wrote to Joseph Wilson at Sault Ste Marie concerning the judgeship of the new district of Algoma. Late in September Prince's offer to serve in the Crimea was politely refused [363].

Prince's last jab at his old enemy William Lyon Mackenzie was delivered in October 1854 [364]. It was in reply to Mackenzie's questioning of his title to the Rondeau property, which had been the cause of so much unhappiness between him and Mary Ann. Prince's strenuous efforts to change his circumstances apparently blotted from his mind the possibility that he might be forced to remain at The Park Farm; his unhappiness would then have been compounded if Mackenzie had accepted his sarcastic offer of the Rondeau lease.

The railroads of the mid-nineteenth century were notorious for their lack of safety, and the Great Western was typical. On 27 October an accident occurred [365] that involved Prince, partly as a lawyer acting for the railroad and partly as a queen's counsel.[8] His position in court was therefore ambiguous [366, 367].

The rivalry between Prince and Arthur Rankin gained new impetus when it became apparent that both had volunteered to raise troops for the Crimea [368]. Soon each was trying to outdo the other in feats of patriotism [369, 370]. This tasteless episode did little to enhance Prince's reputation with some groups [372]. Others, perhaps more sophisticated, had mastered the art of dealing with people like Prince with creative inefficiency. His offer to the War Department was referred back to Canada [373] at the same time as a confidential opinion of him was requested. Governor-in-chief Sir Edmund Head's response must have been a source of satisfaction to the Imperial authorities who had so cautiously handled Prince's proposal. The rashness of 1838 still dogged

---

8 This apparent conflict of interest is left unexplained by Prince's diary statement on 28 October: 'I attended the Coroner's Inquest as Q.C. & Counsel for the G.W. Railway ...'

his career, and more recently he had acquired the reputation of being a drunkard [375]. Still Prince persisted [376], and still the authorities resisted [377].

Meanwhile, never one to concentrate all his efforts in one direction, Prince pursued the Sault Ste Marie judgeship [371]. The refusal of the Huron judgeship in March 1855 [374] was only a slight setback in comparison to the blow he suffered that June, however. Albert, who was living in Sandwich and who had already shamed his father by losing an election – and to Arthur Rankin at that – was to heap scandal on the family name by marrying a divorced woman [378].

Early in July Prince journeyed to New York to settle the affairs of his former servant, William Stevens, who had recently died. In the turmoil of New York, strangely, he found a few days' peace of mind, although he was still troubled by what he considered to be his dreary prospects. On his way back to Sandwich he missed, or avoided, Albert at Niagara Falls.

Although he had resigned his command of the Third Essex in 1846, in the summer of 1855 Prince offered himself as commander of the Ninth Military District [379]. His bitterness towards Arthur Rankin deepened when that worthy was awarded the post early in 1856 [387].

Prince's intense desire to turn his back on his circumstances was further revealed when, following more trouble with Mary Ann in August 1855, he offered The Park Farm and his other properties near Sandwich for sale to pay his debts. He succeeded only in selling what he called his back or wild farm that fall to Henry Banwell, and Mary Ann's accusation that he had cheated the family of the money led to even more unhappiness [384, 385].

Meanwhile, with considerable success Arthur Rankin had been promoting a scheme that was variously known as the Southern Railroad, the Great Southern Railroad and the Amherstburg and St Thomas Railroad. In large measure it was a revival of Prince's old Niagara and Detroit Rivers proposal, and consequently it was not calculated to endear Rankin to Prince, who was put in the difficult position of having to support the railroad while opposing its proponent [380–382]. Complicating his railroad interests still further, he was corresponding during this episode about the possible solicitorship of the Great Western [383].

Following a quarrel between Albert and Rankin, Prince was forced to deal out rough but impartial justice by having both arrested to prevent a duel [386]. He had not jailed anyone in personal contact with him since 1850, when he challenged W.D. Baby's election as reeve of Sandwich Township. Baby had been appointed sheriff in 1851, and Prince's role in his removal from that office [388] began in August 1855, when Prince became convinced that a charge of theft against Baby was valid. Prince had written the governor general on the subject that September. It was another of the many ironies in Prince's life that he was reconciled to Baby in the spring of 1856 [391], but when he finally met Governor General Head personally that summer he disliked him [392].

It was probably a grievance against Attorney General John A. Macdonald, for failing to employ him as a queen's counsel [390], that led Prince to ingratiate himself with another old adversary, the then member for Lambton, George Brown [389]. Early in 1856, in a fit of parliamentary excess, Macdonald had accused Brown of extracting perjured testimony from witnesses during an investigation of the penitentiary at Kingston by a royal commission in 1849. Brown's icily restrained response to this groundless charge, a call for a committee of enquiry, appealed to Prince, who was something of an expert in his own right at dealing with personal attacks in the Assembly, and so he offered his congratulations.

The complexities of party politics were to be set aside, however, and Prince was on the move again. The splendid Park Farm (Prince had won no fewer than thirteen prizes at the county fair in October 1855) was for sale once more in the summer of 1856 – or half of it, or whatever portion would produce a minimum $10,000 down payment – and John Prince would seek to represent the Western Division (Essex, Kent, and Lambton Counties) by winning one of the new elective seats in the Legislative Council [393, 394].

The Sandwich *Maple Leaf* had no difficulty in coming out early (31 July) for Prince, but the Windsor *Herald* maintained its independence a little longer, quoting Prince's remark regarding Canadian newspapers, that 'there was not one of them but could be bought for £20.' Indeed the *Herald* seemed to have a little trouble at first working itself up to its contemporary's enthusiasm [395]. Soon, however, both papers were devoting almost all their space to the election of John Prince. At a meeting on 2 August [396] the central issue in the contest for the Western Division emerged. Arthur Rankin suggested that he was available, but Prince held that no sitting Assembly member was eligible for election to the Council.

Such was Prince's popularity [397] that at first the outcome seemed a foregone conclusion, and, in fact, he found himself campaigning against a number of non-candidates [398]. The *Planet*, however, remained steadfast in its opposition to Prince, and perhaps because of this James Dougall entered the race [400]. On 1 September he was joined officially by Arthur Rankin [401].

In the contest that followed, Prince was widely supported by all elements of the population, including the blacks [402]. He was assisted to a great extent by Albert, who made it a practice to attend Rankin's meetings on behalf of his father, much to the discomfort, as the Prince press had it, of the hon. member for Essex. The *Maple Leaf* indeed seems to have had its candidate in mind to the near exclusion of all other subjects. In one story it succeeded, twice, in referring to the deputy reeve of Sandwich Township, Gabrielle Bondy, as Prince Bondy.

Prince was presented throughout the campaign as a man of experience, which Dougall was not, and a man above party, which Rankin was not; the ideal choice, in short, for a new set of circumstances in the Upper House. 'We all know,' rhapsodized 'An Elector' in the *Maple Leaf*, 'that Col. Prince never was, and never can be a self-interested man; it is contrary to his nature. His policy is to carry out the wishes of his constituents, always with an eye to the good of the country at large.'

The nomination was held at Chatham [403] where, despite Prince's earlier objection [399], John Mercer acted as returning officer. In his speech [404], Prince discussed the railroad that had been projected for so many years, and flourished a nicely timed wire announcing the salvation of the scheme. But that was not all. His proposed canal between Lakes Erie and St Clair would probably have split Essex from Kent and the rest of the province even more effectively than nature had, and might well have sent Essex and even southeastern Michigan into a permanent decline. However, it was just the thing for the voters of Kent; small wonder that Edwin Larwill, who represented Kent in the Assembly, promptly came out for Prince.

To the surprise of few, Prince headed the polls [405–407], with a majority of 511, although he was beaten by Rankin, 358 to 326, in his home territory, Sandwich. The arrogant tone of his remarks at a railroad meeting in Sandwich in August 1855 [381], had been remembered. Still, Rankin had been defeated, Dougall had done surprisingly well, particularly in Kent, and John Prince had been elected [408].

There was one other ramification of all this. A dispute among the directors and stockholders of the Southern Railway had led to the election of two sets of directors, and a lawsuit. John McLeod was president of one faction, and Arthur Rankin of the other. John Prince, in his capacity as solicitor to the McLeod company, obtained a grand jury indictment against Rankin for perjury. The case was dismissed on a technicality, but the alliances for another election contest had been formed.

The beginning of Prince's career as a member of the Legislative Council [410] was similar to the beginning of his career in the lower House in the 1830s. He was chosen to second the address from the throne [411] and, as he confided to his diary, he spoke well. In top oratorical form in 1857, Prince laid his emphasis on engineering schemes for the improvement of the Western Division – a lighthouse for Rondeau, canals to connect Lake Erie with either Lake St Clair or Lake Huron [404, 412], a pier for the residents of Gosfield Township, and a bridge across the Detroit [409]. This latter was a reversal of an earlier attitude on the same subject, expressed to a different and presumably more selfishly interested audience [382].

There was a flurry of legislation, some of specific concern to his constituents, such as bills to incorporate the towns of Sandwich [414, 418, 420] and Windsor [423]. Others, such as a cruelty to animals bill, were of personal interest to Prince. There was also a bill to amend the procedures for election to the Legislative Council itself, to prevent the Arthur Rankins of the world, sitting members of the House, from running for the Council, and also to ensure the impartiality of the John Mercers at election time [413]. Prince could even find Detroit River connotations in such an apparently remote subject as the Newfoundland fisheries, as on 5 April 1857, when he remarked on the American practice of fishing in the waters of his constituents.

Participating in debates on other subjects, having perhaps a wider appeal, Prince ridiculed the notion that the provincial capital should alternate periodically between Toronto and Quebec [415], he supported tighter controls on the granting of credit [416], and he inveighed against the spread of patronage [423].

There was also the matter of two Essex County magistrates, Thomas Woodbridge and John A. Wilkinson, who had been dismissed for wrongfully surrendering an American black into the custody of a sheriff from the United States [424], through the conniving of some mischief-maker whom Prince believed to be Arthur Rankin. In defending Woodbridge and Wilkinson, Prince expounded what he considered to be his own and his constituents' enlightened and liberal attitude towards the refugee black population from the United States which at this time was reaching a peak in Essex and Kent. Blacks were objects of amusement at best and disdain at worst, and they were to be tolerated at all other times as long as they kept their distance [424, 425]. In his response to the Toronto *Colonist*'s criticism of his attitude, Prince appears to have forgotten the black support he received in the campaign of 1856 [402].

Woodbridge was of particular importance to Prince because of his involvement with the Southern Railroad. Railroads such as the Grand Trunk were to be encouraged, just because they were railroads, it would seem, with the possible quibble that they should as a rule have been begun at their western ends [421].

INTRODUCTION   li

As in his cruelty to animals bill, Prince's speech on a fishing bill [422] again revealed his concern with the ethics of the hunting and fishing practices that were widespread in his day. Still, true to form, he managed a reference to his own bailiwick on the Detroit. This time, however, he seemed to be looking to the interests of Americans, who would be inconvenienced by having to confine their fishing to American waters. For some time a growing admiration for things American had been discernible in Prince's speeches [417] and other pronouncements. Many an Independence Day, for example, called for some appropriate sentiment in his diary. Also, as in earlier years, Prince felt little uneasiness at reversing his position, as he did when he repudiated his previous stand on the Court of Chancery [419].

Early in 1857 the unsettled John Prince, having determined to give up The Park Farm, made enquiries about Bois Blanc Island, opposite Amherstburg in the lower Detroit River. In August he volunteered once again for military service, this time in India [426, 427] – with the usual result [428].

The election campaign that began late in 1857 provided Prince with an ingenious solution to a difficult problem. As a member of the Legislative Council it would be inappropriate for him to take part in an election for the Assembly, and yet that scoundrel Rankin was running for re-election, against John McLeod. Prince considered that he could take no sides in a political contest – but there was the matter of the Southern Railroad, whose rival presidents happened to be Arthur Rankin and John McLeod. Prince, as solicitor for the McLeod directorship of the railroad, would be doing no more than his duty if he came out foursquare for McLeod as a railroad president, and that is exactly what he did [429]. Could he be faulted if the voters construed his railroading advice as political, and replaced Rankin with McLeod in the Assembly?

McLeod's victory was part of a lopsided Liberal-Conservative sweep, and Prince lost no time in capitalizing on it in an unctuous letter to John A. Macdonald [430] – whom he had berated in a letter to George Brown not two years before [389].

Prince did not escape completely unscathed [431], but the election did him no serious damage. He soon turned his thoughts once again to the judgeship at Sault Ste Marie [432].

The bustle of legislative activity that Prince initiated in 1857 continued into 1858, with the introduction and passage of a bill to provide for vaccination as a means of preventing smallpox. He did not, however, enjoy invariable success. On 8 April he withdrew a bill to make the speaker's position elective, on the ground that it was unconstitutional. He also failed in another attempt to gain compensation for John Montgomery for the burning of his tavern on Yonge Street, north of Toronto, during the rebellion. What was perhaps of greater significance, however, was the first, tentative, public expression, as reported in the Toronto *Weekly Messenger*, of what had been an evolving and possibly frightening private thought:

It was now many years since the events to which the petition referred transpired, but he (Col. Prince) felt abashed that he had taken the trouble he did on that occasion to defend the country. It was the most unfortunate period of his life; and had he done what those now in power controlling the destinies of Canada had done, he would now have been plain John Prince, of a Western county. But he did his best to protect the dominions of his Queen, and had brought upon himself hatred and malice and all uncharitableness, in consequence of his loyalty.

The judgeship of the provisional district of Algoma soon became the subject of a protracted series of discussions with Attorney General John A. Macdonald [433], whose promises, however, Prince profoundly distrusted [435, 446, 447]. Still, a politician lives on promises, and those of William Cayley and Philip Vankoughnet regarding patronage in the Western Division [434] put him in a position of advantage when Rankin's protest of the Essex election was considered [436]. The validity of Rankin's petition was challenged, and Prince's satisfaction when the matter was referred to a select committee was evident.

Prince's ambiguous outlook, part privilege-conscious English, part populist American, was never more apparent than in May 1858, when almost simultaneously he questioned American intrusions in the Hudson's Bay Company territory, and introduced a bill to admit English attorneys to practise in Canada, and another to abolish property qualifications for candidates for election to Parliament [436, 437]. By extension the latter raised the unsettling questions of universal suffrage and vote by ballot, and Prince won a nervous laugh when he told the Council, 'They will come next.' He lost both bills.

Although Prince was wavering in his support of the ministry late in May [438], he remained in control of patronage in Essex and could regard with some equanimity the House's deliberations on the recent Essex election [439]. At 62 he was fully aware of his advancing age, and he was not above reminding his colleagues of his long years in public life. On 16 June he cast his mind back twenty years and more to recall with fondness the days of Sir Francis Bond Head [440].

The resignation of the ministry late in July 1858, on the question of the seat of government, was accepted with some detachment by Prince. He was neither for nor against them, although he could have offered advice if he had been asked [442]. Indeed this seeming lack of concern was apparent a few days earlier when he 'amused the House for a quarter of an hour with stories of hunts, night adventures, his love of beer, &c.'

On 2 August he complained that the Council had been insulted by the short-lived Brown-Dorion government, which had sent a member to the Council who was not able to enunciate policy, and he foresaw the ministry's early demise. Five days later he supported its successor [443], the 'Double Shuffle' ministry of Cartier and Macdonald, the mirror image of the administration whose resignation had precipitated the crisis. The reason might well have been that Prince needed government support for the advancement of his private interests. He had become involved in railroading once again [434] and, to the discomfiture of Arthur Rankin, the N & DR scheme had been resurrected [444] – but this time with an imposing embellishment, a bridge across the Niagara River [445].

The matter of the Algoma judgeship dragged on, despite Macdonald's promises [446, 447], until on 24 February 1859 Prince received a letter from Sir Edmund Head formally offering him the position [449]. Curiously, that communication came only a few days after Prince had come out in support of confederation (albeit with the qualification that Canada should be independent) [448]. With its emphasis on a happy union, 'independently, thoroughly British at heart,' this proposal seemed to be a re-phrasing in positive terms of remarks he had made on the subject the previous July [441]. Then, in supporting the principle of confederation, he had feared 'Frenchmen ruling over us.' The pro-British tone of these proceedings was also reflected in the form of a bill to outlaw that Yankee devil's invention, the bowie knife [450, 451].

Determined not to miss the opportunity to deliver a farewell speech, Prince attended the Legislative Council on 3 May 1859, even though he was seriously ill [452]. As it turned out, however, this was not to be his final appearance. Later that month an inspection of the land around the Soo cast doubt on the wisdom of settling there [453]. An accident that summer on the steamer *Ploughboy* [454] vividly reinforced his impression of the tenuous link then connecting Algoma to civilization. Whether he accepted the judgeship or not, however, he announced his determination to end his career in the Legislative Council [455].

On Prince's return to Sandwich, the importunities of mankind, in combination with an independence celebration, made so powerful an inducement that he overcame his resolution to forsake public life, and found himself playing host as well as speaker to a large gathering of blacks on 1 August [456]. Public life would not forsake *him*.

Prince's long-cherished dream, the Niagara and Detroit Rivers Railroad, had to be virtually abandoned when it became apparent that the contractor would be unable to carry out the work [457]. The only consolation seemed to be that the hated Rankin could gain nothing, but the episode had another significance: one of Prince's options for the future had closed. It was doubtless this enforced re-examination of his prospects that led Prince, in the light of his disappointing inspection of the Soo, to postpone his resignation from the Legislative Council [458].

The following months were a period of transition for Prince. He last saw The Park Farm on 24 February 1860, and later noted in his diary, 'I do not desire *Ever* again to place my foot on the ungrateful Soil of ungrateful Essex.' On 2 March he was arranging patronage in Kent as well as at Sault Ste Marie [459].

Legislation sponsored by Prince early in 1860 was in the familiar pattern, arising for the most part out of his personal experience and interests. It included a bill requiring steamers to be equipped with sails for emergencies, and still another game bill [460].

For a time the Toronto *Globe* alleged that Prince had deferred his acceptance of the judgeship because of the danger that an opposition member would be elected to replace him in the Legislative Council [461], but the charge was turned aside easily enough with the tabling, on 19 April, of all correspondence on the subject. What really troubled Prince was the news that George Bullock, the Essex County treasurer, for whom he had gone surety [285], was in default to the amount of £1,800 [462]. Prince, of course, paid his share immediately, but in consequence, for some months he suffered severe financial embarrassment.

Still, there were Macdonald's promises [463, 465] to keep him going, and another of those local-interest bills. This one, for the division of Sandwich Township into East and West [464], was passed on 1 May.

On 26 May Prince finally received his appointment to Algoma [466]. The next few days were spent in leavetaking, and in composing another fawning letter to Macdonald [467], making some arrangements, including those concerning a possible successor to his seat in the Western Division (which was finally won by Sir Allan MacNab).

Prince arrived at Sault Ste Marie on 7 July, 1860 [468]. He took up residence in a boarding house operated by Maria Hetherington, who had been his landlady in Toronto the previous year [437], but within three days he had been disillusioned as to his newfound retreat [469]. His last bit of influence in the patronage of Essex and Kent was exerted on 29 July [470], and a month later he was qualifying magistrates for Algoma [471]. The transition was over.

By virtue of his appointment as judge of the District Court, Prince automatically became chairman of the Court of Quarter Sessions and judge of the Surrogate Court. He was also responsible for choosing the locations of division courts at various places in addition to the Soo, which was to be the district town. Richard Carney was appointed sheriff, and the loyal Septimus Prince, who moved with his father to Algoma, became District Court Clerk, registrar of the Surrogate Court, and deputy clerk of the Crown.

At the close of his parliamentary career Prince counted 62 acts that he had originated. No such stocktaking would be complete, however, without a suggestion or two as to the choosing of his successor in the Western Division [472]. To be avoided at all cost was any man with Arthur Rankin's shortcomings.

Through John A. Macdonald's error the Quarter Sessions began on 20 November [473], whereas they should have been held in December. When the error[9] was discovered, they were held on the correct date [474]. To Prince's credit, he revised his first, uncharitable opinion of Richard Carney [467], which apparently had been based largely on hearsay and physical appearance. As to the life that confronted his father, Octavius reported (a little ungrammatically) to the Windsor *Herald*:

His District is of vast extent, and the distance between his Eastern Court at Manitowaning, in Lake Huron, and his Western Court at Fort William, is no less than 420 miles! accessible only at certain seasons of the year, (to say nothing of the Courts which he is required to hold at the Sault Ste Marie and the 'Bruce Mines,' which is about 40 miles from the 'Soo,' and the incessant calls upon him for advice and assistance in this hitherto unorganized and remote part of Canada where law is, comparatively speaking, unknown,) gives him anything but a 'bed of roses.' That remoteness, if I understand him correctly, forms, in his Honor's estimation, its principal charm: but he is grievously disappointed in his favorite sport of shooting and hunting, there being no game of any sort whatever up here; nor even fishing, with a rod and line, worth mentioning.

The absence of sport was a bitter disappointment to a man like Prince. On 16 April 1861 he lamented, 'Oh this *horrid Canada*, this *detestable* Canada, for a sportsman of 45 years standing such as I am, and who, *Even now*, will back my Gun in the Turnip fields, & stubbles, & *Coverts* of England, at *feather or fur* for £100 against *any shot in England*, be [he] whom he may!.' But that was not the only blow. By 4 February excavation had begun for the foundation of a new house, at Grant's Point, east of the village, for Prince and, if they chose to move, his

---

9 Macdonald inadvertently wrote the wrong month in his instructions to Prince.

family. The word that they would not join him, that he would spend the rest of his life alone, reached him on 17 April [475].

For Prince there was no escape. Regardless of personal unhappiness and impoverishment, judicial duties such as the opening of a division court at Bruce Mines [476] – a community owing its existence largely to the despised Arthur Rankin, who had opened the first mine there in 1846 – had to go ahead, and it seemed Rankin's presence tormented him whenever a visitor from the south stopped by [477].

A poor start had been made on the building of a jail and courthouse [478], so for a time Prince had to rent suitable premises while various alternative sites were considered [484]. These were trivial, local matters, however, and as before, what lay at a distance was more interesting. Below, an election for the Assembly was in progress, and it went without saying that in Essex Prince would support whoever was running against Rankin [479]. In Kent, Albert was running; Rankin, of course, won in Essex and Albert lost in Kent. Virtue's reward, as it had been since the days of his youth, was martyrdom [481].

Meanwhile, construction of the new house has been moving ahead [480], and on 28 September it was named Belle Vue Lodge [482]. It had turned out well, and Mrs Hetherington deserved the credit [483].

Early in 1861 Prince recognized that public affairs were mismanaged at Sault Ste Marie because the Algoma District was only a judicial division and had no municipal function or authority. He pressed Macdonald in the matter, and as usual he was put off. The failure to erect a jail and courthouse was a case in point, and petitions for their construction and the creation of a municipal authority were sent to Ottawa in late 1862 [487, 488]. Indeed, a return to the dear, old, simpler days of yore, to the arrangement prior to the inception of the district councils in 1842, when the magistrates in quarter sessions dispensed both justice and local government, was in Prince's opinion the solution to Algoma's problems. He was so convinced of this that throughout his northern career he struggled with unaccustomed consistency to achieve these two ends [489, 493, 497, 500, 503, 504, 507, 508, 513–515, 518, 519, 532]. In Ottawa he must have seemed a hopeless anachronism.

An impending Indian surrender on Manitoulin Island [485] afforded Prince the prospect of a quasi-diplomatic function in the days ahead, but as 1862 drew to a close he was once again revealing his love of the military life. He volunteered yet again for service on the frontier [486], despite the militia law that exempted the judges of county courts from service.

Another of the dominant themes in the old soldier's last years was his forceful response to physically dangerous situations. The threat of

Fenian invasions frightened him not one bit. On 28 March 1866, for example, he was 'promising them if they Came as much of *"Prince's Mixture"* as I gave the Pirates at Windsor in Dec'r/38.'

Belle Vue Lodge was for sale [489, 503], as it had been almost from the day it was named. At various times during his northern career Prince's attempts to escape what he was fond of calling the hyperborean cold of his New Siberia turned his envious eye to such greener fields as the United States [492], to Toronto [500], York County [528], and the Red River – but not, it seems, to Welland, which was too civilized [533, 534].

Indian affairs occupied much more of Prince's time at the Soo than they had previously, and they usually had judicial or municipal overtones. A journey to Fort William in 1863 [490] to apprehend a murder suspect prompted him to appoint constables at that outpost. Fort William had hitherto been forced to rely on the remote and infrequent services of Messrs Hynes and Hughes, of Sault Ste Marie. There was also a replacement for Indian Superintendent George Ironside, Junior, lately deceased [491]. There were surrenders of Indian land on Manitoulin Island [485], lands at Mississagi River [505] and Whitefish River [506], and a mill site at Garden River [526]. There was also a problem in that the Indians had many responsibilities but few of the white man's privileges, and Prince foresaw trouble [497].

Another difficulty in 1863 and 1864 appears to have centred on relations between Sheriff Carney and the two constables, Hughes and Hynes [494–496, 499, 501]. In the past, Prince had clearly sided against 'Old Nick,' as he had styled the sheriff, but a mellowing process was under way. He demonstrated, in a letter to Macdonald in 1864, that his command of the classics and his celebrated wit were as sharp as ever, but he also had kind words for Macdonald's new political ally, George Brown [498]. By 1866 there was even a distinct warming, not only towards Carney [512], but towards that erstwhile arch fiend Arthur Rankin [521].

There was also a perceptible shift in his religious attitude. Whereas previously Roman Catholicism had been 'all mummery & humbug,' by 1865 Prince was defending Catholics against an Anglican priest [502], and he did so again in 1867 [526].

Prince's remarkable resiliency enabled him to survive a series of misfortunes in his old age, any one of which would have been a serious setback to a younger, lesser man. An accident with a horse forced him to amputate his own thumb [509], a bank failure caused him further financial loss [520], Septimus died of alcoholism [510, 525, 527], and in September 1868, accompanied only by the guide Kenosh and the latter's twelve-year-old son, he was marooned by a gale for several days, utterly unprepared, on an islet south of St Joseph's Island.[10]

As John Prince completed the seventieth year of his eventful life, he was given an opportunity to shape the image of him that would be passed on to posterity, in the second volume of Fennings Taylor's *Portraits of British Americans*. The memoir he produced was only lightly edited, if at all, and presented in the third person. It was reasonably close to the truth, but, on occasion, sought to improve on it [507, 510]. The essential idea was there, but as the sketch said of his oratory, the idea could not be separated from 'those beauties and embellishments which seemed playfully to glisten about it like spray around a rock.' It was 'the compact material, whereon his fancy could tack an attractive fringe':

On his father's side, Colonel Prince comes of a good old Gloucestershire family, and on his mother's from such an one in Devonshire. He received the rudiments of his education from his uncle, a clergyman of the Church of England, resident in his native county. At an early age he was removed to the College at Hereford, one of those notable English schools of which the old land is justly proud.

The 'good old Gloucestershire family' among his paternal ancestors was probably the Hoopers, who appear to have been his grandmother's rather than his grandfather's blood relatives. The clergyman uncle from whom he received his early education must have been the Reverend Thomas Hooper of Elkstone and Syde in Gloucestershire. It must also have been the uncle, not Prince as the beginning of the sentence implied, who was 'resident in his native county.' The 'College at Hereford' was the Collegiate Grammar School (the modern Cathedral School), not 'the Old College' nearby, which, paradoxically, is associated with Hereford Cathedral.

Readers of that sketch learned what Prince wished them to learn, and no more. They were given some account (but no specifics) of his political career. They found a paragraph in praise of his legendary hunting skill and sportsmanship, and about the same on his judicial career; but more than half the sketch was devoted to his military exploits. There was nothing at all about the railroad or mining interests that had cost him so much energy; nor, for that matter, was there anything about his wife and children. Prince's autobiography was in the tradition

---

10 The trip was from Bruce Mines to Belle Vue Lodge, and involved stopping probably on Salt Island, then hopping to Butterfield Island, also south of St Joseph Island, and to Hen Island between Neebish and Sugar Islands, before reaching home. The ordeal began on 14 September and lasted a full week.

INTRODUCTION lix

of cunning that had been elevated to a fine art by his father, whose very existence John Prince had spent a miserable lifetime trying to conceal.

Shortly after his arrival in Algoma Prince had perceived the need for a free port at Sault Ste Marie, as a means of increasing commerce in that border town, and for once his lobbying had succeeded. By the spring of 1866 the experiment had proved a failure, however, and Prince changed his position with his accustomed ease [511]. There was similar flexibility in his attitude towards the Fenians. In the spring Prince was prescribing his own remedy for them, which had been so effective in 1838, but by the summer the hardships of 1838 had returned [516]. Once again the idea of independence commended itself, this time as a means of avoiding the pressure on Britain that the Fenians, with the support of a large part of the American population, were applying by their threat to Canada [517]. In Prince's mind colonialism led inevitably to the very worst abuses of which a civil service was capable [522], and so it is small wonder that he viewed British North American union, without independence, with disgust [524].

The Fenian threat continued into 1868 [529], and Prince came to suspect the loyalty of at least one of the villagers, Charles Bampton [530]. Ironically, tragically, less than two weeks later John Prince himself faced the fact that his personal philosophy over the years had evolved away from monarchy and towards republicanism – and the extension of this was that he concluded he had fought on the wrong side in 1838 [531].

The reclusive Prince, who had so often wished for death during his sojourn in Canada, was at last beginning to sense its approach. By the summer of 1867 he had selected the spot for his lonely grave, on what was then an island in front of Belle Vue Lodge [523]. Still, he remained active until the summer of 1870, when in July it is said that he journeyed to Toronto for medical assistance.[11] Back at Belle Vue Lodge early in August, he was still, although a little quaveringly, shaking a fist at the world [535]. As the end came near it is reported that he turned to Chicago for help in September, and to Toronto again in October. In November, back once more at the Soo, the nearly indestructible Prince, having already lost his left thumb in 1866 [509], inspected his farm and later recorded:

Find that the wolves are again ravaging the young cattle and set out traps along

11 Alan Charles Prince, John Prince's great-grandson, read a short paper (unpublished) to the Essex Historical Society, 28 May 1923. There are some slight inaccuracies throughout, but it ends with material that must have been based on a diary volume for 1870, since lost. Details from this source concerning Prince's last days are incorporated here.

the back farm. Had the misfortune to catch my left forefinger in one almost severing it and unable to get medical assistance cut it off with my paring knife.

Prince weakened rapidly, and on 30 November he died.

He had spent nearly forty years in a desperate search for peace of mind, struggling to escape from whatever his circumstances happened to be at any given time, perhaps never dreaming of the ultimate irony: that he might be removed from office. Possibly Prime Minister and Minister of Justice John A. Macdonald pressed a year's leave of absence on the ailing Prince when he visited Toronto in October, but the truth was that it was planned to replace him [536]. Prince's death, however, spared him this humiliation, and brought him peace at last.

JOHN PRINCE

DOCUMENTS

1 PRINCE TO THE EDITOR OF THE *Canadian Emigrant*
[*Sandwich* Canadian Emigrant, *5 September 1835*]

Sandwich, August 27, 1835

In your paper and Supplement of the 15th instant I observed the following paragraphs:

(For the paragraphs to which Mr. Prince alludes the reader is referred to Nos 6 and 7 of the Emigrant.)

Now, Sir, I am of all men the least ambitious to figure in the columns of a Newspaper, and I have always held it as an unfortunate disease to be afflicted, as some learned persons are, with the "Cacoethes Scribendi"[1] for Country Journals. But there are circumstances under which a man ought not to remain silent; and as the latter of your paragraphs contains a direct reflection upon the decision of our late GRAND JURY, I, as their Foreman, cannot submit that it should pass unnoticed or unanswered.

On reading that paragraph I thought it did not originate with you. I thought it was suggested to you by some weak, designing, cunning person, who was bent rather on annoying the feelings of others and on distorting and mis-stating things, than on furthering the ends of Justice. I therefore called on you in person, and in the presence of a fellow juryman and Magistrate demanded from you the author of the paragraph in question. I had my suspicions, and they turned out right. With manly candour you informed me that you had written it, *but that the information had been supplied to you by* MR. CHARLES ELIOT, *of Petite Cote.*[2]

I now take the liberty of telling this Mr. Eliot, through the medium of your columns, that a more impudent, artful, unfounded or ungenerous attack was never made upon a highly respectable body of men than that which he has been the cause of making. This Mr. Charles Eliot – this would-be-learned "*Judge*" as he is called (God save the mark!) knows or ought to know that a Grand Jury before entering upon their duties are sworn to secrecy. He knows or ought to know that to impugn their decisions or their motives is at all times highly indelicate and indecorous, and I will add highly culpable. He states, through you, that "the Prisoners at their examination had both acknowledged the *charge* against them to be true, and that one of them had actually signed a written confession of their guilt." And you, Sir, pinning your faith to this learned Lieutenant – this paragon of veracity, gravely remark that "In this statement

---

1 Uncontrollable urge to write.
2 Eliot, judge of the Western District Court, 1833–45, resided below Sandwich on the Detroit River.

there can be no error." Now, Sir, I happen to differ from you in that assertion. I happen to know and to have learned from my youth upwards that Human Nature is always liable to error; and not even the erudition of the Editor of the "Canadian Emigrant," nor yet the inferior learning and eloquence of his Provider can upset or shake the ancient truism, "humanum est errare."[3]

....

To your friend the learned Lieutenant (if he be your friend) I also offer my affectionate and well meant counsel – let him too ever abstain from meddling with the decisions of Grand Juries, or he may not long retain the gown which adorns his learned shoulders. Let him check, curtail, and moderate that sad disease, that aforesaid "Cacoethes Scribendi" under which as I am credibly informed, and as the columns of your earlier papers, I believe, will prove he has so long unfortunately labored. Let him shun as he would the Devil all the evil passions of our nature – envy, hatred, malice, jealousies, and all uncharitableness. Let him cultivate a good understanding between his neighbours and himself; and above all things let him behave gratefully to old friends. Let him return with abject contrition and repentance to the "Church of his Forefathers" from which he so unrighteously and without a cause withdrew himself. Let him do these things, and act and live in charity with all mankind – and then – he may with an easy heart and cheerful mind, in the romantic solitudes of Petite Cote, beneath the shade of the last remnant of his (wisely no doubt) depopulated orchard, enjoy the "otium cum dignitate"[4] to which all learned persons are undoubtedly entitled – and there he may continue to strum his "light guitar" – and there indulge in the highly useful, pure and patriotic avocations of raising the earliest saucerful of peas for himself and the earliest pretty nosegay for the pretty girls – avocations for the exercise of which and for which alone his high transcendant natural and acquired talents so eminently qualify him.

2 CHARLES ELIOT TO THE EDITOR OF THE *Canadian Emigrant*
[*Sandwich* Canadian Emigrant, *12 September 1835*]

Petite Cote, September 7, 1835

When a stranger comes into a community, his character can be discerned only from his actions. When, therefore, he hastily employs language detractious to the common courtesies of life, he cannot wonder if he be estimated accordingly. The Persians have a proverb, "The leper is discovered by his leprosy, and the gentleman by his language." Had the writer of the letter, in your last paper, signed, John Prince, been the sole person concerned in the Stamborough controversy, I should, most assuredly, have never troubled myself about a reply; because, Mr. Editor, I am not *au fait* at the *vulgar* tongue, an accomplishment wherein that individual is immeasurably my superior, I exult not in the "tougher pellicle" to cope with him on the gladiatory stage of

3 To err is human.
4 Leisure with dignity.

grossness. In faith, in such contests, without any feeling of envy, I yield him every leaf of the palm.

....

Since Mr. John Prince has been pleased to fancy and tell you many things that I have done, Mr. Editor; I will tell you one that I cannot do. I never can, and never will, commit a nuisance by placing a brewery on one side of the public street and encroaching on the other; at the same time, issue my summons and sit in judgment over others for an obstruction on the highway.

3   PRINCE TO THE EDITOR OF THE *Canadian Emigrant*
[*Sandwich* Canadian Emigrant, *19 September 1835*]

Sandwich, September 18, 1835

If Mr. Eliot means (as I infer he does) to charge me with committing "a nuisance by placing a Brewery on one side of the public street and encroaching on the other; *at the same time* issuing my summons and sitting in judgment over others for an obstruction on the Highway", I, in return, charge him with being the author of a wicked, wilful, and malicious falsehood. It is due to the public and to myself to explain the matter. In a few weeks after my arrival here in 1833 I removed the large building which is *now* my Brewery from the river side to where it stands. I could not place it further back because of buildings in the rear. I took advice upon the subject, and was told, and I believe, that it does not encroach upon the street. It formed my stables, waggon house, &c. until the last Spring, when I turned it into a Brewery ... If it be a trespass are the public injured or incommoded by it? The street is bettered; for I keep it dry and clean; and I *know* that the kind and courteous feelings of the Canadians are with me, seeing as they must, that I am bent on general improvements, that I spend all I have among them, and that my wharf (to me a most expensive one) and my private property along the river side (extending as it does by *grant* into the very channel, and therefore liable to be shut up by me at pleasure) has been ever freely open to them for sleighing and every other accommodation they require from me.

4   ELIOT TO THE EDITOR OF THE *Canadian Emigrant*
[*Sandwich* Canadian Emigrant, *26 September 1835*]

Petite Cote, September 21, 1835

Mr. John Prince may boast his doing so much for the country; but I rather think, upon examination, those mighty feats would never have astounded us had there been no expectation of private emolument; his language, at all events, is not indicative of much affection for the place.

....

If it be true what some ancient author has handed down to us 'nullum magnum ingenium sine mixtura dementiæ'; and as our own poet, Dryden, expresses it,
'Great wit to madness sure is near allied'

there can only yet, unfortunately, have been disclosed the gloomy part of the comprehensive intellect from which all this has been elutriated.

5 DIARY, 6 JUNE 1836. *The Park Farm, Sandwich*
[*Hiram Walker Historical Museum, Windsor (loaned to the Archives of Ontario), John Prince Papers*][5]

A fine growing day, With occasional Showers. Sowed the field (which I sowed on Saty last with oats) with a mixture of *red top, timothy,* & *clover*, most of the former. Dr. Johnson[6] & Mr. Charles Baby[7] called and Solicited me to offer as member for Essex. Busy planting Potatoes & hauling dung.

6 DIARY, 27 JUNE 1836

A fine day. Great Excitement. Sandwich full of people. Gave a public breakfast at my House. Upwards of 50 breakfasted here. *Open house here & at Sandwich.* The election commenced at 11. Mr. Girty[8] nominated me. Mr. Lavallee[9] seconded me. I spoke 2 hours from the Hustings. Eliot & Langlois[10] opposed me. Polling began at 2 o'clock. I get on well. Lots of people here day & night.

7 DIARY, 28 JUNE 1836

Fine weather. Attended the Poll all day long. Sandwich all life and Spirits. *My Colours* flying and Band playing. Open house here & at Sandwich. All friends anxious in my Cause. At the Close *I* head the Poll Considerably.

8 DIARY, 29 JUNE 1836

Fine weather. The Same Scene as Yesty. It now appears that neither Langlois nor Eliot have any chance, yet they will not resign. How every unhandsome. We dine now at Mrs. Hawkens'.[11] I head *the Poll.*

---

5 To avoid tedious repetition this citation is omitted hereafter. Abbreviations of certain other references are listed in the *Preface*.
6 This is probably Dr D.D. Johnson, who advertised in the *Canadian Emigrant* in 1831.
7 Thomas Charles Baby was a son of the Hon. James (Jacques) Baby and nephew of Jean Baptiste Baby. He was clerk of the peace of the Western District, 1836–71.
8 Prideaux Girty, of Gosfield, a son of Simon Girty, appears as a justice of the peace of the Western District from 1836.
9 Benjamin Lavalée was a justice of the peace in 1837. He owned property in Sandwich in 1846.
10 Dominique Langlois was an innkeeper at Petite Cote.
11 Mrs Honor (Honour) Hawkens was a Sandwich innkeeper.

9 Diary, 30 June 1836

Fine weather. All gaiety & excitement. Sandwich never Saw Such an Election before. *Eliot resigned.* My friends vote for *me & Caldwell*[12] by my wish. All goes on well. I head the Poll. C. Eliot only 42.

10 Diary, 1 July 1836

Fine weather. The same Scene as before. All Noise, Gaiety, & uproar (tho *at my expence!*). Langlois declines resigning although he has not the Slightest Chance. I head the Poll. Caldwell *next*.

11 Diary, 2 July 1836

A fine day. Langlois resigned at 1/2 p. 10 a.m. The poll then closed, when the number of votes was

> Prince   364!!!!
> Caldwell   341!!!
> Langlois   116!!
> Eliot   42!

I & Caldwell declared elected. *Chaired* with music &c. We addressed the Electors. I Gave a public Dinner at Mrs. Hawkens' Tavern. All went off admirably.

12 Diary, 20 September 1836. *St Thomas*

Mr. Gardiner,[13] Cahoon[14] &c. there. We all met at breakfast. Busy all the morning in making Arrangements. Attended the Great Rail Meeting, I in the Chair. I was aftwds made one of the Directors, & was subsequently made the President. All went off well. Met several friends, & got rather tipsy. Retired to bed at about 2 *o'clock*.

13 Diary, 7 November 1836

A lovely day. Left Niagara with my family & Carriage & horses at 8, & reached Toronto in health & Safety (thank God) by 12. Drove to The North American. Engaged all the Evening with Mr. McClean[15] & his friends relative to the approaching election of speaker. Engaged till past 12 at night.

---

12 Francis Caldwell represented Essex in the Legislative Assembly, 1835–40.
13 Samuel Gardiner was a justice of the peace in 1839.
14 Benjamin P. Cahoon was a partner in the Colborne Iron Works or Furnace, Gosfield Township, and a railroad promoter.
15 Archibald McLean was a member of the Legislative Assembly, for Stormont.

14 DIARY, 8 NOVEMBER 1836

A lovely morning with the usual hoar frost. Attended the opening of Parliament at 3 p.m. Aftwds attended the Election of a Speaker when Mr. McClean was duly Elected by a Majority of 15. We afterwards dined at the North American house & I went to bed most *awfully tipsy* I regret to say.

15 DIARY, 16 NOVEMBER 1836

A drizzling morning. Attended the House all day. Brought in my Bill for preventing the dissol[utio]n of P[ar]l[ia]ment by the Crown's demise & *spoke thereon*. Spoke also on Mr. *McNab's*[16] bill as to *members vacating their seats* on accepting office. D[ea]r William ill with the Measles. D[ea]r Charly & Henry also very unwell. Dined with a large Party at the Mess.

16 DIARY, 28 NOVEMBER 1836

A fine day, bright & sunny. Busy all day long at the House. Spoke at length on the *Court of Equity* Bill & was much applauded. House adjourned at 1/2 p. 5. At Rudyerd's[17] as usual.

17 COURT OF EQUITY SPEECH, 28 NOVEMBER 1836
[*Toronto* Christian Guardian, *7 December 1836*]

MR. PRINCE, on rising to support this bill, said he could not help expressing the pleasure with which he had listened to the speech of his hon. and learned friend, the Solicitor General.[18] The learned Solicitor had clearly elucidated and explained the subject in such a manner as to convince every person of the necessity of a Court of Chancery[19] in this Province.

....

There was one thing in the bill which he would never consent to. It confined the practice in this court, should it be established, to Solicitors and Attorneys in this Province. He for one would never submit to that; and would move an amendment, that any practitioner of five years standing in the Courts of Equity in England, Ireland, and Scotland, should be permitted to practice in this court, provided such Solicitor produces testimonials, not only that he had been five

---

16 Sir Allan Napier MacNab was a member of the Legislative Assembly for Wentworth in 1836. He was a prominent Tory leader, a co-premier of the Province of Canada from 1854 to 1856, and an important railroad promoter.

17 Henry Rudyerd, as a lieutenant in the 15th Foot, was stationed at Amherstburg in 1834. He was a personal friend of Prince.

18 Christopher Alexander Hagerman.

19 Chancery, or equity, was a system to overcome the limitations of the common law, through the application of conscience or natural justice to the resolution of controversies.

years in practice, but that he had never been struck off the rolls of any court, and had never been suspended on account of any malpractice. He ought also to take the oath of allegiance, &c.

18 DIARY, 15 DECEMBER 1836

A fine Cold day. The House again occupied all day in the question of The Clergy Reserves. Dr. Rolph[20] spoke 2-1/2 hours. *At 4 I rose to reply to him. Spoke 'till 5, when the House adjourned till tomorrow morning.*

19 CLERGY RESERVES SPEECH, 15 DECEMBER 1836
[*Toronto* Christian Guardian, *28 December 1836*]

The hon. and learned Doctor had told them a great deal about the connection between Church and State, and the consequences of upholding a dominant Church. He (Mr. P.) was not aware that the appropriation of the Clergy Reserves in the way pointed out in the Constitutional Act, would have the effect so much deprecated by the hon. and learned member. This Province was essentially different from the old country; there he did not approve of what they called toryism, and his great objection to it was, that it tends to support an union of Church and State. (Hear, hear.) – But when a gift was made for the support of religious teachers, for the purpose of keeping up an equilibrium between our own and the Catholic Church, which possesses more wealth, he could see no danger to be apprehended from it; if he could discover a probability of its leading to an undue coalition, as hon. members seemed to dread, he would at once vote against it. (Hear, hear.)

. . . .

As long as these Reserves exist there could be no tythes, but if they were taken away from the Church, tythes must be collected and he cared not how soon. – (Hear, hear.) Let us be taxed an hundred fold rather than let our Ministers of religion depend upon the voluntary contributions of the public.

. . . .

It was contended that education required the assistance of public endowments rather than religion; he would ask what was education unless founded upon religion. He (Mr. P.) cared not what a man's education might be, he cared not if he were ten times more eloquent than the learned Doctor himself, unless that learning were founded upon proper religious principles, it would go for nothing. (Hear, hear.) He might be able to astonish and amuse, he might strike us with wonder and with awe, but destitute of religion and its powerful influence, it would be of little worth. Let us then place our children under the tuition of those who will imbue them with a correct and proper sense of religion, or let them be uneducated altogether; let them rather be serfs of the soil than be learned by irreligion. (Hear, hear.)

20 Dr John Rolph was a member of the Legislative Assembly for Norfolk. He was a radical Reformer, a rebel and subsequently a Clear Grit.

20 Diary, 16 December 1836

A fine cold day. Walked from the Garrison into town with the Lieut. Governor.[21] Engaged at the House all day. Spoke in Continuation of the debate in reply to Dr. Rolph. The Solr. General followed for 2-1/2 hours. The Question disposed of at 6 pm by a Majority in favor of *Religion* thank God. Home by 7.

21 Clergy Reserves Speech Continued, 16 December 1836
[Toronto Christian Guardian, *28 December 1836]*

The Clergy Reserves as they were familiarly termed, might be looked upon as a simple gift from his late revered Majesty George the Third to the Protestant Church. His object was not to make the Church dominant, it could not be so. It would be found a very moderate provision indeed for the Protestant Church of this country when it comes to be established as he hoped it would be ere long in its pristine glory, and slender as the provision was he hoped it would be secured to them.

. . . .

He believed the committee would concur in rejecting the preamble; if the bill were carried it would be signing the death warrant of the protestant Clergy. He trusted that every hon. member of that house would stand up in defence of the church and not allow her to be despoiled of her rights. The moment had arrived when she must either stand or fall, and he confidently hoped that by their vote that day they would enable after ages to look back upon the page of history and say, that it was the thirteenth parliament which supported and secured to them the protestant religion.

22 Diary, 17 January 1837

A fine but Cold day. I do not think that the Cold is more Severe here than it is in The W. District. Engaged all day long in the House & spoke several times against a grant of £200,000 for the Great Western Rail Road from *Hamilton to Sarnia*, which was nev[ertheles]s Carried by a Majority of about 9.

23 Diary, 25 January 1837

A fine day and mild. Busy in the House as usual all day. *Read the Western District Bank Bill a 2nd time*, & overcame the opposition offered to it. Third reading appointed for Friday next. House rose at 1/4 p 10 am. William & Albert ill at Garrison.

21 Sir Francis Bond Head was appointed lieutenant governor of Upper Canada in 1835. His reactionary attitude contributed to the outbreak of the Upper Canada Rebellion.

24 DIARY, 26 JANUARY 1837

A fine day. Suffering from a bad cold all day. Occupied at The House. Spoke in favor of The British North American Bank Bill. William, Albert, & dear little Henry all unwell at The Garrison with colds. I also suffering much from the Same Cause. The House rose at 9 p.m.

25 DIARY, 27 JANUARY 1837

A fine mild day. The winter, upon the whole delightful. Engaged in The House of Assembly all day long. *The Western District Bank Bill passed a 3rd reading. Home by 1/2 p 9 pm*, tired & suffering from Cold. The children a good deal *better*.

26 DIARY, 1 FEBRUARY 1837

Not very well. Intended to stay at home all day, but was sent for in The Great Western Rail Road debate. Withdrew my opposition because certain amendments of mine were agreed to. At the house all day, & got 2 Bills read for the first time. Walked home with Rudyerd & Dewson.[22] Fine weather & cold.

27 DIARY, 2 FEBRUARY 1837

A very cold day. The Chancery Bill debated and Carried, after 8 hours violent debate. My clause in favor of English Solicitors strongly opposed. The Solicitor General & I had some violent *personal* discussion on the subject, But I carried my point in toto. Home by 1/2 p 10. Mr. & Mrs. Rudyerd & my dear M.A.[23] went to Mrs. Bolton's[24] pty.

28 DIARY, 3 FEBRUARY 1837

A lovely day. Hard frost & very cold, but bright and fine. Busily engaged all day long in the House. Had another violent Conflict with the Solr. General in the discussion of The Chancery Bill. The Bill passed after a long debate at 10 o'clock p.m. Home by 1/2 past 11 tired & out of humour.

---

22 This is probably Alfred Kinsey Dewson, M.D., who was a surgeon of Sandwich and Chatham.
23 Mary Ann, Mrs Prince.
24 Apparently this is Mrs D'Arcy Boulton.

29 EXCERPT FROM CHANCERY BILL DEBATE, 3 FEBRUARY 1837
[*Toronto* Christian Guardian, *15 February 1837*]

MR. PRINCE remarked that he was certainly not a little surprised when the hon. and learned Doctor from Norfolk seconded the motion of the hon. and learned Solicitor General, to expunge that clause of the Bill which allowed English lawyers to practice in this Court; and the Solicitor General had surely acted ungratefully towards the learned Doctor in not seconding this motion for him. But he now saw the reason of the learned Doctor's conduct since he came out and declared himself opposed to the Bill altogether; – he saw that, if he could succeed in keeping English barristers, solicitors, and attorneys out of this Court, confusion and every evil attendant on ignorance would ensue, and the Legislature might be compelled to repeal the Act and abolish the court.

30 DIARY, 7 FEBRUARY 1837

A fine & mild day. Engaged at the House 'till 9 pm. Mr. Hepburn[25] was brot to the Bar of the House & there admonished. *Spoke in his behalf.* They wronged him. Occupied all day aftwds in various Matters of bus[ines]s. My dr. M.A. Mr. & Mrs. Rudyerd & Captn Pinder went to an Evg party at Mr. Hagerman's.

31 DIARY, 9 FEBRUARY 1837

A fine & lovely day, bright, not too cold, & air clear. Rather better. Occupied in the *House 'till past 1 in the Morng* upon the Clergy Reserve Rectories. Home by 2 o'clock. I had another breeze with Mr. Solr. General Hagerman. The House most *uproarious*.

32 EXCERPT FROM DEBATE, 9 FEBRUARY 1837
[*Toronto* Constitution, *15 February 1837*]

Mr. Boulton,[26] seconded by Mr. Cartwright,[27] moves that it be

Resolved, That it is expedient to pass an Act declaring that the Rectories lately established for this Province, do not confer on the incumbents thereof any ecclesiastical power or jurisdiction over any of the inhabitants of the province, except over members of the respective congregations attending the Churches in such Rectories.–

Mr. Richardson[28] began speaking – the hour midnight – when Mr. McNab

---

25 William Hepburn was registrar of the Court of Chancery.
26 George Strange Boulton represented Durham in the Legislative Assembly.
27 John Solomon Cartwright sat for Lennox and Addington. A supporter of the 'Family Compact,' he later opposed the union of Upper and Lower Canada, and he refused the proffered post of solicitor general in united Canada.
28 Charles Richardson represented the Town of Niagara in the Legislative Assembly.

gave a tremendous yawn and the laughter rendered Richardson's speech inaudible – he sat down.

Mr. PRINCE (of Essex) rose and read the House a severe, and as it appeared to this reporter a deserved lecture on order – he declared that the Speaker had been wantonly insulted, parliamentary decorum violated, and that the honble and learned Solicitor General had a most unparalleled stock of assurance and most unwarrantable IMPUDENCE.

Cries of Chair, chair, order, order, stopt the learned gentleman.

The SPEAKER said such language, applied as it had been by one member to another was very disorderly and deeply to be regretted.

Mr. PRINCE. – I withdraw the offensive expressions – I bow to the Chair. – What an uproar have we not witnessed within these walls during the last 4 hours! It is discreditable to us, and those who look upon us (turning to the bar) will go away with an impression very unfavourable, and such as I do not think we should have made.

Mr. HAGERMAN. – If the conduct of the House is disgraceful to it this evening, the exhibition the hon'ble and learned gentleman has made will not be likely to raise it much in the public esteem. (Hear, and laughter.)

Mr. CARTWRIGHT, (of Lennox and Addington.) The House instead of speaking "peace and good will towards men" have this night agreed to a declaration of war and prevented the settlement of the Clergy Reserve question for the present Session.

Mr. PRINCE regretted the vote he had given, and would he believed, now be willing to re-invest these Reserves in the British Crown.

33 DIARY, 14 FEBRUARY 1837

A fine day. The 3rd reading of my *Alien Bill* came on & *after some hours debate it was carried by a Majority of 12.* I spoke at great length in reply. Better though still very weak. *I drink bottle porter which strengthens me & does me much good.* Home by 1/2 past 11 fatigued. Pinder & o[the]rs here.

34 DIARY, 17 FEBRUARY 1837

A deep snow & a very cold day. Busy at The House all day. *Carried the Second reading of my Bill to prevent the Dissolution of Plment happening by the demise of The Crown. Maj[orit]y 11.* Home by 10 tired. Mr. & Mrs. Rudyerd & my dr. M.A. at a grand ball at The Garrison.

35 DIARY, 18 FEBRUARY 1837

A fine but a very cold day. Snow deep & drifting dreadfully. At the House all day. *Carried my Bill to prevent a dissolution of Plmt by demise of ye Crown.* Returned to The Garrison by 6. So Early mirabile dictu.[29] Found the dear boys there. A Very cold and very Comfortless day.

29 Strange to say.

36 DIARY, 20 FEBRUARY 1837

A very Mild Morning. Engaged at the House all day long & 'till 9 p.m. *in a Com[mittee] of the Whole on Supply*. Carried a vote of £1500 for a bridge over the Thames at Chatham. Called on His Exc[ellenc]y as to the Indian Reserve, *Rudyerd* &c.

((This day Mr. McNab prom'd me in the Ho[use] of Ass[embl]y that he would next Sess. support any claim I May make to Plmt for a loan to our R. Road.))[30]

37 DIARY, 9 MARCH 1837

Reached St. Thomas (20 miles) at 12 p.m. Met there Mr. Wilkinson[31] Mr. Wm. Elliott[32] & the other Commissioners for locating the Niagara & Detroit Rivers Rail Road. *Resolved* that it shall commence at *Fort Erie Rapids & end in the town of Sandwich*. Some opposition thereto. Sat up very late & retired to bed very much fatigued. The Horses still more so.

38 DIARY, 11 APRIL 1837. *The Park Farm*

Attended at the Quarter Sessions all day long. Mr. *Chas. Eliot* resigned the Chair and the Magistrates unanimously elected me their Chairman. Addressed the Grand Jury upon the *New Laws* &c. &c. & tried several prisoners. The Court rose at 6. Major Lachlan[33] gave up the Agr[icultura]l Soc[iet]y.

39 DIARY, 5 JUNE 1837

A fine day & exceedingly warm. Busily engaged at Sandwich all day, at the rail road meeting, &c. &c. *The Militia paraded in Sandwich as usual.* Dined at Mrs. Hawken's with some of the Directors. They Elected me their President for the ensuing Year. Mr. Rudyerd attended, & slept at The Park Farm.

40 DIARY, 1 JULY 1837. *Toronto*

A fine hot day. Rather Sick from the effects of medicine taken last night. Attended the House & introduced my Bill *Enabling Aliens to hold lands.* Also

---

30 Marginal notes are indicated thus (( )).
31 John Alexander Wilkinson, of Sandwich, a surveyor, was a member of the Legislative Assembly for Essex until 1836.
32 William Elliott, of Sandwich, was colonel of the Second Regiment of Essex Militia.
33 Robert Lachlan, formerly of the British 17th Regiment, was newly settled in Colchester Township in 1836. He was briefly president of the Western District Agricultural Society.

gave notice of introducing my Bill for *preserving Game* from being Killed out of Season. Also Moved *a Call of the House* for Tuesday next. At the Ontario House all the Evg & rather better from having taken Medicine.

41 DIARY, 5 JULY 1837

Very very heavy rain all night. I know not what will become of the Wheat Crops &c. if we do not have dry weather. It cleared up towards the middle of the day & became fine. Attended the House of Assembly and passed my *Game Protection bill through a 3rd reading.* The Bill to Enable aliens to hold Lands read a 2nd time. Engaged at the House 'till 5 p.m. The dear boys drank tea with me. My hound "Trimbush" arrived from Pickering U.C. Price $10.

42 DIARY, 6 JULY 1837

A fine, bright & warm morning. At the house all day & till 7 p.m. *Spoke* at length & voted agst the Bill enabling Bankers to suspend their payments in Specie *voluntarily*. The Bill nev[ertheles]s passed by a large Majority. Passed my Bill enabling Foreigners to hold Lands in this Province thro' a 3rd reading. Returned to The Ontario by 8 pm & went to bed at 9.

43 DIARY, 30 JULY 1837. *The Park Farm*

A fine hot day. In the Morning I rode over to Detroit & called on *Captain Marryatt R.N.* (the author of *Peter Simple, Jacob Faithful*, &c., &c., &c.) Called also on Brush[34] & others. At home in the Evening tired. Marryatt rather disappointed me as a *Conversationalist*.

44 DIARY, 31 AUGUST 1837

A fine day. The Sale of The Indian Reserve nr. Amherstburg took place. Mr. Rudyerd attended, & aftwds dined & returned home. I took the dear boys out shooting thro' McKee's Marsh. Shot 1 wood-duck, a bittern & 2 English Snipes. At home all the Evening afterwards, and rather tired. Lowspirited as usual.

45 DIARY, 18 DECEMBER 1837

A very hard frost & the coldest day we have had this winter. Went with Mr.

---

34 This is probably Edmund A. Brush, who had railroad interests in lower Michigan.

Charles Eliot to Detroit and Called on *Governor Mason*[35] & others about the state of Canadian affairs, the Rebels &c. &c. &c. Got home by 1/2 past 5 very cold. Mr. Eliot took tea with us. At home all the Evg, & executed Westaway's[36] counterpart Lease & Jessop's[37] 2nd Lease.

46 DIARY, 22 DECEMBER 1837

A very cold but a very fine day. Busy at home all day long in receiving visitors and in writing letters. Priest McDonell,[38] Mr. Whiting[39] and others Called. Very much Engaged as usual. Mr. Gardiner & Mr. Dougall[40] Called twice. I wrote to the Lt. Govr. & to Mr. McNab about sending Troops to protect this Frontier.

47 DIARY, 26 DECEMBER 1837

A fine but very cold day. Occupied all day in Sandwich. Attended the public meeting and enrolled myself as a volunteer to defend the Frontier. At 6 p.m. repaired to the Court House (our head quarters) with little *William*, And he & I did duty all night long in the open Weather and in relieving Guard &c. until 6 o'clock in the morning.

48 PRINCE TO COLONEL JAMES HAMILTON
[*MTCL*, James Hamilton Papers]

The Park Farm, December 28, 1837

I send this by Mr. Jessop, the Express, who will receive your directions for tomorrow morning & who will Call at our Post office in his way up, and will carry to you any thing that may be there for you.

I find, on Enquiry, that the present force collected in Sandwich is about 150, Most of whom are without fire arms, and raw, undisciplined recruits. I do not think the force ought to be rated at more than 60 effective Men. I am in Expectation of seeing here tomorrow upwards of 150 coloured me[n] from Malden & Sandwich, most of whom will have fire arms of their own, and are I am told, brave and true fellows. They will probably be commanded by Lieutenant Charles Eliot (one of our Magistrates) & by Mr. Rudyerd (late a Lieut. in the 15th Regt foot) and I hope & believe they will prove to be an efficient Corps.

None of the Essex Militia have yet arrived from below, nor can I inform you

35 Stevens T. Mason was governor of Michigan, 1835–40.
36 William Westaway, of Sandwich, for a time worked The Park Farm on a sharecrop basis.
37 This probably refers to George Jessop, a Sandwich innkeeper.
38 Father Angus MacDonell was the priest of Assumption Church, near Sandwich, 1831–43.
39 This is probably W.L. Whiting, who was a commission merchant in Detroit.
40 James Dougall at this time was a Windsor merchant and notary public.

when they will come. Col: Reynolds states that his men will assemble at Amherstbg tomorrow or on Saturday.

I [expect] to hear fro[m] Captn John Caldwell of Malden that *Every one* of his men (French Canadians living in & about the town of Amherstburg) *refuse to turn out!* They shall receive the full benefit of the Law. He has reported their conduct to Colonel Reynolds this day.

Many of the French Canadians in Petite Cote (about 6 miles from hence) have al[so] refused. Upon the whole I am of opinion that the French Canadians, *as a body, Cannot be relied on.*

I have nothing further, of importance, to Communicate This Evening. Should any thing transpire I will write to you, instanter.

49 DIARY, 30 DECEMBER 1837

A cold, raw & very uncomfortable day. Rode my young Horse down to Amherstbg to confer with the Militia officers & authorities as to the threatened attack on Amherstbg. Cold & wet. Many Militia at Amherstbg. Met a party of Officers &c. at Mr. Rudyerd's. I slept there. A very wet night. Rudyerd quite unwell.

50 DIARY, 6 JANUARY 1838

A fine day & mild. Saw a Rebel Schooner Sail past Sandwich full of men arms & 3 Cannon for Gibraltar with a view as we supposed to attack Amherstburg. All Excitement here. In the Evening about 150 Embarked on board the SB "United" & my Scow, & went to Malden to defend the place. Heavy rain. Reached Malden at 4 am. Wet & cold.

51 PRINCE TO STEVENS T. MASON
[Journal of the House of Assembly of Upper Canada, *February 15, 1838*]

Sandwich, January 6, 1838

As the organ of the Magistrates here, and by their desire, I lose not a moment to inform you that, from clear and unquestionable authority, who were eye-witnesses to the fact last night, we learn that a schooner laden with arms, ammunition, provisions, and from 80 to 100 men, left Detroit this morning, on her way down the river, with the intention of either attacking this Frontier or taking possession of the islands belonging to our Sovereign, called Bois Blanc and Fighting Island, or one of them.

The schooner, I am informed, is called *"The Anne."* She is at this moment slowly proceeding down the river and close upon your side below Spring-well, and is towed by a boat with several men in it. She has also *two cannon* on board.

I am also credibly informed that a large body of men are met at Fort Gratiot[41] for the express purpose of joining the rebels and fugitives from this country – and that the steam-boat "Macomb" has proceeded from Detroit to afford them succour; and we are also correctly informed, that our enemies possessed themselves last night from the Gaol in Detroit of a large quantity of arms, and also of a waggon-load of gunpowder from the Powder-House in your City. We are further correctly informed that they are raising Volunteers, arms, and ammunition at Monroe, to support the Rebels and their adherents.

We rely on the sincerity of your declaration that you, as Chief Magistrate of the opposite State, will do all in your power to preserve the peace – to prevent your people from committing a breach of their laws, and to maintain the amity which at present subsists between Great Britain and the United States. We beg leave to repreat our former assertion that we are prepared for any attack; but we again earnestly call upon you to take such immediate and energetic steps as will prevent bloodshed, and secure the peace of your countrymen and ours from being broken and destroyed. We at the same time beg to assure you that no exertions on our part shall be wanting to attain that very desirable object; but unless prompt and immediate steps are taken, we will not conceal from you our firm conviction that hostilities will have commenced and blood be shed within the next few hours.

52 MASON TO PRINCE
[Journal of the House of Assembly, *15 February 1838*]

Detroit, January 6, 1838

Your favour of this morning has been received. I most sincerely regret that matters are assuming so dangerous an aspect on our borders. We have despatched a Marshall to seize the Schooner now proceeding down the River. The "Macomb" was stopped, her Captain arrested, her lading examined, but nothing could be found to justify detaining her in Port. A Deputy Marshall has been despatched to Monroe and one to Fort Gratiot with authority to call out the power of the respective Counties to arrest all persons found in arms. A meeting of our citizens will be held at 3 o'clock this afternoon to enrol a Volunteer force to aid in enforcing the laws in this city. I need not again express my determination to do all in my power to prevent the violation of the amity now existing between our Governments.

53 DIARY, 8 JANUARY 1838. *Amherstburg*

A fine day & much Snow on the Ground. We left the Island for a few hours in the Morng. About 3 p.m. alarm was given that the Enemy had set sail from Sugar Island and was about landg on Bois Blanc. We hurried over there, & saw

---

41 Present Port Huron, Michigan.

the Enemy (2 or 300) comg over. Waited for them 3 hours, but they hovered abt the Island & kept off. We thought they meant to take Malden, & we therefore evacuated the Island & returned to the Town. The Enemy Schooner fired several shots, & we attacked her with rifles and musketry.

54 DIARY, 9 JANUARY 1838

A very cold day. Up all night, as usual, & our duty is most severe. The Enemy's Schooner at Anchor at the head of Bois Blanc, & we occasionally give her shots, but at too great a distance to hurt her. In the Evg she cannonaded the town, slipt down to Elliotts point, & went ashore. Our men then continued the attack with redoubled vigour. Killed several of the Enemy and took the rest Prisoners, also a large quantity of arms & ammunition & 3 Cannon.

55 DIARY, 15 JANUARY 1838

A fine but cold day. Rode up to The Ferry,[42] & aftwds went over to Detroit Where I met The Governor & a large number of the Most respectable Citizens. Spoke to them at Great length and Explained to them the Whole state of our affairs Civil & political. I believe I altered their opinions as to our Supposed Grievances &c. Did not get back till 6 p.m. My dear M.A. alarmed.

56 EXCERPT FROM PRINCE TO MASON
[Journal of the House of Assembly ... *15 February 1838*]

The Park Farm, January 25, 1838

I learn from good authority that the man calling himself *General Sutherland*[43] is gone into the interior of Michigan, (it is supposed in the direction of Pontiac) to raise Volunteers. I do hope and trust that your Authorities will arrest and secure him and his adherents if possible. It is painful to reflect upon the immense expense attending the constant guarding of this country. Upon whom that expense will eventually fall it is not for us perhaps to enquire at this moment: but I am sure Your Excellency will agree with me in opinion that it is the bounden duty of all good citizens and subjects to prevent the invasion of Upper Canada from being proceeded with if possible, both with a view to save the effusion of human blood and also the enormous cost of keeping thousands of men in arms. I beg to enclose a copy of some acts which our Legislature has felt it incumbent upon them to pass in these disastrous and most critical times.

---

42 Present downtown Windsor.
43 Thomas Jefferson Sutherland was a lawyer and journalist from Buffalo, New York. He commanded the Patriots at Detroit in 1838. After his capture he was sentenced to banishment in Van Diemen's Land, but he was released at Quebec and made his way back to the United States.

57 Diary, 24 February 1838

A fine cold day. On duty all the Morng. At 3 p.m. was informed while Rudyerd was here that a large body of the enemy had taken possession of "Fighting Island". We all marched down there & saw them but night comg on & the Ice bad to cross over we delayed making an attack until tomorrow Morning.

58 Diary, 25 February 1838

A fine day. Marched at 1/2 past 3 with Haggerty[44] & the militia to attack Fighting Island. Met Col. Townshend with his regulars[45] & Captn Glasgow with his Cannon.[46] At 1/2 p 7 we marched over the Ice to attack the Enemy. They were about 300 in number, & before we got half way across they fled before us like kill-sheep dogs. We took 1 prisoner, 1 gun, some small arms & swords, a drum, & some ammunition and Provisions. Got home by 1 very much tired. At Sandwich in the Eveng.

59 Diary, 2 March 1838

A fine cold & clear day. Mr. Mills[47] & Ebberly[48] left. At home all the morng, and very busy in writing letters &c. &c. &c. At 3 p.m. I recd a message from The Honble Colonel Maitland[49] to march to Point Pelée Island to fight the Invaders there. Set out at 4 p.m. & travelled all night long with The Revd A. McDonell, Major Lachlan & Angus McD.[50] A very Cold night.

60 Diary, 3 March 1838

A lovely bright day. Reached Point Pelée Island with the Troops just after Sun-rise. Occupied the Island at once. Released the Inhabitants who were prisoners to the Rebels & Invaders. The latter fled! We scoured the Island. At 2 an action took place. We killed 8 rebels & wounded many others. We lost 2 regulars & 1 Cavalry volunteer, & had about 25 regulars wounded ((4 of whom afterwards died)). Drove to Mr. Girty's by 9 p.m. very cold & very much fatigued, & went to bed there quite exhausted.

---

44 This is probably James Haggerty, of Maidstone Township.
45 The reference is to Colonel (or Major) H.D. Townshend of the 32nd Regiment of Foot.
46 Glasgow's cannon were the Royal Artillery.
47 Either Dr Edward Mills or a brother is intended. Both were from Caradoc.
48 This is probably John Eberle, who owned a tavern on the Talbot Road in Orford Township.
49 Lieutenant Colonel John Maitland commanded the 32nd Regiment in the London and Western Districts.
50 The repetition of the name appears to be a slip. It seems unlikely that Bishop Alexander Macdonell of Kingston, Angus's uncle, is alluded to here.

61 Diary, 4 March 1838

A fine day. Returned home after 12 p.m. with Mr. Girty. About 8 miles below Malden I had the good fortune to capture *General Sutherland & Captain Spencer*[51] of The Patriot (or Rebel) Army! Conveyed them Prisoners to Malden. Arrived there at 5 p.m. Put up at Middleton's[52] as usual. Spent the Evening at Rudyerd's & called on The Hon. Col. Maitland & others. In good spirits.

62 Henry Rudyerd Diary, 4 March 1838
[*MTCL*, Boulton Papers]

Brig: Genl. Sutherland and Captn Spencer were captured by Lt Col'l Prince they were observed by him on the ice about 2 miles from our shore and nearly opposite to big creek about 7 miles below Amherstburg. Col P. was on his way to the latter place from the Island in comp'y with Cap Girty in a Sleigh, Myself & two other officers in another Sleigh. the horses being tired Prince proceeded[?] in two one horse cutters and followed the two men he observed on the ice. after a long chase [he] came up with them and to his great delight recognised Gen Sutherland, who at once recognised Prince and half drew his Sword Prince told him to put it back or he wd. shoot him, he then collared Sutherland and took his sword from him as also Cap Spencer, and *introduced* them to Girty and Myself who came up at the time. we escorted them to Amherstburg, and on the following day I was ordered to take charge of them to Toronto.

63 John Prince Diary, 22 March 1838. *Toronto*

A mild & moist day. Attended Sutherland's Trial again, when the same was postponed till *Thursday next* in order that he May have time to produce his witnesses!! He has none, to my knowledge, and I am sure he has none. Busily engaged in Town all day. *Took leave of Sir Francis Head*. I deeply regret that he is leaving us.

64 Diary, 4 April 1838

A lovely day, but rather Cool. Never was a finer Spring than the present one is. Attended and gave Evidence at the Trial of *Theller*[53] who was found guilty

---

51 Patrick Spencer was aide-de-camp to Sutherland.
52 John Middleton was an Amherstburg innkeeper.
53 Edward Alexander Theller, born in Ireland, was a wholesale grocer, physician and druggist, who arrived in Detroit in 1832 after a sojourn in Montreal. In 1838 he joined the Patriots. He was later imprisoned at Quebec, but escaped and fled to New York City.

of *High Treason*. Returned to The Ontario Hotel to dinner, and did not stir out all the Evening afterwards. At bed by 10! Henry Sherwood[54] called.

65 DIARY, 5 APRIL 1838

A lovely day. Sun bright and fine. Engaged all the morning as usual at Toronto, & Especially at Hagerman's with Sherwood about the *witnesses Expences*. Had warm words with Hagerman (the Atty General) upon the subject & he behaved rather mean respecting it. Busy in the City all day afterwards & at home all the Evening, & low spirited & much out of humour at the meanness & indifference shewn to the Party who accompanied me & the Militia.

66 PRINCE TO SIR GEORGE ARTHUR[55]
[*PAC, R.G. 1, E3, Vol. 64*]

Toronto, April 5, 1838

I take the liberty of addressing you by the request of The Attorney General and Mr. Henry Sherwood (two of Her Majesty's Law Officers) upon the following Subject.

Two persons named Andrew Stewart and James Tofflemire were summoned by Col: Fitzgibbon, the Judge Advocate, to give Evidence upon the Trial of Sutherland, at Sutherland's desire and on his behalf. They came from the Western District in obedience to their Summons and they arrived here on Tuesday. They have been occupied 9 days in coming and will be occupied quite as long in returning – and as Sutherland does not Call any witnesses they are most anxious to get off today if possible. They are without funds, having expended all their Money in travelling Expences down for themselves and their Horses. Twenty five Pounds will be a Moderate Sum to pay them, but the Attorney General and Mr. Sherwood decline paying it out of the £3000 granted by Parliament for defraying the Expences of State Trials unless Your Excellency authorizes them to do so, because a question presents itself to their minds whether the Expences of a Court Martial ought to be paid from that fund.

On applying to the Judge Advocate I find that he has no means at his disposal from which to pay these witnesses their £25, and as they unquestionably ought to be paid, I respectfully beg to Express my hopes that Your Excellency will direct Mr. Sherwood to pay it out of the Sum granted by the Provincial Parliament, so that the men may return home this day.

I am to meet Mr. Sherwood at The Attorney General's this Morning at ten o'clock to arrange as to the Expences of the Trial of Theller (who was yesterday

---

54 In 1838 Henry Sherwood was a reporter for the Law Society of Upper Canada. In the 1840s he represented Toronto in the Legislative Assembly, and served in the Executive Council as, first, solicitor general, and subsequently, attorney general.

55 Sir George Arthur was lieutenant governor of Upper Canada, 1838–41.

Convicted [of] High Treason); and as I am anxious to return home with all the witnesses tomorrow morning, I will do myself the honour, with Your Excellency's permission, of waiting on Your Excellency after I have finished my business with the Attorney General.

67 DIARY, 19 APRIL 1838. *The Park Farm*

Very Cold & snow on the ground! What a climate! Went to Sandwich & attended the opening of the N & D Rivers Rail Road near my Brewery. Present, The Revd W. Johnson,[56] Teakle & Son,[57] J.B. Robinson,[58] Gatfield,[59] Captn Campbell Queen's Light Infantry, Mr. Mercer,[60] Col. Elliott & several other Gentlemen. We afterwards dined together at Mrs. Hawken's Tavern & drank a good deal of Brandy & Water. Home by 8 p.m. & went to bed with a dreadful Headache.

((This day at 12 o'clock we commenced the Construction of The Niagara & Detroit Rivers Rail-Road.))

68 DIARY, 20 MAY 1838

A fine warm day. Sent Wm. to the woods for the Young Stock & turned out the old mare & her foal & the 2 other Colts. At home all day & I drew the Indictment & Case against the Point Pelée Island Prisoners. Susan, & Ann Clarke here. In the Evening Sir Allan Napier Macnab & Mr. Justice Jones[61] Called & Sat with me.

((My dearest Mary Ann delivered of a fine boy at 1/2 p. 12 this day. Thank God they are both doing well.))

69 DIARY, 23 MAY 1838

The Assizes commenced. Declined taking my Seat on the Bench as an associate Judge. Appeared in Court to prefer a bill of Indictment against the Point Pelée murderers. Judge declined to Entertain the Matter. I spoke at Considerable length upon the subject. At home all the Evening.

((The objection made by Sir A. Macnab & Judge Jones to my going before

---

56 William Johnson was rector of the 'English Church' (St John's, Sandwich), 1829–40.

57 George Teakle, an innkeeper after immigrating to Sandwich in 1833, and his son Thomas.

58 Sir John Beverley Robinson was chief justice of Upper Canada and speaker of the Legislative Council.

59 William Gatfield, of Anderdon Township, was a partner of William Stevens, Prince's former servant, as a brewer at Sandwich. By 1839 the partnership had dissolved.

60 Robert Mercer immigrated to Sandwich Township in 1833, from a mercantile background in London, England. He was a justice of the peace.

61 Jonas Jones was puisne judge, 1837–48, of the Upper Canada Court of Queen's Bench.

the Grand Jury occasioned a great sensation. The Grand Jury and Every person approved of what I stated to and urged upon the Court.))

70 EXCERPT FROM ADDRESS TO MR. JUSTICE JONES, 23 MAY 1838
[*Sandwich* Western Herald, *29 May, 1838*]

My Lord, a most foul, atrocious, and unnatural murder was lately committed at Point au Pelée Island within this District by an armed band of ruffians and lawless banditti, some hundreds in number, from the opposite country – and almost all of whom were citizens of the United States. These ruffians took possession of our soil – imprisoned our inhabitants and fellow subjects – closely imprisoned them within their own heretofore peaceful habitations, robbed and plundered them of all they possessed – and finally murdered several of her Majesty's loyal subjects who went to Point au Pelée to relieve the inhabitants and drive the invaders from the soil. All these are well known, well attested facts. They are capable of instant proof, and the witnesses to prove them now stand around me, and have been brought here by me (at considerable expence and at great inconvenience to themselves,) by the request of Her Majesty's Law Officers; and on Monday week I saw the prisoners, I informed them that they would be tried this day for murder, and I advised them to prepare accordingly. To our utter amazement, nay, my Lord, to our utter consternation and dismay, while the injured objects of these most atrocious, unprovoked, uncalled for and unheard of villainies, stand before your Lordship and this Court demanding reparation for their injuries by a due enforcement of the Law, while the whole country claims through me their representative that retributive and evenhanded justice should be fearlessly, firmly and promptly administered, yes, my Lord, administered too in the face and almost at the very doors of that most unfriendly race (*pointing to the opposite shore of Michigan*) who have so cruelly assailed, so wantonly, so unprovokedly attacked, and robbed, and murdered us, I say, my Lord, at this most anxious and interesting moment we are told by your Lordship and by Her Majesty's Counsel that it is the pleasure of His Excellency the Lieutenant Governor and of his advisers the Executive Council that these scoundrels are not to be tried by this Court, but they are to be considered PRISONERS OF WAR!

My Lord, they are not prisoners of war – I deny that they can, by any Law, be known or recognized as such. This I am quite prepared to prove, had this trial been proceeded with. I deny also, my Lord, the right of any person – the right of the EXECUTIVE COUNCIL, the right of THE LIEUTENANT GOVERNOR – the right of even MAJESTY itself to step between the accuser and those accused of murder, and to prevent the incipient proceeding of an inquiry into the matter by the Grand inquest of the country. The Executive may pardon even a convicted murderer: but the Executive cannot prevent the humblest subject of this country from indicting such a criminal; and God forbid it should be otherwise!

71 DIARY, 2 JULY 1838

A fine day. Indeed the weather is lovely. Busily engaged all day in town and Elsewhere on Magisterial business. Published a long Proclamation as to Non-intercourse with Michigan Except by means of Steam Boats. My dearest M.A. rode out in her Carriage.

72 DIARY, 11 AUGUST 1838. *Toronto*

A fine & very warm day. Very ill all the morning from another attack of dumb ague, & extremely weak. Could Scarcely get to the Law Convocation. *At 1/2 p. 11 was called in the Most handsome Manner possible by The Benchers of The Law Society to the Bar, so far as they could act.* Afterwards engaged in Toronto all day on various matters. Went to bed at 10 very weak & unwell.

73 DIARY, 15 AUGUST 1838

A fine but cool, & rather a Cold day. My beloved Mary Ann (thank God) is improving. Attended the Court of King's Bench & was there introduced to the Judges by Henry Sherwood Esqr Queen's Counsel and was Called to the degree of Barrister at Law; also admitted as an Attorney. At home at Bottsford's[62] all the day afterwards.

74 DIARY, 19 NOVEMBER 1838. *The Park Farm*

Another tremendous frost. Threatened attacks by Brigands from Michigan. Very much engaged all day in preparing. In the Evening placed a picket of my volunteers on duty, Patrol &c. Marched to the Ferry and *was on duty all night.* A bitter frost & Cold indeed it was. No attack, but many threatened.

75 DIARY, 24 NOVEMBER 1838

A fine but cold and Comfortless day. Rather better & much stronger thank God, but greatly Mortified at the sad apathy, indifference, & dis-loyalty of our Militia in hesitating to turn out. Busy at home all the Morning. In the Evening attended Parade, &c. &c. &c. at Sandwich. No attack as Yet. The Rudyerds here from Sunday last.

---

62 David Botsford was the proprietor of the Ontario House, referred to in document 40, at the northwest corner of Wellington and Church Streets, Toronto.

76 Diary, 28 November 1838

A fine but very Cold day. Col. Reid[63] Called & took leave, & *he left me in command at this Post*. He & Rudyerd left for Toronto. Mrs. Rudyerd & Tatty[64] extend their visit here 'till his return. Very ill all day. In bed most of the time, and took from Dr. McMullin[65] some very strong Medicine.

77 Prince to General Hugh Brady[66]
[*Fort Malden National Historic Park, Amherstburg*]

Headquarters, Sandwich,
December 1, 1838

I am unwilling to increase the Anxiety & labour which these Critical & Extraordinary times, no doubt, impose upon you; but as the Officer Commanding at this Post, I feel it my duty to inform you, who I understand Command on the opposite Frontier, that I have Ascertained from unquestionable authority that upwards of 1000 men left Buffalo a few days back in Steamers, and that they were to be reinforced all along the Shore of Lake Erie until they mustered about 5000 men; and that their determination is to make a descent upon Malden or some part of this frontier *tonight*.

I have also this very afternoon been informed by one professing to be (but not being in reality) a "Patriot", that there is a Camp of no less than 400 of these Scoundrels in the woods about 2 Miles back of Springwells, opposite this Post – that they are well armed, and that they *have a Cannon deposited in some building at Springwells*; and that their fixed determination is to attack us here or at Windsor this *night*. He was at their Camp last night.

We were under Arms until day light this Morng, and the same harassing duty will be repeated tonight – & so on.

I thus put you in possession of what I verily believe to be *facts*, and I leave you to deal with them as you please.

I only regret that I am Compelled thus to trouble you.

78 Diary, 4 December 1838

A cold day. Awoke at 6 am by an alarm gun at Sandwich. Rose & saw a fire at Windsor. Proceeded there with the Militia & found it in possession of Brigands & Pirates. We attacked them & killed 27 & took about 20 Prisoners. *I ordered the first 5 taken to be Shot.* We lost 4 men, & poor Dr. Hume Asst Staff Surgeon who was cruelly Murdered by them!

---

63 Reid, of the 32nd Regiment, was officer commanding at Sandwich. Another source calls him Major Reid.
64 Charlotte ('Tatty') Rudyerd was a daughter of Henry. Later she married Henry John Boulton.
65 Patrick McMullin moved to Sandwich from Chatham about 1830.
66 Hugh Brady was commander, from 1835, of the Northwestern military Department of the United States.

79 HENRY RUDYERD DIARY, 11 DECEMBER 1838.
TORONTO
[*MTCL*, Boulton Papers]

Saw Lt. Govr. but did not receive any appointment from him, tho he expressed much regret at My services not having been called on in the W. District, was very much annoyed at Princes having ordered four of the Prisoners at Windsor to be Shot. Dined with Attorney Genl. Haggerman.

80 JOHN PRINCE DIARY, 14 DECEMBER 1838

As Cold and as wretched as Ever. This climate is not bearable by Man or beast. Col. Airey[67] & The Asst Qu'r Mr General Col. Fraser Came to Sandwich and I went with them to The Ferry. Occupied all day long in Militia business 'till 7 p.m. Lectured my Qr Mr (Anderson)[68] at Mr. Hall's.[69]

81 DIARY, 29 DECEMBER 1838

A very Cold day. Rather better but weak & unwell. Rode to Sandwich & Windsor & there transacted Militia Business all day long. Home by 5 p.m. & Major Girty dined with me. Captn Leslie[70] & Mr. Foote of Chatham[71] here all the Evg. An attack on My house Expected.

82 DIARY, 5 JANUARY 1839

A cold day. At my Orderly room all the Morng. Was grossly insulted by *Robert Mercer Esqre* behind my back whom I gave a good sound Horsewhipping to in the public Street before my officers & many others. Mr. Richardson[72] & Captn Leslie spent the Evening & slept *at my house.*

83 DIARY, 11 JANUARY 1839

Very mild and very dirty. At 10 o'clock I started for Amherstbg to meet & have a Conference with Sir Geo. Arthur the Lt Governor. Roads dreadfully bad.

67 Richard Airey in 1838 purchased his commission as lieutenant colonel of the 34th Regiment.
68 Charles E. Anderson was a son-in-law of William Elliott, and quartermaster of the Second Regiment of Essex Militia, of which Elliott was colonel.
69 William Hall was a Sandwich innkeeper.
70 G. Leslie, adjutant in Colonel Prince's (Third) Regiment of Essex Militia, was commissioned 3 September 1838.
71 George Wade Foott resided at Thornberry Cottage, near Chatham. He became sheriff of the Western District in 1840.
72 Henry Wellington Richardson, an Amherstburg barrister, was a half brother of Major John Richardson, the author. He died in 1841, aged 26.

Called on His Excellency and had a very long and Satisfactory interview with him. Slept at Liberty's Tavern,[73] on the floor. *A wet night.*

84 DIARY, 12 JANUARY 1839

A mild day. Returned from Amherstburg to Sandwich on my young horse. Roads very bad. Received and waited upon His Excy. Sir George Arthur at The Ferry & also at Sandwich, and in his & their presence I quite defeated the plans of all my enemies. *I crushed them,* as I said I would. The Lt Governor left for Malden.

85 EXCERPTS FROM A PRINTED PAPER PUBLISHED AT DETROIT ENTITLED THE
Battle of Windsor
[Transcript in PAC, R.G. 5, B39]

Captain Sparke[74] finding the pursuit in excellent hands, halted his party when about half a mile from the main road, preparatory to marching back to dislodge any party, who might have remained in Windsor. Just at this time Col. Prince made his first appearance on the field Though some think he may have arrived a few moments sooner, as being dressed in a fustian shooting coat and fur cap, he might not have been immediately recognised. However that may be at this important moment, he informed Captain Sparke and the other officers of the party that he had just received intelligence that upwards of two hundred Brigands were marching down from Detroit on the American side for the purpose of crossing over and attacking Sandwich in front, and that another body had gone round through the groves to attack it in the rear. From this statement of Col. Prince it was deemed advisable to retire to Sandwich without delay, in order to defend that place, where all our ammunition, provisions and the only gun we possessed were deposited.

The men who were in triumphant pursuit of the flying foe, were immediately recalled, and Col Prince ordered the whole force to march back to Sandwich at double quick time. Before the party left the field adjutant Cheeseman of the 3d Essex, who had acted as a volunteer brought up a prisoner whom he had taken. He surrendered him to Col. Prince, who ordered him to be shot upon the spot and it was done accordingly.

. . . .

On our forces reaching Sandwich it was positively ascertained that no body of men had been seen, either on the American side of the river opposite Sandwich, or in the groves in the rear of the town, *as stated by Col. Prince's informants.* Intelligence was also given by James Dougall Esq. and other

---

73 Jean Baptiste Laliberté (or John B. Laliberty) was an Amherstburg innkeeper.
74 Captain Sparke commanded a company of Provincial Volunteer Militia.

respectable inhabitants who had been reconnoitring at Windsor that the Brigands remaining at that place certainly did not exceed one hundred men; and that they were evidently preparing to leave it, as they had fallen back from the spot where they had murdered Doctor Hume to a position in front of the Store of Babcock and Gardner. Colonel Prince was made acquainted with these facts and earnestly solicited by Mr. Dougall and others, as he had now 200 men upon the ground, to send up a force to dislodge the enemy. This he refused to do, giving as his reasons, that the information could not be correct, – that the party at Windsor must be much stronger than represented, that his post was at Sandwich, and if he should leave it, he would by so doing, subject himself to trial by a Court Martial and the liability of being shot. He further stated that he had on the first alarm, despatched an express to Malden, for some Regulars and a field piece, and that he did not think it advisable to move against the enemy, until their arrival which might be expected in two or three hours. The appearance of this reinforcement was now most anxiously looked for, as it was plainly seen that no movement would be made until it had arrived.

. . . .

When we had waited an hour or longer for the expected reinforcement, a prisoner who had been wounded and taken after the engagement was brought into town. He was conducted surrounded by several of our men towards Col. Prince, who was then standing in the most frequented part of our main street. As the prisoner approached he was told by one of the officers to make his peace with God, as he had but a few minutes to live. The wretched man holding up both his hands pleaded most earnestly for mercy, but Col. Prince commanded him to be shot upon the spot, and the same officer, who had first addressed him, probably to disengage him from those by whom he was surrounded, ordered him "to run for his life", and in an instant a dozen muskets were levelled for his execution. At this moment Col. William Elliott of the 2d Essex who chanced to be near at hand exclaimed, "D – n you, you cowardly rascals, are you going to murder your prisoner". This Exclamation for one instant retarded the fire of the party but in the next the prisoner was brought to the ground he sprang again to his feet, and ran round the corner of a fence, where he was met by a person coming from an opposite direction and shot through the head.

From papers found upon his person it appeared his name was "Bennett". It is to be regretted that this painful affair took place in our most public street, and in the presence of several ladies and children, who had been attracted to the doors and windows by the strange events of the morning, but who little expected to witness so awful a tragedy. Another Brigand named Dennison also wounded and unarmed was taken after the action, and brought in during the course of the morning. Charles Elliott Esq happening to be present when the prisoner was about to be shot by Col. Prince's orders, entreated that he might be reserved to be dealt with according to the Laws of the Country, but Col. Prince's reply was "D – n the rascal shoot him", and it was done accordingly.

To the great satisfaction of our anxious people about 11 o'clock A.M. a detachment of 100 men of the 34th under Capt. Broderick, a few artillerists, and a field piece under Lieut. Airey,[75] and some 40 or 50 Indians under Geo. Ironside Esq.[76] galloped into Sandwich. Waiting only a few minutes to enquire the state of affairs at Windsor, which place they were told was still in possession of the Brigands (although it had actually been evacuated long before), they proceeded at full speed up the road in search of the enemy. Col. Prince followed the regulars, with the whole of his command and all the male inhabitants except some 16 or 18 men of the artillery Company under Capt. Chewitt.[77]

This small force, with a nine pound field piece were posted at the north entrance of the town, and to it was committed the defence of the Stores, ammunition & &. When Col. Prince reached Windsor, he was informed that one of the Brigands was lying wounded in the house of Mr. Wm. Johnson.[78] The man whose leg had been shattered by a musket ball, had been found by Francois Baby Esq.[79] after the action and by his orders, was removed to Mr. Johnsons, with a promise of surgical assistance. Col. Prince gave the order for his execution, and he was dragged out of the house and shot accordingly.

The regulars and artillery in waggons, and the Indians on horse back, were by this time two or three miles in advance of Col. Princes party. They had discovered no enemy at Windsor and so continued the pursuit to the windmills,[80] where they found the reported escape of the Brigands but too correct. Nothing could be seen of those whom the militia drove to the woods, nor of those who had so long held possession of Windsor, except one man who was made prisoner and 5 or 6 others who were then crossing in canoes to Hog Island.[81] The captured Brigand made earnest appeals for mercy, to which Capt. Broderick replied "you have fallen into the hands of a British Officer".

. . . .

Captain Broderick finding there was nothing further to be done commenced his return to Sandwich, leaving the prisoners whom he had taken to be brought down under the charge of a dragoon and some others. Col. Prince after meeting the regulars on their return continued his march to the Windmills, and about 1/4 mile below them fell in with Broderick's prisoner. He ordered the man to be taken from the guard, and to be shot upon the spot which was done accordingly.

About the time Capt. Broderick had commenced his return, the Indians had gone in pursuit of some of the enemy who had taken to the woods. After a sharp chase they succeeded in making 7 prisoners, one of whom in attempting to

---

75 Lieutenant Dionysius Airey of the Royal Artillery was a brother of Richard Airey of the 34th.

76 George Ironside, Senior, was Indian superintendent at Amherstburg, 1820–30. He was commissioned captain in the First Essex Militia, 2 September 1838.

77 Alexander Chewett, a Sandwich barrister enrolled in 1825, commanded an artillery company 1837–38.

78 William Johnson, a teacher, should not be confused with the Reverend William Johnson, of St John's, Sandwich.

79 François (Francis) Baby, a member of the Legislative Assembly for Kent (1792–96) and Essex (1820–30), was the proprietor of the land on which the Battle of Windsor was fought. He was an uncle of Charles Baby.

80 A pair of windmills forming a prominent landmark about 1-1/2 miles above The Ferry. One stood at the present foot of Lincoln Road, in Windsor; the other, a little west of Walker Road.

81 Present Belle Isle, a Detroit park.

escape after being captured, was fired upon, wounded and retaken. When the prisoners were first brought out of the woods, the cry was "Bayonet them" but Martin one of the Indian braves replied "no we are Christians – we will not murder them – we will deliver them to our Officers to be treated as they think proper." They were then brought to Col. Prince who had now commenced his return to Sandwich. When he arrived opposite the burning barracks, he ordered the waggon in which the prisoners had been placed to be wheeled off the road. As soon as it had reached an open Spot in the rear of the ruins he commanded the men to be taken out and shot. At this critical moment Charles Eliot and Robert Mercer Esqs and the Rev. Mr. Johnson and Mr. Samuel James rushed forward and entreated Col. Prince not to commit murder by shooting the prisoners, but begged him to leave them to the laws of the country. In making this appeal Mr. James made use of the emphatic language – "For God's sake do not let a white man murder what an Indian has spared". Col. Prince yielded to the entreaties of the gentlemen remarking to Mr. Elliott that he would hold him responsible for his interference, as his (Col. Prince's) orders were to destroy them all.

86 Diary, 15 January 1839

An Exceedingly Cold & raw day with hard frost. Busily engaged at home all the morng in writing letters &c. &c. After dinner at my orderly rooms all the Evg upon Militia business which I transacted there. My situation by no means pleasant. A Cabal of *disappointed* persons Col. Elliott, Cowan[82] & others are formed against me.

87 Prince to the Editor of the Detroit *Daily Advertiser*
[*Sandwich* Western Herald, *29 January 1839*]

The Park Farm, Sandwich,
January 19, 1839

Your papers of the 10th and 14th instants, contain two scandalous and malicious *libels* against me. The first is an *anonymous* letter purporting to be addressed to you from Sandwich, and grossly misrepresenting my conduct and motives as a magistrate, and Chairman of the Quarter Sessions. The second is also *anonymous*, and pretends to give a narrative of what it terms "The Battle of Windsor," but which is utterly false and fabricated as to nine-tenths contained in it about me.

I repeat that those articles are libels upon my character in a civil and military capacity, and I am desirous of punishing the author of them in a court of law – the only tribunal before which falsehood can be thoroughly unveiled and truth elicited.

I therefore request that you will favor me with the authors' names, and that you will also permit a friend of mine to peruse the original manuscript.

---

82 John Cowan was the former publisher of the Sandwich *Canadian Emigrant*.

I cannot anticipate a refusal to my request, because I think you will admit that if real worth is to be the standard of a newspaper, truth ought to be the object.

88 Diary, 6 February 1839

A fine day. Occupied at Sandwich at an Adjourned Quarter Sessions all the Morng, afterwards walked up to The Ferry & there also Engaged in business 'till 3 p.m. At half past 4 I started for Malden on horseback with a view of seeing my friend Rudyerd and prevailing on him to stand my friend as against Col. Elliott, Chas Eliot, & the other Conspirators.

89 Diary, 8 February 1839

A mild morning, & the snow and Ice going away fast. At home all day long and very busily engaged in writing &c. *Mr. Rudyerd called on and wrote to Chas Baby & other Enemies of mine for Satisfaction.* Answers tomorrow. Mr. Gatfield went with my horse to the back farm for Cordwood. At home all day & did not stir out. Unhappy at the base Conduct & ingratitude of C. Baby and others towards me.

90 Diary, 9 February 1839

A hard frost and very Cold. What a changeable climate! Engaged at Sandwich & at The Ferry all day. *Horsewhipped Mr. Charles Baby because he refused to meet my challenge Except upon Hog Island, American Soil*, and I afterwards posted him at Windsor, Sandwich and Malden as a Coward, a Liar, & a Poltroon. At home all the Evening. Lt Cameron[83] Called.

91 Diary, 11 February 1839

A snowy morning. Rose at 5 & accompanied Captn Rudyerd to the place of meeting. We arrived there half an hour before the Enemy. Very cold. Mr. W.R. Wood[84] was attended by Lt Cameron, & I by Rudyerd. Distance 12 paces. At the first shots my Pistol missed fire. On the 2nd shot I hit Mr. Wood in the Jaw & the ball lodged there. He missed me both shots. Home by 8 to breakfast. I sent him home in my sleigh, & Rudyerd and I walked all the way.

92 Diary, 18 February 1839

A fine day. Captain Leslie & Mr. Gardiner breakfasted with us. I was Engaged all day afterwards at the Court of Inquiry about the Windsor affair.

83 Lieutenant Allen Cameron, of the Second Provincial Volunteer Militia.
84 William R. Wood, an architect and art teacher, was appointed treasurer of the Western District in 1836.

The Court Consisted of Colonel Airey, Major Deedes[85] & Major French.[86] Home by 6 tired & vexed, & wretched at the base ingratitude of the Babys and others.

93 Prince's Testimony, 27 February 1839.
Amherstburg
[PAC, R.G. 5, B39]

With reference to No. 1 Prisoner Evidence states that a man (a prisoner) was brought up to him in an orchard, who, there was no doubt, was one of the Rebels – firing and skirmishing were going on at the time close by – Evidence ordered a Couple of Men to shoot him.

With reference to No. 2 Prisoner Evidence states that he was standing with his Militia, who were drawn up in the Streets of Sandwich in front of Mrs. Hawkins's Tavern, with the full impression at the time, from the Reports that were brought in, that they were about to be attacked.

Evidence saw a small posse of men coming up towards him amongst whom were Mr. Anderson and Dunn, the Blacksmith with about a dozen others – they had a Prisoner with them.

Evidence thinks Mr. Anderson Exclaimed "We have got one of the Rascals who was taken on the Field", when several cried out "shoot him, shoot him". Evidence addressed, he thinks, Mr. Anderson (but there were several around at the time) saying, take him into a field, pointing to one at the back of Colonel Elliott's, and shoot him. As soon as Evidence had mentioned those words, the Prisoner breaking off from those who had charge of him, ran off as fast as he could, evidently with a view of escaping. Evidence ordered the Men around him to fire at him, previous to which, however, Evidence thinks several shots were fired at him the Prisoner. He did not fall, but ran around Colonel Elliott's rick of Hay at the back of his house. Evidence heard after that he was shot, but did not see him, nor take any further trouble about him. Evidence adds, that that part of the Statement, which says "the man pleaded for Mercy" is untrue – he might however have done so to those, who brought him up, but Evidence did not see it. It was not represented to Evidence that the Prisoner was wounded, nor had Evidence the least idea he was. Evidence did not hear Colonel Elliott make use of the words mentioned in the Paragraph "Damn your eyes, you cowardly rascals, are you going to shoot your Prisoner" nor does Evidence believe he made use of those Words. Evidence further states, that that part of the Paragraph which says that "this exclamation of Colonel Elliott's retarded for one instant the firing of the party" is false. Evidence also denies that part of the statement "that many females witnessed this awful tragedy."

With reference to the Prisoner mentioned in No. 3 paragraph, Evidence states, that the Man was brought in to him as a Rebel taken in the Field, and that Evidence ordered him to be marched under the Gaol fence to be shot, but that he

---

85 Deedes was an officer in the 34th Regiment.
86 Of the 85th Regiment.

was in fact shot by the impetuosity of the men, who could not be restrained from shooting him at once.

Evidence denies, that the man was reported to him by any one as being wounded. Evidence also denies the words of Mr. Charles Eliot mentioned in the printed statement "that the Prisoner might be reserved to be dealt with according to the laws of his Country".

With reference to the Prisoner mentioned in No. 4 Paragraph Evidence states, that that man was shot by his order, but denies, that it ever was reported to him, that the man was wounded. Mr. Anderson rode up, as they were marching on (anxious to overtake the Regulars, who were in Waggons, and whom they expected would be engaged immediately) saying, "there is one of the Enemy lying concealed in a house" when Evidence said "take him out and shoot him". Evidence did not see Mr. Cowan there on that occasion. Evidence knows nothing about Mr. Francois Baby (as mentioned in the statement) having ordered the man surgical assistance, nor of his being wounded, as it was never reported to him.

With reference to the Prisoner mentioned in No. 5 Paragraph, Evidence states, once for all, that the paragraph in the Statement commencing with the words "Capt: Broderick", and ending with the words "done accordingly", is a fabricated Statement, and false from beginning to end.

Evidence adds, he did order a Prisoner to be shot near the Windmills, but it was a Prisoner brought to evidence by his own men, taken by his own men, and stated to be taken by his own Men in Arms. They were marching on quick to join the Regulars at the time, who were nearly a Mile in advance of them. There was an American Schooner sailing at some little distance from the shore with a man on the top-mast on the look out, full of men, Enemies as they appeared to them.

Evidence was desirous of letting them know, how they would treat such fellows, if they caught them, and therefore ordered the man to be shot in a field off the Road opposite to the Schooner, which was done accordingly, and which Evidence has no doubt the men on board must have witnessed.

Evidence states his reasons for ordering these Prisoners to be shot – were – that according to his opinion they richly deserved it, having satisfied himself beforehand that the Laws would authorize it, and having made up his mind to execute, as soon as he possibly could, every Prisoner that was brought to him.

Evidence considered the example of immediate execution would have the good effect of preventing further aggressions from the Brigands and Pirates who for twelve months previous had kept the Country in a state of fear, excitement and apprehension.

It had moreover been generally understood, published and promulgated among his friends, acquaintances, and the Public at large, that no Prisoners were to be taken or quarter given – which was so generally understood by the Inhabitants and Country at large. Evidence had himself declared his resolutions to that effect *twice* to the men under his command at Parade, when a great number of the Inhabitants were present – once at Windsor and once at Sandwich

– every Body appeared then to approve of the course, and of Evidence's intention – and Evidence has no hesitation in saying, that by far the larger majority did approve of it, and does still.

Evidence further adds, that he has received the most ample testimony of the approval of his general conduct on that occasion, as also an address signed by One Hundred and Sixteen of the principal persons in and about Toronto.

Evidence adds as another reason for refusing to take Prisoners, that not having above One Hundred and Thirty men, under his command, he could not afford a force to guard them – particularly as he was fully impressed from the Reports that were brought in, that they were about to be attacked by a force of a much larger number. Evidence was informed they were crossing over from Detroit to reinforce the persons who were in possession of Windsor, that the Enemy at Windsor were upwards of Four Hundred in number – that an attack was likely to take place below Sandwich from the other side – that the Enemy at Windsor were about to march down upon Sandwich, and that a Party of the Enemy were actually in the Woods at the back of Sandwich with an intention of attacking it.

It would be impossible for evidence to remember the names of all the parties, who made these Reports to him, but Evidence will mention a few. The above Reports were conveyed to Evidence amonst others by Mr. Calhoun [Cahoon] of the Furnace who had been a Prisoner amongst them, and that he had it from the Enemy themselves, from Mr. Forsyth of Sandwich, Mr. Morrow of Sandwich, Captain Hall of Moy above Windsor,[87] Mr. Moring[?] who named a Mr. Kennedy, who had come down from Windsor and stated they were going to march down on Sandwich immediately. Several others brought in Reports of a similar nature, whose names it would be impossible for Evidence to recollect.

Evidence would also add, that he knew the Gaol was too insecure and too small to hold any number of Prisoners taken.

94 DIARY, 11 MARCH 1839. *Toronto*

A fine day. Went to the House of Assembly at 12 o'clock, and when I Entered it the Members *cheered me Enthusiastically*! A very high & most unusual Compliment. Brought up 3 Petitions & gave one notice, and spoke upon Mr. Cameron's[88] Restriction [of] Fishery Bill. The House adjourned at 3 p.m. Dined at The Ontario. Supped with Mr. Charles.

---

87 William Gaspé Hall, from Quebec, bought the Moy farm about 1835, was appointed inspector of licences for the Western District in 1836, and was commissioned as paymaster in Prince's regiment, the Third Essex Militia, in 1838.

88 Malcolm Cameron, the founder of the Perth *Courier*, was a member of the Legislative Assembly for Lanark.

95 Report and Opinion of Court of Inquiry
[*PAC, R.G. 5, B39*]

Fort Malden, Amherstburg,
March 14, 1839

The Court having gone into the most minute and detailed investigation of the particulars contained in the printed paper, headed,
"BATTLE OF WINDSOR"
in so far as relates to statements of a very painful nature respecting the treatment, by order of Colonel Prince, of certain Brigand Prisoners, who were captured at Windsor U.C. on the 4th of December last, – and having carefully and patiently examined, individually, the several gentlemen who signed the address to His Excellency the Lieutenant Governor, transmitting the said document, in which it is stated that,
"As the several particulars, (which joined together form the connected State-
"ment) are Known to some one, or more of the subscribers, they pledge
"themselves individually for the truth of the parts to which they were respective-
"ly eye-witnesses, and collectively to the accuracy of the whole narrative in all
"its essential points", –
is of opinion, that the invidious colouring which characterizes the detail of the facts alluded to, reflecting so painfully upon the conduct of Colonel Prince, is not in any way substantiated by evidence, and, that the court cannot but observe the existence of a spirit of personal hostility and enmity towards Colonel Prince from which alone, in the opinion of the President and Members, has emanated the narrative in question, – nor can the Court refrain from expressing deep regret that at any period, but more especially so at a time like the present, when unanimity and good feeling ought to be conspicuous amongst all classes of Her Majesty's Subjects, – that statements of the nature of those, which form the basis of this investigation (the circulation of which will not be confined to these Provinces only) should have been presented to the public without the fullest, the clearest, and the most indisputable Knowledge of their accuracy.

96 Diary, 20 March 1839

A hard frost & fine day, but towards Evening it came on to rain, and sleet, rain, & hail fell. At the House of Assembly all day & 'till 1/2 past 5. I then dined with The Hon. Mr. Fergusson[89] and Mr. Shade,[90] meeting Mr. Hn. Merritt,[91]

---

[89] Adam Fergusson, of the Gore District, was a newly appointed member of the Legislative Council. He was prominent in the Reform movement.

[90] Absalom Shade was an entrepreneur in Dumfries Township, Gore District, with extensive mercantile, land management, milling, distilling, banking, railroading and roadbuilding interests. He was a Tory, representing Halton in the Legislative Assembly from 1831 to 1841.

[91] William Hamilton Merritt was a member of the Legislative Assembly for Haldimand, and later for Lincoln. He was a promoter of the Welland Canal, and in 1850 he was made commissioner of public works. In 1860 he was elected to the Legislative Council.

The Hon. Mr. Moffatt from Montreal,[92] Hon. Mr. Crooks[93] & others. A pleasant party, & we discussed the projected Union of the Provinces.

97 DIARY, 25 APRIL 1839

A fine day, but rather raw and Cold. Busily engaged at the House all day. Spoke at great length against the *Executive Council* in whom *I declared I had not the smallest Confidence whatever*. Pointed out their injustice in the Case of Howland Hastings'[94] Bail and the Schooner Ann Prize Money &c. &c. &c. House broke up at 11 p.m. Went to bed *at 1*.

98 DIARY, 6 MAY 1839

A fine & warm day. Very busy at the House all day long, and spoke several times on several Subjects of Finance, Supplies, &c. Debated and passed my Bill granting £40,000 to pay sufferers & claimants by reason of the late Rebellion & Invasion of this Province. Messrs. Gardiner, Girty, Nelson[95] Smith[96] & Wright[97] from the Western D[istrict] attended. Sergeant Miller also here.

99 DIARY, 8 MAY 1839

A fine day. Occupied all the morning in writing, & took a walk up Yonge St with Mr. Biscoe.[98] In the Evg again attended The House, & repassed my £40,000 Grant or bill of Indemnity, The Leg[islative] Co'l having *ruinously* amended it, being a Money bill. Passed it thro' *all its readings* this Evening. The Clergy Reserve Debate revived. Home by 12 & in bed by one as usual.

---

92 George Moffatt, an important Montreal merchant and a member of the 'British' Tory group in Canada East, in 1839 was a member of the Executive Council of Lower Canada. He sat for the City of Montreal.

93 James Crooks, a prominent merchant and papermaker of Flamboro West, a conservative, was first elected to the Assembly in 1821, and appointed in 1831 to the Legislative Council of Upper Canada.

94 Howland Hastings was an American, jailed at Sandwich as a would-be assassin of Prince, but ordered released on bond by the provincial authorities. One of Hastings's sureties was Charles Eliot. Prince withheld the warrant for Hastings's release, and was reprimanded.

95 Horatio (also Horace) Nelson of Gosfield Township was captain in the Third Essex Militia and a justice of the peace.

96 Probably Charles Smith of Tilbury West and, later, Chatham Township, is intended here.

97 Apparently the reference is to Thomas H. Wright, a lieutenant in the First Essex Militia during the Patriot troubles. Wright was trained as a civil engineer, and worked on the survey for Prince's Niagara and Detroit Rivers Railroad in 1836. Later he became a Colchester storekeeper and an Amherstburg miller. In 1863 he became treasurer of Essex County.

98 Captain Vincent Biscoe, of the Royal Engineers, was posted at Amherstburg in 1839.

100 EXCERPT FROM HOUSE OF LORDS DEBATE,
27 MAY 1839
[*Sandwich* Western Herald, *17 July 1839*]

Lord Brougham[99] made enquiries relating to the outrageous conduct imputed to Colonel Prince, of Upper Canada. He wished to know whether any steps had been taken to punish him: saying that he had disgraced the name of a British Officer. Alluding to the justification of Colonel Prince's conduct by Sir George Arthur, Lord Brougham said that nothing but insanity could excuse it.

The Marquis of Normanby[100] said that disapprobation of Col. Prince's conduct had been communicated to Sir G. Arthur by her Majesty's Government. He complained, however, that Lord Brougham had said nothing about the extenuating circumstances of the case.

Lord Brougham moved for a return of the papers. He had read the report of the court of Enquiry, which was anything but satisfactory. As a lawyer he had no hesitation in saying that Col. Prince was guilty of murder. Governor Wall[101] had been hanged for an act similar to this.

Lord Normanby said that he had no objections to produce the papers, and repeated that disapprobation had been expressed of Col. Prince's conduct.

Lord Brougham said that was not enough, there must be punishment and severe punishment too.

101 NOTICE, 4 JUNE 1839
[*Sandwich* Western Herald, *6 June 1839* et seqq.]
SPRING-GUNS.

Having received certain *threatening letters* against my life and property, I hereby give NOTICE that from this day, on every evening at sun-down, I shall cause 12 SPRING-GUNS with wires and strings complete and each loaded with 30 *buck shot*, to be set about my house and farm buildings, also 2 MAN-TRAPS.

All persons are therefore hereby warned not to come within the grounds on which my premises are built, between *sun-set and sun-rise*.

JOHN PRINCE.

102 DIARY, 9 JULY 1939. *The Park Farm*

A very fine & very warm day with a heavy shower in the Evening. Attended the Quarter Sessions at which no less than 21 Magistrates were present. Rose &

---

99 Henry Peter Brougham, first Baron of Brougham and Vaux, was chancellor of the exchequer, 1830–34. He was known as a mischief-maker.

100 Constantine Henry Phipps, first Marquis of Normanby, was secretary of war and the colonies in 1839.

101 Joseph Wall, governor of Senegal from 1779, was executed for excessively disciplining the troops under his command.

proposed Mr. J. Gardiner[102] as a fresh Chairman in the place of Mr. Charles Eliot. Mr. Gardiner declined. Mr. Anderton[103] then proposed me, and I was Elected by a large Majority. Presided all day and tried some Prisoners &c. &c. Dined with a large Party of my friends at Mears's.[104] Aftwds att'd road meeting.

103 Diary, 12 August 1839

A fine day. Sir George Arthur arrived & inspected the Troops here. Waited on His Excellency several times, and in the Evening he did me the honor to Confront me with the horrid *Clique* that has for so long a time harassed me here. *He lectured them well.* Drank 'till 2 in the Morning with the officers at their quarters.

104 Diary, 21 September 1839

A very hot day. The Case of Wright vs Baxter came on at 1/2 p. 9. Lasted 3 hours. I got a Verdict for £50 Damages, and £25 in Wright v Rendt, & £400 in Drew & Dods vs Baby. I was very successful during *the assizes generally*. The Court rose at 7 p.m. leaving about 15 Causes "Remanets".[105] Rudyerd slept at The Park Farm. This Evening I was Reconciled to my *enemies*, the authors of "The Battle of Windsor".

105 Diary, 31 December 1839. *Toronto*

A fine cold & clear day, and a hard frost. Wrote several letters in the Morning. Had an Inverview by appointment with His Excellency The Rt. Honble Poulett Thompson [sic].[106] He is a plain, sensible and affable man. I like him. Sir George Arthur also Called upon him. Went to the House for an hour (which had adjourned) and afterwards made several Calls. At The Ontario all the Evening. So Ends the Year!

106 Diary, 13 January 1840

A mild day with some little fall of Snow. Went to the house for a couple of

102 Samuel Gardiner appears to be intended here; James Gardiner of Chatham did not become a magistrate until later.

103 William Anderton was a magistrate and captain of the First Essex Militia. Some believe that Anderdon Township was named for him.

104 John Mears was a Sandwich innkeeper.

105 Postponed.

106 Charles Poulett Thomson, first Baron Sydenham, was governor of Canada from the autumn of 1839 until his death in Kingston on 19 September 1841.

Hours and also to the public Offices on business of various sorts. Did not stop long in the House because I could not Concur in the view the majority of the Members take with respect to The Clergy Reserves and The Union of The Provinces. Called on The Chief Justice of Montreal & Lower Canada.[107]

107 DIARY, 14 JANUARY 1840

A snowy and unpleasant day, but by no means cold. Attended at the public Offices in some business. Did not go to *The House at all*, because I find it useless to raise my single voice against the System of Spoliation going on against the Church of England with regard to The Clergy Reserves. Attended a Meeting of The St. George's Society in the Evening at The Ontario House. Went to bed at 11.

108 DIARY, 20 JANUARY 1840

A fine day but rather raw & Cold without frost. Busily engaged all day long at The House of Assembly & spoke upon The Usury Laws and the confiscation of Traitors' Estates. Dined at The Ontario and went to bed at 8 p.m. very low spirited as usual, & Cursing the unlucky Star that guided me to this wretched Country.

109 DIARY, 21 JANUARY 1840

A fine & cold day but not much frost. The Sleighing Continues Excellent in & about Toronto. Attended at The House all day and spoke upon several questions. Introduced, & spoke upon, & Carried a Resolution agreeing to grant £50,000 for the payment of all losses, claims, and demands arising in Consequence of the late Rebellion and invasions of the Country. Dined at The Ontario and went to bed at 11. Spent an hour with *the Patricks*.[108]

110 DIARY, 5 FEBRUARY 1840

A mild day, comparatively speaking. Occupied at The House of Assembly all day long and spoke at some length against Mr. Murney's[109] bill to repeal the Court of Chancery Act, which bill I strenuously opposed as being an unwise, unstatesmanlike and unjust Measure. But the House divided in favor of it. Heard from home, & thank God my Mary Ann is better.

---

107 Apparently Sir James Stuart, chief justice of the Court of King's Bench at Quebec, is intended here. The Montreal post seems to have been vacant at this time.
108 Alfred Patrick entered the civil service in 1827. He was the author of a work on contested elections in Upper Canada. In 1873 he became clerk of the House of Commons.
109 Edmund Murney was the member of the Legislative Assembly for Hastings.

111 Excerpt from Editorial
[*Sandwich* Western Herald, *22 February 1840*]

Notwithstanding the late rumors from the seat of Government, propagated through the columns of the *Commercial Herald*, that our honored representative had signified his intention to withdraw from public life, after the dissolution of the present parliament, his friends – and they are not few – could not consent to lose his valuable services without making an effort to retain them. – They could not consent to let the faithful and steadfast friend of the Western District – the independent and fearless advocate of the rights of the people of this province – the staunch and zealous supporter of British honor and British Justice, retire to the peaceful shades of private life, when they reflected that the political struggles in which we have been some time involved, and in which he, their representative, had acquired no small degree of honorable notoriety, and accomplished for them so much good, were not yet brought to a close; and that the time was fast approaching when the services of such men as COLONEL JOHN PRINCE would be wanted in the United (perhaps, *dis*-united) parliament of the two Provinces, to assert British principles, and maintain British rights, in the face of a faction composed of men "fit for treason stratagems and spoils," who would in all probability, attempt at the first onset, to separate these noble provinces from Great Britain, and hand them over to the tender mercies of the Yankees.

112 Excerpt from Report of Requisition, 10 March 1840
[*Sandwich* Western Herald, *14 March 1840*]

On arriving at the house of their honorable friend, they were received by him with that gentlemanly courtesy and urbanity which have ever characterized his attentions to his friends.

DR. MCMULLIN, the zealous chairman of the Sandwich committee, then presented a requisition, signed by three hundred and fifty-three freeholders, soliciting Mr. Prince to represent them in the ensuing parliament. Mr. P. thanked them in becoming terms for the honor shown him, &c., &c., but begged to decline giving a definite answer until next week, when we hope to be enabled to present the same to our readers.

The company were entertained by Mr. Prince with his usual generous hospitality. A barrel of choice ale was "knocked in the head," and a variety of other liquids were brought forward, which caused many of his *ardent* friends to deviate considerably from the straight path, which led to their several homes.

113 Diary, 12 March 1840

A very fine day. Busily engaged at home all the morning in writing and in Seeing People. After dinner walked into Sandwich and called at The Brewery.

Afterwards went up to The Ferry where a large Party of my friends met me, and drank my good health, and we had quite an *Electioneering Jollification*. Returned home by 8 o'clock rather the worse for *Toasts*. Called on The Chewetts. Mrs. Blackburn[110] there. Quite Merry, mirabile visu![111]

((My Birth Day. 44 Years old! How awful!!))

114 DIARY, 2 APRIL 1840

A very hard frost!!! But the day turned out bright & fine. Engaged as usual all day long in the house nailed like a bad shilling to the Counter and utterly unable to stir out in consequence of being so much Engaged in Law business and with people Calling on me. In short my life is one of almost *Slavery*. Not an hour Can I Call my own and I am miserably unhappy.

115 DIARY, 30 MAY 1840

A very hot day. At the office and busily engaged until 1 o'clock. Went on horseback to my back-woods with Bella[112] at 3 o'clock. Home by 6 a good deal tired. The boys went to *McKee's Point fishing*. In the [evening] I attended a large Party of my friends and Constituents at Hall's Tavern. Spoke often, of Course. Home by 1/2 p. 1 a.m.

116 DIARY, 1 JULY 1840

A fine day. Very busy at the office & for the Askins,[113] in drawing their affidavits &c. &c. for the Heir and Devisee Commission. In the Evening attended a large party of my political electioneering friends at Chappu's tavern Petite Cote. A rainy Evening which will do good, and rather Cold. Home by 10 p.m. with as much Grog on board as I could Conveniently Carry. Went to bed tired.

117 DIARY, 9 JULY 1840

A lovely day. Rose early and rode to Shaffer's Inn on Lake St. Clair[114] to breakfast. Spent the day with my political friends at Markham's Tavern on The

---

110 This is probably the wife of Thornton Blackburn. Both were former slaves who had escaped to Sandwich in 1833.

111 Strange to see.

112 Arabella Prince, eleven years old in 1840, was also known as Bell.

113 Charles Askin, a former Western District clerk of the peace (succeeded by Charles Baby), and his brother James, registrar of deeds from 1831.

114 Jacob Shaffer's inn was in Maidstone Township, near Pike Creek.

Belle River. A very large meeting. A great number of Speeches made and all went off admirably well, notwithstanding a great many got very drunk. Returned to Shaffer's Tavern by 8 p.m. where I slept, and Dr. McMullin staid there with me. A fine & very warm night.

118 DIARY, 11 JULY 1840

Rose at 1/2 p 3. A very hot day. Tremendously hot! Drove five of my friends to Malden where we took breakfast. Proceeded on to Colchester and attended there *a very numerous meeting*. Spoke at great length to the assembled Multitude. *Considerable opposition*. Returned home (by way of Major Lachlan's) to Rudyerd's where I slept. Dined at Bullock's Tavern[115] at 9 pm! Went to bed at Rudyerds at 1 or half past. Dreadfully *hot*.

119 DIARY, 1 AUGUST 1840

A very hot day with some showers. Messrs Read and Fisher Executed their Deeds at The Park Farm. Rode out to my back woods with Albert in search of a Deer, but found none. Home by 4 wet thro' and much tired. Afterwards went to an Electioneering meeting at Hutton's Tavern about 4 miles above the Ferry. A large meeting, and I had to speak at some length & give explanations. Home by 2 a.m. and went to bed with more Whiskey (so Called) than I could Conveniently Carry.

120 DIARY, 11 AUGUST 1840

Very hot. Excessively engaged all day long at Amherstburg on all sorts of conceivable and inconceivable business, drawing Deeds &c. &c. &c. &c. &c. &c. &c. &c. &c. Every body seems to think that because I am to be their M.P.P. they may *demand* legal advice, professional *labour* & all sorts of things of me. Left Malden with my carriage full of friends at 4 & reached home at *12!* Calling at houses & drinking all the way home. Got to bed at about 1 a.m.

121 DIARY, 20 OCTOBER 1840. *Gosfield Township*

A very fine and bright day with a hoar frost. After breakfast we proceeded to Mersea, and met the Mersea Companies there at Leonard Wigle's Inn. We dined there and spent a jovial day. Got home to H[enr]y Leighton's[116] by 6 p.m. and sat up drinking until about 12 as usual, having had but very little sleep the

---

115 George Bullock was an Amherstburg innkeeper.
116 Henry Leighton was a Gosfield Township innkeeper, beginning in 1840.

night before. Oh how I do detest all this, and how I regret that I ever Consented to stand again for the representation of Essex. Went to bed in low spirits, as usual.

122 DIARY, 14 JANUARY 1841. *Sandwich*

Weather milder. Occupied at Court on this day also. The Grand Jury presented my Brewery as encroaching on the Highway. This was done at the instance of Mr. Wm. Elliott and Mr. Charles Baby. But I could not urge them on to Trial. *I defied them*. The Sessions ended and I returned home & went to bed at 11.

123 DIARY, 31 JANUARY 1841

A very fine & warm day. Started at 1/2 p 7 with Dr. McMullin & others for *Belle River* where there was Mass performed at The New R. Catholic Church, in the woods. Thought it a good opportunity to speak to the Electors which I did after the Service was over and they were all unanimous in my favor. *Caldwell & Charles Baby there*. They appeared not to have a friend. Made several Calls & after drinking a good deal got home by 9 pm. Captn Talbot[117] here & slept.

124 DIARY, 8 MARCH 1841

A fine day and quite mild. After breakfast we commenced canvassing round Gosfield Furnace (Colborne) and reached *Leonard Wigle's* in Mersea where we dined and slept, and where I had to Entertain all sorts of *Hottentots* Called Electors "free & independent Electors" until 3 in the Morning! I then went to bed overwhelmed with whiskey, wine, and worrying of *all Sorts*.

125 DIARY, 9 MARCH 1841

A fine day & bright, but a great deal of snow on the ground. Canvassed all the way from Leonard Wigle's up to Robinson's Tavern in Gosfield where we slept. Met Mr. Caldwell, my opponent, and his party numbering about 60. *Shook hands with all of them*, much to their amusement. Proceed[ed] on & Called on several persons. Very lowspirited, as usual.

126 DIARY, 22 MARCH 1841. *The Park Farm*

A fine but rather a raw day. The first day of the Election!! Several gentlemen breakfasted with me. We then proceeded to meet my friends with their Flags,

---

117 Captain Talbot was an officer of the 43rd Light Infantry, then stationed at Fort Malden.

Banners, *Rigged Man of War* (a 6 oared boat) &c. &c. at Jessop's Tavern to Conduct me to The Hustings. An immense Concourse of People. My friends by far the Most Numerous. Addressed the Multitudes at great length from The Hustings. My opponent Mr. Caldwell said very little, & his supporter, C. Baby, made a fool of himself. I polled a great many more votes than Caldwell did. My House full of friends.

127 EXCERPT FROM ELECTION REPORT
[*Sandwich* Western Herald, *31 March 1841*]

After Col. Prince concluded his manly address, which he did amidst the heartiest cheers of the vast assemblage, CHARLES BABY, Esq., came forward and addressed the people in favor of his friend, Mr. Francis Caldwell; and, unfortunately for the equanimity of some of the opposite party, and his own reputation as a legal gentleman, he adverted to matters of a local nature, (and which had not the least reference to Col. Prince's qualifications,) with the view of casting reproach upon that gentleman. Various charges were brought forward by Mr. Baby, of rather a delicate nature, which, Col. Prince, with more bluntness than we could exactly justify, promptly repelled and denied on the spot, and he subsequently proved them to be unfounded and incorrect.

128 DIARY, 24 MARCH 1841

Another fine day. The polling commenced at 10 and Continued very slowly throughout the day. It was nevertheless Kept up 'till *half past 5 when Mr. Caldwell resigned the Contest!* I was immediately thereupon declared duly elected, and deafening cheers rang throughout the Hall & air. I was then chaired & carried *on men's shoulders throughout the Town* with the Band of the 2nd Batt'n of Militia. Occupied in Sandwich 'till 12 p'.m. in receiving the Congratulations of my friends & in paying visits. Addressed the People twice, & got home by 1 o'clock in the Morning.

129 DIARY, 14 JUNE 1841. *Kingston*

A fine day. This day at 2 o'clock I attended at The New Parliament House & took the Usual oath and subscribed The Parliament Roll. A very full attendance of Members. We then proceeded to elect a speaker & I was the third person who spoke thereon. *Mr. Cuvillier*[118] was chosen, & then, after a great deal of debate & discussion, the House adjourned until tomorrow at 3. *Dined & Spent the Evening at The Governor General's*. Rather warm.

---

118 Augustin Cuvillier was a member of the Legislative Assembly for Huntingdon, and one of the few French Canadians who were prominent in the Montreal business community.

130 EXCERPT FROM DEBATE, 14 JUNE 1841
[*Sandwich* Western Herald, *24 June 1841*]

Colonel Prince had much pleasure in supporting the nomination, he thought Mr. Cuvillier admirably adapted for the high office of Speaker, for these reasons: first, that his great experience in the parliament of Lower Canada rendered him especially eligible; secondly, that he was a moderate reformer, the same as he, (Col. Prince,) was; and thirdly, that he wished to pay a compliment to his own constituents, a majority of whom were French Canadians, and he felt proud they should know he was the third person who spoke in support of a French Canadian as speaker of the Assembly. He also thought it due to Lower Canada that the selection of a speaker should be made from among her representatives, seeing that her privileges had certainly not been extended by the union; and he trusted that the gentlemen from that part of the province would accept it as an earnest of his desire to see all parties acting together in harmony, and having but one object in their proceedings – the furtherance of the prosperity of United Canada. He could not sit down without paying a compliment to the high character of the late Speaker, Sir Allan McNab, and this he could not express in a more appropriate manner than by hoping that Mr. Cuvillier might emulate the ability, impartiality and intelligence of his predecessor.

131 EXCERPT FROM SPEECH OF 23 JUNE 1841
[*Sandwich* Western Herald, *7 July 1841*]

I can imagine, sir, that some Honorable Member, who having crossed the broad Atlantic, to embark his fortune in this Colony, and invested his capital on the banks of one of our noble rivers, in the just hope and expectation that he would be as safe there under the ægis of the British Constitution as he would on the river Thames in England, but whose hopes and expectations had been bitterly deceived – who had here spent the prime of his life in counselling the weak, the disappointed and the restless, and had kept them in the straight line of duty, to their Sovereign and their Country – one on whom they had leaned on all occasions – whose time had been entirely devoted to their service and to the service of an ungrateful Government – one who had risked his life too often – and had spent his means, his time, his almost every thing, in repelling from the soil of his adopted country bands of ruffian invaders, who came there to insult the Crown, to change our Laws and Institutions, and to murder and rob his fellow citizens – one whose services thus gratuitously bestowed had met from the Government of other days neglect and coldness, and that indeed which was far worse than mere indifference – ingratitude. I say, sir, I can well imagine that any Hon. Member, used and treated in the manner I have just described, may naturally be expected to oppose this address, and the measures of His Excellency. But, sir, no true Briton will oppose it even on such grounds as those. – (Hear, hear, hear.) No sir, a loyal man, a sincere supporter of Lord Sydenham's administration – he who has an earnest desire to see this country prosper, will not divide the House on this occasion, but he will express as I do now, a hearty hope that there shall be no dissension in the camp – and that the world shall see that the first parliament of united Canada are united in the first important measure upon which they have deliberated (hear, hear.)

132 DIARY, 9 JULY 1841

Busy at the House & in town all day. Called on Mr. & Mrs. Dykes.[119] & Mr. & Mrs. Thos Wilson.[120] Charles Baby in Kingston and he is very friendly with me! Whether Sincerely so or not I cannot tell. The House adjourned early for want of an *Election Committee*. A party of us met and Settled the dispute between Messrs Hamilton & Christie[121] *MPPs*. Home by 10 and went to bed at 11. Tired.

133 EXCERPT FROM SPEECH OF 12 JULY 1841
[*Sandwich* Western Herald, *28 July 1841*]

COL. PRINCE rose and said, that as he observed every hon. member of the Executive Council who had seats in that house were [sic] present, he would give notice that he would, on Thursday next, put the following questions to them, namely, whether it was the intention of Her Majesty's government to introduce any measure for the relief and pardon of certain persons charged with political offences alleged to have been committed within the last four years. Col. Prince said that many worthy men had been entrapped into the traitorous schemes of artful and cowardly leaders, and undeserved banishment from their country and homes had been the consequence. – He was not at this moment prepared to say where the line of mercy should be drawn, but he sincerely hoped that it would be speedily established, and that very many of the exiles from the soil would be very soon recalled.

134 EXCERPT FROM DEBATE OF 16 JULY 1841
[*St Catharines* Journal, *29 July 1841, in* Nish, *Vol. 1*]

Col. Prince said, his question was a very simple one, and required only a plain answer. Was it, or was it not, the intention of the Executive to show mercy to those who, the dupes of knaves and villains, by whom they had been betrayed, were now dragging out a miserable existence in that land, which had once dazzled their imagination with dreams of happiness and liberty – the

---

119 This probably refers to a Kingston dry goods dealer named Deykes.
120 Thomas Wilson was a Kingston magistrate, notary public, and entrepreneur.
121 J.R. Hamilton was a Government member of the Legislative Assembly, representing Bonaventure. Robert Christie, historian, was an independent member, for Gaspé. The dispute concerned Christie's allegation that the judge of the Gaspé District Court was incompetent.

United States – or who, still more unfortunate, were withering beneath the degradation of the felon's brand, in remorse and agony, in New South Wales?

135 SPEECH OF 23 JULY 1841
[*Sandwich* Western Herald, *11 August 1841*]

Col. Prince rose for the purpose of bringing under the notice of the House a paragraph which had been published in a certan newspaper. – (Cries of "name, name.") – The *Montreal Herald*.

....

Col. Prince read the article referred to by him, being the leading article in the Montreal Herald of the 20th instant.

The Editor (Col. Prince said) he imagined would be somewhat puzzled to show that he (Col Prince) had ever moved for the introduction of a bill to pardon universally and indiscriminately. He never even gave notice of such a bill.

Col Prince read another extract, in which a portion of the House was stigmatized as "rebels." (A laugh.)

Col. Prince said, hon. gentlemen may laugh at this – I do not. I stand here to assert and to protect the rights and privileges of this House and of myself; I will not quietly submit to hear it asserted that there are rebels among the representatives of the people – (Hear, hear.) The time may come when every honest and honorable opponent of a ministerial measure will be branded as a rebel. I make these observations to show how necessary it is that we should have a committee of privileges.

Colonel Prince concluded by explaining that the simple question put by him a few days back to His Excellency's advisers as to whether any relief was intended to be offered to any of the misguided men who had left this country, had been (as he could not but imagine wilfully) misconstrued by the Editor of the *Montreal Herald* into the actual introduction of a bill for the indiscriminate pardon of all; a measure which every lawyer must well know would be unconstitutional and a direct interference with the prerogative of the Crown, and therefore illegal. (Hear, hear.)

136 DIARY, 26 JULY 1841

Quite a Cold & chilly day, with a strong North Wind. How very Changeable is this climate! It however became as warm as Ever towards Evening. Called on Lord Sydenham and received from him some rather encouraging Conversation as to *my future professional prospects*. Whether he was sincere I Cannot say. In the Evening I went to the House for 6 hours; and then met the Wilsons at Mr. Askew's of The British North American Bank and spent the Evening there. Home by 12, very lowspirited at not having heard from home.

137 EXCERPT FROM ALIEN BILL SPEECH, 28 JULY 1841
[*Kingston* Chronicle, *4 August 1841, in* Nish, *Vol. 1*]

The bill is certainly a very good measure as far as it goes, but it is not sufficiently comprehensive. We want our country populated: we want foreigners from all nations: there should be no line of distinction drawn. We want Prussians, Belgians, Hollanders, Swiss, and Americans. (Hear, hear.) Yes, Americans, for I am far from imputing to the American nation the crime of their worst citizens, the injuries which we have sustained from a portion of the lowest class of society. (Hear, Hear.) I would make no invidious distinction. We talk of sending Emigrant agents to England; we have one there already, a talented and sensible man, but what description of emigrants does he send us? They are of that class which we do not want; they are paupers. (Hear, hear.) We want capitalists, and if they are American capitalists so much the better.

138 DIARY, 30 JULY 1841

A very fine day and not too warm. Not well by any means and lowspirited and bilious. Engaged in town during the Morning, and went to the House in The Evening where we sat in debate until 11. I spoke upon Mr. Small's[122] Bill for Vote by Ballot, and destroyed it by Moving that the Committee *do rise*, which was Carried & the bill was therefore lost. Walked home with Mr. Wilson and got to bed at 12 o'clock, much pleased at having *hoisted* Small's bill.

139 EXCERPT FROM SECRET BALLOT SPEECH, 30 JULY 1841
[*Kingston* Chronicle, *7 August 1841, in* Nish, *Vol. 1*]

I say that every man who possesses health and strength may, if he chooses, be as independent as the Lord of the land. (Hear, hear.) Yes, the backwoodsman of Canada is far more independent than the office holder who relies upon the fleeting fancies of the popular will for his continuance in office. I will never acknowledge that the Canadian freeholder has any necessity for resorting to this underhand mode of giving his vote; no, he may go boldly to the hustings, and defy any human being to injure him if he gives an honest vote.

140 273 MAGISTRATES AND FREEHOLDERS OF ESSEX TO PRINCE
[*Sandwich* Western Herald, *25 August 1841*]

Sandwich, July 31, 1841
The undersigned beg leave respectfully to express their approbation of your

---

122 James Edward Small, member of the Legislative Assembly for the third riding of York, was an Ultra-Reform supporter of Sydenham.

past and present political course as their Representative in parliament. Yet satisfied as they are with the whole tenor of your political conduct, they cannot refrain from expressing the peculiar gratification they enjoy by your late notice relative to those of our countrymen now suffering for political offences. They fully agree with you, sir, that many of these exiles are the victims of deception; that they have been led into error by designing demagogues, and hurried into rebellion, and consequent banishment, by traitors and cowards; and while the undersigned would not for a moment justify or palliate those offences, they cannot but wish that as justice has claimed and received her due, mercy might be heard on their behalf, and on behalf of their suffering families.

141 EXCERPT FROM EDITORIAL
[*Niagara* Chronicle, *in Sandwich* Western Herald, *4 August 1841*]

Colonel Prince is pursuing as erratic a course as any honorable member of the Assembly, for he is pushing measures which his personal experience must have convinced him are contrary alike to the good of the country and to just legislation – measures which the province would quite as soon have expected to find an advocate for in Sir Francis Head as in the hero of Windsor Chase – he whose "I ordered them to be shot, and it was done accordingly," did more to check "sympathy" than all the paper proclamations which the patriot war saw issued. The exiled "patriots" and the unbaptized "sympathisers," have become the objects of the gallant Colonel's tender solicitude. He is anxious to open the province to both these offshoots of the human race – in plain English, to fill this dependency of Britain with Britain's enemies. He is a remarkable man, Colonel Prince is!

142 DIARY, 5 AUGUST 1841

A fine morning, and it turned out a lovely day. In the morng I called on The Govr General & had a long & satisfactory interview with him. Dined at 2, and then went to The House of Assembly. The Municipal Corporation Bill came up for debate, and we debated it *until 3 in the morning*. Much warm language used on both sides. We Carried the three first Sections of the Act. House adjourned at about 1/4 past 3, and I got to bed at 1/2 past 3 not a little fatigued, as may be supposed.

143 DIARY, 25 AUGUST 1841

Another fine day & warm. But it is not so warm here as it is at Sandwich. Very unwell all day, owing to my having drank an extra glass yesterday, *and having no appetite. I cannot eat.* The House of Assembly met at 10 am, and adjourned at 1/2 past 5. Spent an hour in town with Aylwin[123] MP. Mr. Atty General Draper[124] informed me that Ld Sydenham would give me a Silk Gown & that I was to go the Western Circuit this Summer. At home & in bed by 12.

144   EXCERPTS FROM DEBATE OF 30 AUGUST 1841
[*Montreal* Gazette, *2 and 3 September 1841, in* Nish, *Vol. 1*]

"It might be thought," said Mr. P., "very singular that I should be the advocate for the pardon of these persons – I care little or nothing for what is said or thought upon the subject – I am guided by principles of Christianity and honesty, which I hold to be above all other considerations." ... He knew that three hundred of his constituents, Magistrates, farmers, and men of the most respectable character, have approved his conduct, and he cared not for a vicious and malignant press.

145   REPORT OF A TRIAL AT SANDWICH,
12 OCTOBER 1841
[*Sandwich* Western Herald, *21 October 1841*]

The whole town was thrown into a state of excitement and ferment on Tuesday, the 12th inst., in consequence of the unlicensed use of that unruly little member, the tongue, in the Court Room, by JOHN PRINCE, Esq., the leading (and driving) member of the bar in this town, M.P.P. for this county, Queen's counsel, and last, though not least, Colonel of the 3d Essex Militia! This 'learned,' 'gallant' and 'honorable gentleman,' was employed by Lieut. Augustus William Schweiger, of the 2d batt'n I.M., as counsel in a case of assault which took place in the month of June last.

. . . .

On Tuesday afternoon, the 12th inst., Mr. Prince opened the case in behalf of his client, Mr. Schweiger, in his usual bland, but most discursive style; and after alluding to the correspondence, and reflecting in sarcastic (but perfectly harmless) terms on the 'Western Herald,' which he designated as a contemptible little sheet, he launched forth in a most grandiloquent and sentimental strain in praise of Mr. Keating[125] and his aboriginal lady, expressing himself most desperately smitten with the Indian character, and the innocence, amiability and independent bearing of the squaws. After almost sickening the Court and Jury with his fulsome adulation of Mr. Keating and the squaws, he spent a

---

123 Thomas Cushing Aylwin in 1841 was a Reform member of the Assembly, representing Portneuf, L.C. He was solicitor general for Lower Canada from 24 September 1842, to 27 November 1843, and again, briefly, in the spring of 1848.

124 William Henry Draper, a moderate Tory, was appointed attorney general (west) by Lord Sydenham in 1841.

125 John W. Keating, of Moore Township in 1841, was a magistrate of the Western District and, from 1839, an assistant Indian superintendent.

portion of his eloquence in "soft sodering" our esteemed friend, Mr. Woods,[126] M.P.P. for Kent, Mr. Woods, we believe, was in the Court room, and must have been considerably "raised" in his own esteem by what fell from the learned counsellor's lips. Having rambled about from Bear Creek to our printing office, he at last lighted on our friend, Mr. Wiggins,[127] the defendant in the case, and such a regular black-balling a poor wight never got. He called him a "*young ruffian*," a "*printer's devil*," (Mr. W. had been employed in our office a short time as a compositor) and he daubed him and rolled him all over with printer's ink in a very uncomely manner. Then, unfortunate "we" had to take it, knowing full well that nothing he could say would injure us in the estimation of any one who knew us. At last, by candle light, the case was brought to bear with "full force, virtue and effect" on the minds of the jury, who, notwithstanding the counsellor's repeated attempts at wit and humor, were as sedate as an Indian council.

....

Mr. Prince put several questions to Mr. Watson which were quite irrelevant to the case, but which suited his purpose very well, as it enabled him to vent his personal dislike to that gentleman in the most insulting, and abusive terms. He particularly aimed his sarcasm at the circumstance of Mr. Watson being a "shop-keeper," an occupation which he Mr. Prince, looked upon with the utmost contempt; and he laboured hard to show that Mr. Watson, being (as Mr. P. expressed it) "*a petty shop-keeper – a dealer in stay-laces and ten-penny nails*," – could not, therefore, be a gentleman. He enlightened the court with a long definition of what constitutes a gentleman, and then turned upon Mr. Watson again the "vials of his wrath," his countenance at the time exhibiting the blackest malignity, and pointing to him with his dexter hand, he called him a '*wretch*,' a '*fool*,' an '*animal*,' and a variety of other epithets which were anything but complimentary.

146 EXCERPT FROM WIGGINS TO THE *Western Herald*
[*Sandwich* Western Herald, *28 October 1841*]

Sandwich Jail, October 24, 1841

The fact of Mr. Prince having *supposed* me to have written certain political articles, which have appeared in the Western Herald newspaper, reflecting on his conduct in the House of Assembly, has had the effect of bringing down his wrathful indignation upon my head. The *redoubtable* Colonel is altogether wrong in his sapient *supposition*, as I have never written ten lines concerning him (before the present communication) in the whole course of my life.

---

126 Joseph Woods, formerly of Sandwich, in 1841 was a Chatham land speculator. He represented Kent in the Assembly.
127 Charles Wiggins was formerly a clerk to Charles Baby. Subsequently he became a partner in the Chatham *Gleaner*.

147 DIARY, 14 DECEMBER 1841

A fine day. Busily engaged all the morng at the Office. In the afternoon attended J.A. Wilkinson Esqre J.P.W.D. & had *Grant*,[128] the Editor, brought before him for Libel, & held to Bail to appear to an Indictment at the next Assizes. Sat 2 or 3 hours with several at Bill Hall's. Home & in bed by 11 fatigued & not well.

148 PRINCE TO COLONEL RICHARD BULLOCK[129]
[*PAC, R.G. 9, I, B1, Vol. 61*]

The Park Farm
December 30, 1841

As all apprehensions of a Rupture with the United States have happily passed away, and as my Services are not likely to be required by the Government; and especially as I have learned by dear-bought experience that the Command of a Militia Regiment in this Country entails upon one (if one does one's duty) "Envy, hatred, and malice, and all uncharitableness"; and as I, moreover, have other reasons for desiring to be relieved from my Commission, I beg leave to tender, through you, to His Excellency The Administrator of The Government,[130] my resignation of the Command of the 3rd Regiment of Essex Militia, Which I earnestly hope will be at once accepted.

149 DIARY, 3 JUNE 1842

A very fine day and very warm. Attended Court all day, and was Excessively fatigued. The *Special* Jury gave a Verdict of 6d Damages against *Grant*! for a Most atrocious libel. No such thing as a *special* Jury ought to be empannelled [*sic*] in this Country! Home by 10 *much tired*.

150 EXCERPT FROM REPORT OF THE ASSIZES
[*Sandwich* Western Herald, *16 June 1842*]

On Tuesday evening the 7th, previous to the Judge passing sentence on the unfortunate criminals, Mr. PRINCE generously came forward and prayed His Lordship to stay judgment with respect to Mr. Chas. Wiggins, who had pleaded guilty to the authorship and publication of two alleged libels, the one against Mr. Prince, the other against certain Magistrates. – Our contracted limits will not admit of our giving even the substance of his remarks, but they went far to

---

128 Henry C. Grant was publisher from 1838 of the Sandwich *Western Herald and Farmers Magazine*.
129 Bullock was adjutant general of militia from 1837.
130 Sir Richard Downes Jackson.

show that in the prosecution of Mr. Wiggins he was actuated by no other motive than that of putting a stop to such publications, which had so direct a tendency to create breaches of the peace, and all manner of ill feeling.

Mr. Wiggins briefly thanked Mr. Prince for his interposition, which he assured that gentleman was received with the same sincerity and heartiness with which it was offered.

Having also been indicted for publishing an alleged libel against certain Magistrates, to several counts of which we were instructed by our counsel to plead guilty, we were also made the subject of Mr. Prince's gracious interposition, who prayed His Lordship to stay judgment against us also. His remarks indicated a commendable desire for the restoration of harmony in this distracted town, and were otherwise well adapted to allay any bitterness of feeling which may have existed in the bosoms of any present.

We acknowledged our obligations to Mr. Prince for his gratuitous intervention, and we sincerely responded to the sentiment expressed, that all past differences might cease from that moment.

The Judge then admonished Mr. Wiggins and ourselves in a manner that could not but prove his goodwill and solicitude, and was graciously pleased to discharge us both from the infliction of any penalty.

151 DIARY, 24 FEBRUARY 1843

Another hard frost and very cold, but a fine & bright day, and sleighing incomparable. Busy at the Office & in Sandwich all day long. *This day I attended at Mr. Charles Baby's Office and there qualified as a Magistrate of this District.* William Vidal[131] dined with us and sat until 1/2 past 10 when we all went to bed, a good deal fatigued in consequence of Sitting up so late last night. A Cold night & hard frost again! *What a Climate!!*

152 DIARY, 12 MARCH 1843

An extremely hard frost. My Bella, thank God, a great deal better. We went to Church in the morning, but it was *bitter Cold*. A great deal of Snow fell today. At home all day after Dinner. Spent the Evg in reading &c. Dr. McMullin spent an hour with us. A Cold night with frost. Heard from Hon. Mr. Baldwin (the Atty Genl, West),[132] offering me the Western Circuit at the next Assizes.

---

131 William Penrose Vidal, a son of Richard Emeric Vidal, of Sarnia Township, was a Sandwich barrister in 1851. He moved to Sarnia in 1853, and became reeve of Sarnia Township in 1856.

132 Robert Baldwin, Reform member of the Legislative Assembly for Hastings, with Louis Hippolyte LaFontaine had formed the first Baldwin-LaFontaine administration in September 1842. Baldwin was the leader of the Upper Canadian Reformers during the post-Rebellion period and until his retirement from politics in 1851.

153 PRINCE TO ROBERT BALDWIN
[*MTCL, Robert Baldwin Papers*]

The Park Farm, March 12, 1843

I am this day favored with your letter of the 7th informing me of the Commission days for the Ensuing Lent assizes on The Western Circuit, and desiring to be informed by return of Post whether it will be convenient for me to take the Crown business on that Circuit for those Assizes. In reply I beg to say that I shall be most happy to do so. I take your offer as a Compliment to myself, and I beg to thank you for it.

154 EXCERPT FROM PRINCE TO BALDWIN
[*MTCL, Robert Baldwin Papers*]

The Park Farm, March 24, 1843

The "materiel" composing the Magistracy of this District is, for the Most part, of an Extraordinary sort, and but ill adapted to vindicate the Laws or to protect the Subject. Such facts have Come to my knowledge within the last Six or Eight Months that would appear incredible, and I forbear to trouble you with their detail. But I have witnessed in men, now in the Commission of the Peace, such ignorance, corruption, and wickedness as is rarely seen elsewhere; and much as it was against my will to do so, (having for the first 6 years of my life in this District been a *Slave* to the public in my magisterial Capacity) I was prevailed upon a few days since to qualify and again incur the very troublesome duties of the office of a J.P. because I saw justice witheld [*sic*] from many and tyranny and oppression Exercised over not a few.

155 DIARY, 19 APRIL 1843

A fine day and mild. Busily engaged in Sandwich from 10 am 'till 8 pm. Bothered almost to death, & heartily sick am I of the *legal profession* in this detestable Country, & among such a *Set*. William & Bella went out riding & Came home late. My man Richard[133] very unwell as is always the Case with all men in this hateful Country, just as the Spring & fall work on farms Commences! Went to bed at 10 just as unhappy & miserable as any wretch Can be.

156 EXCERPT FROM PRINCE TO BALDWIN
[*MTCL, Robert Baldwin Papers*]

The Park Farm, September 3, 1843

As regards the Indemnity Bill, we really must do something to satisfy the Country about it, or you and I will lose some of our best, and Staunchest, and

---

133 The reference is probably to Richard Hunter, a Negro farm hand.

most influential friends. Besides, Common Justice demands that Something sho'd be done, and she Never can appeal in vain to *you*, my dear Sir. I see, and I have for a long time seen, the perplexities to which you allude. But I think they are to be dissolved. However, more of this when we meet, and that will be, I hope, in a very few days after the opening of the Session. We cannot differ, I apprehend, upon this important Matter.

157 PRINCE TO BALDWIN
[*MTCL, Robert Baldwin Papers*]

London, Canada West,
October 1, 1843

As the representative of a People lying "far west", I could *not* vote for the Seat of Govt being Carried far "East", though you, being differently situated, may feel it your duty to do so. "Entre Nous", I, as far as my own private feelings go, would just as soon have it at Montreal or Quebec as where it is – perhaps *rather*. But my Conscience, as a representative, points one way, while my disposition leads toward another.

....

P.S. Should any thing come up in the House relative to the removal of the Western District Gaol and Court House from *Sandwich to Chatham* please stave it off until I come down.

158 DIARY, 25 OCTOBER 1843. *Kingston*

A wet morning. My Corns have foretold rain for the last 2 days, and so it has come. At the Russell Election Committee all the morning. Then dined and attended the House till 9 p.m. & past. Spoke upon the bill for preventing unlawful meetings and also upon my Game Law Bill which I introduced for the first time and it was well received. The unlawful meeting bill occasioned a good deal of debate but it carried by a large majority. Took tea at 9 and went to bed at 11.

159 PRINCE TO BALDWIN. *Private*
[*MTCL, Robert Baldwin Papers*]

Kingston, October 26, 1843

The almost impossibility of procuring half an hour's quiet conversation with you and the almost unfairness of asking you for it at the present time are reasons why I trouble you with this instead of with a personal interview.

You are aware that the Office of District Judge for the Western District is at present filled by *a Lieutenant in the Army on half pay*. His qualifications, or rather his want of Qualification for the office, is too ridiculous to dwell upon, and it has long since been the earnest desire of the Profession that a Barrister should be appointed in his stead. It is, moreover, against the spirit of the Law passed in 1841 that any other person than a Barrister should fill the office of D. Judge, and Mr. Charles Eliot never having been bred to the Profession, and being also a person without any *legal turn of mind*, sometimes decides Cases in a manner not very satisfactory to the Suitors or the Profession. I never practice in his District Court, but his frequent references to me for advice and the observations I hear from others, all go to shew that he is (and indeed how Can he be otherwise?) a very unfit person to preside as District Judge, principally for want of a legal Education. He declared a short time since that he would give it up.

I do therefore hope that, with this example before you (and there are other Districts Similarly Circumstanced) you will introduce your Bill for altering the District & Division Courts, and will press it through the present Session. And I really see no reason why the District Court should not be allowed, by Law, an Extended Jurisdiction – say, in liquidated demands to the Extent of £100 and in unliquidated to the extent of £50; and if the Clerks and Practitioners were to have Q[ueen's] B[ench] Costs taxed, the Fee Fund would, I think, pay the expences, and the Profession and Country be better satisfied.

Should such a Bill pass and should Mr. Eliot be removed upon such Compensation made to him as may be just and reasonable, I beg permission to offer my Services as Judge for that District. It is my intention to abandon Practice as an *Attorney* from the 1st of next January, and I am of opinion that no D. Judge ought to be permitted to act as an *Attorney within his District.* Indeed, I think he ought not to practice either as Atty or Counsel within the same, but the Country will not, I fear, submit to pay that increased Salary which a Judge ought to have on relinquishing his Practice. There are many other points connected with this Matter which I much wish to speak to you about when an opportunity offers, and I think I can Satisfy you (what I know from experience) that the peace, and welfare, and good Conduct of the inhabitants of a District are in no small degree dependent upon the officer who necessarily mixes amongst them so much as their Judge does.

I therefore solicit your good offices in my behalf; and I ground my pretensions to the office mainly upon the continuous Service which as a Magistrate, a lawyer, and a friend I have unreservedly bestowed upon all classes of the People Throughout my district for the last ten years & upwards, and which (I speak without vanity) have secured to me that *Popularity* (a very unprofitable one by the bye, "entre nous") Which Nothing can, I apprehend, dissipate or lessen so long as I remain their friend and neighbour.

160 EXCERPTS FROM SPEECH, 3 NOVEMBER 1843
[*Kingston* Chronicle, *15 November 1843, in* Nish, *Vol. 3*]

He (Colonel Prince) considered the inhabitants of Kingston to have almost a vested right in the premises in question, and he for one would not disturb that right but would vote for its remaining with them ... And for reasons ably demonstrated by many honorable and learned members during the debate and in accordance with his own feelings and opinion on the subject – an opinion which he doubted not his constituents in the far West would sanction and approve of – he felt himself constrained to vote against the first Resolution introduced by his honorable and learned friend the Attorney General (West) for removing the Seat of Government to Montreal – as an Upper Canadian he protested against its leaving Upper Canada (hear, hear, hear;) and he would now emphatically call upon the honorable members from Lower Canada to pause before they voted for the Resolution in favor of Montreal.

161 Diary, 27 November 1843

A beautiful day and a hard frost. *The Ministry resigned office!* All Kingston in great Excitement. The Governor General[134] sent for me and Consulted me about a New Ministry. Went to bed at 10 much fatigued.

162 Excerpt from Debate, 1 December 1843
[*Toronto* British Colonist, *8 December 1843, in* Nish, *Vol. 3*]

MR. HENRY SMITH[135] – With reference to the member for Essex's admiration of the late government, he would like to know what government *he* was *ever* opposed to? No! discreet and cautious, the hon. and learned member always looked around him and voted with the *strongest* party. (Hear, hear.) His opinions would no doubt be supported by a majority in the House, but they would do him *but little credit out of it*. (Hear, hear.)

163 Diary, 7 January 1844

A very hard frost. About 3 inches of Snow on the Earth. Blowing hard. *The Most splendid Hunting day I ever knew*; but it is Sunday. Violent wind & cold weather all day. No going to Church in the Morng. Messrs. Wingfield,[136] Sloane,[137] & Liberté[138] & his Son waited on me with the Address of the Inhabitants of Malden and Anderdon & dined with us at The Park Farm. The boys went to Church in the afternoon, and I went into town and made several Calls. Home to tea, and went to bed at 10 o'clock.

---

134 Sir Charles Theophilus Metcalfe.
135 Smith represented Frontenac in the House of Assembly from 1841.
136 Rowland Wingfield, an English immigrant in 1831, soon thereafter settled in Anderdon Township where he sold small parcels of land to blacks. In 1843–44 he was a justice of the peace of the Western District.
137 John Sloan was an Anderdon Township member of the Western District Council. He kept a shop and tavern on the river road just above Amherstburg.
138 Jean Baptiste Laliberté.

164 DIARY, 20 JANUARY 1844

A fine but cold day. The same persons breakfasted and dined with us as did yesterday. William returned with Bell from Malden. Sheriff Foott slept at our House. This day *The Great Political Meeting took place at Sandwich.* Court House crammed to suffocation almost. I spoke for upwards of 1 hour and a half, and we Carried our *"Resolutions"* by sweeping Majorities. The same Party dined here. Home by 8 & in bed by 11.

165 PRINCE TO BALDWIN
[*MTCL, Robert Baldwin Papers*]

The Park Farm, January 23, 1844

We have had an immense *County* Meeting here which was Convened at my suggestion. Such a demonstration of public Opinion upon the late resignations &c. has not been Exhibited since the recent Prorogation, and it will afford you pleasure to hear that *all our "Resolutions"* (which I need hardly mention to you were drawn by myself and placed in the hands of friends to move, and which they did Move with admirable effect) carried unanimously ... The result of this meeting will, I think, have a strong effect upon the public mind; and it is highly flattering to you and your late Colleagues as well as to myself.

Mr. Wingfield's resolution as regards *myself* I, of Course, knew nothing about until it was moved.

166 DIARY, 22 FEBRUARY 1844

A Most lovely day & although a slight frost it is as warm as April & the heat of the Sun makes Every thing very *muddy* by 11 a.m. Received a letter from Mr. Daly the Prov[incia]l Secy[139] offering me the Commissionership of Bankruptcy for this District. At home and within doors all day and busy in writing a long letter to Mr. Daly in reply to his rec'd this morng. Wrote also a private note to him & one to *Mr. Draper. Mrs. Woods* left for *Beeman's.*[140] She starts tom[orro]w on a visit to her mother at Smooth Rock. *Beautiful* weather but roads muddy. Went to bed at 10 in rather better spirits.

167 DIARY, 5 APRIL 1844

A very wet Morng. Heavy Rain. The family went to Church in the Morng notwithstanding. Saw Wingfield & Laliberté for half an hour, and after Church Called on The Chewetts & Sat an hour. Mr. Chewett very unwell again. Heard

139 Sir Dominick Daly, 'the perpetual secretary,' was Governor Metcalfe's only constitutional advisor; from November 1843, until August 1844.
140 Elam Beeman was a Sandwich innkeeper.

from Mr. Draper offering the Sandwich & London assizes to me as Q.C. at the ensuing Circuit. Much pleased with the offer. The Country is inundated with water owing to the late rains. At home all the Eveng & went to bed at 11. A wet night.

168 EXCERPT FROM PRINCE TO COLONEL RICHARD BULLOCK. *Private*
[*PAC, R.G. 9, IB1, Vol. 64*]

London, Canada West
May, 18, 1844

I know you are a friend of mine & I know you will feel much gratified at the Contents of Sir F.B. Head's letter which I inclose herewith.

Do me the favor to shew it to Sir Chas Metcalfe (to whom I am Comparatively a Stranger) when you lay before him my official letter to you, as I am Naturally desirous that he should know I stand well with so good a Man as Sir Francis is.

169 DIARY, 23 JULY 1844. *The Park Farm*

Robinson ploughed 1/2 the day. A very fine & hot morning. Wrote some letters and busy among my men on the farm. Hauled several loads of Hay when heavy Thunder, Lightning, & tremendous Rain came on and stopped us, so that we were not able to draw any more. Mr. Wingfield dined here, and Messrs. Sloan & Wingfield sat an hour or two and drank & talked Politics. We think of starting Mr. Wingfield for the County in my stead when I resign at the forthcoming general Election. Went to bed at 10, tired. A very hot night.

170 EXCERPT FROM PRINCE TO LOUIS HIPPOLYTE LAFONTAINE[141]
[*PAC, M.G. 24, B14, Vol. 5*]

The Park Farm, Sandwich
August 30, 1844

This will be handed to you by my old friend Mr. J.B. Laliberté of Malden, than whom a better or a worthier man does not live in Western Canada.

He will tell you all about our Politics, etc. etc. etc. and I hope you will be able to tell him in return, (*but I doubt it*) that Sir Charles Metcalfe *has* at length formed an administration *which the Country will support.* What a strange

---

141 Louis Hippolyte LaFontaine, thanks to Robert Baldwin, was at this time the member of the Legislative Assembly for the fourth riding of York, Canada West. He was the post-Rebellion leader of the Lower Canadian Reformers until he retired from politics in 1851.

position are we in, and how *tamely do the People* submit to be treated as they have been! But they will not endure it much longer; and they have a right to ask and they will *demand* why their Constitution has been suspended; and I presume that Parliament (if it does again assemble) will ask and demand the same.

171   356 FREEHOLDERS OF ESSEX TO PRINCE
[*Sandwich* Western Express, *12 October 1844*]

Sandwich, September 30, 1844

We the undersigned Freeholders of the County of Essex have learned with dismay and unfeigned regret that your political connexion with us is likely to be severed by your acceptance of a trifling and unprofitable office which we fear you must have taken with no other view than to be relieved from going to Parliament ... We are therefore naturally more than anxious to secure a continuance of your political services; and although some of us may have wished that you had supported His Excellency the Governor General during his late difference with his Ministry, yet even these few of us cannot but admire your Independence, and we now tender you our support.

No other Candidate whom we know can stand in competition with you. You, sir, are the man of the people, as was that great statesman, Charles James Fox, in whose politics you were educated and whose praises you have so often sounded. And Sir, we ask you to continue our chosen Representative and to allow us to return you to the next Parliament as the Independent Member of the equally independent Electors of this County.

172   DIARY, 7 OCTOBER 1844

A beautiful day. Went into town in the morning & Called at Chewetts'. Killed a fine fat heifer. She turned out good beef. At 12 near *100* Freeholders Called on me with addresses from various townships requesting me to go to Parliament again, And after much entreaty I consented to be put in Nomination. We all drank freely. Sheriff Foott supped and slept here. Laliberty & others here in the Eveng. They too drank tea. Went to bed at 11 a little worse for liquor.

173   DIARY, 8 OCTOBER 1844

Another fine day. Drove out to my back farm & brought in a good load of wood. Home by 3 p.m. Mrs. Holland[142] spent the day here. Walked round my farm in the Evening, & after dusk was Engaged in making out my accts. against the Government as Queen's Counsel. Made very uncomfortable by Elec-

---

142 The widow of Edward Holland, postmaster at Sandwich until his death in 1843.

tioneering news brought from Malden (from Lachlan & Wingfield) by Wm. D. Baby.[143] Went to bed at 12, unhappy.

174 EXCERPT FROM ROWLAND WINGFIELD TO PRINCE
[*Sandwich* Western Express, *12 October 1844*]

Onslow Cottage, October 8, 1844

Without any feeling of personal ill will or anger, I enclose you my retiring address, which will give you an opportunity publicly of refuting a conviction very prevalent in this neighborhood, that you *always* intended to come out as a representative for the County of Essex, and that I have either been a party to your scheme of finesse, or that I have been most shamefully duped.

175 EXCERPT FROM WINGFIELD TO THE FREEHOLDERS OF ESSEX
[*Sandwich* Western Express, *12 October 1844*]

Onslow Cottage, October 8, 1844

Did I give way to personal feelings or the request of my numerous friends, who declare they will support me to the last, my inclination would lead me to contest the County with a person, who to say the best of it, has treated me in a very uncourteous manner, but duty to my Country, at this all important crisis, forbids that I should be the means of giving the Tory Candidate any chance of success and therefore I shall not be the means of dividing the Reformers, but record my vote for Col. Prince, as the Constitutional Candidate, supporting Responsible Government, as understood by the late Ministers.

176 DIARY, 9 OCTOBER 1844

A beautifully fine & warm day. The Indian Summer, I think. If so, I also think it portends a *hard* winter. Black Squirrels numerous but other game scarce. At Sandwich in the morning and *resolved on Retiring from the Representation of Essex*, much to the Chagrin of the *Canadians*.[144] *Wrote Major Lachlan and Mr. Wingfield to that effect*. Thus Ends my public life as an M.P. W.D. Baby took the letters to Malden. Went to my back farm & brought in a Load of wood. At home all the Eveng and wrote to Mr. Daly P. Secretary & Mr. Cary Dy Inspt Genl.[145] In bed by 10.

---

143 William Duperon Baby was a nephew of François Baby. For a time he was articled to Prince, but the partnership of Prince and Baby broke up in 1846.

144 i.e., the French Canadians.

145 Joseph Cary was inspector general of Lower Canada from 1826. He served as deputy inspector general of the Province of Canada, 1842–67.

177 PRINCE'S REPLY TO 356 ELECTORS,
9 OCTOBER 1844
[*Sandwich* Western Express, *12 October 1844*]

I cannot sufficiently thank you or in adequate terms convey to you my grateful feelings for your address and for your good opinion of me as your Representative for the last eight years. You are well aware that until the last few days I had fully determined upon retiring from public life, and that upon no one occasion have I, since the general Election in 1841 solicited the vote or interest of any Freeholder. But when *upwards of one hundred of you* did me the honor of presenting me, in person, with this address at my own house, you pressed me at the same time with so many kind and irresistible arguments in favor of my continuing to represent you that I promised you I would not refuse to go if you were fully determined as you said you were, to send me to Parliament again; and I at the same time told you that I should not canvass or interfere, but should remain at home quite passive until the day of election came. We separated with this understanding; and the gratification which I derived from that meeting, attended as it was by upwards of *one hundred Freeholders of the highest respectability in Essex*, can never be effaced from my memory. At that time there were (and I believe still are) as we were given to understand from report, three Candidates for the honor of your suffrages, namely, Major Lachlan, Mr. Wingfield, and Mr. Watson. The two first are personal friends of mine, and they came forward in the first instance because I told them (and as it was well known) I had declined the honor. They both assured me over and over again that if it was my intention to stand again, they would not present themselves as Candidates. I am sure they were sincere; and I admit that I had not, nor have I since had, a right to ask them to retire in [my] favor. But I thought it due to them as my friends and gentlemen to inform them of what had taken place and that I had become, to a certain extent, pledged to the Electors. I therefore lost no time in addressing Major Lachlan and Mr. Wingfield on the subject. I did not ask them to resign, nor did I intimate the slightest wish that they should change their course. All I told them was that "I was pressed by the Electors beyond all my expectations or desire – and that they had determined upon electing me and no other person – that my friends told me I should be guilty of Ingratitude if I declined – that I was therefore in the hands of the Electors – that they would deal with me as they thought fit, and that I should remain entirely passive, as I hitherto had done until the election was ended."

Little [did] I suppose, gentlemen, that there was anything in the above communication that could give offence to Major Lachlan or to Mr. Wingfield. As friends of mine and coming forward as they did (though on principles somewhat but not so very opposite as many seem to think,) I conceived it to be [m]y duty to app[r]ize *both*, in terms alike, of the resolution to which your confidence and kindness had driven me. But, gentlemen, no sooner had my letters been received and read than I was branded by the Parties with political dishonesty, with duplicity in having written similar letters to both of them, with insincerity, a want of candour and various other epithets too numerous to mention, and above all, I was charged by both with having "sold" them (as the "slang" has it), with having all along had in view an intention of coming forward though not honest enough to declare that intention openly, and also with having made Fools as well as Tools of them. A worthy young friend of theirs and mine did his utmost to convince them of my sincerity – others did the same, but no change could they effect in these gentlemen's opinions of my conduct. It therefore remained for me to be under the imputations and obloquy thus unjustly heaped upon me or to prove the sincerity of my motives by *at once retiring*.

....

It now only remains for me to add that I have addressed letters to Major Lachlan and Mr. Wingfield expressing "my deep regret that my former letter had given them umbrage, and that they should have conceived that *I had all along intended* offering myself as a Candidate in opposition to them though my professions tended the other way – in short that I had made or attempted to make Tools of them to serve my own selfish purposes – that I was informed they could not be convinced to the contrary – that I was much pained by these reports, and that I should best satisfy them of the purity of my motives by *declaring that I renounced all claim to the representation of this County in the ensuing Parliament*, and that my withdrawal should appear in the next Sandwich Paper, and I concluded thus; 'I take this step, not from any doubt of my being returned, had I offered, (because a majority of the Freeholders have already signed a requisition to me, and upwards of a hundred of them presented it to me here on Monday last,) but I take it as being the most conclusive – perhaps the only way of convincing you that I am not, nor have ever been, governed by those selfish and insincere motives which have been imputed to me, and which I look upon as equally disgraceful to the public as to the private gentleman. I therefore now leave the field open to all Candidates who may offer.'"

178 "SHAMEFUL EXPOSE"
[*Sandwich* Western Express, *12 October 1844*]

On Tuesday last the Town of Amherstburgh was the scene of the most disgraceful exposé that has ever fallen to a public Journal to record.

It is well known to the public that Major Lachlan, and Rowland Wingfield, Esq. have for some time past been named as rival Candidates for the representation of the County of Essex in the next Parliament. It is also well known that public opinion has been decided [divided?] on the question of *which* of the Candidates came out under the auspices of the late member, Mr. Prince. The friends of the Major roundly asserted that Mr. Prince, not only drafted the Requisition to that gentleman, with his own hand, but that he had authorized the Major to write to a certain influential friend in Gosfield and ask his interest in that quarter – nay farther – that he had requested the Major to write to the Private Secretary[146] of the Governor General, to assure His Excellency that he, *Mr.*

---

146 Captain J.M. Higginson was private secretary to Sir Charles Metcalfe from 1843.

Prince would support His Excellency and promote the Major's Election. On the other hand, the adherents of Mr. Wingfield, as strenuously insisted that *their* Candidate was the favorite and had received the written promise of Mr. Prince's support for himself *and the measures of the late Baldwin and Lafontaine ministry.* These conflicting assertions, and the notorious fact that a constant correspondence was maintained between the late member and Mr. Wingfield, at length aroused the suspicions of the too-confiding Major, who came to the resolution to call upon Mr. Wingfield and "compare notes" – The call was met in that spirit of candour and urbanity so characteristic of Mr. Wingfield, and resulted in the most "damning proofs" of the duplicity of Mr. Prince. Indignant at such dishonorable conduct, these insulted gentlemen repaired to a meeting, then being held in Amherstburgh, and there, in the present of a large number of the most respectable and intelligent Electors of the County publicly exposed the baseness of the late member.

Mr. Wingfield produced a letter from Mr. Prince, which was read, and proved to be "verbatim et literatim,"[147] the same as one addressed to Major Lachlan, promising *him* his support, with this *slight* difference, which to a gentleman of Mr. Prince's *consistency*, was a mere *trifle*, that, in that to Mr. Wingfield he avowed himself the *supporter of the measures of the late ministry*, while in that to the Major, he pledged himself TO SUPPORT SIR CHARLES METCALFE. The proofs were clear, undisputable – *palpable*; and have convicted Mr. P. of an act of heartless imposition upon two of his most intimate and devoted personal friends, and of political dishonesty without a parallel in these most unscrupulous times. And this, Freeholders of Essex, this is the man who hopes for your support at the coming election. This man, who merits the indignant scorn and withering contempt of every *honorable* man in the County, has the presumption to anticipate your unsought suffrages! has the vanity to believe you will return him *even against his will* – has the unblushing effrontery to think that you can lightly look upon such deeds of private turpitude and political dishonesty as mere bagatelle. – But shew him his mistake. Let him learn at the polls that the man who can be faithless to his friend is not to be trusted with the sacred interests of our country. Let him remain in the solitude of retirement to brood over his blasted hopes and aimless ambition. – Leave him to his own reflections –

> "For 'tis vain to curse,
> 'Tis folly to upbraid him,
> HATE cannot WISH him WORSE
> Than guilt and shame have made him."

179 DIARY, 13 OCTOBER 1844

A beautiful day. Indian Summer certainly. Wm. Baby breakfasted & afterwards went off to Lachlan & Wingfield to demand of them for me a refutation of the Editorial Calumny in yesterday's Paper. Miss Innes, Miss Wright & Wm.

---

147 Word for word and letter for letter.

Johnson dined here. No Church. Mr. Ritchie[148] gone to Toronto. Dr. McMullin and W.D. Baby here in the Evening. *Determined upon standing for this County*. Much Excitement in consequence. Wrote to Mr. Daly with Resignation of My Commission of Bankrupts for this District. W.D. Baby mailed the letter. A good deal of Excitement in Sandwich in Consequence. W. Baby here again at 10 p.m. Could not meet Lachlan or Wingfield. Went to bed at 11 fatigued.

180 DIARY, 14 OCTOBER 1844

A rainy morning. It will do much good. Wrote also to Mr. Higginson, Private Secy, with my resignation of Commr. of Bankrupts. W.D. Baby mailed the letter under cover to Thos. Steers Esqre, Land Agent, Montreal.[149] Very busy at home all day. Mr. W.D. Baby obtained from Lachlan & Wingfield denials *in writing* of the truth of the Shameful libel on me in last Saturday's "Express" (Called "Shameful Exposé") and I had 100 Copies printed & Circulated. A good many persons Called in the Evg, Chewett, Mr. Woods & others. Went to bed at 11 tired.

181 DIARY, 16 OCTOBER 1844

A damp Morng. Mr. Gardiner breakfasted here. This was the day of Nomination for Candidates to serve in Plment. Very busy with my friends Calling on me. Went to hustings at 1 o'clock and was proposed by Mr. Lavallée and seconded by Mr. Vitus Villair.[150] Opposed by Lachlan & Wingfield. I addressed the Electors at much length. Compelled to use violent language agst Lachlan. The shew of hands in my favor. A Poll demanded which was granted. Great Excitement in the Town. A vast many people Came home with me to The Park Farm. Major Girty slept here.

182 DIARY, 23 OCTOBER 1844

A beautiful day. Mr. Gardiner breakfasted with me, and several persons met me at Mrs. Beeman's Tavern and accompanied me from thence to the Polling place at Mrs. Mears's. Polling Commenced at 9, & when it ended at 5 p.m. I was a large Number a head of my Opponents Lachlan, Elliott, & Wingfield. Adjourned to Beeman's Inn, drank freely altogether and home by 11 & went to bed at 12.

---

148 William Ritchie was rector of St John's Church, Sandwich, from 1843.

149 Thomas Steers' jurisdiction as a crown lands agent was Kent County. He was normally domiciled at Chatham.

150 Along the upper Detroit the sobriquet St Louis is usually employed in place of the proper surname Villaire. There is a diary reference on 12 August 1846, to Vitus St Louis.

183   EXCERPT FROM PRINCE'S VICTORY ADDRESS,
      28 OCTOBER 1844
      [*PAC, M.G. 24, B14, Vol. 5*]

Gentlemen: – *The contest is ended, and you have won the* battle nobly. Essex is freed from Tory tyranny, which aimed to usurp your rights and liberties. In defiance of Tory lies of the vilest kind, of Tory machinations, calumnies, and scandal of the most inconceivable and indescribable sorts against my private as well as public character, not only disseminated here but throughout the Province, by the venal, ignorant, hireling and lying Press of this Western District, you have *independently* returned to Parliament the *man of your choice* – him who has represented you for the last eight years.

184   EXCERPT FROM PIERRE HECTOR MORIN[151]
      TO LAFONTAINE
      [*PAC, M.G. 24, B14, Vol. 5*]

Sandwich, November 15, 1844

Sachant que la force d'un parti dépend de la nomination de L'Orateur en Chambre, c'est avec plaisir que je vous annonce que Notre Respectable Membre le Colonel Prince a exprimé à plusieurs de ses amis intimes la résolution où il est de proposer et de supporter L'Honorable Monsieur Morin[152] comme réunissant les talents et les qualités requises pour occuper ce post éminent dans L'Assemblée Legislative – Il n'y a aucun doute que le Gallant Colonel Prince entrainera plusieurs des Membres du Haut-Canada pour le supporter dans une démarche aussi louable et patriotique. Mais dans le cas où les Membres du Bas-Canada voudraient reciproquer dans le prochain Parlement et choisir l'Orateur parmi les Membres du Haut-Canada, je me permettrai ici de vous rappeler le nom du Col: Prince qui a fait preuve de ses sentimens [*sic*] libéraux dans le dernier Parlement et aux débats du quel je vous refère pour plus amples informations.

Je me contenterai seulement d'ajouter ici que le Col: Prince peut être considéré comme Canadien français, car en tous temps il s'est montré le défenseur des Canadiens du District de L'Ouest – et aujourd'hui ce sont les Canadiens d'origine française qui le députent au Parlement pour défendre leurs droits, advocasser le Gouvernement Responsable tel qu'entendu par l'ex-Ministère et conformément aux résolutions de 1841.

185   DIARY, 28 NOVEMBER 1844

A fine day. I like Montreal. It is a fine & substantially built City, and reminds one a good deal of Lombard Street & many of the Streets about the City of

---

151 Pierre Hector Morin was collector of customs and postmaster at Sandwich, beginning in 1843.

152 Augustin Norbert Morin, newly elected member of the Legislative Assembly for Terrebonne, was formerly the member for Nicolet. He was LaFontaine's lieutenant, and succeeded him as leader and co-premier in 1851.

London. The House met at 12, Went to the Legislative Council, and then returned to their own Chamber to Elect a Speaker. I proposed The Honble *Mr. Morin* & was 2d by Mr. Christie M.P. for Gaspé, But Sir Allan N. McNab Carried it by 3 votes & he was Elected. Dined & spent the Evening at Rasco's,[153] where Sir Allan gave the Company Champagne. My Dear William came to me.

186 Excerpt from Prince to Baldwin
[*MTCL, Robert Baldwin Papers*]

Noon, December 6, 1844

I think it proper and only Courteous towards you to mention to you and Mr. Price[154] (to whom I request you will be so good as to shew this note) that after the speeches from The Treasury Benches and *the promises & pledges* so liberally made on the part of the Government I have, after giving the matter my *deepest & Most anxious consideration*, arrived at the Conclusion that I cannot Conscientiously oppose the Address.

In the few remarks which I shall make upon the Subject in my place in the House, you will hear my reasons for Coming to this Conclusion, and as it results from the Conviction of my *own* mind that I should do wrong in adopting an opposite Course, I hope you will give me credit for Sincerity, though you may fancy me mistaken.

187 Diary, 20 December 1844

A fine but dull morning. Snow threatens daily but does not come! It is much wanted. Sat all the morning upon the Durand & Webster Election Committee. House met at 1. The Governor General came down and gave his assent to 2 or 3 Bills. Our House then went up to him at the old Govt. House, & presented 3 addresses. I Returned to House of Assembly and carried the address on behalf of The Exiles in Van Dieman's Land, & bro't in the New Registry Law Bill. House adjourned at 10 to meet again in 17 days. Mr. Johnson[155] sat with me in the Evening. In bed by 12.

188 Excerpt from Sir Charles Metcalfe to Lord Stanley.[156] *Private*
[*PAC, MG 24, A15*]

Montreal, December 28, 1844

Colonel Prince – formerly supposed to be a staunch supporter of Her

---

153 Rasco's Hotel, St Paul Street, was then Montreal's best hotel.

154 James Hervey Price was a Reform member of the Legislative Assembly for the first riding of York.

155 James Johnston, a Tory, represented Carleton in the Legislative Assembly.

156 Edward George Geoffrey Smith Stanley, 14th Earl of Derby, was colonial secretary, 1841–45.

Majesty's Government and professes to be so still. When the late Council resigned he volunteered to me a most unqualified assurance of his devotion. He afterwards made a violent speech on the other side and voted accordingly. He has since played a double part, coquetting with both sides. Having in view a District Judgeship expected to be vacated, he accepted a Commissionership of Bankruptcy as a step to the other which was to be joined with it. On the approach of the General Election he professed not to stand – then sent in his resignation of his Office in order that he might stand – then recalled his resignation – then pressed it again & finally became a Candidate. His election was chiefly owing to a French Canadian Population in the Western Extremity of Upper Canada and he must have been indebted for their suffrages to the belief that he was in favor of the Ex Councillors – Nevertheless he obtained other Votes by professing to support me and came down to the Legislative Assembly with similar professions. But he proposed Mr. Morin for the Speakership and voted with the Enemy on that occasion. On the Address he avowed his intention of voting with the Government but was absent on the Division alleging sickness. He has since professed adherence to the Government & the Members of the Exec. Council appear to believe him.

189 Diary, 19 February 1845

As mild as April. Very lowspirited owing to William's absence. Wrote several letters, and sent a Parcel of them to him at Chambly,[157] for Col. Chichester[158] and Col. England.[159] At 1/2 past 3 went to The House & remained there debating several matters until *2 in the morning*. My bill for the preservation of wild-fowl occupied 3 hours, and it was lost owing to the clause for preventing hunting & shooting on the Lord's Day. Shameful to dismiss it on that account! At Gould's[160] & in bed by 1/2 p. 2. Killing work!

190 Sabbath Desecration Bill Debate, 24 February 1845
[*Montreal* Gazette, *27 February 1845*]

Col. PRINCE moved for leave to introduce a Bill to provide against the desecration of the Sabbath. The announcement was received upon the opposition side with ironical cheers.

Mr. MURNEY congratulated Col. Prince upon his change of sentiment. When that gentleman had introduced his Game Bill, it had been without the clause providing against hunting on the Sabbath. Upon the third reading of that Bill, he (Mr. M.) had moved for the introduction of this clause, but the motion was

---

157 A reserve battalion of William Prince's regiment, the 71st Foot (Highland Light Infantry), arrived at Chambly on 5 May 1844.
158 Colonel Chichester was in command at Chatham from about 1838.
159 71st Regiment.
160 Gould's Hotel, College Street, Montreal, was also known as the Mansion House.

rejected. He had then begged that it might be extended to Upper Canada, but that had also been refused, and he believed that Col. Prince had voted against it. He trusted that the Bill would be received, at least so far as Upper Canada was concerned.

Mr. Solicitor General SHERWOOD vindicated Col. Prince; there was no inconsistency in that gentleman's conduct, he had been always in favor of such an enactment. He trusted that the Bill would pass the House.

Mr. MOFFATT would vote for the reception of the Bill; but when it came up for discussion, he would not vote for its application to those of the Roman Catholic Religion, if they did not desire it.

191 DIARY, 25 FEBRUARY 1845

A beautiful day. Sun bright & atmosphere as warm & mild as May! What Most Extraordinary Weather. Busy at the House & in Town all the Morng. Went to The House again at 3 and remained in debate 'till 12 at night. Carried an Address of Congratulation to H.E. *Lord Metcalfe*. Much opposition. Withdrew my Profanation of the Sabbath, & introduced another applicable to U.C. only. Debated *the Rebellion claims* Resolution warmly. That also much Contested by the Opposition. Messrs. Draper and Woods took their Seats. A full house. In bed by 1.

192 SPEECH ON ADDRESS TO THE GOVERNOR GENERAL, 25 FEBRUARY 1845
[*Montreal* Gazette, *27 February 1845*]

Col. PRINCE rose to make a motion, which he had no doubt would be accepted by both sides of the House with great favour. In a few words, he begged leave to move, that an humble Address be presented to His Excellency the Governor-General, to congratulate him on his elevation to the Peerage of the United Kingdom of Great Britain and Ireland, and to express their gratitude to their august Sovereign for thus rewarding His Excellency's distinguished merits. He was seconded by his Hon. friend, the member for Prince Edward.[161] He was quite sure, that all who had the pleasure of knowing the character of the Governor-General in private life, would be gratified by this mark of Her Majesty's favour, which had been offered him, of her high approval of his public character and private worth. He hoped he should meet with the full assent of the House; and, that setting aside all form – if any gentleman should think his motion informal – they would recollect the old adage, "*qui cito dat, bis dat*,"[162] and agree at once to pay the compliment which was so justly due to the illustrious individual at the head of the Government. He hoped the House would

---

161 John Philip Roblin.
162 He that gives quickly gives twice.

pass the motion without any forms. If he were asked what precedents existed for such a course? he would reply, that he had precedents ready, if they were called for; but he hoped they would not be, because it might imply a holding back, on the part of those who might demand them, from paying their meed of praise to the Governor-General.

193 DIARY, 3 MARCH 1845

A very fine & mild day with some snow. Called on The *Honble Mr. Draper* (Atty General West) respecting Chewett & the W.D. Judgeship and also respecting the Ensuing Western Circuit in all of which he promised to meet my views & wishes. Afterwards Called on ye *Honble Mr. Sherwood* at Rasco's on the same subject. He promised the same. Sent home & to The West & Elsewhere lots of letters and Papers. At 3 I went to The House of Assembly and the Customs Bill was debated until *past* 2 a.m! Back to Gould's & in bed by 3 o'clock! Hard work.

194 DIARY, 10 MARCH 1845

A fine bright Morng and a hard frost. Healthy & fine. Occupied for an hour in the morng & sent off a great many Parliamentary Papers & some letters. Then went up to the public offices on business. The House met at 3 and I passed thro' 2 Committees of the Whole my Bill to prevent the *Profanation of the Sabbath* and also the bill to preserve Wild-fowl and to prevent the Trapping of Quail & Grouse. The Speaker being rather unwell, The House adjourned at 10. Quite early. I went to bed *at 11*.

195 EXCERPTS FROM SABBATH PROFANATION BILL DEBATE, 10 MARCH 1845
[*Montreal* Gazette, *13 March 1845*]

Col. PRINCE said the Bill now applied only to Upper Canada, and the preamble, which set forth that the Lord's Day should be kept sacred, was concurred in by all the hon. members from that part of the Province. He read an extract from Blackstone's Commentaries which conveyed his feelings in respect to this subject, and stated that at present there was no Statute in Upper Canada which prevented persons from following their occupations on the Lord's Day.

. . . .

Mr. ROBLIN said that as hunting and shooting were to be prohibited, he thought fishing should be so also.

Col. PRINCE gave as a reason why it should not, that in certain parts of the river Detroit, the run of the whitefish took place at particular seasons, and it would be a hardship to prevent the fishermen, who were principally poor Frenchmen from making their harvest at that time, through they should infringe on the Sabbath day.

....

Col. PRINCE said, he thought that the question was not properly understood in the House, and that in England and Scotland, where shooting was prohibited, fishing was regarded as a work of necessity, and was not. Sooner than lose the bill, however, he would consent to introduce the word fishing, though his own feelings were against it.

196 DIARY, 20 MARCH 1845

A Snowy morng & Cold. Winter appears to have come again. Busily engaged at the House both Morng & Eveng & we did not adjourn 'till 12 at night. Paid a visit to Lord Metcalfe, The Governor General, and Sat an hour with him in chat on various Matters, and nothing could be more generous, & affable, & indeed friendly than he was. *Took leave of him.* Returned to the House, & remained there 'till near 12. Dr. Dunlop[163] & Jemmy Johnson took horns with me & I went to bed.

197 DIARY, 13 APRIL 1845. *London, Canada West*

A beautiful Spring Morning. No frost & quite mild, but windy. How changeable is this climate! Occupied till 12 in preparing Indictments &c. when (while Albert & the people were attending divine Service) a terrific fire broke out which in a few hours destroyed more than half of London! Such a Scene I never witnessed! Poor Probett's[164] House was burnt to the Ground and I had great difficulty in saving my papers books & clothes &c. By the invitation of Dr. Cornish[165] Albert & I went to his house. Hundreds here are at this moment *houseless*, having lost their *All*!!

198 DIARY, 23 APRIL 1845

A fine day. Growing weather. Reached Chatham at 6 a.m. & after a thorough good wash was visited by a great many persons, and an Address was presented to me approving of my parliamentary Conduct in the last Session just Ended. Went to Sandwich by "The Kent", and was met at Windsor by my Constituents,

---

163 Dr. William ('Tiger') Dunlop, a surgeon, hunter, and literary contributor, came to Canada, where he settled in the Huron District, in 1826. There he became general superintendent of the Huron Tract, on behalf of the Canada Company. He was elected to the Assembly in 1841, representing Huron as a Tory until 1846.
164 Stephen T. Probett, a former Chatham innkeeper, had moved to London *ca.* 1841.
165 Dr William King Cornish was, at various times, a roadmaster, lawyer, and physician.

on my landing, with flags & banners & a Band of Music & Escorted to my home in great style. Reached The Park Farm at 1/2 past 5, & thank God, found all well there. The large Cavalcade returned home immediately.

199 DIARY, 28 APRIL 1845

A lovely day. Court met at 11 and passed Sentence on the Prisoners. *Four sent to The Penitentiary!* Occupied in Sandwich on various Matters of business, and Called on The Chewetts and Mrs. Hands[166] and Mrs. Blackburn. The Chewetts then drove me home & spent the Evening at our House, & *he & I finally arranged about the District Judgeship being taken by him for one year.* Albert went to a Party at Mr. Chas Eliot's & returned at 2 a.m.

200 DIARY, 8 AUGUST 1845. *Montreal*

Another broiling day. Very busy in & about town, dancing attendance at The Government House & offices about the Mines & Minerals when I at last obtained an answer to my application which is any thing but Satisfactory. In the Eveng Messrs. Penner[167] & Son & Captn Grundy[168] dined with me at Orr's hotel. The night dreadfully hot. In bed & asleep by about 1/2 p. 10.

201 DIARY, 12 SEPTEMBER 1845. *The Park Farm*

A beautiful day. Tried Arthur Rankin[169] on 2 of the 3 Indictments and he was *acquitted on both*, though The Judge told the Jury that the publications *were libellous* and that they ought to find him *Guilty*. Great Excitement Exhibited in Sandwich in Consequence, & in favor of Rankin. Dixie[170] left. Mrs. W.D. Baby took Tea. Occupied 'till late in writing letters & preparing to start for London tomorrow.

202 DIARY, 12 DECEMBER 1845

A fine day. Vidal left us. I have a dreadful head-ache and am lowspirited. In the Morng went to town on business and drew and signed a requisition to The

---

166 The widow of William Hands, a government official at Sandwich who had died in 1836.

167 Charles Penner, of Lachine, was a former friend of Prince's parents. His son John was a Montreal businessman.

168 Grundy appears to have been a captain in William Prince's regiment, the 71st.

169 Arthur Rankin, a brother of the well-known surveyor Charles Rankin, recently returned from taking a Wild West show to England, was now embarking on a career in mining speculations.

170 Wolston Alexander Dixie was living in Colchester Township in 1845. In 1851 he was an attorney at Amherstburg.

Sheriff to Call a meeting to address Lord Metcalfe on his departure from The Province. Mr. Sheriff Foott dined with us at 4 & I walked into Town with him. In the Morning I called & sat *an hour with Mrs. Chewett, who is lowspirited.* Chewett has been ill again. At home & in bed by 10.
 ((Made a Solemn Promise *not* to))

203 Diary, 21 January 1846

A deep snow! Unhappy, & more than unhappy at the Sad differences between M.A. & me about The Ritchies & other Nonsense which she has got into her head. Within doors all day & very busy in writing & seeing People. Miss Jane Foott here & dear Henry. Mr. Charles Eliot dined with us. The Chewetts Called in the Evening. Air & weather dull. I went to bed miserable.

204 Diary, 23 March 1846. *Montreal*

A fine day & very mild. Busy about Town all day and at the public Offices. Attended the House in the Evening and moved The "Address" & Resolution in answer to The Speech from The Throne. Spoke at Consdble length; and afterwards replied to Malcolm Cameron M.P. for Lanark. House adjourned at 12, & I went to bed at 1 tired.

205 Speech, 23 March 1846
[*Montreal* Gazette, *25 March 1846*]

Col. PRINCE ... could not help here remarking upon the few addresses which had been presented to Lord Metcalfe upon his departure – an omission which might be attributed to a wrong cause; the Western District had set an example to the rest of Canada in that respect ... With regard to the Militia Law, he (Col. Prince) had the most unbounded confidence in the loyalty of the colonists, in their devotion to the Mother Country, and their determination to preserve their connection with it; but the militia were in a disorganized state, and individual bravery would be of little avail against an enemy, but might lead to disasters, if their commanders were not only able to lead them into danger, but competent also to lead them out of it. He (Col. P.) knew the state of the Militia of Upper Canada, and he was well aware that it was at present inefficient, and he should be glad to see any measure introduced which would put that force upon an efficient footing. But while he wished this, he trusted that their services would not be called for; he sincerely trusted that there would be no war between Great Britain and the United States; he believed that it would be the greatest curse, the most afflicting calamity which could happen to both countries and to this Colony. He trusted that the world had become too civilized, that it was too far advanced in morality to go to war about trifles. But if such a calamity were to occur, it was upon the Militia of the Province that the greatest dependance was to be placed for the defence of our homes and the honour of the British Empire.

206   CONTINUATION OF SPEECH, 23 MARCH 1846
[*Montreal* Mirror of Parliament]

The hon. member next adverted to that part of the close of the Speech which referred "to the rising growth of this rapidly improving colony"; he was delighted to read that passage, he trusted that the eyes of the present Administration, that the eyes of the country at large were open to the necessity of improving the grand resources of Canada; ... lately hundreds of square acres of minerals have been discovered; five years ago he (Col. Prince) had ascertained the existence of this important source of wealth, but then we had no united Parliament, the little Parliament of Upper Canada could not aid in its development; he hoped, however, that now such an extent of advantage would not be neglected, in the neighbourhood to which he referred copper sufficient to supply the whole of England could be found; a part of it was brought out under his (Colonel Prince's) superintendence, and at his expence; facilities should be immediately afforded for bringing it into full play; no narrow policy should be adopted, – Ministers should not start back, – they should look well to it, they should attend to the granting of licences to all who would apply to them; let them look to the extent of enterprise in England, look to the railroad progress – there great men are obliged to allow railroads to go through their very parks, because the public voice demanded it; he (Col. P.) lately saw that seven hundred applications for railroads had been entertained. – Whatever project private enterprise chose to embark in, there should be no refusal; if injury occurred, it would be not to the country but to individuals; there should then be no hindrance to operations to draw forth the revenues of the country, no matter whether it was railroads or mining schemes. The hon. member concluded by again alluding to the necessity of action on the part of the Government and union amongst the people in order to promote the public good.

207   EXCERPT FROM DEBATE, 23 MARCH 1846
[*Montreal* Gazette, *25 March 1846*]

Mr. MCDONALD, of Glengarry,[171] spoke in favor of Mr. Baldwin's amendment. In the course of his remarks, he accused Colonel Prince with having

---

171 John Sandfield Macdonald, a lawyer, was elected to the Legislative Assembly from Glengarry in 1841. By 1844 he was identified with the Reform cause, and in 1849 he entered the Cabinet. With A.A. Dorion he became also co-premier of Canada in 1862, and premier of Ontario in 1867.

gained his election by professing to come forward on the principles advocated by the ex-Ministry.

Colonel PRINCE declared the assertion to be "false," and again and again reiterated the term, refusing to retract the expression, or to apologise to the House.

The SPEAKER called upon the House to maintain him in his endeavours to preserve order.

Mr. ATT. GEN. DRAPER trusted that Col. Prince would, upon reflection, see the propriety of apologising to the Chair; putting aside all other considerations, he hoped that so old a Member would not set so bad an example to the House.

Col. PRINCE said that some little allowance must be made for the infirmities of humanity. He had smarted under false imputations, and regretted that he had, in the presence of the House and the Speaker, made use of the language he had done. But, it was to the Speaker and the House alone that he apologised, and not to the individual who had called forth the remark.

208 Diary, 28 March 1846

A beautiful day. Wrote home to my dear M.A. & also other letters. Occupied within doors pretty much all day in writing letters &c. &c. In the Evening dined with Lord & Lady Cathcart[172] and spent a very pleasant Evening. Left at 1/2 p. 11 and home to Gould's by 12 & then went to bed. His Lordship is a fine old fellow.

209 Diary, 1 April 1846

A beautiful, mild, & bright day. Just like May! Occupied on Captain Vidal's[173] Committee all the morning, and Called on The Govr General & introduced Col. Wm. Elliott of Sandwich to him. He gave me encouragement about my mining speculations. At the House all the Evg. House adjourned at 6. Went to Rasco's. Supped at Dolly's.[174] Home & in bed by 10.

210 Diary, 2 April 1846

A beautiful day. Busy about Town and sitting on Election Committees all the morng, and spent the Evening at The House. Spoke fully on the 2d reading of my Rail-road bill. It was opposed strongly. Spent 2 hours at Rasco's and went to bed at 12.

---

172 Charles Murray Cathcart, Earl Cathcart, was administrator of the government of Canada from 26 November 1845, and governor general from 24 April 1846 to 29 January 1847.

173 This is probably Captain Richard Emeric Vidal, R.N., a lawyer of Sarnia Township. Captain Vidal was the father of William P. Vidal.

174 Dolly's Chop House, St Francis Xavier Street, Montreal.

211 RAILROAD DEBATE, 2 APRIL 1846
[*Montreal* Mirror of Parliament]

Mr. PRINCE ... was desirous of entering into a few explanations designed more especially for the use of the members from Lower Canada; in 1834 the London and Gore Rail Road, or rather the Great Western Rail Road bill was passed in the Upper Canada Parliament by which the work was to be finished in ten years; but the law remained a dead letter to 1837; two years after the bill had been granted, a bill was applied and obtained for the Niagara and Detroit Rail Road Company of which he had the honor to be President; the work to be completed in ten years, power being given in the act to Great Western Rail Road Company to join the Niagara and Detroit Rail Road should they see fit. But the Great Western was never commenced; the Company always being crippled by want of funds, and although the Government had granted them money to carry out the project.

Mr. BOULTON.[175] – He did not think this was the proper time to enter into any discussion upon the measure; the hon. member should wait until the House entered into the merits of the bill.

Mr. PRINCE. – He would persist in his explanations as he wanted to shew the members that it was only justice he demanded; and that hon. members opposed it only because they had an interest in a rival undertaking; the Niagara and Detroit Rail Road Company was organised, subscriptions raised, and scrip issued, of which he (Mr. P.) had some on his desk. Officers and Directors were appointed from time to time, and the Company was in full operation, until the invasion, he could not call it rebellion, took place, which paralysed the Company, and the Rail Road slept; and such was the case with the Great Western Rail Road; the time within which the work was to have been completed had expired, and it was now necessary to have the Provisions of the present bill extended in order to enable them to get the work completed, and was there, he would ask, any pretence for opposing the petition of thousands of respectable inhabitants of that part of the country; there was no petition against it. The shares have all been subscribed for. He had five hundred himself, and they were waiting to proceed; and were they now, after all the trouble and expense they had undergone, to have all their plans destroyed because the railway was going to be a profitable one?

....

Mr. Sol. Gen. SHERWOOD... The present rail-road forms no part of any great line in Canada, and would principally benefit the two large American cities, Buffalo and Detroit. The great mass of the stock was taken up by the people of the United States; it was in fact an American railroad, merely running through the British territory skirting the shores of Lake Erie, and would be but a small benefit to Canada.

....

Col. PRINCE ... Certain members opposed this Railroad, because they supposed it would injure the Great Western Railroad among the British Capitalists,

---

175 William Henry Boulton, a Tory, represented Toronto in the House.

why, he (Mr. P.) thought that the whole of the stock of this Company had been subscribed for, and the first instalment paid. The hon. member for Lanark is perfectly willing for his measure to go before the Committee, as he only wishes some trifling amendments made, his company having had an Act passed during the last Session, giving them five years to commence their road, and two to finish it; while he (Mr. P.) wished the house to grant his Company only five years longer to finish the Railroad. If the house contrary to all the principles of justice should decide against him, he (Mr. P.) would say with O'Connell, "sentence has been pronounced against me, but justice has not been done me."

212 DIARY, 3 APRIL 1846

Busy all the morng (very busy) on The West Halton Committee & public offices. Had another interview with Lord Cathcart. Sent in to the Council another Petition for putting me into possession of my mining Lands forthwith. At the House all the Eveng, and returned to Gould's Early & went to bed at 9. Heard from my dearest M.A.

213 PRINCE TO COLONEL O'HARA[176]
[*PAC, R.G. 9, I, B1, Vol. 66*]

Montreal, April 4, 1846

In reply to Your letter of the 30th ulto in which you acknowledge the receipt of Mine of the 24th and are pleased to remark that should the present unsettled relations of this Country result in hostilities my name shall be submitted to His Excellency the Administrator for "*favorable Consideration*", I beg leave to say that you appear to think me a Candidate for office and as *soliciting* a Command. That is not so. My sole object was to place at the disposal of His Excellency my services in *any way* acceptable to him, should a rupture with the United States occur; and I have to request that you will, without delay, submit my offer to Lord Cathcart. I have no desire that my letter should sleep among the Archives of your office but I wish that my desire to serve the Country should be made known to His Lordship.

214 DIARY, 7 APRIL 1846

Another *May day*. No weather can be finer. Sat on Special Committees again this day 'till one o'clock. House met at 3. The correspondence between Mr. Atty General Draper and Hon. Mr. Caron[177] discussed. I spoke at some length,

---

[176] O'Hara was the assistant adjutant general of militia, i.e., assistant to Colonel Richard Bullock.

[177] René Edouard Caron was a member of the Legislative Council of Canada from 1841, and speaker from 1843. Draper entered into negotiations with him, as a French-Canadian leader from Quebec, in an attempt either to divide the French-Canadian bloc or to wean it away from LaFontaine's leadership.

and trimmed LaFontaine & Draper's opponents *well*. Drank too much. In bed by 1.

215 DIARY, 9 APRIL 1846

Another lovely May Day. Vegetation is springing finely on this Island of Montreal. Busy in town & at the public offices all the morng. Attended The House in the Eveng & 'till 11 when it adjourned. Spoke on Several Subjects & on Draper's assessment Bill, & pronounced the W'n District Council a Nuisance to the Country & their Clerk (John Cowan) a rascal. Went to bed at 12.

216 DISTRICT COUNCILS DEBATE, 9 APRIL 1846
[*Montreal* Mirror of Parliament]

Col. PRINCE said, he was one of those persons who had voted for the establishment of District Councils, and he was now sorry that he had done so. He was against placing any more power in their hands than they now possessed, because they were utterly incompetent to perform the duties already imposed upon them. They were elected for party purposes only, and had neither brains nor principles; and they only went to the Council Chamber for the purpose of badgering each other. He had no confidence in District Councils. He (Col. Prince) referred particularly to the Council of the Western District, with whose proceedings he was more particularly acquainted. So grossly ignorant was that Council of its duties, that when the Clerk was petitioned against, although it was notorious that he was a highly disreputable character, they would not even allow the petition to be read.

....

Mr. CHALMERS[178] ... If the people of the Western District are so bad as the hon. member for Essex represented, he (Mr. C.) could not see how such a corrupt people could send to that House a jewel so pure as the hon. member – (laughter).

Col. PRINCE explained that he did not mean to condemn all the people of the Western District; and he would say that it was not by the bad portion that he was returned, – it was not by the Port Sarnia men. The hon. member reverted to his charges against the clerk, and challenged the hon. member for Lanark, or any other, to contradict them if they could.

Mr. CAMERON said, that he must again contradict the statements made by the honourable member for Essex. The men sent by the Northern Townships of Kent were generally men worthy a seat in this House; ... he asserted that the petition alluded to was too indecent to be read, and that the character of the clerk was as good as that of the hon. member for Essex himself, and he again demanded of the member for Kent to aid and defend not only his constituents but his native district from aspersions so false and foul, and would only make

---

178 George Chalmers was a Tory member of the Assembly, representing Halton East.

one remark that he (Mr. C.) could conceive nothing so damnatory to any man's character as an admission that he was at war with all his neighbours! The hon. member for Essex took pains to represent himself in this position, and it was he thought correct.

217 Excerpt from Mining Speech, 14 April 1846
[*Montreal* Mirror of Parliament]

He (Mr. P.) agreed with the hon..member for Quebec[179] that the Government is not entitled to give any preference to one part of Her Majesty's subjects over another; but he did think that it was their duty to encourage the enterprise of the people, that the hidden resources of the country might be developed. He (Mr. P.) did not see any partiality in allowing a person who discovers a hidden treasure or mine, that requires many thousand pounds to work it, to work it at his own expense. With respect to the copper mines on the north shore of Lake Superior, he (Mr. P.) and a few friends had been *graciously* permitted, under the great Seal of the Province, to spend as much of their own money as they pleased in exploring the country, and if we did discover a mine, we were to have the liberty of working it at our own expense, upon such terms as the Government might see fit to impose. He (Mr. P.) did not thank the Administration for these favours, for if the people of Canada had half the enterprise of the Americans, many of them would have gone into the region possessed of mineral wealth, and *squatted* there, without the permission of the Government. Large fortunes have been made from the copper mines on the southern shore of Lake Superior, while our mineral wealth lies dormant. He (Mr. P.) would repeat what he stated in moving the address to His Excellency in answer to the speech from the Throne, that a government to be strong, must be liberal to those who are willing to develope [*sic*] the resources of the country.

218 Railroad Debate, 16 April 1846
[*Montreal* Gazette, *20 April 1846*]

Col. PRINCE ... There was an hon. friend of his in the House who had got up in his place last session, and had asked the promoters of the Great Western Bill, whether that measure was to interfere with the Niagara and Detroit Company, and his honble. friend was told distinctly, no! His hon. friend knew that the hon. gentleman who had charge of that Bill had had it in his pocket for several weeks, and that he took the opportunity of bringing it forward after he (Col. Prince) had obtained leave of absence from the House. He said that that Bill had been obtained by fraud, for, so far from interfering with the Niagara and Detroit line, it had received powers to extend its road beyond the original limits indicated by the Act of 1837, as far as Detroit River, the terminus of his (Col. Prince's) line, and the only place whose traffic could enable the Great Western to pay its

179 T.C. Aylwin formerly represented Portneuf.

expenses. He now called upon the Committee to prevent the Company to which he belonged from being deprived of their rights.

....

The American gentlemen connected with the Niagara and Detroit Railway Company were prepared to advance £300,000 upon the renewal of the charter, to build the railway as far as that sum would go. – He considered the Great Western project as an impossibility, that the physical difficulties in the way of its construction would entail such an enormous expense as to defeat its object. He could not conceive what reasonable objection there could be to allow American capitalists to make public improvements in this Colony.

219 Diary, 18 April 1846

Quite a May day. Very much Engaged about Town and with Major Ward from Boston, & others about my Mining operations. I think it likely to turn out profitable. Attended a Meeting at Tetu's[180] respecting the Ministry's threat to resign. Passed a Resolution. Sat at *Dolly's* with Johnson 'till 10, and home to Gould's & in bed by 11.

220 Diary, 20 April 1846

A fine day. Excessively engaged about town and at *Tetu's* on mining business. Finally arranged Matters. Took leave of The Ministry and several other friends. Very much engaged indeed & had hardly half an hour to myself. Spent 3 hours with Gowan[181] at Captain Grundy's & went to bed at 1/2 past 1.

221 Diary, 26 April 1846. *Hamilton*

Rose at 7. A fine morng. This Hotel of Weekes's is a very good & a very Comfortable one. Occupied within doors all the Morng in writing letters, & preparing for our assizes &c. Mr. Malcolm Cameron, M.P.P. here, & we shook hands & occupy the same room & are *friends* as heretofore. Left Hamilton by stage at 4 and arrived at Brantford by 8 p.m. A horrid road thro' *"The Swamp"*.

222 Diary, 4 July 1846. *The Park Farm*

Another broiling day. The Revd. Mr. Ritchie came to The Farm by my desire, and heard Mrs. P's statement & mine about Mrs. Chewett. Nothing

---

180 This probably refers to Têtu's Hotel, at 23–25 Great St James Street.
181 Ogle Robert Gowan was the editor of the Brockville *Statesman* and a Tory member of the Assembly, for Leeds. He was a founder of the Orange Association of British America.

satisfactory resulted. M.A. & Bella went to a Pic Nic at Major Forsyth's[182] nr Detroit, & returned at 10 p.m. I was down in town in the Eveng. Called twice on Dr. Bower[183] who is rather better. Went to bed at 10 as miserable, as usual, as any body Can be.

223 DIARY, 28 JULY 1846. *Montreal*

A very warm day. Occupied on my legs about town all day & greatly fatigued. Sent in the *map* of my mining Location & *Mr. Kinzies*[184] report thereon to Mr. Secy Daly. Also applied for Mining licences for Rudyerd, *Mercer* & Albert. At 6 p.m. Dr. Dunlop and Mr. Grundy dined with me at Daly's.[185] I then attended a meeting of the B.N. American Mining Co. at The City Bank, and we passed divers *resolutions*. Called afterwards at Mr. Townshend the Jeweller's thereon & went to bed at 11 tired.

224 DIARY, 25 AUGUST 1846. *The Park Farm*

Another very warm day. Exceedingly Engaged all day at home in business. Mrs. Partridge[186] a little better, but her Step-daughter Maria very ill also. Mr. Rudyerd and Henry went down to The River "Rouge", Duck shooting. He killed a Couple only. Birds very Scarce. In the Eveng hard words bet'n M.A. & Me in Mrs. Rudyerd's presence about Mrs. Chewett. Went to bed at 10 perfectly Miserable as usual.

225 DIARY, 5 NOVEMBER 1846

A hoar frost, but beautiful day. Sun bright & fine. *Had a dreadful quarrel with M.A. while dressing this Morning.* I see nothing but a *Separation* in prospect. She *hates* me, and why, God only knows. At home all day busily occupied (*tormented*) as usual, but unprofitably. Walked to McKee's Marsh & Called on Janisse. Wretched. I wish I was *dead for Ever*.

226 DIARY, 12 JANUARY 1847

I am so unhappy that I wo'd *shoot myself* if I was not a *Xtian*. Oh! But what a

---

182 Major Robert A. Forsyth, land registrar, resided at Springwells, Michigan, opposite Sandwich.

183 Dr Martin Bower, formerly of Gosfield Township, was a resident of Sandwich from 1841. He had recently been injured in a fall from a wagon. In 1849 he was a Sandwich innkeeper.

184 'Col. Kinzie on Lake Superior' (diary, 9 June 1846) was probably John H. Kinzie, an Indian agent at Fort Winnebago, Wisconsin, in 1830.

185 Daly's Hotel was formerly Rasco's.

186 The former Mrs Woods (mentioned in Document 166), of Elm Cottage on the Thames in Kent County, married William Partridge, Prince's tenant on The Park Farm, 24 December 1845.

wicked and Most wretched Xtian am I! However, is it my own fault? God grant that in the "day of Judgment", he may say *"not altogether"*, & extenuate my Crimes! I am worse than *Miserable*. Walked to The Ferry & pd monies to Litchfield[187] & Brown, & did a good deal of business. Wade Foott[188] with me. Home & in bed by 10.

227 DIARY, 4 FEBRUARY 1847

A very hard frost. Much Snow fell yesterday. Good sleighing. Busy all day in my office. In the Evening went into Town and saw a great many of the District Councillors on behalf of young James M. Cowan whom I advised them to appoint District Clerk in the place of his father. At home and in bed by 11.

228 PRINCE TO D.A. MACDONALD[189]
[*PAC, R.G. 9, I, C1, Vol. 51*]

The Park Farm, March 21, 1847

I rec'd your letter, and I have been from home, or it should have had my attention sooner. I herewith send the *certificate* you wish for. Seeing of what *Materials* some of [our?] Militia Regts are Composed, I [think it?] almost a burlesque upon *Arms*. My worthy *Blacksmith*[190] is actually a *Lieutenant Colonel* under the new Law! Thank God, I have nothing more to do with Militia Matters, having retired, & resigned the Command of the 3rd Essex rather than be *bothered* any longer with such things.

229 EXCERPT FROM BALDWIN TO LAFONTAINE. *Private*
[*PAC, M.G. 24, B14, Vol. 7*]

Toronto, May 8, 1847

If Cameron was to offer for Essex could any one of our Lower Canada friends such as Mr. Cartier[191] for instance make it convenient to pay that county a visit and give a filip [*sic*] to our French Canadian friends there that would help to get them out of the leading strings of Col Prince. It would do much good if it could be accomplished. I confess until lately I had abandoned all hopes of Essex for

---

187 This is probably E.C. Litchfield, a Detroit banker.

188 A son of Sheriff George Wade Foott.

189 Donald Alexander Macdonald, an engineer and surveyor, was a younger brother of John Sandfield Macdonald. He was a lieutenant in the Essex Militia in 1837–38, and Prince was sending him a testimonial in regard to his military services. Macdonald succeeded his brother as the member for Glengarry in 1857, and became lieutenant governor of Ontario in 1875.

190 Antoine Ouellette.

191 George Etienne Cartier, a Montreal lawyer, was a supporter of LaFontaine. He represented Verchères in the Assembly from 1848, and entered the Executive Council in 1855. He was the leading French-Canadian member of the 'Great Coalition,' and was a persuasive pro-Confederation force in the 1860s.

Prince seemed to have succeeded in establishing such a notion of his being paramount that I thought it would be useless to contest the matter with him. But they are beginning to move over there and they seem to think that Cameron would be a good candidate to run against him. I however expect Cameron down before long and will know more then.

230 DIARY, 11 MAY 1847

A fine day. Rose at 5. Miserable & almost ready to destroy myself. Parted from The family at 10; and oh! such a Parting it was!! I am the *unhappiest of men!* Reached Chatham by boat at 8, and then I had to undergo the *miseries* of *a public dinner* given to me by The People. Went to bed at 2 a.m. with a *heavy heavy* heart.

231 REPORT OF DINNER, 11 MAY 1847
[*Chatham* Gleaner, *18 May 1847*]

... the Chairman then, in a neat speech, alluded to the object of the meeting, and spoke in terms of warm eulogy of the public merits and private virtues of their distinguished guest, closing his remarks by proposing the health of 'Colonel John Prince.' The enthusiasm with which this toast was drank is past description. The learned gentleman responded in a strain of eloquence and feeling which drew from the assembled company continued and deafening applause: He, John Prince, would remind ministers of their promises to him; he would teach those eminent gentlemen something of the geography of Canada; they should know there was such a place as the Western District! He alluded to the deplorable condition of our roads, the Chatham bridge, the works at the Rond d'Eau,[192] the extravagance of the Board of Works, their recklessness in expenditure, and of the necessity of reform in that department. There was one object he supposed the inhabitants of Kent felt deeply interested in accomplishing: the division of the present District, and the erection of Kent into a separate one. The Western District was certainly too large; it was inconveniently so. The measure should have his warmest support, and our own member, Joseph Woods, Esquire, (of whom he spoke in the most respectful and feeling manner,) should have his cordial assistance. Gentlemen however must support their representative; petitions should be forwarded to him from every township; and there could then be little doubt of our being successful.

....

Upon the whole this dinner was the most brilliant affair we have ever witnessed in this part of Canada: in number, intelligence, and influence, it was all that could be desired. Persons of every shade of politics, from the two

---

192 Rondeau was then undergoing development as a shipping facility. Prince also spelled the name Round O, Rond Eau, etc.

extremes to the loose fish, were there; and amidst the flash of wit and flow of soul, all seemed to enjoy themselves.

232 EXCERPT FROM DEBATE, 2 JUNE 1847. *Montreal*
[*Montreal* Gazette, *3 June 1847*]

The Hon. W. DRAPER then rose and announced the resignation of his seat in the House, but from the noise without, and his distance from the gallery, we did not exactly catch his words.

Col. PRINCE enquired in what capacity the Hon. and learned gentleman occupied his seat? It had been currently mentioned that he had accepted a situation which precluded his sitting there. The common report was that he had succeeded to the vacant situation on the Judicial Bench of Canada West.

Col. PRINCE was proceeding with some remarks on the impropriety of Mr. Draper's occupying his seat, when –

The SPEAKER intimated that it was out of order to put a question and, without waiting for the answer, to make a speech.

Col. PRINCE said that the answer would be a very simple one, and required no "dodging." (Laughter.) It was publicly stated in the newspapers that the Hon. and learned gentleman had vacated his seat, and Hon. gentlemen seldom vacated their seats without a "con-si-de-ra-tion"; in fact that he had accepted a Judgeship.

Mr. DRAPER had no hesitation in saying that he had not accepted any such office.

233 REPORT OF SPEECH, 4 JUNE 1847
[*Montreal* Gazette, *7 June 1847*]

COL. PRINCE would vote for the motion, though he was [by] no means certain, that there had not been an acceptance on the part of the Speaker. It appeared to him from the wording of the Act, that a very slight intimation of an intention to accept office, was enough to vacate his seat, nevertheless, you, Mr. Speaker, shall have the benefit of my vote; what were the facts, a gentleman who had done good service to the country, was brought into contact with the head of the Government, an arrangement was entered into between them as binding as any arrangement could be, yet his Excellency[193] was forced to break through his engagement, and that too by a ministry who are too fond of reflecting on others for attempting to coerce the crown. It was not services to the country that led to rewards and honors – that now exploded notion was abandoned; and the honorable Speaker was the first victim. But what could be thought of an administration, who took upon themselves to Gazette so prominent a Public Officer, without having first obtained his consent. He had heard it called a

---

193 James Bruce, Earl of Elgin, was governor-in-chief from 30 January 1847 to 19 December 1854.

blunder, he must say that it was a very gross blunder, so gross a blunder he did not believe had ever been heard of before. As his learned friend from Quebec had said, had the circumstances occurred during the Session of the House, it would have afforded room for corruption, and he would apply that remark to a case before them. He saw the late Attorney-General West, sitting in the House where it was well known that he was to be made Judge – Before the next assizes there was little doubt that that gentleman would be one of the Judges perhaps the vice Chancellor, yet this gentleman was still bolstering up the ministry. At the last sitting he was to be found seated at the utmost extremity of the House – to-day he was to be found among the Ministry. Probably the hon. member has been told by his former colleagues, that if he deserts them so, that unless he is a very good boy, and gives them all the assistance which he can, he would not get his Judgeship after all. (Laughter). That was the only construction that he (Col. Prince) could put on the matter. To return to the Speakership, he must say that he was sorry that the honorable Speaker had not received the appointment in question[194]; but, although such was the case, he must congratulate the country on the present Adjutant-General[195] and his Deputy.[196]

234 Diary, 5 June 1847

A cold raw & damp morng. More rain threatened. Occupied in town all the morng in writing letters, and at Mr. Badgley's[197] office, with Mr. Child[198] about Mining Matters. In the afternoon attended a meeting of *Mining Interests* at The Montreal M. Co's office in Gt St. James' Street. Mr. Moffatt in the chair. Agreed to the terms of a Bill which he read. Then went to Daly's & took wine & sat an hour with The Recr General McDonald[199] & others. Then sat an hour with Aylwin & others at *Tetu's* talking Politics and making some political arrangements with Aylwin as a leader. Home by 1 & went to bed, having drank rather too much to do good.

235 Excerpt from Editorial
[*Toronto* Globe, *5 June 1847*]

We are glad to find that the Reformers in the County of Essex are bestirring themselves in the choice of a Representative. Meetings have been held in the

---

194 Speaker MacNab was appointed adjutant general of militia, but he declined to accept.
195 Colonel Plomer Young.
196 This is either Deputy Adjutant General (East) Lieutenant Colonel E.P. Taché, or Deputy Adjutant General (West) Lieutenant Colonel D. Macdonell.
197 William Badgley, a Tory member representing Missisquoi County, C.E., was attorney general (east) from April 1847 to March 1848.
198 This is possibly M. Child or Childs, the member for Stanstead, 1841–44.
199 John Alexander Macdonald, first elected a member of the Legislative assembly for Kingston in 1844, rose rapidly among the Tories. He was made receiver general in the Draper government in May 1847.

Town Hall of Amherstburgh, and in the Townships of Anderton [*sic*] and Colchester, for the purpose of appointing Delegates to a Reform Convention. The gentleman most talked of as the candidate is Malcolm Cameron, Esq., at present member for Lanark. We feel confident that should Mr. Cameron be persuaded to stand, he would be returned by a large majority. The people of Essex are tired of, and disgusted with the base political dishonesty of Colonel Prince, and they will never permit him to misrepresent them again.

236 Diary, 7 June 1847

A beautiful day. Occupied at The House in the morng writing letters and sending off Newspapers &c. Went to The House at 3 which did not sit above an hour and then adjourned. Walked about town, & sat an hour with Gowan and Aylwin and talked over some new Ministerial arrangements probably to arise. Home by nine, & went to bed tired & lowspirited.

237 Excerpt from Report of Speech, 10 June 1847
[*Montreal* Gazette, *12 June 1847*]

Col. PRINCE ... Again, is it not a matter of regret that there are no Municipalities Bill or Education Bill? These measures, he said, had long been promised, and yet there was no appearance of them. Look at the promises conveyed in the Speech from the throne, at the first meeting of the present Parliament. Have they been fulfilled? Where is the University Bill? Has the Clergy Reserve question been settled? The [first] paragraph contains an expression of regret at the ministry not being able to complete the Cabinet sooner. Was not that a matter of regret among themselves? Then why do they object that the House should sympathise with them? Had the Ministry been able to complete the Cabinet, would they not have taken good care to have had them returned? Was it not, then, a matter of regret to them that they could not accomplish this.

238 Excerpt from Report of Speech, 10 June 1847
[*Montreal* Transcript, *12 June 1847*]

Col. PRINCE said, that if Ministers suffered themselves to be defeated, it would be their own palpable and visible neglect. He had formerly supported them, on the promise of their sustaining Responsible Government, but they had failed to do so. He objected to the appointments lately made, especially of the Solicitor General,[200] not on account of talent or personal character, but because there were many other men, equally fitted for the office, who had served their

---

200 John Hillyard Cameron represented Cornwall in the Legislative Assembly.

country for years in Parliament. The Administration, he said, was too weak to carry on the Government. The Commissioner of Crown Lands[201] was unfit for his office, and if he did not retire it was the duty of the Administration to force him out. The member for Leeds[202] had been talked of, and would be a fit person for the office.

239 Excerpt from Report of Speech, 10 June 1847
[*Toronto* Globe, *16 June 1847*]

Col. Prince gave the speech of the evening. We never heard a more masterly address. He stated that he had been induced to support the present Administration, through the positive pledge given him by Lord Metcalfe and Att'y-Gen'l Smith,[203] that the great liberal measures wanted by the country would be brought in by them. These pledges had not been kept, and he had found, after two years' trial, that the present Administration was incapable – weak – cowardly – ungrateful – deceitful – and corrupt to the core.

240 Diary, 25 June 1847

Very hot weather. Engaged as yesterday. In the Eveng went to The House, and sat late. Passed my Niagara & Detroit Rivers Rail-road bill, and also the Western District Division Bill thro' The Assembly. Very Successful. House adjourned at 12. In bed by one, & not before.

241 Diary, 30 June 1847

A very fine day & not too hot. Attended a Special Committee at which Sir James Stuart, Ch. Justice of Lower Canada was Examined. Then engaged about Town. Several here from The Western District. Attended The House & debated several matters. Carried my own & Hincks's[204] Mining Bills after a stormy debate & *factious* opposition from Baldwin & Aylwin. House adjourned at 12. Went to bed at 1.

---

201 D.B. Papineau, a brother of Louis Joseph Papineau, was the member for Ottawa County. He was one of the few French Canadians willing to take office after the clash between Metcalfe and the Reformers, led by Baldwin and LaFontaine. His deafness probably accounted for the reference to his unfitness for office.
202 Ogle R. Gowan.
203 James Smith, representing Missisquoi, had been attorney general (east) immediately before William Badgley.
204 Francis Hincks in 1847 was a former member for Oxford, who had served as inspector general, 1842–43. Prince was acting in his behalf, to get his mining bill passed.

242 EXCERPTS FROM MINING DEBATE, 30 JUNE 1847
[*Montreal* Gazette, *2 July 1847*]

Col. PRINCE ... They had paid four shillings an acre for land, which, if it did not possess minerals, was not worth four cents an acre; they had not purchased land containing valuable minerals, they had purchased on the chance of finding minerals, and he considered the amount they had paid to be enormous; they purchased the land on a speculation; they took all the expenses of exploring and surveying upon themselves, and, should the speculation turn out unprofitable, they would be exposed to a great loss, but they themselves would be the only losers. He repeated there had been no favour, scarcely, he thought, even the justice they were entitled to ... Now, let the honourable member for Quebec make a practical experiment as to whether partiality is or is not shown in the disposal of their lands; let him become a purchaser of a vacant lot alongside of him (Col. Prince), who would be proud and happy to have his honourable and learned friend for a neighbour. (Mr. Aylwin – you'll not catch me up there; and laughter.) Well, he would be happy to catch him up there, for, were he to go there, he would entertain pretty much the same idea of the favouritism shown by Government that he (Col. Prince) entertained; and, under these circumstances, he trusted the honourable member for Quebec would not oppose the second reading of the Bill.

243 DIARY, 11 JULY 1847

Dreadfully hot. I am by no means well, but still not actually ill. The Heat nearly broiling. Never Experienced any thing like it in The West. Within doors all the day 'till 3 p.m. and occupied in writing letters and drawing final agreement between Sir Allan Macnab & Mr. Carroll[205] & myself as to the Great Western Rail-road & The Niagara & Detroit Rivers Rail-road. Then walked over to Dr. Dunlop's & dined with him. Excessively hot. Home by nine & in bed by 10, fatigued.

244 DIARY, 13 JULY 1847

A good deal of Rain fell this morng, which had had beneficial effects, no doubt, on vegetation. The Earth was parched before. Wearied in writing letters. About Town all the morning. In the Evening did not go to *The House* at all (tho' I *have much business there*) but remained in my room writing letters, & the slave of melancholy broodings & forebodings, & went to bed at 9 perfectly wretched & miserable!

205 This is possibly P. Carroll, who protested Hincks's election for Oxford early in 1848.

245 DIARY, 30 JULY 1847

A fine & Cool day. Very busy all day in town. Occupied at The Donagana's [*sic*] Hotel with Messrs. Rankin, Keating, Cuthbertson,[206] Crawford, Robt. S. Woods,[207] & Meredith Q.C.[208] in discussing the dispute as to the "*Bruce*" Mines, and the *ore* therefrom which is seized at Detroit. *Settled it*, fortunately for all Parties, and dined with them. Then occupied with Messrs. Castle,[209] Jobin,[210] & Badgley at The Bank, and arranging as to our B.N.A. Mines. Left at 12. A wet night.

246 DIARY, 31 JULY 1847

Another fine & Cool day, but it became very hot towards Evening. Occupied very much in and about town all day long. Attended a meeting of our *Mining Co.* at The *City Bank*, and assigned my right to The Location Ticket, I rec[eivin]g a certificate or declaration that I am Entitled to 1000 shares unassessable 'till after 5$ per share is assessed & pd. up by others. Sat one hour at *Donagana's* & at *Daly's*. Home to dinner at 6. Wrote & read a short time, & went to bed at 9.

247 DIARY, 2 AUGUST 1847

Could not go home today, as I intended, because the Bruce Mine business is to be finally settled. Occupied at Meredith's office with all Parties thereon 'till 2 p.m. Then drove in a Caleche out to Mr. Penner's and spent 2 or 3 hours there, & took leave. Called also on Dr. Dunlop & took leave. At Mrs. Steele's[211] till 9 p.m. Then went to Donagana's by appointment & met all Parties, and signed articles of Copartnership as to The *Elgin* Mines (in which I am to have 1000 Shares) and as to The *Huron Copper* mines (in which Rankin generously gave me 500 Shares). Sat 'till 2! when I went to bed.

248 PRINCE TO THE COMMISSIONER OF CROWN LANDS[212]
[*AO, R.G. 1, A-1-6, Vol. 26*]

Montreal, August 2, 1847

In the Course of next Month I shall visit the *Rondeau* Harbour in company of

---

206 James Cuthbertson was a Scottish-born speculator, resident in Sandwich Township.
207 Robert Stuart Woods, born at Sandwich, was called to the bar in 1842.
208 Edmund Allen Meredith was appointed assistant provincial secretary (west) in 1847.
209 This is C.H. Castle, of the City Bank, Montreal.
210 A. Jobin sat for Montreal County in the Assembly.
211 Prince stayed in boarding houses operated by Mrs Steele in Montreal and, later, Toronto and Quebec City.
212 D.B. Papineau.

friends who are desirous of Establishing a *Fishery* there upon an Extensive Scale if our Experiments will warrant the outlay. If they do, I shall apply to you soliciting a *Lease* or *Licence of occupation* of the *waste Lands* of the Crown and of the *Waters* and beach there, upon such Terms as Government may be pleased to grant it; and I request you will have the goodness to Consider this as my first application, to be renewed in a more full degree after my friends and I have practically demonstrated the Capabilities of the Place for Fishing purposes.

249 DIARY, 13 DECEMBER 1847. *The Park Farm*

A mild day. Octy[213] better, but he was very sick all night. Busy in my office 'till past 12. Then went into town, and was invited by a Committee of Gentlemen to stand for Essex. Drove Col. Elliott to Windsor & met another numerous deputation at Mason's Tavern. Agreed to Comply with their request. Stopt an hour at Beeman's. Home by 7, having drank rather too freely.

250 24 DECEMBER 1847

A very fine & bright day, but rather cold. A good deal of Snow on the ground. *The Essex Election* took place & I was nominated by the *Warden*[214] who was Seconded by Mr. *Luc Montreuil*[215] & I was returned by acclamation. No opposition! The town full of People, and I addressed them at great length in The Court House, which was filled. We then dined together at Beeman's (Prince Albert) Hotel (about 150 at my expence) & I remained in town till 1/2 p 9. Mr. Barstow[216] at The Park Farm.

251 PRINCE TO JOHN A. MACDONALD
[*AO, Miscellaneous Mss.*]

The Park Farm, January 6, 1848

Permit me to congratulate you upon your return for Kingston, and to offer you the Compliments of the Season. About 2 months ago I forwarded a Petition to Lord Elgin accompanied by a letter to Mr. Secy Daly, requesting to be permitted to Establish a Fishery and to lease certain Government Lands &c: at The Rond-Eau in this district. Mr Daly wrote me that the Petition had been transmitted to The Crown Land office; and as I have heard nothing more about it, I fear it may linger there. May I request the favor of your attending to it, (as

---

213 Octavius was Prince's son, born 14 April 1841.
214 George Bullock.
215 Luc (Luke, St Luc, St Luke) Montreuil, of Sandwich, had canvassed for Prince in 1836.
216 Samuel Barstow, a Detroit lawyer and personal friend, at this time was president of the Detroit Board of Education.

the head of the department[217]), because if the prayer of it is to be granted, as I trust it will, it is almost time for me to begin making preparations for the *Spring Fishing*.

252 PRINCE TO THE EDITOR OF THE TORONTO *Church*
[*Hamilton* Spectator, *26 January 1848*]

The Park Farm, January 11, 1848

In your paper of the 7th, you think proper to set me down as a "rather doubtful" M.P.P. You are right so far. I am "independent," and unlike *bigots*, I vote according to my sense and conscience, after having heard both sides of the question fully argued. I have always shunned "PARTY," and always shall; and therefore I am always "rather doubtful." But, pray why omit the asterisk to my name, which showed I was *unopposed?* I'll tell you why; because you, like many others of your way of thinking, despise the *English* gentleman who has anything like *independence* about him, and you were vastly afraid that, from the fact of my having been elected by *acclamation, and without stirring from my house to visit a single voter, and without writing to a single voter, I should stand higher in public estimation* (which, God knows, I care not one straw for in such a Country as this Canada is) than "The Church" would desire I should.

All I demand of you men of "The Press," is to do justice and report faithfully. I want no partiality or favour from any of you.

253 EDITORIAL RESPONSE
[*Hamilton* Spectator, *26 January 1848*]

We will mention one or two circumstances connected with the recent general election, which will show the "English gentleman" in his true character. At the election for Kent, Col. Prince wrote to Mr. Solicitor General Cameron, congratulating him on his prospects, and volunteering to come down to Chatham to second his nomination. A week after Col. Prince had proffered his assistance to the Conservative Candidate, he wrote to Mr. Malcolm Cameron, who was running on the Radical ticket, to the effect that "it was most disgraceful that the large and populous County of Kent should send 250 miles to Toronto, for a young lawyer to represent it," when it possessed capable men within its borders, and intimating that he (Col. Prince) would support Mr. Malcolm Cameron, and bring a number of electors with him to the poll! ... "Such a country as this Canada is," must be altogether too contracted for his operations, and we shall not be disappointed if the gallant Colonel, finding that there are too many applicants for District Judgeships and Queen's Counsel fees, should shake the dust from his feet and depart for a more congenial clime. Humbug! thy name is Prince.

---

217 Macdonald had been appointed commissioner of crown lands, 8 December 1847.

254 EXCERPT FROM PRINCE'S REPLY
[*Hamilton* Spectator, *5 February 1848*]

The Park Farm, January 29, 1848

Of course I have read your comments upon my recent letter to "The Church." I shall merely condescend to remark that they contain a tissue of malignant and unfounded *falsehoods* from beginning to end! – that I *never* "wrote to Mr. Solicitor General Cameron volunteering to come down to Chatham to second his nomination" for Kent; but that on the contrary, I declined the written invitation of that gentleman's Committee, and of himself, to do so; and I stated in writing, my reason for declining – that I never wrote to Mr. Malcolm Cameron in the terms you have so falsely described, nor did I ever "intimate that I would support him, and bring a number of Electors to the Poll["], or anything of the kind – but that, on the contrary, I addressed a letter to him (in reply to one he wrote to me) in which I distinctly stated that "I could not congratulate the County upon the prospects of *the Opposition* attaining unto Power, and that I could not support his *Party*" and I gave my reasons why – that consequently no such correspondence as that described (and invented) by you in your precious article, "and was made public at the Hustings," or produced "Shouts of Execration" from any body – and, lastly, that the whole article is *untrue*, and is the offspring of your malignant heart and distempered brain. As you conduct one of the most corrupt, unprincipled and licentious presses in "This Canada," I doubt whether you have the *honesty* or the *independence* to publish this letter. I have therefore sent it to a paper which possesses both those virtues – The "Western Standard."

255 FURTHER EDITORIAL RESPONSE
[*Hamilton* Spectator, *5 February 1848*]

The petty quibbling of the learned Colonel deserves little attention. He humbugged both parties in Kent; and all the sophistry of which he is master, will not redeem him from the disgrace which invariably follows the path of the political mountebank. Col. Prince denies that he promised to nominate Mr. Solicitor General Cameron. This we have already corrected. The promise, however, amounted to the same thing, being nothing more or less than an offer to come to the polls, and bring some friends with him, to vote for the Solicitor General.

. . . .

Col. Prince boasts that the Western *Standard*, a miserable apology for a paper maintained by the Col. himself, comes up to his idea of perfection. Not a doubt of it. *Tel maitre tel valet*; and the only difference between the Colonel and his organ is that the reputation of the man is notorious throughout the Province, whilst the newspaper is never heard of beyond the precincts of the village of Sandwich.

256 DIARY, 25 FEBRUARY 1848

A fine but a very cold day tho' clear. Good Sleighing in Montreal, the Streets being covered with Ice. Busy about town in the morning. The House met at 3 p.m. The Hon. Mr. Morin chosen *Speaker* by a large Majority. Hon. Mr. Cayley[218] nom[inate]d Sir Allan McNab, & *I* seconded it. But we could not succeed. At Donagana's for an hour afterwards.

257 DIARY, 26 FEBRUARY 1848

Another bright & Cold day. Very busy in and about Town 'till 6 p.m. Attended meeting of Directors of The British North American Mining Co. at Mr. Secy Badgley's office whereat I was unanimously elected President for the ensuing Year. Home to dinner at 1/2 p 6. Wrote letters, & in bed by 1/2 past 9.

258 DIARY, 3 MARCH 1848

Rose with a head-ache. Much Snow falling & good sleighing. Very busy in & about Town. Went to The House at 3, and moved "The Address" in ans'r to "The Speech" from the Throne. Spoke at much length, when Baldwin introduced an Amendm't including *Want of Confidence* in the present Ministry. Division at 1/2 past 11, when the Am't carried by a large Majority, & so the Ministry's fate is Sealed! Home by 12 and went to bed at 2.

259 REPORT OF PRINCE'S ANSWER, 3 MARCH 1848
[*Toronto* Globe, *15 March 1848*]

But who, asks our shrewd reader, moved and seconded the answer? Who were hardy enough to be the champions of such an Administration? What men could be found in that or any other House, courageous enough to avow confidence in Daly, Cayly [*sic*], & Co. Men fit for such a task must be no ordinary characters – men of assured self-reliance they must be – men of the world, who value consistency at what it is worth – men of large and fanciful imaginations, who could paint the light and dark shades of the subject with a *feeling* brush – men, in short, as bad, or if possible a little worse than the Ministers themselves! And truly they found such men.

Col. John Prince moved the address, and *Mr. Christie* seconded it! Could any selection have been more proper?

....

Never before did men make such speeches, in the position they occupied. "How happy could I be with either, were t'other dear charmer away," was the burden of their song; but they took care to let it be seen how much more fondly

---

[218] William Cayley, a Tory, represented Huron and at this time was inspector general of provincial accounts.

they would have hugged the Reform side, had the white flag been floating out for them.

. . . .

Col. Prince spoke for an hour and a quarter ... He strongly advocated the Great Western Railway scheme, and asked that minor schemes should not be allowed to interfere with this great national undertaking ... What are Reformers? He wanted to know, and hoped some hon. Member would explain the difference between a Reformer and the present Ministers. He contended they had done a great deal in the cause of Reform; that the former Administration had not done so much, and, therefore, the present Administration did more than the self-styled Reformers. Why, then, did I withhold my support from them at the commencement of last session. Because there had been a leader amongst them whose hypocrisy and cunning, and whose silver tongue could deceive mankind; and I withdrew my confidence from the whole flock because there was a black sheep amongst them ... True, they continued in power with small majorities: Pitt did the same; Melbourne did the same; and the Grenville Administration did the same – Grenville that paragon of political perfection – that old English Whig, like myself!!! No; here, a Whig is called a Tory; here, a man to be liberal, must be destructive; and with such examples before them, are my hon. friends opposite, to be taunted with tenacity for place.

260 'NIAGARA AND DETROIT RAILROAD AND THE
ENGLISH GENTLEMAN'[219]
[*Toronto* Globe, *22 March 1848*]

A very rich scene occurred on the presentation of a petition by Mr. McFarland[220] for the renewal of the Niagara and Detroit Rivers Railroad Charter. The petitioners take the opportunity of petitioning to denounce Colonel Prince for the way in which he sold them to the Great Western Company last Session, and the "gallant gentleman" fired up at it at once.

. . . .

On the petition being read Colonel Prince rose and pronouncing the document a "tissue of gross and malignant falsehoods," he "pitched into" the hon. member for Welland in his most approved style, for presenting such a petition and especially for not previously showing it to him. He then went on to consider the petitioners – "Who are they?" asked the Colonel, "why Mr Speaker, two or three petty shopkeepers in a paltry little village called Bertie[221] – a dirty little fishing place with half a dozen houses in it!" And these people, forsooth, to tell ME that I betrayed trust with them! that THEY entrusted me with carrying

---

219 Misdating in the original assigns this to Monday, 11 March. Actually Monday was the 13th, probably the true date.
220 D. McFarland was a Reform member for Welland.
221 Correctly, Waterloo (modern Fort Erie), in the township of Bertie.

through the Railroad Charter!! That I did not consult them!! Was ever such assumption – such impudence heard of? Mr. Speaker, I brought in the Charter myself, of my own free will and accord – I advertised my intention to apply, through the *Gazette* – I asked no one's consent. But forsooth I must consult these people before I withdraw my own Bill! Such impudence! What care I for the people of Bertie, or all the people of "glorious old Norfolk, to boot?" A parcel of whiskey makers and fishers of black bass!!!

261 EXCERPTS FROM DEBATE, 16 MARCH 1848
[*Montreal* Transcript, *17 March 1848*]

Mr. MCFARLAND moved that an addition be made to the present Railway Committee.

....

Col. PRINCE said he would vote for the measure – and that he agreed with hon. members that an increase of committee was necessary, he thought the present committee sufficient for all useful purposes – but he would not oppose it because he thought it should go forth to the country that this *liberal* parliament should be the first to throw obstacles in the way of public improvements, and the hon. gentleman, in reference to the expected prorogation said, that it evidently showed that the Government had neither the desire, the means or the ability to carry on the business of the country.

....

Mr. BILLA FLINT[222] ... made some facetious allusions to the tavern, or at least the bar, in the House, which was very frequently visited by hon. members, especially by his hon. friend the member for Essex ...

Col. PRINCE rose, and good humouredly alluded to the expressions which had fallen from the hon. member for Hastings. He said he had spent the previous hour at the bar of the refreshment room with the hon. member, and never spent an hour more pleasantly. In fact, he thought the hon. member for Hastings would make a good lawyer, for he was calculated to "shine at the bar." He should support the motion as far as the refusing licences to improper houses. And he thought not only should drunkenness be made an indictable offence, but that persons who charged those with drunkenness who were sober, should also be indictable. He was no friend to drunkenness but he was opposed to temperance meetings. A man was not worthy of the name, who had not sufficient self command to abstain from brutal intoxication. The hon. member then entered into an eulogy on the virtues of "Sir John Barleycorn," to whose merits he attributed the surpassing energy, talent, and courage of the British nation. Besides, said the hon. member, what would become of the barley, which is so largely grown, if beer and whiskey were not manufactured? Amidst much laughter he sat down.

---

222 Flint, a Belleville merchant, was a Reform member of the Legislative Assembly for Hastings.

262 DIARY, 18 MARCH 1848

A mild day & weather very fine. Sent off a good many letters and Papers by Mail. Sat from 10 to nearly one on The Oxford Election Committee. *Hincks declared duly Elected.* I the only dissenting voice. After dinner I went out to Mr. Penner's with Mr. Somerville, who dined with me. Got there at 7 & remained the Eveng.

263 DIARY, 21 MARCH 1848

A rapid thaw & very mild. No frost last night. Streets sloppy and most unpleasant to walk in. Busy in the City & at Mr. Court's & in The House all the morng. Went to The House after dinner, & remained in debate there 'till 1/2 p 12. Mr. *Vansittart*[223] brot to the Bar of The House. Sir Allan Macnab & I & others defended him. Debate adjourned. In bed by 1 o'clock!

264 DIARY, 22 MARCH 1848

A very fine Spring like morning with but little frost. Busy on The Great Western Rail-Road Committee all the morning. Attended The House from 3 p.m. 'till *3 am*! discussing Van Sittart's Case chiefly. I examined George Brown,[224] & spoke at much length giving the Ministry & their supporters a good lashing and defending myself as regards the Windsor affair.

265 'THE COUNTY OF KENT'
[*Toronto* Globe, *5 April 1848*]

We have a letter from a correspondent in Kent stating that it is expected that Mr. Malcolm Cameron will be opposed in that County – and by whom? By Col. Prince!!! Our correspondent must have been imposed upon. There is but one constituency in the British Empire that would have anything to do with that unprincipled man – the County of Essex, in Upper Canada.

266 DIARY, 10 APRIL 1848. *Chatham*

A lovely day. Wrote to my dear M.A. by Ralph Dynes. Busy in my room 'till 1. Then The Kent Election took place, and I addressed the multitude at great length on general subjects and against the present administration. Malcolm

---

223 Vansittart was registrar of the Surrogate Court of the Brock District.
224 The Reformer George Brown founded the Toronto *Globe* in 1844. He was a supporter of Hincks in this case, but he soon took a dislike to him. First elected in 1851, for Kent, he ultimately became the leader of the Grits.

Cameron also addressed them at much length. He was Elected by acclamation. Went to bed at 1/2 p. 12 having (as usual) drank too much.

267 DIARY, 18 SEPTEMBER 1848. *The Park Farm*

It rained all day yesterday but is finer today. Sick all night with fever & a pain in my head, & was attended by Dr. Bower, & *in bed all day*. Very unwell. Had a long conversation with M.A. and *mutual explanations took place*. Both to blame. Got a little better towards Eveng but [sentence not completed.]

268 EXCERPTS FROM DEBATE, 22 JANUARY 1849. *Montreal*
[*Montreal* Gazette, *24 January 1849*]

Col. PRINCE withdrew his notice of motion for an Address to His Excellency, for copies of Indictment, &c., against George Brown, at the last Spring Assizes, in the London District. He accused the Attorney General West[225] of great neglect in this particular. The explanation of that learned officer was satisfactory as far as regarded the want of trial at the Fall Assizes of 1847; but he maintained that the duties of Mr. Brown in the Penitentiary Committee were no excuse, such duties came within the province of Inspectors, and in that Commission there were others named, so that it could not be urged as a reason for the frustration of the ends of public justice, towards an individual against whom a true bill had been found by a Grand Jury, for a most gross Libel, the matter of which he very well knew to be false, and which he had reiterated.

. . . .

It was amusing, it was funny, he thought, to hear a Speech from the Throne, in a British Colony, delivered by the Representative of Her Majesty in a foreign tongue, and it must have tickled the ears of more than him. No doubt His Excellency was advised to do this, and he had no doubt he would soon be advised to do many more amusing and absurd things. It was, no doubt, done to please the French Canadians; but why did they not get His Excellency to read it in French first? It might have pleased them more, it was a desperate thing to be obliged to be contented to play second fiddler. But they need not think they would gain any credit by it, they could not so easily blind fold the Canadians, who, he was sure, would only look upon it as an attempt to throw dust in their eyes ... He would refer them to the case of the three associate Judges at London – (Hear, hear.) ... He found they had filled up their places with other gentlemen, which had been done, no doubt, by the advice of the member for Kent;[226] ... He would now refer them to the case of Mr. Gzowsky,[227] an atrocious case; that

---

225 Robert Baldwin.
226 Malcolm Cameron.
227 Casimir Gzowsky, born in Russia, was a civil engineer and financier. In 1841 he was employed as an engineer in the Department of Public Works, at Toronto. He left the public service in 1848. In 1853 his private company undertook the building of the Grand Trunk Railway between Toronto and Sarnia. In the 1870s he built a bridge across the Niagara River.

gentleman was a foreigner, and came to this country about 6 years ago, when he was invited to join the Board of Works as an Engineer, and since that time till lately he had performed his duties to the satisfaction of every one – and when he was suddenly deprived of his salary of £6000 a-year, (and he is a man with a large family,) and informed that his services were no longer required, and that in a letter of great politeness, – (Hear, hear,) – which bore testimony to his skill and good conduct; and why was this done? It was done to make room for Mr. Killaly,[228] who was immediately appointed to his situation, at a far higher salary; ... They had in England a Board of Works, but it was filled from top to bottom with eminent Engineers. – But whom have they put at the head of the Board here? – a most respectable gentleman and a first-rate physician no doubt, one who could physic his patients well, but he was a person who knew no more of Engineering than he (Col. P.) did, and that was very little; and, then, who was called upon to assist him; was it an Engineer? It was the member for Kent, who, no doubt, knew the value of lumber, the value of a bale of goods very well, but was totally ignorant of Engineering ... The hon. member then proceeded to speak about the conduct of the Ministry in employing other members of the Bar to conduct the Crown business when there were Queen's Counsel to do it. – It might be ascribed to him that he spoke from personal feelings, and that he complained of this because he had been deprived of the Crown business, but it was not because they had done so that he complained of it; he never expected it, and it was on behalf of the other Queen's Counsel, and for the sake of the profession, that he spoke; ... The Address spoke of the amendment of the Emigration Law with a view to encourage emigrants, intending to settle in Upper Canada or the Western States, coming by the St. Lawrence. What had they to do with emigrants coming to settle in the Western States? What had they to do with the Union? Nothing; but he would tell them that the conduct of the Ministry was altering the views of many of their best citizens regarding the Union, and many of them would be obliged to leave their country to go there, if the conduct of the Ministry in excluding all that were good and virtuous from office was persisted in. – (Hear, hear.) The hon. members opposite cry hear, hear. He had no doubt that they would be happier under a Republic than under England, – (hear,) – but they had not the courage to come forward and say so. – (Hear, hear, and laughter.)

269 EXCERPTS FROM SPEECH ON THE VANSITTART
CASE, 8 FEBRUARY 1849
[*Montreal* Gazette, *9 February 1849*]

They had called upon George Brown for what purpose – for the purpose of proving the fact alleged in the resolution. He was a witness of the hon. gentleman opposite, in fact, a witness for the part of the prosecution ... It could

---

228 Hamilton Hartley Killaly was chairman of the Board of Works, 1841–46, and represented London in the Legislative Assembly, 1841–44. After 1848 he was in charge of the Welland Canal and other works.

not be concealed, because they had it from his own lips, that he was the agent of Mr. Hincks in the county of Oxford, he was a very strong partizan of that gentleman, and canvassed the county of Oxford; and it had also been proved, from his own lips that he was actuated by a very strong feeling against Mr. Vansittart, ... He [Prince] was placed in a position where he had to decide on some points which would have puzzled some of the ablest members in that House. Was there no allowance to be made to Mr. Vansittart supposing that he acted wrongly. Was there no ground for his believing himself to be right, and if there were grounds he (Col. P.) would ask upon what grounds they would condemn Mr. Vansittart? He would not detain the House any longer; he would hear what other members said upon the subject. He was not so much wedded to his opinion that he might not alter it if he was convinced it was erroneous. He had endeavoured to apply his mind to the evidence as he was in the habit of doing in Courts of Law; and his conviction was that the testimony of Brown was erroneous, and that the evidence of Mr. Vansittart acquitted him of any intention to do wrong, and he thought he should therefore be sent away from the bar, free from any stain on his character.

270 EXCERPT FROM REBELLION LOSSES DEBATE, 13 FEBRUARY 1849
[*Montreal* Gazette, *14 February 1849*]

Col. Prince hoped that the Administration would not have the House into Committee, but that they would give the Constituencies of the members from Upper Canada some opportunity of expressing their opinion on the measure; he lived 600 miles away from this, and he asked for such delay as would enable him to consult his Constituents. He did not ask it as a favour, he demanded it as a right. It had been said by the Attorney General East,[229] that it had already been before the House, but so monstrous a proposition was never brought them, and he would die before he would consent to its passing, he was certain that three-fourths of the people of Upper Canada were against it.

271 DIARY, 16 FEBRUARY 1849

A fine frosty morning. Went to The House at 10 and remained there 'till 1. Then attended The annual general meeting of *The British North American Mining Co. Then spent an hour or two with good & Jolly fellows at *Dolly's* but drank a *leetle* too much. Home & in bed by 11 fatigued & rather lowspirited.
((*I was re-elected a *Director*.))

---

[229] L.H. LaFontaine. He regarded the Rebellion Losses Bill as a test case, to prove to French Canadians that they could enjoy power and obtain justice within the union.

272 DIARY, 17 FEBRUARY 1849

A remarkably cold day, 20 below Zero. Attended The *Standing Committee on Rail-Roads* of which I am a Member. Lunched at Dolly's in Gt. St. James' Street. Saw Mr. Moffatt on business. Sat at The "Ottawa" (Lavine's) 'till 6, then went to the great meeting at The "*Bon Secours*" new market. Was called on to speak when I addressed upwards of 4000 persons, and about 1000 afterwards from *Donagana's* steps. Sat there with Vansittart & others 'till 1. Then went to bed.

273 EXCERPTS FROM REBELLION LOSSES SPEECH, 20 FEBRUARY 1849
[*Montreal* Gazette, *23 February 1849*]

It had been said by a Member of the Government that the Member for Hamilton and the Member for Toronto, and all those who supported the Government of that day, were the cause of the Rebellion. This was distinctly stated, and he did not choose to submit to it, and he threw back the statement as an utterly absurd and false statement. What, Sir Allan McNab a Rebel? and the late Attorney General[230] a Rebel? – they who had been brought up in principles of allegiance to their Sovereign were Rebels, because they had supported Sir F.B. Head and his government. He denied it ... And he had been charged with causing rebellion. The greatest curse which ever fell upon him or his family was, that he had ever heard the name of Canada, because there his loyalty had been no advantage to him ... He would not call certain persons rebels in return, but he would detail them a few facts which history and public notoriety furnished him ... He had been told that Hypolite Lafontaine had done some naughty things, ... He did not think he was a rebel, but he was told that one James Harvey Price was charged with doing some naughty things, ... there was another gentleman of the name of Francis Hincks, – he (Col. P.) did not know any such person – (laughter) ... There was another famous gentleman of those days, one Robert Baldwin, ... As he, (Col. P.) had been charged with being a rebel, he retorted it upon those who did so, and he told them, and the whole of Canada, "*nemo me impune lacessit.*"[231] He was quiet when let alone, but they would not raise his blood by charging him with the greatest crime which a man could be guilty of with impunity. In his opinion the Union of the Provinces had been a curse to Upper Canada, he would not go into figures to prove it – he was above them – he looked to the peaceful home which he had expected to find in this land, and had he known the one hundredth part of what he now knew, he should have opposed such a measure – he should have in the name of their common country, which he had adopted – in the name of public safety – he should have forbidden the bans of this unhallowed Union. (Cheers.) ... He

---

230 Henry Sherwood, a Tory sitting for Toronto, was attorney general 1847–48.
231 No one attacks me with impunity.

(Col. P.) would now tell them why he could not vote for the resolutions before the House; he could not vote for them because he looked upon the Lower Canada rebels as having been the cause of the loss and misery which he and his constituents in the western Districts sustained ... His life, instead of being a happy one as he expected it would be when he came to this country, had been rendered an unhappy one; his life had been [made] miserable by these occurrences, and by the feelings which still existed in consequence.

274 AMENDMENT
[Journal of the House of Assembly, *27 February 1849*]

Mr. *Prince* moved in amendment to the said Resolution, seconded by Mr. Malloch,[232] ... that the loyal subjects of Her Majesty, and no others in *Lower Canada*, should be indemnified for the just Losses they sustained, but that such Losses should be paid by *Lower Canada* alone, and from her own local resources, and that *Upper Canada* and the Consolidated Revenue Fund of the Province should be wholly and entirely exempt from the burthen of any portion of those Losses; because it would, in the opinion of this House, be the height of injustice to saddle Upper Canada, and especially the Western Districts thereof, with any part of these Losses, there having been no Rebellion nor any symptoms of Rebellion there; it being, on the contrary, a fact that the peaceable inhabitants along the frontier were the victims of various invasions, ...

275 DIARY, 28 FEBRUARY 1849

A mild day like April! Busy about Town all the morng. In the Evening went to The House, and remained there until late, as usual. *I turned William Lyon McKenzie,*[233] *the Traitor, out of The Library*. Much Excitement created thereby. Home & in bed by 12 o'clock.

276 SECOND READING OF REBELLION LOSSES BILL, 2 MARCH 1849
[*Toronto* Globe, *10 March 1849*]

Colonel Prince entered a vehement protest against the passing of such a nefarious measure. He rated Mr. Lafontaine for always addressing the House in "that confounded French language;" and referring to the nickname of "the lily of the valley," applied to Mr. Ex-Secretary Daly, compared the Attorney General to the "dandelion of the valley."

---

232 E. Malloch was a Tory, representing Carleton in the Assembly.
233 Mackenzie had just returned to Canada from exile in the United States following the Upper Canada Rebellion, under an amnesty act.

277 DIARY, 14 MAY 1849. *London, C.W.*

A wet night last night & a wet, cold, & blowing day. Any thing but Congenial or seasonable! *March*-like! The Indictment agst George Brown for Libel on myself was tried. I was Examined at Considerable length by The Counsel for The Crown & x examined by Brown. He was found "Guilty", & sentenced to pay a fine of £30 & give Security &c. Spent the Evening with friends and drank rather too freely.

278 EXCERPT FROM REPORT OF TRIAL, 14 MAY 1849
[*Toronto* Globe, *19 May 1849*]

The charge arose out of a report of a trial in the London District Court, published in the *Globe* of 30th November, 1847. Mr. Horton, Attorney, was the plaintiff, and Mr. Thomas Partridge was the defendant – the former suing the latter for a bill of costs incurred in defending Partridge on a Queen's Bench suit, including £5 for a Counsel fee to Col. Prince. Partridge defended the action brought by Horton, on the ground that he had received no value. He called Mr. John Wilson, M.P.P.,[234] and proved by him that Mr. Prince was the Counsel in the cause – that in his opinion Mr. Prince was drunk at the trial – that he declared in Court he knew nothing of the case, and if Partridge had any defence none was offered. Of this trial we published a true and accurate report, without any comment – and on this publication the first count of the indictment was laid.

In the *Western Globe*[235] of the week following, however, (7th Dec'r, 1847,) we published some brief criticisms on Col. Prince's conduct in the matter, assuming the truth of Mr. Wilson's evidence. On this publication the second and third counts were grounded.

The Jury acquitted Mr. Brown on the first count – thereby acquitting him of all moral guilt; but on the two last they found him guilty under the charge of the court.

279 DIARY, 19 MAY 1849

Rose at 5, Boat off at 1/2 p. 4. We descended The "Cedar" and other furious "Rapids" & reached Lachine at 7. Then went by The Rail-road Cars to Montreal. Reached my hostess's (Mrs. Steele's) by 8. Busy about town 'till 1, when I went to the Chamber of the Assembly and spoke & voted against Hy. Sherwood's address to The Govr. General to remove Parliament 4 years alternatively to Quebec & Toronto.

---

234 John Wilson represented the Town of London in the Legislative Assembly from 1844. He crossed to the Reform ranks in March 1849.

235 A western edition of the Toronto *Globe* was begun in 1845. It was published in Toronto, but was given a London dateline.

280 DIARY, 25 MAY 1849

A finer day than yesterday but still very Cool. Lt. General Sir Benjamin D'Urbain died suddenly at Donagana's Hotel! He commanded in Canada. Attended the House 'till 5 p.m. & spoke at some length on Christie's amendment to the Supply Bill that The House should pledge itself to curtail, next year, all Salaries above £500. Blamed the Ministers severely. Dined at 6, and then Morris[236] & I spent a couple of Hours at Dolly's.

281 DIARY, 30 MAY 1849

A fine warm and growing day. At the House for an hour in the morng. Then walked up to *Monklands*[237] and spent an hour or two with Lord *Elgin* & conversed at much length with him about his position as Govr. General &c. &c. The Dep'y Govr. *General Rowan*[238] prorogued Parliament at 4 p.m. Lord Elgin in low spirits. Wrote many letters, and went to bed at 11 fatigued and "out of Sorts".

282 DIARY, 16 JULY 1849

A very fine day. Rose Early. A great public political meeting convened at Sandwich by The "Rads". Malcolm *Cameron* & Mr. *Cauchon*[239] M.P.P.'s addressed them. So did I, & demolished those Gents and the Rads Most Completely. In town 'till 10 pm. Mr. Anderton & Mr. Gatfield slept at our house. Drank a great deal too much.

283 REPORT OF A POLITICAL MEETING AT CHATHAM, 19 JULY 1849
[*Chatham* Chronicle, *7 August 1849*]

COL. PRINCE BEING CALLED UPON SAID:

....

As an Elector, therefore, of this County, I rise to call to account for his past acts the person who holds my interests in his hand. And certainly we have just

---

236 This is probably James Morris, who was appointed to the Legislative Council in 1844 after having represented Leeds in the Assembly from 1837.
237 Monklands was the governor general's residence, on Mount Royal.
238 Sir William Rowan. In 1849 he was appointed commander in chief of the British forces in North America, a post which he retained until he left Canada in 1855. Rowan, a personal friend and confidant of Lord Elgin, prorogued Parliament on Elgin's behalf to spare him any possible harassment arising out of violent disturbances in Montreal over the Rebellion Losses debate, recently concluded.
239 Joseph Edouard Cauchon was a French-Canadian member of the Legislative Assembly for Montmorency.

cause to be proud of our Hon. Member for the high compliment he has paid to us for placing him in the position of our representative. He has told us that it is not his intention to offer again as a candidate for your suffrages – that he will, when another election comes, resign the trust you have reposed in him, and advises you to look out for some person else, as he has now pitched upon Essex as the next place he must storm and carry, by his humbug, his knavery, and deceit.

....

Lord Elgin has stooped from the high, and dignified position of Governor General, and becomes a mere tool in the hands of men, who rule him as they please – has sunk to the degraded, and contemptible position of an apologist for the acts of those, whose duty it was to restrain from trampling on the rights and liberties of a people over whom he is called to rule.

....

It has also been stated that I have come here to-day to solicit the votes of the electors of Kent at the next election, this I likewise pronounced a falsehood. I have (said the Gallant Col.) now represented the County of Essex for nearly 14 years, they have honored me during that long and eventful period with their confidence. I am not conscious that from any act which I have committed either in the House or out of it, where their interests locally, or generally, were involved, that I have forfeited that confidence, nor will I, like the member for Kent, turn round and betray them, by throwing myself on another constituency. It is neither my advantage nor my wish to appear again in the walls of Parliament, as the representative of that or any constituency. I have long desired to retire from public life, but never shall I do so, while I have a tongue to speak – as long as I behold one portion of the people trampled upon, their rights and liberties invaded, to appease the tyranny and rapacity of the other – till justice and equitable rights are fully extended to all.

284 DIARY, 23 JANUARY 1850. *The Park Farm*

A cold day but Seasonable and healthy. Bad travelling, the roads being full of rough and broken Ice. Occupied in town all day. Had Wm. D. Baby committed to Sandwich Gaol for Contempt of Chancery. Attended the Magistrates for Dr. Russell[240] and dismissed Mr. F. Baby's complaint agst The "Argo"[241] with Costs. Home to dinner at 6, and found Henry returned (with 2 deer) & Cam. Parry[242] & Marion Forsith at our House. Went to bed at 10.

285 DIARY, 30 JANUARY 1850

Another hard frost & Cold, but healthy day. Occupied all the Morng in Town and with Rankin on business. *Became Surety for Bullock* the new Co[unt]y

---

240 This is possibly Dr George B. Russell, of Detroit.
241 The second ferry so named, built at Detroit in 1849.
242 A contemporary and friend of the Prince children, from Gosfield Township.

Treasurer, and signed his Bond for £2000 in presence of Horace Nelson at Laughton's[243] Tavern. Home to dinner at 5, and in my office all the Evening. Went to bed at 1/2 9 unhappy as usual. Mr. Colley[244] here.

286   DIARY, 31 JANUARY 1850

A fine mild day, much the same as April generally is! Busy in my office all day long, drawing aff[idavi]t &c. as to the illegality of W.D. Baby's recent Election.[245] Then read for an hour at night, and went to bed miserable as usual!

287   DIARY, 17 FEBRUARY 1850

A fine day but Cold. Very unhappy all day, & shut myself up in my office. I often wish I was dead! Did not stir out of doors once all day, but was occupied in addressing a long, a very long letter to Mr. Rankin & my Constituents on the subject of *Annexation* and *Independence*. Henry & Miss Newton[246] returned from Anderdon. Went to bed at 12, miserable!

288   PRINCE TO ARTHUR RANKIN ('INDEPENDENCE MANIFESTO')
[*Detroit* Daily Advertiser, ca. *25 February 1850*]

The Park Farm, February 19, 1850

I thank you for having called my attention to a paragraph in the Toronto "Independent" of the 30th ultimo., which intimates that I have declared in favor of *Annexation*, and that my constituents will sustain me in it; and you very naturally and very properly desire, on behalf of yourself and other Freeholders of this County, to be made acquainted with my views upon that all-engrossing subject. I will give them to you freely. At once, then, I proclaim to you and to my constituents at large, that *I am against the Annexation Manifesto*, but am decidedly in favor of *Independence*; and my earnest desire is to see all the noble Provinces of British North America confederated, and that one great nation shall spring therefrom – a nation free and independent of all other nations – a nation based upon the broadest principles of liberty, and possessing the freest institutions, and a sovereignty within itself! ... I demand, what reason have we, or our friends who signed that document, to doubt that this country, mighty as she already is, through nature's gifts, and mightier still as she must become, *if free*, will take her place among the nations of the earth, at

---

243 John Betton Laughton was the proprietor of the Free Mason's Arms, Sandwich.
244 A visitor from England.
245 As reeve of Sandwich Township, Baby sat on the Western District Council from 1846, and was elected to the Municipal Council as reeve of Sandwich Township in 1850. He occupied his seat for the remainder of 1850, following Prince's challenge, but it was his last term on the Council.
246 Mariane ('Munny') Newton, apparently a governess for the younger Prince children.

the proper time, without forcing herself upon our neighbors of "*The Union*" as a sort of Protege? ... Nor can I approve of the manifesto upon other grounds. It assumes to do that which the Sovereign and Government of England cannot do, that is, to unite us to a Foreign Nation, with the mere consent of the Crown and Government. – The people, surely, should be first consulted. – They should first appeal to Parliament, and they will in my opinion, degrade themselves if they do not make INDEPENDENCE (not Annexation) the TEST at the general elections ...

Secondly, I go for Independence from the mother country, because (and I desire not use the term offensively) I think her domination baneful to us ... We cannot legislate for ourselves; we are controlled by the executive of England in that respect; and, after all our boastings about "Responsible Government," the Parliament *here* is but little better than a mere board of advice to her. We are trammelled by the Head – the transient, ever changing Head of that Colonial Office there, in Downing Street – a Head and a place four thousand miles away! ...

I should like to know what *capitalist* would settle here in the present state of things – here, in this the fairest, mildest, and most fertile part of Canada, when he learns that, for the last twelve years, the country has gradually retrograded; that sixteen years ago, a man of ample means, of a liberal education, of energy and enterprise and industry, not given to that pride of "pomp and circumstance," or to that extravagance and profligacy which ruin thousands, and are so incompatible with life in Canada, or in any other infant country, a man whose chief delight and object were to be of service to his adopted land and people, to add to its improvement, and to carve out, by honest means, that estate for his numerous family which he never could obtain at "home" – one who invested here and hereabouts nine thousand pounds of sterling gold in such laudable pursuits, which sum, for the last ten years, has not returned to him an income of twenty pounds per annum! Who spent a thousand pounds in the erection of a brewery and malt-house in his district town, which yields him a yearly rent of just *one solitary dollar*! One whose property is worse than valueless – a mill stone round his neck – but which, if it were but in another land, within even musket shot of where it is, would be worth *treble what it cost him*. I ask what man of capital, or of intelligence, or of enterprise, or of industry would pitch his tent and settle down in such a country, with such warnings as every day's observation gives of its "ruin and decay!" None but a lunatic would do so ... Then, let me ask, of what advantage is England to us, or we to her? Of none, in my opinion, whatever. Each is an incubus upon the other. I came hither as an "Emigrant – not as a Knight Errant to sustain the fame and glory of my native land." The "days of chivalry" are past with me; but I came here to mend a fortune which the "going surety for friends" at home had cruelly impaired, and to enjoy in peace on the banks of our beautiful St. Lawrence, my new home, with the same security and quietude, as I thought, that belongs to an Englishman's home on the banks of our own old "Father Thames." But alas, how bitterly has one been deceived! – Peace and rest and contentment have vanished from us for the last ten years, ne'er to return so long as we remain dependent on that distant land called "home." The pride of power there – the many petty quarrels that may arise between distant nations of which we desire to be entirely free, added to the jealousies which the very name of *monarchy* involves, amidst the greatest power in the Western Hemisphere, may hurry us, as has been the case before, in some unholy strife with our friends and neighbors opposite, and we may be *forced* by the "baneful domination" under which we groan, again to waste our blood, our fortunes, and our health, in sustaining what is called the honor of the crown – a glittering diadem, which our imaginations view at the interesting and influencing distance of four thousand miles!

....

But as to her Majesty's Attorney General, Mr. Robert Baldwin, *daring* to charge those with *impiety*, who are advocates for independence, I tell him now, as I told many of his admirers, and more of an opposite "kidney" two years ago both here and in the London District, (and it is no new notion of mine) that without Independence and freedom from the stubbornness and ignorance of Downing Street, we never can be prosperous – that he who opposes it is an enemy to the principles of *Radical Reform* – (the only Reform worth having now,) and that he the learned functionary, puritan though in truth he be, will be chargeable with little short of blasphemy if he dare hereafter to assume the title of "Reformer." ... I trust I shall yet live to see the views which I entertain, and as explained in this letter, carried out; and I also trust that Essex will, through me, her representative, petition Parliament to address the Queen for emancipation.

289 PRINCE TO THE HON. JAMES LESLIE [247]
[*Detroit* Daily Advertiser, *11 April 1850*]

The Park Farm, March 30, 1850

I presume that my letter of yesterday (Good Friday) duly reached your office. I now presume also to send to you for the Governor General's perusal and your own, (as an *earnest* of my intentions to carry out the meaning of that letter,) a petition to Parliament praying for "Independence." It may probably relieve his Excellency from cogitating much about my "Silk Gown," and I trust I shall be permitted to carry it through the House next Session.

290 DIARY, 9 APRIL 1850. *The Park Farm*

A very fine day. Busily occupied about my garden & farm all the morng. At Sandwich from 2 till 7 p.m. and busy there with Mr. Hyde, the Warden,[248] & others. *Wrote Lord Elgin my resignation of my Silk Gown &c.* Very much engaged at Laughton's Tavern. Home by 8 to tea, and went to bed at 10 fatigued & troubled with the Rash.

247 James Leslie was a Reformer who represented Montreal East and then Verchères in the Legislative Assembly. He was president of the Council, 1848, and provincial secretary, 1848–51, in the second Baldwin-LaFontaine administration.

248 George Hyde, of Plympton Township, was the newly elected warden of the United Counties of Essex, Kent, and Lambton.

291 PRINCE TO THE HON. JAMES LESLIE
[*Detroit* Daily Advertiser]

The Park Farm, April 13, 1850

Your letter dated the 5th, (but mailed at Toronto on the 6th) written by command of the Governor General, and informing me that Her Majesty has no further occasion for my services as one of her Counsel, or as a Justice of the Peace, arrived here on the 11th inst.

The Governor General and you both well know that I publicly resigned the office of Justice of the Peace *many months ago*, and that of Queen's Counsel *before* my services, as such, were dispensed with.

. . . .

I swerve not from the opinions which I have formed upon a subject of such magnitude as the independence of this country; and I now cease to write further, leaving it to His Excellency and his "Liberal" advisers the enviable 'duty' of attempting to put down, by an arbitrary assumption of power with which they are not clothed, *the subjects' right to petition their Sovereign and to exercise freedom of speech* upon important State affairs.

292 DIARY, 17 MAY 1850. *Toronto*

A warm & fine growing Morng. Rain & Thunder about day light. At the House in the morng. In the Evg at 3 a debate upon Baldwin's motion that my Petition for *Independence* sho'd not be received took place, & it was Carried by 50 Majority. So much for the "Liberals"! To refuse to receive & hear a Petition indeed! Monstrous. Went to bed at 12 much wearied.

293 PRINCE'S REPLY TO SPEECH FROM THE THRONE,
21 MAY 1850
[*Toronto* British Colonist, *24 May 1850*]

The first part of the speech to which he would allude, is that where His Excellency says, that the occurrences of the past year had induced him to remove the seat of Government from Montreal. This was very singular language ... Was it forgotten that £100,000 was voted at Kingston, a few years ago, for the erection of public buildings at Montreal? Why was not that sum of money used for the purpose for which it was intended? It was reserved to pay Rebels ... Last Session, the Hon. Commissioner of the Public Works,[249] told the House, that they would positively have Reciprocity, – but what was the result? Why Congress had met, and refused it, and public notoriety says, (which was good evidence now-a-days,) that we were as likely to get Reciprocity now, as he was to become Prime Minister to the Moon. Public notoriety also said that the hon. member for Kent had visited Washington in regard to that question; and he hoped he should hear from him that there were good grounds for that which was stated in the address, because he believed that reciprocity

---

249 William Hamilton Merritt was appointed commissioner of public works 8 April 1850. He was a champion of both the Welland Canal and reciprocity.

would do much good to the country, and would relieve the people of the Western District of many of the burthens which they now bear in consequence of the late commercial changes made by Great Britain ... He now came to the Court of Chancery ... That court must be abolished, or the whole country would be ruined in time (hear). It was created last session merely to give offices to the friends of the ministry. He regretted that he was absent, on leave, last session when the bill creating that court was passed ... He would merely say, that its whole machinery was bad, that its costs were too high, and before the session closed, he would ask the House to support him in a bill which he intended to bring in, by which cheap and speedy equity might be obtained ... He now came to the 19th and 20th clause of the address. They were couched in language with which he could not agree, that is, in approving the conduct of the ministers in dismissing from office those who had petitioned for Independence or Annexation. Their conduct with those gentlemen was unjust and tyrannical. All the threats of the ministers, nor of the united Press of Canada, could prevent him from expressing his opinion. What right had they to dismiss those from office who signed the Annexation Manifesto? None ... Why they deprived men of talent from office, and filled the vacancies thus created by ignorant boobies, because the former chose to express their opinion. He knew a Queen's Counsel who, six months ago, resigned his silk gown, because he would no longer serve under such a government; but four days after he sent in his resignation, a paragraph appeared in the Gazette, stating that that gentleman had been *dismissed* from his office. Was anything so contemptible, so unbecoming, so pigmy? ... He would delay the House no longer, but he must add, that he had never seen anything so worthless as the speech from the Throne. A parcel of old Dowagers would have concocted something better over a tea-table. It was composed of old Dutch Flummery. – (Laughter.) No good could come from it. It was conceived in folly and ignorance; and he could also tell the ministry, that since the last session they had been an unjust, an unconstitutional, and unprincipled Government. (Hear, hear.)

294 REPORT OF SPEECH, 23 MAY 1850
[*Toronto* British Colonist, *28 May 1850*]

Col. PRINCE spoke for nearly two hours in favor of annexation, elective Institutions, and concluded by saying that none knew better than the Attorney General East[250] the necessity of an elective Legislative Council, although, perhaps he would not think it policy to vote in its favour just at present. But the hon. gentleman would be in office long enough to do so some other time, for he freely confessed he had no objection to ministers remaining in, for he did not see enough talent on his (Col. Prince's) side of the House to form an administration. Of course, no one would appoint him to office, he was too loose and slippery a fish, therefore he did not oppose ministers to get their places, but

---

250 Louis Hippolyte LaFontaine.

because he had found their measures to be universally unscrupulous, tyrannical, and unjust.

295 REPORT OF SPEECH, 27 MAY 1850
[*Toronto* British Colonist, *28 May 1850*]

Col. PRINCE, seconded by Mr. DEWITT,[251] then moved the amendment, of which he had given notice, condemnatory of the course taken by ministers, in dismissing the magistrates and militia officers for signing the Annexation Manifesto ... He said that he conscientiously believed that the majority of the inhabitants of Canada were in favour of Annexation or Independence; but, for the most part, it was not convenient for them to acknowledge it. He stated that in spite of the declaration of the hon. member for Kent, that not twenty influential persons in the Western District were in favour of Annexation. He had received four petitions, word for word, identical with that which he had before presented, and signed by hundreds of influential farmers and merchants in the West; but he would not disgrace or insult them by presenting these petitions to this House.

296 SPEECH ON ABOLITION OF THE SEIGNEURIES, 14 JUNE 1850
[*Toronto* British Colonist, *18 June 1850*]

Mr. PRINCE said it might be presumptuous for any person to offer an opinion which was adverse to the views held by the head of the Government, especially on a measure relating principally to Lower Canada, but he felt it his duty to protect and assist Lower Canadian members against any infringement of their rights ... The language of the resolutions conveyed the assurance that there was an intention on the part of the proposed committee to rob the proprietors of those lands of their lawful properties. Their lands were held upon the same principle as the manorial rights of England – by conquest ... As a legal character he was anxious to protect vested rights, and even though Seigneurs in this House were favourable to disturbing the right under which they held their own property, he would guard them against their own acts.

297 DIARY, 29 JULY 1850

A very fine but a very hot and very uncomfortable day. At the House all the morng & about Town. Met R.S. Woods & others at the Athenæum at 1, about The *Rail-Road*. The debate thereon Commenced at 7 & lasted 'till 1/2 past 12 pm. I spoke for 2 hours agst Sir Allan & our opponents; but they beat us by a Majority of 2 only, So that our Road is stopped for the present. Home by 1 disappointed.

---

251 J. De Witt, a Liberal, was a member of the Legislative Assembly for Beauharnois.

298 Diary, 24 September 1850. *The Park Farm*

Another fine day, and I as wretched as Ever. I fully mean to leave this detestable Canadian Country *for good* at the first chance. At home & in town all day, *un*profitably engaged, and went to bed at 10 *half* deranged, as usual.

299 Diary, 23 May 1851. *Toronto*

A windy, rough, & cold morng, for the time of year. Occupied at Osgoode Hall and about town and for half an hour in The House in the morning. Then went to The House again in the afternoon & spoke against Ministers. *McKenzie* very polite to me! House adjourned at 8. Took Bell & William to the Theatre. Could not get to the Concert at St. Lawrence Hall.

300 Diary, 28 May 1851

A fine, growing morning, but dull & more rain threatens. Very busy about Town at The Banks &c. At The House & with Mr. Harrington on Patent business. At Three p.m. went again to The House and presented *J. Montgomery's* Petition (the quondam Rebel & Traitor).[252] Spoke upon it & 2 other Subjects. The House adjourned at 8 p.m. William at an Hotel. C. Baby & Vidal spent an hour there in Evg. Went to bed at 11.

301 Speech on Mackenzie's Conciliation Courts Bill, 11 June 1851
[*Toronto* British Colonist, *13 June 1851*]

Col. PRINCE found it exceedingly funny to see such a bill introduced by the hon. member for Haldimand, as no man had ever more successfully evaded the law ... He continued at some length to ridicule the bill in a facetious manner and amid roars of laughter. He was surprised the Solicitor General[253] should have condescended to a serious argument in answer to such a palpable absurdity. He thanked God we lived in a land of liberty, a great country to which nature had been liberal of her favours, and where every man could have such courts, without the bill of the hon. member for Haldimand, if his constituents wanted it, they were great jackasses that was all he could say. (Loud laughter.)

302 Excerpts from Debate, 13 June 1851
[*Toronto* British Colonist, *17 June 1851*]

He should never again come back to that House, and he therefore desired to say

---

252 John Montgomery, the proprietor of Montgomery's Tavern, north of Toronto, fled to the United States after the Rebellion, but returned under amnesty in 1843.
253 John Sandfield Macdonald had been solicitor general of Upper Canada since 1849.

this much, that he threw his silk gown to the four winds, but that if he ever spoke with disrespect of the hon. member at the head of the government, it was because he was stung, and he should feel stung by the gratuitous insult offered him, by sending his dismissal after he had tendered his resignation.

....

Col. PRINCE had very carefully studied the dates and could say that, unless the post miscarried, his letter must have been in the hands of the Government forty-eight hours before the dismissal was despatched. But this was the real arrow corroding in his bosom – there was a patent of dismissals despatched a month afterwards. He repeated, this was a bitter insult, and he would have brought the man at the head of the Government to justice – not to the justice of the bar – if he could have found any friend to stand by him.

303 DIARY, 27 JUNE 1851

Another beautiful day. Rose early & wrote letters &c. &c. Then busy about Town. Went to The House at 3 and remained there 'till 11, and spoke several times upon The County division Bill & Carried an amendment to leave the Sites of the Co. Towns to be fixed by The Govr. & Council. Much Excitement thereat. Went to bed at 1 hot & fatigued.

304 DIARY, 28 JUNE 1851

A very warm & fine day. Wrote several letters and to *Tom Webb*[254] with the release Executed by William & Albert. Then, about Town all day long. At 6 attended a grand public Dinner given to The Honble. Mr. Howe of Nova Scotia[255] and acted as *Vice President*. Lord Elgin there, & I spoke twice. Home by 12, but drank a great deal too much Champagne.

305 EXCERPT FROM SPEECH ON BALDWIN'S RESIGNATION, 30 JUNE 1851
[*Toronto* British Colonist, *1 July 1851*]

Col. PRINCE said it was doubtless affecting to the feelings of the House to lose a friend, even though that friend were a political opponent. He had listened to the hon. members speech, and sympathized with his feelings, and with those of his friends around him; and although many a rough word had fallen from him, (Col. Prince,) called forth by injuries which were, perhaps, only fancied injuries, he hoped that in the words of Sterne, a recording angel had dropped a tear upon the book, and blotted them out for ever.

254 Webb, a cousin, of Hereford, was Prince's agent in England. He died in 1859.
255 Joseph Howe, a member of the Nova Scotia Legislative Assembly, and provincial secretary 1848–54, had come to the Canadas to seek their cooperation in building a railway to link them with New Brunswick and Nova Scotia.

306 Prince to Thomas Park[256]
[*Fort Malden National Historic Park, Amherstburg*]

Toronto, July 22, 1851

I was much obliged to you for your kind letter as to my return to Parliament. But, my dear Sir, it is *impossible* for me to go there any more. I have written an address to the Freeholders of Essex, which the County Clerk[257] will have inserted in The Sandwich "*Oak*" of Saturday next, and I hope the other Editors will give it Circulation. In it you will perceive *some* of my reasons for retiring into private life – to my Profession and my Farms. I hope you enjoy good health, & that all my friends around you are well. I think we shall be prorogued about the 12th or 15th Prox'o.

307 Excerpt from Debate, 4 August 1851
[*Toronto* British Colonist, *5 August 1851*]

Mr. MACKENZIE moved the second reading of the bill to authorize Her Majesty's subjects to plead for themselves.

....

Col. PRINCE opposed the bill, contending that it was an absurdity; but he was in favour of abolishing the office of Queen's Counsel, and he ridiculed, in a severe manner the calling of judges "my lord!" He looked upon such a practice with contempt. He went over an argument that he had before used, that the term "your honor" was the proper appellation to apply to judges.

308 Excerpt from Speech, 12 August 1851
[*Toronto* British Colonist, *15 August 1851*]

Our experience has taught us that private enterprise was insufficient to give Canada the railways she required; and to this lack of enterprise had been added petty jealousies between localities and individuals. There would have been a line from Bertie to Sandwich long ago; but for the narrow views and monopolising tendencies of what was called the Great Western Railway, which was still far from being built. His opinion of that undertaking was more favourable than it was twelve months ago, but he was still disposed to apply to it the maxim – *parturiunt montes nascitur ridiculous mus.*[258] He concluded by some remarks personal to the ministry.

309 Diary, 12 September 1851. *The Park Farm*

Another broiling day. Heat Scarcely bearable! Occupied in business all the

---

256 Thomas Park was a member of the Amherstburg firm of Park & Co., general merchants, wharfingers, and steamboat owners.

257 Samuel Smith Macdonell was a lawyer who by 1850 had arrived in Windsor from Toronto.

258 The lab'ring mountain scarce brings forth a mouse; Horace, *Ars Poetica*, line 168, translated in 1680 by the Earl of Roscommon.

morning. At 1 p.m. upwards of 50 good old Freeholders paid me a visit, and presented me with a requisition signed by upwards of 400 to allow them to nominate me as their M.P. at the next General Election. I consented and wrote Them my reply. They all got tolerably *Mellow*, and I went to bed at 10, much the same.

310 Excerpt from Prince to Lieutenant Colonel McDonald[259]
[*PAC, R.G. 9, I, C1, Vol. 57*]

The Park Farm, October 20, 1851

Nothing new here. Mr. Rankin is canvassing Kent upon the *Radical* ticket – he having suddenly "chopped round" *from high conservatism*!; and the Lieges of Essex seem resolved to send me again to Parliament, tho' I do assure you very much against my will!

311 Diary, 15 November 1851

A very dull morng. Published a short address to The "Electors" of Essex. Now, my Electioneering troubles begin altho' I was assured by The "People" I should be put to none. I am nearly distracted with the *Hosts* that infest & annoy me. At home all day, & very busy. Fresh arrivals here at 6 pm!!!! Went to bed at 11, perfectly wretched & miserable.

312 Excerpt from Editorial
[*Sandwich* Essex Advocate, *20 November 1851*]

Now we have a pretty kettle of fish. – Let us look for John Prince's principles. – What are they? In 1844 they were those of a Loyalist and a Liberal Reformer. In 1846, 47 and 48 they were those (if we may Judge from the Company he kept) of a high Church Tory. In 1849 they were those of the shouting demogogue. In 1850 they were, INDEPENDENCE as preparatory to a marriage with that "GLORIOUS REPUBLIC" "within musket shot of him" – in one word Annexation. In September 1851 he cooly tells the men he so much loved in 1844 that they know him too well to demand pledges of him, that he is their "OLD AND FAITHFUL FRIEND" and that "he will represent them as he has done heretofore." Worthy man, is he not a treasure, an honor to Essex!

Is it for such a man the independent Electors of Essex will vote? Will they stamp the seal of their approbation on his Independence Manifesto? Will they by returning him to Parliament acknowledge that the PETITION he presented there praying for separation from the mother Country, expressed their views upon the subject? We propose these questions to the good sense of the freeholders of Essex; and, we trust they will give proper and decisive answer to each of

---

259 This is apparently D. Macdonell, deputy adjutant general of militia for Canada West, 1846–61; see also Note 201.

them at the Polls. On the one hand they have the political weather-cock, Loyal Independence REPUBLICAN John Prince; on the other they have Francis Caron,[260] a sound and consistent Reformer and an upright man. Electors, for which will you cast your votes!!

313 DIARY, 29 NOVEMBER 1851

A fine day but cold, it being a black Frost. This was the nomination day (or first day of Election) for Essex. Hundreds of people flocked into Town. *Caron* (my opponent) and I severally addressed them from The Hustings. I spoke about 2 hours, &, they say, well. The show of hands was at least 3 to 1 in my favor. Caron demanded a Poll. The assembly dispersed in 6 hours.

314 DIARY, 9 DECEMBER 1851

A cold day. Poor Mrs. Stevens [261] still continues very ill. I fear she will not recover. Polling commenced at Sandwich & in Essex County. I was (as was Mr. Caron) at the poll (in the stone building[262]) all day 'till 5 p.m., and then Caron was 70 ahead of me in this Township. Spent the Eveng at Teakle's Inn till 8 o'clock, and then went home & to bed by 11 rather lowspirited.

315 DIARY, 10 DECEMBER 1851

Another Cold day. The Poll opened at 9 a.m. and remained open 'till 5 p.m. I was there (as was Caron) all day. At the close he was about 69 ahead of me here, but the news from the Townships satisfy us all that I am Elected by a very large Majority – upwards of 300! Addressed the Electors at the close of The Poll. Drank too much and got home by 9 p.m. & then went to bed by 10 fatigued.

316 DIARY, 13 DECEMBER 1851

Another very hard frost & extremely Cold. At 11 a.m. upwards of 100 Electors, with Carriage & four & Bands came to The Park Farm and Escorted me into Town where Sheriff Baby[263] declared me duly Elected by a Majority of

260 Prince's opponent, Magistrate François Caron, was probably the 'Carron' who in 1849 discussed establishing a bilingual newspaper in Amherstburg with Prince. In 1851 he was a lumber merchant.

261 Probably Susan, Mrs William Stevens. Both she and her husband, a Sandwich innkeeper in 1851, had been servants of Prince in England, and had migrated with him to Canada.

262 The Western District Grammar School, informally known as 'The Stone College,' stood on the site of the present General Brock Public School, at Sandwich and Brock Streets in modern Windsor.

263 William Duperon Baby.

302 over Caron! Then we adjourned to The Court House where I & Caron & others addressed The Electors. Then I was Escorted to Windsor, and home & in bed by 11.

317 EXCERPT FROM ADDRESS TO THE ELECTORS, 13 DECEMBER 1851
[*Detroit* Daily Advertiser, *18 December 1851*]

The contest is over, and the battle has been fairly and nobly won – and by whom? by those electors and generous friends of mine, whose "*free and independent minds*" minds, unenslaved by bigotry of any sort, maintained our cause triumphantly; and the triumph is the greater, because your exertions were spontaneous and unsought, and unsolicited by me, and because certain secret influences, which you all comprehend, engendered prejudices of a religious kind, which were brought to bear against me when sectarian prejudice should have stood aloof.

318 Diary, 6 January 1852

A hard frost & a Cold day. Rose at 9 and attended the Polls & voted for Woodbridge[264] & D. Langlois and also for Oliver Maisonville. *Gave Arthur Rankin a terrible "hauling over" at Fabien Parent's*[265] *Inn* before a large number of People. Then went to Detroit and transacted a good deal of business & made some Calls. *Much Snow* fell. Rode home by 9 a little the worse for liquor.

319 EXCERPT FROM PRINCE TO WILLIAM ALLAN[266]
[*MTCL, William Allan Papers*]

The Park Farm, January 8, 1852

I have purchased these 600 acres, merely to keep off a Set of people, of *all Colours*, who would have bought the Greater part of it if I had not; and as these lands adjoin one of my best farms, I wish to Keep off such neighbours; and that is the reason why I have agreed to give you much more than their real and intrinsic value.

264 Thomas Woodbridge, a Sandwich harness- and saddlemaker, was deputy reeve of Sandwich Township in 1850.
265 Parent was a resident of the Town of Sandwich and a pathmaster.
266 Allan was a former member of the Legislative and Executive Councils, and a central figure in the 'Family Compact.' He was the first president of the Bank of Upper Canada.

320 DIARY, 8 MARCH 1852

A mild day and thawing fast. Henry left to go back to Detroit. Mr. Gardiner & others Called this morng. People all mad about Rail-Road matters. Every body Expects to have his land covered with Sovereigns, if wanted for the R-Road! At home all day. The Hunts[267] here as usual to dinner &c. I went to bed at 10 lowspirited as usual.

321 DIARY, 10 APRIL 1852

A very fine day. Rose Early and got up to Windsor by 9 where I was occupied 'till 3 p.m. with Mr. Gunn[268] and others on Rail-Road business and the great Western Terminus was *fixed* at Windsor. Drew a Bond & agreement therein. Then walked home, Calling at 2 or 3 places. Within doors all the Evening, and went to bed at 10 any thing but comfortable in mind.

322 EXCERPT FROM DEBATE, 6 SEPTEMBER 1852. *Quebec* [*Toronto* Globe, *14 September 1852*]

The SPEAKER[269]: – The Hon. Mr. Cameron moves for leave to introduce a bill to prohibit the manufacture, importation, or sale of intoxicating liquors in this Province, – seconded by Col. Prince. (Loud laughter.)

Mr. PRINCE could not understand the degree of surprise manifested by hon. gentlemen at the announcement that he seconded the motion of his hon. friend. The applause seemed to come strangely enough on such an occasion; and he could imagine in what light it was intended that he should regard it. If it were meant as a cheer of welcome and pleasure at seeing and old friend once more on the floor of the House, he could understand and appreciate it; but if it were meant as a sarcasm, he could assure his friends on the opposite side of the House that he was as serious in seconding that motion as he had ever been in any act in his life. It is well known that he is a man formed by nature with social habits, and that he has been accustomed to enjoy, as he will still enjoy, the social cup taken in reason and at a proper hour of the day (hear and laughter); but he would tell them that he has observed, and closely observed, for many a long year, in that western country where he resides, – and he doubted whether the virtue of forbearance was much better understood or practised in the eastern country than there, – he had observed, he would repeat, the evils flowing from this vice of drunkenness, and the wretchedness it caused, not only among the young and unwary, but even among the old and the experienced; and he had determined to

---

267 Probably Frank Hunt and his wife, Eliza ('Puss') Knapp, formerly of Grosse Ile, Michigan, but in the spring of 1852 living on the Canadian side, between Sandwich and Windsor. In the 1851 census Frank Hunt's occupation was given as 'loafer.'
268 An agent of the Great Western Railroad.
269 John Sandfield Macdonald.

forego his own enjoyment to make a sacrifice, which to him would be great, and heartily co-operate with the hon. President of the council,[270] for the sake of example, and for the purpose of conferring a real benefit on others. (Hear, hear.)

323 EXCERPT FROM DEBATE, 8 SEPTEMBER 1852
[*Toronto* Globe, *16 September 1852*]

Mr. MACKENZIE moved the second reading of his bill to establish Conciliation Courts.

....

Mr PRINCE heaped unmeasured ridicule on the mover and on the bill ... He did not question the versatility of talent of the member for Haldimand, or his great parliamentary experience, but that gentleman had mistaken his vocation when he conceived that he possessed the talent of drafting Acts of Parliament. The gentleman, doubtless, supposed that he was capable of doing anything and everything; and, whenever he rose, invariably reminded him (Mr. P.) of the old song –

> "For cabbaging and sawing,
> "For bleeding or toothdrawing,
> "Dicky Gossip, Dicky Gossip's the man."

324 DIARY, 9 SEPTEMBER 1852

A lovely morning. Cool, moist, and in all respects beautiful. What a charming place is Quebec, and the surrounding Country. Such Scenery I never before beheld! Busy with Lord Elgin & about Quebec. Major Lachlan dined with me, and we afterwards went to The House together. I spoke twice, & I seconded a Bill of Mr. McKenzie's! House adjourned at 10, and I went to tea & to bed.

325 EXCERPT FROM SPEECH, 9 SEPTEMBER 1852
[*Quebec* Morning Chronicle, *10 September 1852*]

He did not think the Sabbath was desecrated by keeping open the Post-office and receiving letters on business, or social intercourse; but what he did consider desecration was the exhibition of vanity in clothes, on the way to church, or the pomp of horses to carry their owners even to the door of the temple of God. He had, after saying his prayers, last Sunday, taken his quiet, tranquil walk and had admired the landscape; but he met there two men shooting, and two others fishing, and this he conceived to be a real desecration of the Sabbath. This was never seen in Upper Canada; but these persons were not Lower Canadians but Englishmen.

---

270 Cameron had been appointed president of the Executive Council on 28 October 1851.

326   EXCERPT FROM SPEECH, 13 SEPTEMBER 1852
[*Quebec* Morning Chronicle, *15 September 1852*]

He concluded by alluding to the petition he had formerly presented in favour of Independence. He would ever defend that, but he denied that he ever favoured annexation, as had been stated in the public prints. He had only been in favour of asking the Queen to consider whether the time had not arrived when Canada should become independent.

327   DIARY, 14 SEPTEMBER 1852

A dull and damp, but a fine morng. Rose early and wrote letters. Exceedingly busy about Town buying things, & preparing to leave tomorrow. Dined at 1/2 past 1, & made some Calls. Went to The House at 3 and remained there 'till 11, & spoke on Mr. Hincks's resolutions about The Clergy *Reserves* & in favor of his measure & their Secularization. Drew Deed bet'n Torrance & Northwood. At home by 1/2 past 11 & in bed by 12.

328   DIARY, 3 NOVEMBER 1852

A dull, damp & very mild morng. As *mild as April!* & this too in Quebec! Busy about Town all the morng & at the public Offices. House met at 3 and I spoke upon 2 occasions. A good deal of business got through. Carried my motion for an adjournm't 'till 14th Feb'y, after a long debate. House adjourned at 12 and I went to bed at 1. A fine night.

329   EXCERPT FROM RAILROAD DEBATE, 3 NOVEMBER 1852
[*Toronto* Globe, *18 November 1852*]

Mr. RIDOUT[271] moved that the House do go into Committee of the Whole on the Toronto and Guelph Railroad bill.

Sir A. MACNAB opposed the motion. It was his duty to combat this bill to the very last, and he would take every opportunity afforded to a member of Parliament to attempt its defeat.

....

Mr. PRINCE ... Then, two questions arose: would the House be justified in preventing a company from making a railroad through one of the most fertile parts of Upper Canada where at present there is no communication? Then, again, looking at the charter of the Great Western Company, could the House

---

271 G.P. Ridout represented Toronto City in the Assembly.

refuse the applicants their charter on the ground that it would militate against the Great Western Railroad? To this he would reply that he could not bring himself to think that under any shape or circumstance, it would militate against the Great Western Railroad, and as it runs through one of the finest counties (Waterloo) in the world, and as it is not to be built at the expense of the Province, but with the money of the applicants themselves, he could see no reason for refusing their desire.

330 DIARY, 4 NOVEMBER 1852

A most beautiful day again. Sat on the Committee on private Bills. Wrote some letters and sent off a large batch of printed Papers. House met at 3 and I answered McKenzie, & spoke upon a Rail-Road question, in opposition to Sir Allan McNab. Could not avoid doing so & voting for The Guelph & Sarnia R. Road. House adjourned at 12 p.m. Home by half past and in bed by one.

331 DIARY, 9 NOVEMBER 1852

A beautifully bright Morng, with considerable Frost. House met at 10. Wrote a great many letters & occupied thereat 'till 2. Then dined & back to The House where I spoke & voted several times. McKenzie as great a *bore* as Ever in talking. He kept The House about nothing for 2 hours. Adjourned at 12 and I went to bed at one. A fine but rather a cold & frosty night.

332 DIARY, 10 NOVEMBER 1852

A very fine day, & a tolerably hard frost. Exceedingly busy at The House all day. Spoke on the "*Supplies*" and commended Hincks much, and defied Opposition to form another Ministry if these men went out. At 1/2 p. 1 The Govr. Genl. summoned us to The Council Chamber where he gave his assent to about 70 bills. The House then afterwards adjourned 'till 14 Feb'y next. Went to bed at 1/2 past 8 fatigued.

333 DIARY, 14 DECEMBER 1852. *The Park Farm*

Rose at 1/2 past 5 a.m. A mild day & *snow* yet on the ground. Did not go to Chatham by The Boat as I intended because I was invited to a public dinner to be given there tomorrow to Geo. Brown Esq're M.P.P. which I wished to avoid. Hunted for Deer all day but found none. Some Tracks. Went to bed at 10. Wonderful to relate, nobody here but Cam Parry & young White.

334 REPORT TO A HOUSE COMMITTEE ON THE COUNTRY
NORTH OF LAKE SUPERIOR
[*Toronto* Daily Leader, *27 September 1853*]

The Park Farm, January 24, 1853

The first point to be considered is, whether the region above Sault Ste. Marie is susceptible of yielding a prosperous commerce, whether its natural advantages are such as to render it possible by public Works, or legislative enactments, to foster or produce a paying trade? My impressions tend to a favorable reply, but I should conceive it imperative, that any consideration relative to the establishment of such a trade on Lake Superior, should have a reference to the vast country now thrown open for settlements on the South Shore, where success in mining operations is leading to a large influx of population, partly agricultural, and where an immense tract of excellent land in rear of the high and barren range which bears the native silver and copper, affords the means of growing many of the requisites for its increasing thousands.

....

Now, it is almost impossible to conceive that the boundless mineral wealth which continued search seems only to establish on a firmer basis, should be confined to the South Shore of Lake Superior, and its present thriving trade may form no incorrect ground work for a calculation of that which may soon, from the same causes, flow from our own territory.

....

But at the same time that the bosom of the earth offers its varied treasures to the adventurous miners, it is to be regretted that its surface throughout the whole extent of the coast, affords no resting place for an agricultural population. High and barren rocks, scantily clothed with stunted firs or poplar, or covered with grey lichens, often the food of the miserable aborigines, rise from the very verge of the dark green waters and run far inland ...

Nature has not, however, left the future settler in these sterile regions without an equivalent to offer in exchange for the many articles he may require. The clear waters of the lake are his harvest field, and from these he must gather his yearly crop. White fish, trout, and pickerel, of the finest description, abound along the shore, and though now forming no source of profit or revenue, might readily be made to do so ...

The lake with its fish, the land with its mines, could well maintain a hardy population, who would form a home market for much of our surplus produce, whilst our shipping would find constant and profitable employment on their new and more northern career.

....

By cutting a canal round Sault Ste. Marie at once, we should secure the carrying trade of the Americans through our own canals to the Atlantic; offer to those who might be inclined to embark on either of the above named pursuits, increased facilities, and consequently increased incentives; and probably accomplish the object of the present inquiries ... Every ton of goods or copper has to be transhipped and conveyed over a rude railroad, about a mile in length, at a very considerable expense to the public and profit to the owners, who strenuously oppose the contemplated improvement! Passengers are frequently detained at the Sault many days by non-arrival of vessels, and the innkeepers look with jealousy on a canal which would carry the rich harvest past their doors.

....

There is one other matter to which I beg leave to refer, and which the *public* consider, and I too consider, of the utmost importance to the well-being and good government of the country, and upon which I desire to have the honor to report to the Committee. It is hardly conceivable that amidst all the population, and business, and prospective advantages which I have endeavored to portray, there is not in these Northern regions (in British territory too) *a single Court of Law* for the prosecution of criminals, or for the redress of grievances, or for the recovery of debts! ... Surely these circumstances prove, (and they are capable of proof,) that a *Judiciary* ought to be established in that remote though rich and splendid region without delay.

The Sault Ste. Marie being a place of general resort, and which *must* be a grand focus of attraction, if not domicile for all the miners and other settlers on Lake Huron and Lake Superior for many years to come, it is apparent, and it admits of no doubt that, in common justice to the Queen's subjects and the people there, *a Court of Record* (be it Queen's Bench, Common Pleas, or a Recorder's Court, a County Court, or a Division Court, or all combined), presided over by a barrister of admitted competent knowledge in the practice and profession of law and equity, ought to be erected there without further delay; ... In conclusion, I beg leave to inform the Committee, that for the substance of the foregoing report I am mainly indebted to J.W. Keating, Esq, of Chatham.

335 EXCERPT FROM EDITORIAL
[*Sandwich* Canada Advertiser, *3 February 1853*]

However much Reformers may hitherto have distrusted the disposition of Colonel Prince to represent them faithfully upon the all-important principles involved in the settlement of the Clergy Reserves question, his votes in the late Parliament must have convinced them that their fears were not well founded, and that Col. Prince has nobly fulfilled the promise he made in his speech at the Hustings, when alluding to this subject. And hence we were much gratified at witnessing the leading reformers of Essex generally in attendance at, and identified with the deliberations of, the friendly demonstration of approbation of the course pursued by Col. Prince, not only upon the point adverted to, but also because he "stood by" and defended the present Reform Ministry of the Government, in their arduous and untiring exertions to advance the internal and commercial interests of Canada, against the crafty, but delusive schemes, and combined efforts, of the unprincipled representative of Kent,[272] and his reckless, bigot allies in political delinquency.

336 Diary, 23 February 1853. *Quebec*

Very mild again today and a wet Snow still Falling. Occupied all the morng in writing letters and with Ch. J. Sir Jas. Stuart on prof[essiona]l business, he being my Client. Went to The House at 3 & referred some Petitions and moved & brought in my *Strychnine* Bill for killing wolves &c. Home to Lamb's[273] by 10 & went to bed at 11. Lowspirited.

337 Report of Speech, 24 February 1853
[*Quebec* Morning Chronicle, *28 February 1853*]

Mr. PRINCE thought this not unreasonable,[274] and comparing the position of the poor in Upper Canada with that of the poor in Lower Canada, he saw that the poor in the city of Quebec were provided for in a way which ought to make Protestants blush. Where was the law in Western Canada by which the beggar was taken up and protected from the winter's blast? Scarcely any one applied to the Municipal or County Councils without being told that there was no law for their relief. It was not desirable, in his opinion, to invest large quantities of real estate in these corporations; but in England there were numerous grants of land to support the poor, and within proper limits there was no objection to them.

338 Excerpts from Breach of Privilege Debate, 1 March 1853
[*Quebec* Morning Chronicle, *4 March 1853*]

Col. PRINCE called the attention of the House to a complaint of an article in a newspaper, which he considered to be a gross breach of privilege. It was possible he was mistaken in thinking this was the case; but he thought it not very probable. On this occasion he should not talk about the liberty of the press; that was appreciated by no one more than himself. But when the press was turned into an engine of licentiousness and gloated over insults to members, especially to the first member of the House, it was the duty of the House to protect him and themselves from insult. That all public men were liable to the censures of the press was true; and slavish would be the man who would try to prevent that

---

272 George Brown.
273 This antedates Thomas Lamb's hotel in Toronto, 1855–58.
274 The debate concerned a bill to incorporate La Société des Dames Charitables de la Paroisse de St Etienne de la Malbaie. Prince considered an amendment, to prevent the holding of real estate as a source of revenue, to be not unreasonable. The amendment was defeated.

censure; but remarks upon personal appearance of members of that House ought certainly to be restrained by the severest penalties.

....

Mr H. SMITH was astonished that the House should be detained on a government night about a paragraph of this kind in a public newspaper, which seemed to be a criticism upon the personal appearance of a member.

....

He farther [sic] reminded the House that if this reporter was turned out others could be turned out, too, by any other member. Did not the hon. member himself once kick that poor little man the member for Haldimand out of the library, and did not the hon. member of Huron give him a ticket to go in again.

Mr. PRINCE said it was not true that he had kicked the hon. member for Haldimand out of the Library.

....

He then assured the House that he never condescended to touch Mr. McKenzie; but he was indignant under the peculiar circumstances – not necessary to mention – of that gentleman's presence, at seeing him in the Library, and he directed him to withdraw, which Mr. McKenzie did.

339 DIARY, 2 MARCH 1853

A mild but dull morng and the air appears to be charged with Snow. Busy in the morng at The House. Dined at 1. Then to the House again at 3 where I remained 'till 10, when it soon after adjourned. Spoke several times, & defended Chief Justice Robinson agst an attack of McKenzie's. They say I spoke well. Went to bed at 1.

340 DIARY, 7 MARCH 1853

Another very beautiful day. By no means well. Lowspirited, sick and un-nerved. Busy writing letters in the Library all the morng. Went to The House at 3 and remained there until 1/2 past 12 p.m. when the Debate on the repeal of the Usury Laws ended and the House adjourned. I gave a good dressing to *McKenzie* as usual, because he deserved it. Spoke twice. Went to bed at 2.

341 REPORT OF TEMPERANCE BILL SPEECH, 24 MARCH 1853
[*Quebec* Morning Chronicle, *28 March 1853*]

Mr. PRINCE began by confessing himself to be very fond of the social glass, and of society; but fond as he was of these indulgences, he would cheerfully give them up, if to do so would preserve one poor creature from the evils of drunkenness. He then went into consideration of the bill, which he declared was much superior to the Maine Liquor Law, inasmuch as it was simpler and capable of being understood by the most doltish magistrate in the country. It might be said of him, as it was said of Queen Elizabeth by J. Wesley, she had not much religion about her; but he loved her because she patronized religion in others. He had been accused of bunkum. But bunkum was the Parliamentary vice of young members, who wanted to be again returned, but could not be applicable to Col. John Prince, who had represented Essex for seventeen years, without ever asking for a vote. He believed the bill ought not to come into operation, for eighteen months or two years, in order that those who held heavy stocks of liquors might get rid of them, without loss. – But as to the bill, its advantage could not be doubted. All over the country he saw young men wasting time and ruining themselves in barrooms and taverns. It was the keepers of these places that he wanted to prevent from carrying on their iniquitous traffic.

342 DIARY, 26 APRIL 1853. *London, C.W.*

A very mild day and quite Spring-like. Very much Engaged in writing letters Early & in attending Court on Crown business. Bothered just the same as yesterday by all the vulgar folk (& none are half so vulgar as the "Plebs Canadiensis"). *Perfect Beasts, chewing, spitting & belching* Eternally!! Went to bed at 9, utterly disgusted with men & manners & with the whole place called "this *Canada*".

343 DIARY, 10 MAY 1853

Rose at 5 at which hour we reached Buffalo. A cold, windy, & cheerless morng. My spirits no better. Breakfasted on board of The "Emerald". Then went by The Cars to Lewiston where we dined, & took the S.B. "*Cataract*" to Ogdensburg, en route to Quebec. The Lake "Ontario" comparatively still and pleasant. James Wilkinson[275] with me, going down about The Indian business & Chas Baby's Misconduct therein (re Mears). Turned in at 9 very lowspirited.

344 SPEECH ON ELECTIVE LEGISLATIVE COUNCIL, 13 MAY 1853
[*Quebec* Morning Chronicle, *17 May 1853*]

Mr. PRINCE, while not agreeing with all the details of the resolutions, would nevertheless vote for them, as the best which had been submitted to the House. He proceeded to find fault with the council at length; and declared the country had no confidence in it. Its members were seldom heard from, except when they

---

275 James Hands Wilkinson, of Sandwich, was a son of John Alexander Wilkinson.

rejected the best bills of the assembly. He also complained that they did not attend in their places. He went on to criticize the resolutions in detail, expressing his concurrence in some points, and his disapprobation of others.

345 Excerpt from Debate, 20 May 1853
[*Quebec* Morning Chronicle, *24 May 1853*]

The next item was £15,094 for expenses at Spencer Wood. Mr Mackenzie objected to it, saying that he supposed Col. Prince would like to treat him as he had once treated the poor prisoners at Sandwich who were shot accordingly, in cold blood, or as he had treated himself once, when he had the power to offer him petty insult. But if the hon member could do so, it would not prevent him from doing his duty to his country. The hon. member was the last person who ought to touch on these subjects, considering his great declaration of independence. Nor did he think that Sir Allan wanted any deserter from his own camp to take his part. He (Mr. Mackenzie) did not think he had ever said anything unparliamentary respecting Mr. Prince except it were when he stated that no lawyer who did not support his ministry would get the £300 and £400, which were given to the hon. gentleman for neglecting his duty in the House. He then enlarged upon great expenses incurred in this building of Palaces, and going back to Mr. Prince said he of course knew the hon. member was employed and paid as a lawyer to abuse him, and was quite ready to take all the abuse he could give.

Col. PRINCE looked on Mr. McKenzie as a reptile, and trod on him as such. For the member for Haldimand to talk of these times, when he practiced rebellion, murder and mail robbery, for him to talk of his (Col. Prince's) pocket. It was lucky for him he (Col. Prince) did not catch him, for by the Holy Moses, if he had, the hon. member would never have been seen again on the floor of that house. He (Col. Prince) notwithstanding what he had done, had a heart in his bosom; but the hon. member with a heart of lapstone could not feel for those whose deaths he had caused. The first man who was shot accordingly at Sandwich had there said that he owed his death to W.L. McKenzie. The time was terrible, and a terrible example was necessary, and he (Col. Prince) had the moral courage to give it. He wished the hon. member had come over then instead of those five men, and by the Holy Moses he would have speedily sent him to Heaven. He would have given him a soldier's death, and have thus saved the country many thousand pounds. The member for Haldimand was an itinerant mendicant, who earned a fortune by sitting in that House and getting a pound a day, because he could not get a fortune anywhere else. The Queen had approved of his [Prince's] conduct by giving a commission to a son and a fine son: the Duke of Wellington had approved it too. He would therefore, not disgrace himself by noticing the disapproval of the hon. member for Haldimand. He concluded by assuring the member that friendly as he was to independence, if he ever caught him again in the position which he had once been in, he would hang him.

346 REPORT OF SPEECH AT A DINNER TO MALCOLM CAMERON, 22 JULY 1853
[*Detroit* Daily Advertiser]

The Hon. Attorney General[276] was succeeded by Col. Prince, of Sandwich, one of the strongest and most popular men in the Province. His speech was full of eloquence, wit and sound argumentative appeals, and evinced a very high degree of talent. In the course of his remarks he did not hesitate to touch on the increasing friendship and sympathy that seemed to be growing up between the Provinces and the American States, and hinted in the most emphatic manner on the subject of future *annexation*, insinuating that an event of that sort would be attended with the most important consequences to the Provinces, among which he reckoned the fine market which would then be opened to the Canadian girls for energetic Yankee husbands! The Colonel closed with a toast to their American friends, and an invocation of an increasing friendship and sympathy between the Canadas and the United States.

347 DIARY, 31 AUGUST 1853

A dull morng & rain threatens. Drove up to Windsor, & then crossed over to Detroit & Called on Hincks, Hon'ble John Ross,[277] Mr. Jackson M.P.,[278] Mr. Stevenson M.P.,[279] the Civil Engineer & a great many more Rail-Road gentlemen at *The National*. Spent most of the day there. Mr. Hincks & Mr. Ross met a Party at The Park Farm in the Evg, & slept here. We kept it up 'till 2 & then went to bed. A Shower.

348 DIARY, 15 SEPTEMBER 1853

Fog thick. I am any thing but well & feel feverish & Sick. We made the mouth of The River St. Marie at 6 a.m. Obliged to remain in my berth all the way up to The American Village "Sault Ste Marie" where we arrived at 11. Shaved & dressed & went across to The Canadian shore with a Mr. Smith[280] & called on Mr. Wilson[281] *our* Collector. I think The "Soo" a wild & horrid & inhospitable place. Should not like to live there. Turned into my Berth at 7 p.m. very unwell.

276 Lewis Thomas Drummond.
277 Ross, a Reformer, was then the newly appointed attorney general (west). He was married to Robert Baldwin's daughter.
278 The reference is probably to Sir William Jackson, member of the Imperial Parliament for Newcastle under Lyne, 1847–65, and a railroad builder whose work included the Grand Trunk in Canada.
279 Robert Stephenson, an engineer, surveyor, and locomotive builder, represented Whitby in the Imperial Parliament. He built the Victoria Bridge across the St Lawrence River, 1854–59.
280 Elsewhere Prince refers to Smith the Dutchman, S.A. or L.A. Smith, and W. Smith, all at Sault Ste Marie.
281 Joseph Wilson had served as a customs officer at the Soo from his arrival in 1843, and was a sort of one-man local government by default.

349 DIARY, 21 NOVEMBER 1853. *The Park Farm*

Another rainy day. Within doors 'till 10 & then went to Albert's office for an hour or two. Home by 2, and then wrote to Albert and inclosed several letters to him at Toronto. Mrs. F. Hunt supped & slept here. In bed by 10 miserable, M.A. having declared she would not sell this farm which is *daily ruining* us.

350 DIARY, 17 JANUARY 1854

A very fine & bright day and a clear & hard frost. Crow[282] returned home. Breakfasts as late as usual. Occupied all the morng and until 1/2 past 12 in writing letters & arranging Papers &c. At 2 p.m. went to Windsor to meet the Triumphant Cars from Hamilton on the opening of the line all through. A great sight! Crossed over & dined at Detroit by invitation. Upwards of 2500 persons dined at The Depôt. I spoke at some length, but so much noise I could hardly be heard. Had a shake-down at Dibble's.[283]

351 DIARY, 1 APRIL 1854

Albert was very ill last night with Diarrhœa, & M.A. was up with him from 2 a.m. Quite weak. He over-Exerts himself in business, & *must* be quiet or he may have a relapse of his late serious illness. A mild morng after yesterday's rain. Albert did not stir out all day. *Old Barrett* (the assessor) & o[the]rs called & I returned *my Income under £500 pr ann. & My p'sonal property under £500, and my lands the same as last year & in 1852*. Transacted a good deal of business, & went to bed at 10. Miss Brewster[284] still here & Albert better.

352 DIARY, 13 APRIL 1854. *St Thomas*

A very fine day but a hardish Frost & cold. Attended Court at 9 a.m. and was occupied throughout the whole day in trying Prisoners. Drew at these assizes no less than 15 Indictments! Pretty good, for the 1st time the Court ever Sat in this new County of Elgin. Court adjourned over until 1 p.m. tomorrow (it being Good Friday), and Becher[285] promised to attend to my 2 remaining Indictments for me. A very Cold night.

282 This could be John, Robert, or Thomas Crow, Junior, all residents of Kent County.

283 The Biddle House, Detroit, was opened in 1851 by Colonel Orville B. Dibble and his son Charles.

284 Miss Brewster was probably a daughter of Edward Brewster, the proprietor of a farm lot next to that of Arthur Rankin, fronting on the river between Sandwich and Windsor.

285 Henry Corry Rowley Becher was an English-born lawyer and entrepreneur. From 1839 he was registrar of the Surrogate Court, London District.

353 DIARY, 13 JUNE 1854. *Quebec*

A very fine but a broiling hot day. Busy in my room until 10. Then called on Mr. Attorney General Ross, & had a pleasant & Encouraging interview with him. He is an uncommonly nice fellow. Saw a good many friends, MPs from U.C. His Excy Lord Elgin opened The House in state. The Music room makes a good assembly room. House adjourned at 4. William dined with me. I took a walk in the Eveng and went to bed at 10.

354 EXCERPT FROM ALEXANDER CAMERON [286] TO A.N. BUELL [287]
[*AO, A.N. Buell Papers*]

Quebec, June 13, 1854

J.S. McDonald, Prince, Sicotte,[288] D[itt]o Taché, are all displeased with policy of Gov't in holding another session – Prince Complains of management of Crown Lands Dep't; altho he will not say anything about my purchase of Clergy lands.

355 DIARY, 19 JUNE 1854

A fine & warm day. Feverish & not at all well, owing to having drank some *wine* & sitting up late last night. This City life does not suit me at all; and I wish I was living in the Forest away from Even my own race, for I am *never happy*, no not for a day, so help me God! Indeed, I am *always* the reverse! Wrote several letters, one to M.A. among others. Went to The House at 3, and spoke again, & explained to Ministers that they could not legally buy public lands. House adjourned at 1 a.m. In bed by 1/2 p. 2.

356 PRINCE TO LORD RAGLAN
[*Quoted in Prince to the Duke of Newcastle,*[289] *29 August 1854: PAC, R.G. 7, G5, Vol. 38*]

The Park Farm, July 12, 1854

There are many fine young fellows in this Neighborhood who would like to Serve Her Majesty in the present Russian War. If General you think this offer of our services would be acceptable to the Queen, pray tell me so; and if you order me to raise a Battallion [*sic*] of from 500 to 800 men, it shall be done forthwith,

---

286 Probably a Toronto lawyer.
287 Andrew Norton Buell was master in chancery at Toronto.
288 L.V. Sicotte was a member of the Legislative Assembly, representing St Hyacinthe.
289 Henry Pelham Fiennes Pelham Clinton, fifth Duke of Newcastle, was appointed secretary of state for war, 12 June 1854.

as other Regiments have been raised in earlier times, and it shall be composed of men who will do their duty, Men who I undertake shall flinch from nothing. I am well known to Lord Seaton,[290] Sir George Arthur, Genl Wetherall,[291] Col Love,[292] Sir Francis Bond Head and others now at home who are acquainted with the history of Canada for the last Eighteen Years, and I hope I am not unfavourably Known. If my Services are accepted I will venture to ask that my eldest Son Capt. Prince of the 71st now in [sic] duty in Quebec may be honored with the Majority of my New Battallion.

357 DIARY, 15 JULY 1854. *Port Sarnia*

Rose at 7 a.m. Dreadfully hot. Called on Geo. Brown and Hon. M. Cameron. At 12 accompanied the latter to The Hustings, & wound up the Proceedings of the day by speaking to the assembled Multitude in Malcolm's favor & by partly demolishing Brown's speech. All was over by 6 p.m. Then Mr. Hyde & Mr. & Mrs. Cronyn[293] spent the Evening with me. Sat an hour at W.P. Vidal's with some friends and smoked &c., and then back to McAvoy's Hotel & went to bed at 12. A broiling night.

358 DIARY, 23 JULY 1854. *The Park Farm*

Another broiling day! The Heat almost insupportable. Some of The Family went to Church. I am better (thank God) but did not rise 'till 10 a.m. Obliged to write Electioneering letters for Albert, & some other letters also by Mail. Sad & wrongful occupations for this holy day! The Gordons[294] called. Albert & Henry returned home at 9 p.m. Chs. went to Church in the Eveng. A little Rain which, with the Gordons, kept M.A. at home.

359 DIARY, 24 JULY 1854

A broiling day. I am any thing but well. Rose at 5 & wrote some letters, then went up to Windsor intending to go on to Sombra to vote for Malcolm Cameron, but while crossing over Dougall (who was going to vote for Brown) *paired off with me*, and after staying an hour or 2 at Hutton's & drinking some Porter, I

---

290 Sir John Colborne, Baron Seaton, was lieutenant governor of Upper Canada, 1829–36, commander in chief in 1837 and 1838, and very briefly governor in chief of British North America in 1839.

291 Sir George Augustus Wetherall, who had served as a colonel in Canada during the Rebellion, was deputy adjutant general in Canada, 1843–50.

292 Colonel Sir James Frederick Love commanded a movable column of the 52nd Light Infantry in Lower Canada in 1838–39. In 1854 he was governor of Jersey, in the English Channel.

293 This is probably Thomas Cronyn, collector of customs at Rondeau in 1851.

294 Alexander Gordon was Windsor stationmaster on the Great Western.

returned home, where I remained (not well) & went to bed at 9. Albert down the lake Canvassing, with his friends.

360 DIARY, 27 JULY 1854. *Morpeth*

Rose Early & called on The Zimmermans.[295] Not very well on account of the intense heat. Walked there & back. Then went to the Polling Place at *Ridgetown* (a pretty village) & argued there on behalf of Waddell.[296] Met Geo. Brown, M.P.P. for Kent, there. Back to Sheldon's[297] by 6 p.m. Made some Calls and sat an hour with Mr. Duck.[298] Weather oppressively hot. News that Albert will be defeated *in Essex*.

((Albert lost his Election!))

361 DIARY, 31 JULY 1854. *The Park Farm*

Heat almost insupportable. Still very weak and unwell. Did not rise before 2 pm. Wrote several letters, but was greatly fatigued in doing so. *Lolled* about the House & Premises all the Eveng Scarcely able to support ones-self. *Such heat* was never before known in the Memory of Man! Poor Jos. B. Parent[299] died.

((A great day in Sandwich. Rankin duly declared Elected. Bands, Coaches, &c. parading the Streets &c. Such Vain Costs & expences!))

362 EXCERPT FROM PRINCE TO THE COMMISSIONER OF CROWN LANDS[300]
[*AO, R.G. 1, A-1-6, Vol. 31*]

The Park Farm, August 22, 1854

A few days ago I addressed a letter to the Provincial Secretary[301] accompanied by a Memorial to H.E. The Governor General shewing to H.E. that your agent here held the following offices, viz, *Gaoler, Deputy Sheriff, Crown Land agent*, & Clerk to the *Township Council* of Sandwich.

I assure you that he does not perform any one of the duties of Either of these offices *properly*, as I am informed and believe; and, Moreover, he is a violent &

---

295 This probably refers to Samuel Zimmerman, a contractor who built parts of the Great Western Railroad.

296 John Waddell was sheriff of Kent County.

297 William Sheldon's hotel, named after Lord Morpeth, gave the former village of Howard its present name.

298 George Duck was reeve of Howard Township and warden of Kent County.

299 Parent was a Sandwich innkeeper.

300 A.N. Morin.

301 P.J.O. Chauveau, a French-Canadian member of the legislative Assembly for Quebec County, was elected in 1844.

active *political partizan*, & wastes his time in Politics whereas he ought to Employ himself in his local Duties.

I, therefore, beg leave to suggest to you the Propriety of putting him to his Election as to whether he will give up the Crown Land agency or retain it; and if the latter, on terms of abandoning his office of Gaoler &c &c. Only fancy, honest yeomen being compelled to go to a *Common Gaol* to have their Land business transacted! and I am informed that Evidence of the *grossest partiality* on the part of Moynahan can be adduced in favor of *Roman Catholic Irish Against Protestants*, & people differing with him in "political opinions", (so called), who apply to him for lands!!

I hope you will send him a Copy of this letter, & try him upon it here.

363 G.C. MUNDAY TO PRINCE
[PAC, R.G. 7, G5, Vol. 38]

War Department, September 23, 1854

I am directed by the Duke of NewCastle to acknowledge the receipt of Your letter of the 29th ulto conveying the offer of Your Services in raising in Canada a Corps of from 500 to 800 Men for Service in the War with Russia, and I am to acquaint you in reply that as 3 Regiments have been ordered to be withdrawn from Canada and it is expected that a Militia will be raised for the defence of the Province, His Grace does not consider that it would be fair to encourage such a drain upon the fighting portion of the Population as that which you propose without the formal recommendation of the Colonial Authorities but I am at the same time to State that His Grace highly appreciates the loyalty and Zeal which influence you in making the Offer Conveyed in your letter and entertains no doubt that the Sympathy of the Canadian people in all that Concerns the interests and struggles of the Mother Country would ensure the success of your plan if it were Considered expedient to adopt it.

364 PRINCE TO A.N. MORIN
[AO, R.G. 1, A-1-6, Vol. 31]

The Park Farm, October 7, 1854

I see by the Papers that, as moved for by Mr. McKenzie, A copy of my Lease of The "Point aux Pins" (Rond' Eau Point usually called) is before The House. The lease was originally granted by the Govt preceding the last (when, I think, Mr. John A McDonald was Crown Land Commissioner) and it was renewed by the last Govt. when Dr. Rolph held that office. I don't at all regret that Mr. McKenzie carried his motion, but I think The House might have rejected it by informing him that all he wanted to know upon the subject he could get by an application to the Provincial Registrar in whose office the Lease is duly recorded; and only fancy what trouble & what Sacrifice of the public time must necessarily arise, if Members are to Call for Patents &c. &c. at their free will and pleasure. Besides, it has been perfectly notorious, for two years past, that I held this property under The Crown, and it may be fairly asked of Mr. McKenzie why he did not make his Motion *while I was a Member of The House*, and where I could, in person, have replied to his remarks.

If any debate comes up, I shall be much obliged to you to inform the House (as the fact is) that the property in question has been wild & unenclosed for centuries, and that when I leased it from The Crown, the *Cedar*, and *Pine*, and other Trees were nearly all cut down and stolen from off the Premises – that I have, during my tenancy, protected them, according to the terms of my Lease – that I have inclosed the "Point" by running a good fence from the waters of The Rond' Eau to those of Lake Erie – that I have, at *much Expence*, tried to develope [sic] the *supposed fishery* there, but failed, the Coast being unfit for nets, & no fish frequenting it, worth Catching – that the land is Even unfit for raising valuable Stock on, being for the Most part, too Sandy, and for the rest too Marshy & swampy to be good for any thing but shooting & hunting over – and that if Mr. McKenzie will just pay me what I have expended there, he is Most welcome to my Lease, and the Premises, and Every part thereof.

I shall be much obliged to you to submit this Letter to your & my friends in The House and Especially to Mr. Hincks.

365 DIARY, 27 OCTOBER 1854

Another mild & lovely May-Day. Rose Early and went up to Windsor & to Partridge's on business. A dreadfull [sic] accident occurred on the G.W. Railway this morng at 4 a.m. near Baptiste Creek on the Plains. *50 persons killed*! and about 20 wounded, so that many, it is feared, will die! The Express Cars ran into a gravel Train & crushed themselves & the Train too. A Horrible Scene. A heartrending Scene. Home by 12, and then walked over the Farm with Miss Murray.[302] In the afternoon I drove her down to Petite Côte. Back to dinner by 6, and talked with her 'till nine, when I went to bed.

366 DIARY, 16 NOVEMBER 1854

The same as yesterday. In Court all day, and 'till late at night. *Remonstrated in open Court agst The Grand Jury (for Essex) reflecting, in their general Presentment upon the Great Wn. Railway Co. for the recent accident in Kent.* Dined at 8. House full of Company. In bed by 1/2 p. 10.

365 DIARY, 17 NOVEMBER 1854

Another cold & raw day. On opening The Court *Chief Justice McCaulay*[303]

---

302 The Honorable Amelia Murray was the author of *Letters From the United States, Cuba, and Canada*, published in 1856.

303 Sir James Buchanan Macaulay had been chief justice of the Court of Common Pleas since 1849.

alluded to the Course I pursued yesterday towards *The Grand Jury*, & gave me a *whipping* for it, to which I replied at some length, and the Business of the Court proceeded. I was Engaged in several Civil & criminal Cases & was generally successful. Mr. Becher left us for his Home at London.

368   Editorial Comment
[*Windsor* Herald, *13 January 1855*]

A report has been current for some time past that the Member for this county, ARTHUR RANKIN, ESQ., has tendered his services to the Imperial Government in the shape of an offer to raise a Regiment of Canadian volunteers to proceed to the seat of War.

....

We have also much pleasure in directing attention to a communication which we received from Mr. Albert Prince, inclosing the copy of a correspondence between Col. Prince, the late loyal Member for this county, and the authorities of the Home Goverment, from which it will appear that a similar offer was made some time since by that gentleman ... The latter proposition, too, was made after a frightful amount of bloodshed and the most serious disasters had occurred in the East, and when it is too probable that assistance will be gladly accepted from any quarter, while the former, praiseworthy as it was, was made at a time when the allied armies were flushed with confidence of anticipated success, and when there existed not the same demand upon our sympathies as at present.

369   Prince to the Duke of Newcastle
[*PAC, R.G. 7, G5, Vol. 38*]

The Park Farm, January 24, 1855

It is impossible to notice the progress of our Arms in the Crimea without entertaining a strong conviction that Her Majestys Forces there and elsewhere stand in need of reenforcements.

I was duly honored with Your Graces letter of the 23rd of September last, through Colonel Mundy but considering what has since occurred at the Seat of War I now take the liberty of renewing the offer of my Services, which I had the honor of submitting to Your Grace about three months ago.

370   Diary, 30 January 1855

Another fine day but Snow deeper than Ever. Occupied in Town all this morng with Lalonge, Fox & Dr. Guischard[304] on the same bus's. as I was yesterday. Dined again at Hennell's.[305] At 3 p.m. I attended a public meeting at

---
304 These were clients. Dr Daniel Guischard was coroner at Windsor in 1866.
305 William Hennell was proprietor of the Hennell House, Sandwich.

the Court House convened in behalf of *The Patriotic fund* for our army in The Crimea, & spoke at some length & moved some resolutions, & carried them. Home by 7 & went to bed at 11.

371 Diary, 12 February 1855

A snowy, dull, wintry, gloomy and very unpleasant day. Did not stir out of doors, but was occupied with persons on business and in cleaning up & oiling my guns, fishing Tackle &c. &c. all day long, and also in writing letters and in preparing to start for Chatham on *Chancery* & other business tomorrow. Mailed a good many letters & among others one to Sir Allan N. Macnab about The Northern Judgeship, & went to bed at 1/2 past 10 tired and lowspirited.
((Wrote McNab & Christie.))

372 Excerpt from 'Fair Play' to the Editor of the Windsor *Herald*
[*Windsor* Herald, *24 February 1855*]

It is not my purpose to occupy your time with a discussion upon the relative claims of Col. P. and Mr. R. to the merit of originating the patriotic offer which was submitted to the imperial government, because I am certain the public will agree with me in thinking it a matter of very small importance; but I must, through your journal, Mr. Editor, call attention to the Quebec Chronicle's claim of "distinguished service," &c., in behalf of Col. Prince, and put it to the public whether that paper is not more redundant of "Bunkum" than the Mercury[306] in his laudations of Mr. Rankin. Where are Col. Prince's claims to distinction for public service? He certainly was not present at the Battle of Windsor, where Mr. Rankin's humanity was no less conspicuous than his gallantry, since he narrowly escaped the bayonets of his own men when trying to save the life of the poor devil from whose hands he had seized the patriot flag, and who was crying for mercy; nor was he at the capture of the schooner Anne, nor at [the] Point Pelee fight; but, Mr. Editor, I do not mean to insinuate that the Colonel would not have done distinguished service had he been there.

373 The War Department to Prince, 16 March 1855
[*PAC, R.G. 7, G5, Vol. 38*]

I am directed by Lord Panmure[307] to acknowledge the receipt of Your letter of the 24th January last renewing the Offer of Your Services in raising a body of from 500 to 800 Men for Service during the present War, and I am to acquaint you in reply that Her Majesty's Government have recently had under their

---
306 The Sandwich *Western Mercury*.
307 Fox Maule, second Baron Panmure, was secretary for war.

consideration the question of raising a body of volunteers in Canada for a limited period of Active Service, and the Governor of Canada has been instructed after consultation with the Lieutenant General Commanding the Troops to report what are the views which he entertains as to the practicability of the Scheme, and as to the best means of Carrying it into effect.

Lord Panmure would therefore suggest to you to place yourself in Communication with Sir Edmund Head[308] on the subject of your offer.

374 DIARY, 24 MARCH 1855

An extremely Cold day, and as hard a frost last night & this morng & all day long as we have had this winter. Indeed, winter appears to have come again! What a climate!! Yesterday it was spring-like. Walked to Windsor & transacted business there. The same afterwards at Detroit, and walked home in the Eveng to tea by 7 o'clock. Bella returned from Detroit. I am vexed & harassed & disappointed at the dishonest conduct of The *Government* in refusing me (contrary to their promise) the Huron Judgeship.

375 EXCERPT FROM HEAD TO LORD RUSSELL[309]
Confidential
[*PAC, R.G. 7, G12, Vol. 66*]

Quebec, April 27, 1855

Sir George Grey[310] requests me to report on the subjects of the Correspondence with Col. Prince "at my earliest convenience". I proceed accordingly to state that I cannot recommend H.M's Govt to place in Colonel Prince's hands the charge of raising men in the mode proposed by him.

I have no personal Knowledge of Col Prince, but I would suggest that before placing confidence in his Exertions, in so important a matter, it would be necessary to enquire fully into that Gentleman's conduct *whilst in command of a body of Militia in 1837 & 1838*. I am not satisfied either at the present time of the Sobriety of his general habits.

376 DIARY, 8 MAY 1855

Any thing but well, & sick at Stomach with Palpitation of the Heart. A very cold & comfortless day again today. More like November than May! What a horrible climate & country for an Englishman to come to! Oh, how I do detest it! Within doors all day, & the House is as cold & comfortless as in November. Not

---

308 Sir Edmund Walker Head was governor in chief of Canada, 1854–61.
309 Lord John Russell, first Earl Russell, was the colonial secretary from March 1855.
310 Grey was colonial secretary from 10 June 1854, until his successor was appointed in February 1855.

at all well & very lowspirited all day long. Wrote to The Govr. General about the Plan for raising my Battalion. Mr. Sutton[311] called & announced Mr. Gardiner's death. I took medicine & went to bed at 10 pm.

377 SIR EDMUND HEAD TO LORD JOHN RUSSELL
[*PAC, R.G. 7, G12, Vol. 66*]

Quebec, May 12, 1855

I have the honor to enclose certain proposals made by Col. John Prince of Canada West with reference to raising a body of troops in Canada.

I would wish your Lordship to refer in the first instance to a despatch of April 27th Confidential with regard to the terms now proposed by Colonel Prince. I think the bounty which he suggests (£10) is more than is usually given & it will be for the Military Authorities to say how far such a difference might create difficulties.

I could not conscientiously recommend that Colonel Prince should command the Corps and that his son should be as a matter of course its Major under his father.

378 DIARY, 9 JUNE 1855

A very warm, damp and growing day. Busy at home all the morng in writing letters &c. &c. Then went into Town & got my letters & Papers, among others 1 from William and one *from Albert announcing his intended Marriage to Lizzy!*[312] Much distressed at it, as I fear it will end in his Ruin. He says he is to be married in *August*, and this is the first intimation I have had of it!! Returned home by 4 p.m. Spent the Evening most unhappy and uncomfortable in my mind, and went to bed at 10 perfectly wretched!

379 PRINCE TO THE ADJUTANT GENERAL OF MILITIA[313]
[*PAC, R.G. 9, I, CI, Vol. 126*]

The Park Farm, July 30, 1855

I am a stranger to you, as well as to His Excellency The Governor General, but not to His "Council", nor to your Deputy, Lt Col. McDonell, who Knows all about me. But, permit me to say, I am the *first person in* Canada, who, (twelve months ago), offered to raise a Battalion in U.C. for The Crimea Service. There appears to be but little hope of my offer being accepted by The War Department "at Home". It would gratify me to be placed at the head of the *Ninth* Military District in U. Canada, where I have resided for Twenty Two Years, and where I commanded a Regiment of Sedentary Militia for very many

---

311 This is probably A.B. Sutton, a Windsor merchant who was a nephew of Gardiner.
312 The former wife of Frank Hunt.
313 Colonel G.F. de Rottenburg was appointed adjutant general of militia 1 July 1855.

Years, and also a "Contingent" Battalion of my own raising which (they say) did good service then in 1837 and 8, and effectually stopped all Marauders from The U. States from Ever afterwards polluting our Soil. And this the Americans now admit, and approve of *now*, as heartily as they *then* condemned my decisive conduct.

I take the liberty of asking you to promote my views, and of mentioning my name to The Governor General, and also to Enquire of Lt Col. McDonell *who I am*, & what my "*Antecedents*" have been.

I have written to him by this mail upon the Subject. I will merely add that I still hold the rank of "*Colonel*" of Militia in Upper Canada.

380 Diary, 16 August 1855

A very fine Harvesting Day. Busy at home until 11 a.m. writing, & with Col. Lansing[314] about the Coal Mines of Michigan. Then at 12 I attended a very large *public* meeting at The Court House convened to consider whether Essex sho'd take £50,000 Cy. of Stock in the *Southern Rail-road*. Rankin spoke much & so did I & Mr. Woodbridge, & I demolished Rankin Nicely, & carried the measure against his views by about 200 to Six!! He was much Enraged. Then I went up to Windsor and saw Col. Lansing & o[the]rs on business, & returned home with Bampton[315] & went to bed at 10.

381 Excerpt from Report of Southern Railway Meeting, 16 August 1855
[*Windsor* Herald, *1 September 1855*]

Being thus called upon, Mr. Prince rose and spoke at some length. First, he began by expressing his disappointment at the smallness of the meeting. He, however, was not surprised, since he had always (during his long experience) observed, with regret, and often with disgust, that the people of this part of the county generally, but more particularly the inhabitants of this township, were lamentably backward, indeed far inferior to the people of any other part of the Province, in point of intelligence and knowledge of those things which most concerned their own interest. He would, however, proceed to speak to them, farmer as he was, and in his own plain way, and endeavor to make them comprehend the question which they were assembled here to decide. He next briefly reviewed the conduct of Mr. Rankin as the Member for the county, declared that he had read his speeches in Parliament, and did not admire them, and, in fact, there was nothing in them; and as to his receiving credit for obtaining the charter for the Southern Railway, it was ridiculous; there was no difficulty whatever to overcome – no one was opposed to it, it was passed as a

---

314 The reference is probably to E.A. Lansing, a Detroit insurance agent and alderman.
315 William Bampton was a Windsor tavernkeeper.

matter of course, and therefore no particular credit was due to Mr. Rankin for anything he had done in the matter. He warned the people not to sanction the By-Law. He (Mr. P.) was in favour of the Southern Railway – he wished this to be understood; but he was totally opposed to the county's taking any stock whatever in the company – let those who wanted the road find the money wherewith to build it. If we take this £50,000 of stock, we shall be taxed to raise the money "two hundred thousand dollars," and never see a farthing of it back again; and where will the money go? Why into the hands of a set of speculators, adventurers, and land sharks, and into the pockets of Mr. Scott, the Engineer, who was dismissed from the service of the Great Western Railway.[316]

382 PRINCE TO THE EDITOR OF THE WINDSOR *Herald*
[*Windsor* Herald, *8 September 1855*]

The Park Farm, September 6, 1855

My attention has been directed to the partial, garbled, incorrect, and untrue report, in your last issue, of the proceedings which took place in Sandwich Court House, on the 16th ultimo, respecting the "Southern Railway," so called ... I did not "assail" Mr. Scott, as "Our Member" hath it. I opposed Mr. Scott's scheme of BRIDGING OR TUNNELING the mighty river Detroit! and I had every right to oppose it in any terms I pleased, whether Mr. Scott was there or not. He, like "Our Member," is a great promoter of that Utopian scheme I ridiculed.

383 DIARY, 14 NOVEMBER 1855

A slight frost and a beautiful day. Much like May! Very busily engaged in my office all day long. M.A. & Bell went over to Detroit on Henry's and other business. Wrote a long letter to Mr. O'Reilly[317] about rail-way m[atte]rs, and also a "Private" note to him in reply to his very Explanatory letter to me about the *Solicitorship* to the G.W.R. Co., *all confidential*. He is a *good fellow*, & an honourable Man. M.A. returned by 5 p.m. I walked about the Premises a little, but found nothing to interest me. At home all the Evg and went to bed at 10 p.m.

384 DIARY, 26 NOVEMBER 1855

A slight rain this morng & very mild, tho' it got warmer towards noon. *Nailed*, as usual, to my desk all day long in writing letters and in seeing People on professional business. Tom *McKee & Ward* from Amherstbg, & *Emery*

---

316 William Scott arrived at Sandwich from Ireland in 1853, and was in charge of the construction of the great Western between London and Windsor. On 16 January 1855, he pledged his time and best energies to Arthur Rankin's Southern Railway scheme, and by 3 March he was 'late Engineer on the Great Western Railway.'

317 Miles O'Reilly, a Hamilton lawyer, was solicitor for the Great Western.

called on business.[318] Intended to go out Deer shooting, but, as usual prevented by people calling about business of little or no importance. That's how my life is spent. A dreadful fracas between myself & my "amiable" [illegible] wife This Eveng, in which she accused me before the children, Charles & Bell, of having *cheated* them out of Banwell's[319] money. Went to bed, of Course, perfectly wretched. She is not worthy to be *spoken to again* by me as a husband or friend!

385   Diary, 8 December 1855

A wet & steady rainy morng. Disturbed at *1/2 p. 1* by their return [Mary Ann, Arabella and Henry] from Detroit & slept very little afterwards. My mind much hurt & discomposed & made miserable by *the family's misbehaviour towards me*. Menzies from Detroit called, & I settled his a/c with me. In my office, solitary & miserable, all day long and was it not for the *Crime* against *my Maker* I declare to *Him* I would *commit Suicide*, so wretched, so miserable am I!! and leave my thoughtless, useless, & ungrateful family to their Fate. God help them, say I! I read 'till 10 p.m., and then I went to bed as usual, miserable.

386   Diary, 21 January 1856

Another bitter day, with a hard frost & very Cold. Not much better, and I have a cold and Cough into the bargain. Much harassed, not only with the Pains about me, which betoken an Illness coming on, but also vexed & somewhat alarmed at reports about a serious quarrel which has occurred between Albert & that bag-of-wind Rankin. Went to bed at 9 in Pain, and at 11 got an anonymous letter that they were to meet in hostile array tomorrow. Had *both arrested*.

387   Excerpt from Prince to the Editor of the Sandwich *Canada Oak*
[*Windsor* Herald, *25 January 1856*]

I am a true prophet. The "agency of the Government" hath, indeed, transfigured military rights into political expediency. It has perpetrated a "Job" at the expense of men – of tried and well-proved officers.

Mr. Arthur Rankin has been appointed to command the ninth Military District of Upper Canada! Start not at the name, Mr. Rankin (I beg his pardon, I should say "Colonel" Rankin, now) did good service on this Frontier in 1838 and 9. He was a subaltern in one of the then incorporated battalions of Militia, and I strove hard to get him promoted to a company (as my letters to the

---

318 Clients. Joseph Ward was a butcher.
319 Henry Banwell, of Sandwich Township, had bought Prince's 'Back Farm,' about three miles from The Park Farm.

Adjutant General of that day[320] abundantly show), but, much to my chagrin, I strove without success. THAT, I am credibly informed, was the commencement of his miltary career, and, with the disbanding of the regiment in 1839, a cadet, and after that he ceased to hold any commission in the service.

388 PRINCE TO THE EDITOR OF THE WINDSOR *Herald*
[*Windsor* Herald, *29 February 1856*]

The Park Farm, February 27, 1856

It is now a matter of record that no sooner were the [Essex County] Council informed of the intention of the Executive to remove Mr. Baby from his office, than they "Memorialized" the Governor General in his behalf, and upon these grounds, "That Mr. Baby is a man enjoying a wide-spread popularity throughout this county," and "that they (the Council) have the fullest confidence in the integrity of purpose of Mr. Baby." ...

It has been perfectly notorious, for years past, to all practitioners of the Law who have sent their writs and proceedings to Mr. W.D. Baby to be executed, that he regularly and systematically neglected their business and his duties as Sheriff, SCARCELY EVER ANSWERING A LETTER, and proving himself to be utterly unfit and incapable for the office, and inadequate to its responsibilities.

....

Let the Councils attend to their legitimate duties, and properly attend to them, and they will command respect ...

P.S. I have heard that a report is being circulated by the Friends (?) of the late Sheriff that the Executive has offered to reinstate him in office. I pronounce the report to be utterly false and without a shadow of truth or foundation, and to be a gross scandal upon the Governor General.

389 PRINCE TO GEORGE BROWN
[*PAC, M.G. 24, B40, Vol. 2*]

The Park Farm, March 6, 1856

I cannot refrain from writing a few lines to congratulate you upon the Course you have taken to protect yourself against the infamous conduct of that *Coxcomb*, Attorney General McDonald, towards you, and to bring him to condign censure & disgrace. As *a Briton*, I am proud to witness your manly Conduct, and that you so stoutly resisted the tenders of some puny legislators to give way. Every one of the charges brought by him against you are, in point of law, gross *slanders*; and I have no doubt that a Jury would mulct him in heavy Damages, because his language, (tho' uttered where it was, and upon the occasion it was,) *cannot be called privileged*. It was gross, wilful, false, & *Malicious* Slander; and I trust The Committee will do you Justice. I think they

---

320 Colonel Richard Bullock.

will, & I am glad that my friend John Wilson is one of them. You have acquitted yourself *admirably* in the matter. Go on, and The Country will sustain you; and McDonald could not promote your Popularity more than by taking the Course he has.

390 DIARY, 16 APRIL 1856. *Chatham*

A fine day. Rose Early and got into Court by 9 a.m. My leg does not heal or recover from occasional Pains & twitchings so rapidly as I could wish it to do. In and out of Court all day. Defended 2 Prisoners for felony but they were both found guilty. It is difficult to get the better of Crown Testimony. 'Tis generally so clear against the unfortunate Prisoner. Mr Becher transacted The Crown business. What infamous injustice the attorney General and the Government perpetrate against me in not employing me (an old Q.C. & Crown officer) to do all the Crown business, as usual! But such is the treatment all "true men" receive from the "Powers that be" in this horrid Country Called "*Canada*". Curse it & Every thing belonging to it say I!

391 DIARY, 23 APRIL 1856. *Sandwich*

A fine day. Rose Early – not very well & unnerved & lowspirited. Mr Becher conducted the Crown business for the Government. I was in and out of Court all day and had my fair share of business to transact. Home by 8 p.m. *W. Baby* & I shook hands and made friends at Teakles Inn & *I & Mike Fox*[321] & *Windle Wigle*[322] went & Called on Mrs. W.D. Baby & sat 1/2 an hour there. Home & in bed by 10 fatigued.

392 DIARY, 23 JUNE 1856. *Toronto*

A beautiful day. Bright & fine with a delightful air, and growing weather. My health improving daily. Rose Early and ate a tolerable breakfast. Then about the City a good deal and transacted business. Called on H.E. The Govr. General. *I don't like him.* He is a crusty & by no means an Educated or clever man in my opinion. Octy & I went to The House & remained there 'till past 12. A great many of my friends & M.P.P.s there. Back to Inglis's[323] by 1 pm.

393 DIARY, 22 JULY 1856

A broiling day, and rain again much wanted. Busy in Sandwich all day nearly on Magisterial and other business. Dined at Hennell's. Folks very busy in

---

321 For a time Michael Fox kept an inn in Gosfield Township.
322 Wendel S. Wigle, also of Gosfield Township, was a peddler.
323 Russell Inglis was proprietor of the Wellington Hotel, Church and Wellington Streets, Toronto.

preparing for my offering myself to be elected as Member of the Legislative Council for Essex and Kent under the New Law. Drank rather too much beer, people were so numerous and so pressing around me. Went to bed at 12.

394 Diary, 26 July 1856

Another very Sultry day, and I think it will rain before nightfall Tho' I should like to get my clover in before rain comes. But Providence must order all things – &, no doubt, will do so, for the best always. Busy 'till 1; Then went into Town & met a large Party of friends at Dobson's[324] who presented me with a Requisition to become a Candidate for the Seat in the Legislative Council under the new Law. *I assented*. Query have I done right or have I not again sadly involved myself in pecuniary loss and in trouble & anxiety? I fear the latter. Afterwards went by The Stage to Windsor, & home by 8 and went to bed at 10 fatigued, hot & lowspirited.

((Re-Entered Politics again. I fear I have done wrong.))

395 Excerpt from Editorial Comment
[*Windsor* Herald, *1 August 1856*]

Col. Prince has become a candidate for the Representation of the Western Division in the Legislative Council at the solicitation of 675 of the electors of Essex. The requisition was presented to him on Saturday last, at Sandwich, signed by the above number of voters, and returns had not yet been received from three of the townships, which would have increased the number of requisitionists materially. Should other candidates enter the field, the Colonel is certain of having a very large majority in Essex, and it is believed that he will stand as good a chance in Kent as any other man who may enter the arena. But Colonel Prince cannot please all. Three or four newspapers at a distance present a hostile front, refraining, at the same time, from stating the grounds on which their opposition rests. We have decided to support him in the ensuing election, not because we approve of all his political acts, but because we believe him to be one of the best men that could be sent to the Legislative Council ...

396 Report of a Meeting at Maidstone Cross,[325] 2 August 1856
[*Windsor* Herald, *8 August 1856*]

Mr. RANKIN then came forward and stated that, as he had been instrumental in producing the law which had rendered the Legislative Council elective, he conceived it to be his duty to make all the provisions of the Act widely known ...

---

324 Cyrus Dobson's Western Hotel stood near the Essex County Courthouse.
325 The present Village of Maidstone.

His duty to his constituents had dictated to him his proceeding in the present instance, and if they conceived that he (Mr. Rankin) was a fit person to represent them in the Legislative Council, he was prepared to undertake the duties of that important office.

. . . .

Mr. Prince made a few observations, but as the rain was falling heavily at the time, no chance existed for taking notes. The following is perhaps a near representation of what was said: Mr. Rankin had read the Act of Parliament to the meeting in order that they might fully understand it. Did Mr. Rankin himself know its provisions perfectly as far as his own position might be affected? There was evidently a wish for elevation, but was that gentleman prepared to resign his seat in the Legislative Assembly? Is it to gratify ambition that he will now relinquish his seat in the Assembly – a seat which he gained by my resignation? If this is his object I will contest the point against him. A requisition has been presented to me, numerously signed, – Mr. Rankin has solicited support – I have requested no one to favor me with their influence; I come forward because I have been requested to do so; ambition for the office has no place in my views, but if elected, I am ready to undertake its responsibilities.

397 DIARY, 9 AUGUST 1856

Left by The Cars from Windsor at 11 to attend a Great County Meeting at Chatham in Kent as to an elective Leg. Council. Stopt At Mason's Hotel. Addressed the meeting at great length at the Court room over the Town Hall, over The Market Place. The *Majority* was, decidedly, in my favor. Hon. Mr. Boulton,[326] Mr. Rankin & I spoke. Mr. *Woodbridge* & Isaac *Askew*[327] accompanied me, and the latter returned home with me. Both addressed the meeting, and we were all *well received*, and I do consider my Election for Essex & Kent as all but certain. Returned to Hennell's by 10, and took some Supper & went to bed at about 1/2 past 11 p.m.

398 REPORT OF CHATHAM MEETING, 9 AUGUST 1856
[*Windsor* Herald, *15 August 1856*]

During his speech [Col. Prince] denounced the Ministry, and attempted to show that Lawyers were better qualified to fill seats in our Legislative Halls, than any other class in the community. He expressed himself opposed to Separate Schools, and tho' he was opposed to a member being tied down with pledges, he was willing to give one or two, but he believed he would act honest and independent, as he was not corrupt enough to be a good politician. He

---

326 Henry John Boulton was attorney general of Upper Canada, 1829–33. He represented Norfolk in the Assembly, as a Reform member, 1848–51.
327 Isaac Askew was an Amherstburg mason.

would also pledge himself, that if he was returned, and [if] his course in the House did not meet with the approval of his constituents, he would resign on a respectable requisition being presented to him requesting him to do so.

. . . .

H.J. Boulton, Esq., being called to speak, said he was not a candidate ...

A. Rankin, Esq., followed. He also professed himself not to be a candidate ...

James Dougall, Esq., of Windsor, being called for, presented himself. He also was no candidate, but if he were called out he would run, if not, he would vote for Col. Prince.

399 DIARY, 22 AUGUST 1856. *Blenheim*

Rose at 6 a.m. with a Head-ache – the result of last Evening's rollicking, speaking, and drinking. Wrote a long letter to Enoch Stevens[328] about Mrs. Dixies[329] Cases &c: and another to The Govr. General (thro his Secy Mr. Pennefather) not to appoint Mr. Jno. Mercer (Sheriff and a Partizan) Returning Officer at the Coming Election. Then Jno. Sheldon[330] drove me to Morpeth which place I reached at 10 a.m. Wrote several letters. Went down Talbot Street[331] for 3 or 4 hours with Mr Bissell[332] to Geo Baily's at Orford, and called on several friends in returning. At 6 p.m. I addressed a large body of the Electors at The Town Hall in Morpeth very *Successfully*, and spoke for an hour or two. Then at 9 about 15 supped with me, and I went to bed at about 2 a.m. fatigued & rather feverish.

400 'AN ESSEX ELECTOR' TO THE EDITOR OF THE WINDSOR *Herald*
[*Windsor* Herald, *22 August 1856*]

As only one candidate is yet in the field for representing the Western Division in the Legislative Council, namely, Col. Prince, it affords matter for surprise that such strong feelings of opposition should be manifested against that gentleman by a minute clique in Chatham, seeing that the Planet, which heads the opposition, says that there are many better men than the Colonel; if so, why are they not induced to come forward?

. . . .

I believe that if Colonel Prince could invariably have controlled his temper, and treated the Press with that graceful sycophancy which many candidates for

---

328 Enoch Stevens was a native of Darlington Township, Durham County. In 1854 he moved to Harwich Township, in Kent, where he bought 800 acres.
329 The widow of W.A. Dixie, an Amherstburg attorney.
330 John B. Sheldon was an innkeeper in Blenheim.
331 The Talbot Road West (present Highway 3) was often simply called The Street.
332 Bissell was a partner in the development of mail and stage routes radiating from Chatham.

popular favor know how to exhibit, he might have escaped a thousand groundless calumnies, and also have evaded the publication of a few well-founded truths which have circulated to his disadvantage.

. . . .

The Editor of the Planet founds his present hostility to Prince on the fact that he has been stigmatized by that gentleman as "a blackguard, a coward, and a ruffian." I have no wish to excuse the use of such terms; but, if they were used, I think it is probable that they were merited.

. . . .

I have just read the remarks contained in Monday's edition of the Planet, and I find that Mr. Dougall, who was nominated at the Kent Convention, is characterized as an Annexationist and a Doughface. I am not aware that Mr. Dougall has on any occasion said anything derogatory to the Editor of that Journal; but if he should now do so, after this provocation, the Planet will exhibit its refined feelings and classical acquirements by pointing out what share Billingsgate had in the education of the candidate. This refined Editor, who is so guarded and chaste in his language, styles the two candidates at present before the public as "Doughface" and "Dogface!"

401 DIARY, 1 SEPTEMBER 1856

Another fine day just like Yesterday. Rose at 7 quite well, thank God! Intended to go home, but notices were published that Rankin was to hold a meeting at The Town Hall this Evening and so I remained at Chatham. About town all day long & saw a great number of persons upon business and Electioneering Matters. In the Evening I attended Rankin's large meeting and I addressed the Electors at much length, and he came out and avowed himself to be a Candidate for a Seat in the legislative Council. He made but "a poor fist" of it. At 12 the meeting separated and I went to bed. Sent Dr. Guischard to Windsor & Sandwich.

402 DIARY, 18 SEPTEMBER 1856. *The Park Farm*

A beautiful Morng & some rain fell but not Enough of it. Extremely busy at home all the morning. Lisle (the colored man) Called, after having canvassed the *black Folk*, who, he says, are favorable to my Cause. Wrote several letters and sent off many Papers &c. about Election Matters. In the Evening drove up to Windsor about divers things & Called on S.S. McDonell. Returned by The Stage which took me *direct* home, & I went to bed at 11 fatigued.

403 DIARY, 4 OCTOBER 1856. *Near Chatham*

A beautiful day & quite warm. Just like May! How very changeable is this climate! Foott invited Mr. Ronalds,[333] Monck[334] & Dr. Cross[335] to breakfast with us. At 12 we left Thornberry Cottage & arrived at The Court House at 1. Then, Mercer the returning officer opened the *nomination* for a Leg. Councillor. Mr. Ronalds proposed me & Mr. Boismier[336] seconded the Proposal, and Rankin & Dougall were proposed and Seconded by their friends. The *"Shew of hands"* declared by Mercer to be in favor of Rankin. They say he acted *partially*; But I hope not. After the proceedings of the day closed, my friends accompanied me to The Station House where we Embarked on board The Cars and (thank God!) reached home in safety & found all well, but rather *chagrined* because, it will give Rankin & his crew a *temporary Triumph*. Went to bed at 12 very much fatigued.

404 REPORT OF PRINCE'S NOMINATION SPEECH, 4 OCTOBER 1856
[Sandwich Maple Leaf, *9 October 1856]*

"It is remarkable," said he, "that not one of my opponents has, from the commencement of this contest brought forward the subject of internal improvements in these counties. It is remarkable that they have never suggested the vast and feasible project of a ship canal from the Cheneille ecarte[337] to the Thames, and from thence to the Two Creeks on Lake Erie, thereby at an expense of not more than half a million, connecting the waters of Lake Erie and St. Clair, securing to us the entire command of these and the great Lakes above, and draining and thereby rendering invaluable thousands and tens of thousands of acres which now consists of marsh and swamps."

Then he touched upon the Southern Railroad, which he had always supported and meant still to support, and told that he himself was for some time President of the Niagara and Detroit Rivers Railroad, which ran over nearly the same line of country as is proposed for the Southern, but the charter was lost because capital sufficient to build the road could not be raised; and he had the pleasure to announce that within the last 10 minutes he had received a telegraphic despatch that Messrs. Buchanan[338] and Harris[339] had arrived by the "Africa," from England, and that the Southern Railway was safe! (Cheers.)

....

The Council ought not to be a partizan body – they should be an independent

---

333 Henry Ronalds, of Raleigh Plains, became a member of Kent County Council in 1857.

334 Richard Monck was a holder from time to time of various public offices in Kent County.

335 Later (1869–79) Dr T. Cross was inspector of inland revenue for Kent and Lambton.

336 Edward Boismier, of Sandwich, after a brief career as a militia captain during the Rebellion, held various public offices. In 1858 he was the first mayor of the newly incorporated Town of Sandwich.

337 A channel near the mouth of the St Clair River was known as the *Chenail Ecarté*, the out-of-the-way channel.

338 Isaac Buchanan of Hamilton, a former member of the Legislative Assembly for Toronto, was one of Canada West's leading merchants. He had extensive investments in railways, particularly in the Canada Southern.

339 Robert W. Harris was president of the Great Western Railway.

body and not wedded to any party or to any particular line of politics; and it is because they ought to be independent and non-political that they are or ought to be respected by the people. Moreover, the councillor, or a member of the Lower House, who takes his seat as one bound to his constituents by pledges, is not a free man – he is not the people's representative but he is their delegate, their deputy, their slave, – he is not permitted to exercise his own abilities and judgement, or to act with independence – in fact he is a mere *automaton*, and in my opinion, wholly unfit to do justice to the people or to carry out any of the great principles of our representative system." (Cheers)

405 DIARY, 13 OCTOBER 1856. *The Park Farm*

A beautiful day, but rather raw & Cold – good weather, nevertheless, for the voters to travel up to The Poll. In Town, and at The Polling place (the old Barracks) by 9. The voters came up well & briskly in my behalf. I kept at the *head of The Poll* all day long in Sandwich, and was far ahead when it closed. In [and] about town all the Evening, and much fatigued. The Town full of people, of Course, and drinking & all sorts of rollicking swearing & quarrelling as usual upon such occasions. I went to bed at 11 *well tired*, & must be at it again tomorrow.

406 DIARY, 14 OCTOBER 1856

A fine morng. Polling going on briskly. I attended it at Sandwich 'till 10. Then I went up to Windsor & attended it there for an hour. Then took the Cars to Chatham and attended the Polling there for 3 hours. Headed the Poll there by about 21! Town full, and rollicking &c. &c. going on as in Sandwich. I think there is no doubt whatever that I have been Elected! But the State of the several Polls will, tomorrow, "tell the Tale". Put up at Mason's Commercial hotel and went to bed at 11 pm, very much fatigued and none the better for having drank so much as I am obliged to do in these *Exciting* Electioneering Times.

407 DIARY, 15 OCTOBER 1856

In and about town all day long. *The Assizes* Commenced, but I could not attend Court Except for about an hour so Exciting is the Election. The return of The Polls shew my "election sure". Would to God it were as certain hereafter! My Majority will be about 500!! But Dougall has stood well in Kent. Called on the Judge Ch. Justice Draper. Kept up late in talking & Carousing with people, and I went to bed at about 12 p.m. tired.

408 DIARY, 22 OCTOBER 1856

A very smoky morng, & it turned out a very *hot* day – much the same as [it] is in July! It must surely be the Indian Summer. Rose at 8, and at 12 Foott drove Mr. Ronalds and me to Chatham Court House where I was duly *declared* by Sheriff Mercer (the returning officer) the *Elected Legislative Councillor* for the Western Division. Then, I addressed a large concourse of The Electors at considerable length, who had assembled in The Court House, & thanked them, and was heard & received with much applause. Dougall & Rankin also spoke to them at some length. Rankin, as usual, shewed himself a *fool*! Then the meeting separated peaceably, & I spent the remainder of the day in making Calls with Foott, who drove me to Mr. Delmage's[340] & Mr. Ronalds's & he supped with me (as did Monck also) and I went to bed at 11. This has certainly been a *proud* day for me, in being elevated to so high a position as I am by the Electors of these 2 large Counties, and I hope I shall do my duty, and be always alive to the great responsibility thus Cast upon me. Thank God! the Contest is over.

409 DIARY, 7 FEBRUARY 1857

Rose at 7 from my hard Couch, & walked home by 1/2 past 8. As usual found the servants just up, and no work done. Went into Sandwich by 11 to see Mr. Scott the C. Engineer and others upon Business, & I went to his House, & conferred with him as to the contemplated Pier at Pigeon Bay & the Bridge over The River *Detroit*. Occupied in town in waiting for the mail & my letters & seeing & Conversing with persons about all sorts of things. Home by 9 pm. Raining heavily & slushy & dirty. Supped off a Scrap of cold meat & went to bed at 11 miserable as usual.

410 DIARY, 26 FEBRUARY 1857. *Toronto*

A cold, but a bright & bracing day, and a hard black Frost. Occupied in unpacking and in my room all the morning. At 1 p.m. dined & Captain Mackintosh[341] dined with me. Went to The opening of the Parliament and took "Octy" with me. Met there "Tatty" (Mrs. Henry Boulton) and Bell. The L. Chamber crowded to Excess. I was introduced by The Honble Mr. Gordon[342] & Honble Mr. Perry[343] as a L. Councillor, and then I took the oath of Allegiance and subscribed the same, & became one of the Legislative Council. His Excellency The Govr. Genl. then read his Speech in English & French, and retired with the usual Pomp & ceremonies. We then had prayers read by Rev'd Dr. Adamson, the Chaplain to The Council,[344] and Entered upon a few formal

---

340 John F. Delmage was a lawyer, editor of the Chatham *Journal* and secretary of the Chatham and Camden Plank Road Company.

341 This is probably Donald Macintosh, who was a Kingston steamboat captain in 1857.

342 James Gordon, a popular and successful merchant of Amherstburg, was elected to the Legislative Assembly, representing Kent, in 1820. In 1828 he was first appointed to the Legislative Council. He retired to Toronto about 1846.

343 Ebenezer Perry was appointed to the Legislative Council in 1855.

344 William Agar Adamson was chaplain and librarian of the Legislative Council from 1841.

m[atte]rs of business in which I gave a Couple of notices; and the Council adjourned 'till Monday, then to Consider His Ex's Speech. Octy & I took tea at The Wellington & aftwds went up to Lamb's where we sat for 2 hours, and I went to bed at 11 very very lowspirited.

411 Excerpt from Speech, 2 March 1857
[*Sandwich and Amherstburg* Maple Leaf, *5 March 1857*]

The Honorable JOHN PRINCE rose and said that he had been rather unexpectedly requested to second the address, but had much pleasure in doing so. He thanked the old members for the graceful and courteous manner in which they had been received and welcomed in the Council. He hoped and believed that the introduction of the new members would never be a cause of dissatisfaction and regret; as to the address he approved of it generally. With respect to the improvements in the Ottawa and St. Maurice regions, that was all right; but he would have liked to have seen some allusion to the western country. There were improvements, necessary there; and perhaps more imperatively required there than in older and more settled parts of the country which were mentioned.

412 Report of Speech, 4 March 1857
[*Sandwich and Amherstburg* Maple Leaf, *12 March 1857*]

Eighteen petitions were presented, among them – Hon. COL. PRINCE brought up one from the inhabitants of the counties of Essex and Kent, in reference to the construction of a canal from the waters of lake Huron to the harbour of Rondeau; and upon this very important subject he (Col. Prince) was desirous of offering a few observations. It was a well known fact that the Rondeau harbour, in the county of Kent, is one of the finest harbours on the continent, if properly taken care of, and its natural advantages had been improved some years ago, and a light-house had been constructed. Subsequently, however, the natural advantages of this harbour had been lost sight of by the government preceding the present one. The light-house was unfortunately burnt down, since which no other had been erected; and the very circumstances of such light-house being laid down in the charts had proved a snare to mariners, as they naturally looked out for such light after it had been once published; and it could not be too strongly urged upon the government how very important it was to the shipping and other interests that such light-house should be at once restored.

413 Excerpt from Legislative Council Bill Speech, 9 March 1857
[CPD]

Now it was well known that in the district which he represented – the western district – a gentleman who is a Member of the Lower House, at the late election for the candidates for the Upper House, thought proper to continue his suit for the representation of that District in the Legislative Council, he might almost say until the day of the declaration. Surely the gentleman he alluded to ought to have resigned his seat in the other House before becoming a candidate for the Legislative Council. Well, as is well known, the gentleman in question was defeated; but not until there was an enormous expenditure of money, and not before the country had been effectually disturbed ... Another very material point in the proposed Bill provided that no person in the employment of the Government as a paid servant should have any right to interfere at an election, that is, no Sheriffs, or Commissioners of Crown Lands, or registration or retiring [returning?] officers should be allowed to follow a certain candidate through the country, to the prejudice of the other, or in any way interfere in the election beyond the extent of their duty. The power the Sheriff [w]ields on such occasions was so well known that comment was needless.

414 Diary, 11 March 1857

A very beautiful morning. Rose at 7 and was occupied 'till 1 p.m. very busy in my bed-room in writing letters &c. &c., shut up. Gave Ingles notice that I sho'd leave for private lodgings on *Friday Evening next*, and pd. him $40 on a/c of his *enormous* Bill. At 3 went to the House & brought up the Sandwich Petition for incorporating that Town. Spoke upon Mr. De Blaquière's[345] motion as to the Speaker's right to vote in Committees. The motion was lost by a Majority of 7. I think it ought to have carried, & that the Speaker ought only to give a Casting vote, *in the Chair*. House adjourned at 6.15, and I spent some time with Larwill.[346] and then at the Wellington for an hour, and went to bed at 10, thinking of home &c. &c.

415 Excerpt from Seat of Government Debate, 12 March 1857
[CPD]

Hon. Col. PRINCE thought there was no doubt in the world that the resolutions would pass. All over the world the permanent system of Government was what was followed, and he had always looked on the transitive mode of Government as a nuisance. Indeed so much was he persuaded that it was ridiculous that he had thought that a large steam palace constructed to float up and down the St. Lawrence, for the accommodation of the legislators would be preferable, or at

---

345 Peter Boyle De Blaquière was a member of the Legislative Council from 1839.
346 Edwin Larwill, member of the Legislative Assembly for Kent in 1857, had previously represented Raleigh Township on the Western District Council, 1848–49. In 1858 he was appointed registrar for Kent County.

least as good an idea as the system at present in vogue; the steam palace would have this advantage over the present system – it would not cost some £30,000 for its removal every four years.

416 Excerpt from Report of Insolvent Debtors' Act Speech, 18 March 1857
[CPD]

No doubt many rogues had been whitewashed through the operations of this law; but were there no instances where honest men had been relieved? And was it not better that a rogue should occasionally escape free, than that an honest trader should be allowed to be harrassed by his creditor, day after day and year after year, in consequence of his having adopted a course, which, after he had taken it with the sanction of the Legislature, they proposed to render illegal? He would not wish to speak disrespectfully of the merchants of Western Canada, but he would say that in his opinion much of the blame of the state of things which led to the act of last session was attributable to them. By the course which they had adopted of giving young men goods to a large amount of credit, they induced many tradesmen to embark in the business who knew no more of it, than he did. How often did hon. gentlemen see that persons who might have earned an honorable livelihood at farming, had been ruined by the temptation of becoming a merchant. The young merchant was trusted to a large extent no doubt, in the most generous and kindly manner. He got long credit, but at an enormous price. The result was, that, in many instances, these young persons failed – from various causes.

417 Report of Debate, 16 April 1857
[CPD]

Hon. Col. PRINCE rose to move the second reading of the bill to provide for the election of the Speaker of the Legislative council.

. . . .

He did not think that the voting for this motion would injure the state: or that it advanced the state toward Republicanism. He for one admired the American institutions, and there was a great deal to copy from in them. If he had his way, he would nail the Government like a bad shilling to a tradesman's desk. He would not have a man at the head of the Board of Works who knew nothing about public works; or a man at the head of the Crown Lands Department who knew no more about his business than the man in the moon. He regretted to find that the opposition he received came from the members of the Government; at the same time he would ask who supported him, and seconded him? (Hon. Mr. DeBlaquiere) One who was never heard but to be admired, the descendant of a noble family, and his opinion was that the House ought to have right to elect their own speaker.

418 Diary, 24 April 1857

A very fine day. Busy up to 11 a.m. in writing letters. Then dressed and went to a concert (Thalberg's)[347] at The City Hall, with Mrs. Becher, & her daughter, & "Tatty" Boulton & Miss Boulton. Left after the 1st part was over. Then went to The House at 3 and passed the Sandwich Incorporation Bill & got through other business, & spoke several times on divers subjects. Mrs. Becher & her daughter, & Bell, there for an hour. Called at The Boultons after The Concert. Spent the Eveng at Sword's[348] & Smith's[349] & saw Henry & Octy there, and Octy & I got home to our lodgings by 11 and went to bed. Quite a cold night.

419 Excerpt from Report of Court of Chancery Speech, 24 April 1857
[CPD]

The object of the motion was to take the first step towards abolishing the Court of Chancery, which has become an incubus on the country. The hon. gentleman had assisted to form the bill under which the court had been founded; he had seen its working, and was well acquainted with its evils; he therefore hoped that some legal gentleman would second him.

420 Diary, 15 May 1857

Another very wet morng. Went to The House by 10 & sat on another Committee. Otherwise much occupied with Woodbridge & Wilkinson about The Sandwich Incorporation Bill. Rankin proves himself to be a great Scoundrel in that matter as well as in Every thing Else that he is concerned in! Home by 12 to lunch. Then to The House in the Eveng by 3 and attended it till 6 when it adjourned. Wrote several letters, & afterwards took Woodbridge to the Leg. Assembly where we remained for a Considerable time. Drank tea in the Saloon & after taking a few glasses with friends went to bed at 11.

421 Excerpts from Report of Grand Trunk Railroad Debate, 19 May 1857
[CPD]

Hon. Mr. VANKOUGHNET[350] moved the second reading of the bill (from

---

347 Sigismond Thalberg was a German pianist and composer, resident in England.

348 P. Swords had formerly operated hotels in Quebec and Montreal. In 1854 he moved to Toronto, to the site of the present Royal York hotel.

349 Edwin Smith's restaurant was at 52 King Street West, opposite Lamb's Hotel, Toronto.

350 Philip Michael Matthew Scott Vankoughnet, a brilliant equity lawyer, elected a Conservative member of the Legislative Council for the Rideau Division in 1856, was chosen president of the Executive Council and minister of agriculture. He had an important role in Canadian expansion into the Northwest.

the Legislative Assembly) to facilitate the completion of the Grand Trunk Railroad ...

Hon. Colonel PRINCE rose and seconded the motion. He said that he felt much pleasure in seconding the bill, though at the same time that pleasure was not unmixed with lamentation. That the Province would suffer by the bill he had no doubt, but then he felt sure that the suffering would be of short duration, and that the loss to be sustained would not be great. He doubted, indeed, if the Grand Trunk scheme would ever succeed to the extent that had been predicted; but at the same time, he thought that the great undertaking must eventually pay for the money that had been invested in it. The great mistake that had been made in the Grand Trunk enterprise was that it had been commenced at the wrong end. It should have been begun at the western, not the eastern extremity of the Province; if such had been done the result would have been different to day from what it was.

422 REPORT OF FISHING ACT SPEECH, 22 MAY 1857
[CPD]

Hon. Col. PRINCE was glad that a bill was about to be introduced to protect the fish.

....

There was no skill requisite to use the spear; it was a dastardly and mean thing to hold a torch at the surface of the water, waiting until the fish came up, and then to stick it with a fork. It was as bad to do this as to follow the practice of some individuals who go out into the woods with hounds, and hunt the poor deer into the lake, and then take a canoe, paddle over to the poor animal, and shoot it. No sportsman would follow such discreditable sport. He himself would rather take the deer on the bound, or cast fly at the fish he wished to capture. However, there was another clause of the bill he had an objection to, and that was the clause that none but her Majesty['s subjects?] should be allowed to fish in the Province. It would be extremely inconvenient; such as for the people living at the other side of the narrow Windsor River.[351]

423 EXCERPTS FROM DEBATE, 26 MAY 1857
[*Sandwich and Amherstburg* Maple Leaf, *4 June 1857*]

Bill to provide for the separation for judicial purposes of Cities and Counties in Upper Canada. (Hon. Mr. Simpson.[352])

....

Hon. Col. PRINCE said he should like to be informed what necessity there was for the Bill? ... He deprecated such a course, and it would be most unwise to

---

351 The Detroit River.

352 John Simpson, a general merchant and banker, was elected to the Legislative Council for the Queen's Division as a Liberal in 1856. He became a senator in 1867.

break up the established institutions of this country merely for the sake of creating additional patronage.

....

Hon. Mr. MURNEY again moved the second reading of the Bill for the Incorporation of the Village of Windsor.

The Hon. Col. PRINCE agreed to the motion, and told the House that he never intended to offer any objection to the Bill, but that he wished to arrest its progress for two or three days in order to obtain an object he had in view which had been accomplished ... namely, the incorporation of Sandwich (which had been unnecessarily and improperly opposed).

424 SPEECH ON THE DISMISSAL OF MAGISTRATES, 9 JUNE 1857
[*Sandwich and Amherstburg* Maple Leaf, *16 July 1857*]

In December 1855 it appears that a Sheriff from the United States applied to these Magistrates Messrs. Wilkinson and Woodbridge and claimed that a colored man named Lanton, should be given over to his custody on a charge then substantiated on his affidavit, and on other evidence shewing, that he had stolen horses from Ohio ... It had been erroneously stated that Lanton was a fugitive slave seeking the protection of British soil, and considerable sympathy had been elicited, owing to the misrepresentation of an individual from whom one had a right to expect better things but who for the present should be nameless; and the magistrates, the people of Sandwich and of Essex had been libelled by a high functionary who said they entertained an antipathy to the colored race; whereas the contrary was the fact, as that race had been treated with invariable kindness by the people of Essex, a kindness which (Col. P.) was sorry to say had in many cases been met with the basest ingratitude, the recipients rewarding their benefactors by robbing, pilfering and plunder, and committing other crimes.

....

The gallant Col. then gave a succinct detail of the means which had been employed by a certain party, who should for the present be nameless, to accomplish the dismissal of these Magistrates, and that that individual had cozened the Government most effectually; and had deceived them to gratify his spite and malice.

....

He (Col. P.) would now briefly advert to the libel the government had cast upon the people of Essex, by a statement one of its members had made that these Magistrates and the people of Essex had been actuated by a feeling of hatred and bitterness against the colored and fugitive race, than which a greater libel could not be cast upon men who as he (Col. P.) had stated in the earlier part of the debate had ever treated that race with kindness ... Had the learned Attorney General, before uttering that libel looked at the criminal returns, he would have found that a very large proportion of the convicted for larceny and higher crimes, were colored persons – viewing this – viewing the base return, which had been made for kindness and hospitality shown to them, there certainly was a general feeling abroad, not only in Essex, but elsewhere, that if the Government choose to allow these men to escape into British territory and encourage large settlements of them here, The Crown had better appropriate the Manatoulan Islands to them, as their close proximity to others settling around and among the white inhabitants in the majority of cases was anything but pleasant.

425   PRINCE TO THE EDITOR OF THE TORONTO *Colonist*
[*Sandwich and Amherstburg* Maple Leaf, *9 July 1857*]

Toronto, June 26, 1857

Your valuable paper of yesterday has afforded me a rich treat and not a little fun in the report of an indignation meeting of "the colored citizens" of Toronto, held for the purpose of censuring me ... I admit that one company of blacks did belong to my contingent battalion, but they made the very worst of soldiers, and were, comparatively speaking, unsusceptible of drill or discipline, and were conspicuous for one act only – a stupid sentry shot the son of one of our oldest Colonels, under a mistaken notion that he was hereby doing his duty. But I certainly never did myself the honor of "walking arm in arm" with any of the colored gentlemen of that distinguished corps. Then, as to my election. Few, very few blacks voted for me. *I never canvassed them*, and hence, I supposed they supported as a body, my opponent ...

Then how rich have I become among my "colored clients!" I assert, without fear of contradiction, that I have been the friend – the only friend of our Western "Darkies" for more than twenty years; and amidst difficulties and troubles innumerable, (for they are a litigious race), I have been their adviser, and I never made twenty pounds out of them in that long period! The fact is that the poor creatures had never the ability to pay a lawyer's fee.

It has been my misfortune, and the misfortune of my family to live among those Blacks, (and they have lived *upon us*,) for twenty-four years. I have employed hundreds of them, and, with the exception of one (named Richard Hunter), not one has ever done for us a week's honest labor.

426   EXCERPT FROM PRINCE TO LORD PANMURE
[*Sandwich and Amherstburg* Maple Leaf, *26 November 1857*]

The Park Farm, August 24, 1857

I have the honor to propose to your Lordship that I be permitted to raise a Battalion in Upper Canada for service in INDIA at the present alarming position of affairs there; and I propose to raise it upon the terms mentioned in my letters, which (among others) were, *that I should have the command in person, and that my Son, Captain Prince of the 71st Highland Light Infantry, (now stationed at Malta,) should be the Major.*

427 Excerpts from Prince to Lord Palmerston[353]
[*Sandwich and Amherstburg* Maple Leaf, *26 November 1857*]

The Park Farm, August 31, 1857

The inclosed correspondence will inform your Lordship that I offered my services in 1854, to raise a regiment for the Crimea, and that I now offer to raise one here, for INDIA ... I belong to the party called Loyalists and Liberal Conservatives; but I assure your Lordship that we have had great reason to feel dissatisfied and to feel deeply injured at witnessing among the number of our *Rulers*, men of disloyal and disaffected principles, and some of the chief promoters of Rebellion! I trust, however, that the next general election will "tell a different tale;" though Loyalty, my Lord, has no encouragement in Canada.

428 Excerpt from H.R. Storks to Prince
[*Sandwich and Amherstburg* Maple Leaf, *26 November 1857*]

War Office, September 16, 1857

Lord Panmure desires me, in reply, to convey to you an expression of thanks for the offer of service thus made, which, however, his Lordship is unable to avail himself of.

429 Diary, 8 December 1857

A beautiful day and as mild as May! Very much engaged all the morng in my office in preparing the Deed, Memorial &c. to *Vollans*,[354] & sent same off to Albert. At 12 went into Sandwich, where a large political meeting took place. I interfered but little, and spoke in the Court House as to my position as a Legislative Councillor, and stated that though I was precluded from voting or interfering in the Election (Rankin & McLeod[355] being the Candidates), still my Sympathies were all *with McLeod*. Spent the Evening with McLeod & his friends at Hennell's, and trudged home thro darkness & mud & mire by 11 p.m.

430 Prince to John A. Macdonald
[*PAC, M.G. 26, A1(d), Vol. 336, Pt. 2*]

The Park Farm, January 13, 1858

Don't you feel *astonished*, & more than astonished, at the late Proceedings in this, heretofore, well-conducted County – so far as the recent Election is

---

[353] Henry John Temple, third Viscount Palmerston, was prime minister of Great Britain 1855–58 and 1859–65.
[354] This is probably George Vollans (Vollins, Vollens), a farmer, of Sandwich Township.
[355] John McLeod was an Amherstburg distiller, shipowner, and merchant, and a former member of the Western District Council.

concerned? I am sure you *do*. Certes! I am doing my duty and I will continue to do it, as the only *independent* J.P. in Essex; and I will bring *all offenders* to Justice. If I do *not* perform my part, as I ought to do it, the Commission of the Peace will be deemed a *Mockery*, and the fountain of Justice will be rendered stagnant – and ye Freedom of Election will be "Burked"![356] That shall *not* be, as long as I can hold my reason, and use my pen, and my common, as well as my acquired, Sense. Rely on that.

There is much to do here, but I will do it all; & no *Justice* shall sit with me as a Colleague. They are all (more of less) *Partizans*, and I shall cheerfully invite and incur the whole responsibility of my Conduct.

Your, & our Sheriff,[357] has done *well*, & I shall continue to support him. His late Deputy, Mr Moynahan, has acted dishonestly, and in *direct violation* of the Statute Law. He shall feel the effects of his Misconduct, in due time, & shall meet with "his Reward".

Your letter to McEwan is just what an Attorney General ought to have written to such an officer. All will come right at last; and much, to make it right, depends upon me as a J.P., & *I will do my duty*, firmly.

"Entre nous." Don't believe the Newspapers, *that J. McLeod is in opposition*. He will render your Government far more Service than *Rankin Ever did*. Rely on my word for that. You, & he, & I, are all *liberal Conservatives*. Besides, I know the Course he *Must* & will pursue. Pray Excuse this hurried Scrawl, from yr. friend,

431 EXCERPT FROM AN EDITORIAL
[*Sandwich* Western Mercury, *18 February 1858*]

When Col. Prince assumed the honor and the responsibility of the high position of a Legislative Councillor, we felt that he was equal to the task, and we thought he would be – as his ability, eloquence and experience qualify him – an honor to this County, and one whom, whatever his past errors might have been, would take his stand as an adviser of the Crown, and the advocate of the interests of his constituents, above the influence of local squabbles, or the contemptible jealousies of vulgar cliques. The late election has somewhat shaken our faith, yet we would fain still reason, that circumstances connected with the W. Divis'n election have forced the Col. into positions and associations which as a gentleman, he must abhor, and as the friend and advocate of the honor, rights and interests of the county, he must condemn, and we hope that the future will prove that we have not made a false estimate of the man, which cannot be the case if he so far forgets himself as to descend to the *status* of a *follower* of McLeod and his equally vulgar and unprincipled rabble.

---

356 To burke was to commit murder and sell the corpse, in the fashion of William Burke, a murderer and bodysnatcher who was hanged in Edinburgh for his sensational crimes in 1829.
357 John McEwen was sheriff of Essex, 1856–83.

432 Diary, 7 March 1858. *Toronto*

A fine day and much milder than yesterday, but still Cold. Two fires in The City last night. What a place for fires is *this* Canada! Octy went to Church, but I was occupied from 9 a.m. 'till 9 p.m. (I regret to say) in writing letters to England & divers other places, and did not stir out of my room all day! A Most improper Mode of spending The Sabbath, but what Can one do? So heavy is my correspondence &c: and no Clerk! Albert & Jno Waddell Called on me. I went to bed at 10.

((Wrote Honble J. Ross & sent him some letters abt. the *N. Judgeship.*))

433 Diary, 17 April 1858

A very beautiful day & the Sun very bright. Exceedingly busy in my room in writing letters & among my papers 'till 1/2 past 11 am. Then went to meet the Attorney Genl, by appointment, at his Office. The meeting was rather Satisfactory & I am to have his final decision about the *Northern Judgeship*. How difficult these Ministers are to deal with, & how negligent & careless towards their Supporters! Occupied in town for an hour or two – Then wrote letters to William & Charles – not very pleasant ones as to leaving the Park Farm in August or Sept'r next, & the miserable dissensions between *Our* family and *Albert's* which I fear Can never be healed up! Mailed many letters and papers – from The House. In the Eveng Smoked a Cigar by myself & took a glass of Ale at Mrs. Anderson's[358] and went home & to bed by 11 unhappy.

434 Diary, 30 April 1858

A most beautiful Spring day. A Southerly wind & quite warm. Every thing looks green, and things will now grow fast. Busy at the L.C. all the morng, & in writing letters. Afterwards about town on business. Then at 3 went to The Legislative Council & had one of my bills read a 3rd time and introduced my Bill to alter & amend the *Railway Acts*. Busy for hours afterwards in writing letters, and very much annoyed & bothered with people. Gave notice on behalf of Dr. Rees[359] to The Ministry. *Had an interview with Honbles Messrs Cayley and Vankoughnet* in our Speaker's room, *who promised me the Patronage of Kent* when any thing *turned up, & a little in Essex*. Took Lizzy & Mrs. Sivewright[360] & Mrs. McLeod to The Theatre. Mrs. Becher & Henry & Octy there. Home & in bed by 12 at night.

---

358 Mrs A. Anderson operated the Half Way House, Front Street near John, Toronto.

359 William Rees was medical superintendent of the Provincial Lunatic Asylum until an injury forced his retirement in 1844. Thereafter he repeatedly sought compensation from the government.

360 Perhaps the wife of Captain Andrew Sievewright, of Kingston.

435 DIARY, 14 MAY 1858

A very fine day. Rose Early and none the worse for my Journey Yesterday – tho' I hear some of the folks in town had sad head *aches this morng*. Dont wonder at it considering the quantity of *Champagne* (so called) which they drank! Busy at The *land office* and about town all the morng on business. Back to my lodgings to dinner and then to *The Leg. Assembly* (which sat today though the Leg. C did not) and wrote a good many letters and mailed a good many packets to friends. Home to tea at 6. Then went to The House again – & *saw Atty General McDonald* who solemnly promised me that he would give me the appointment of Judge of the Northern Township immediately on the Close of the present Session. Note that. But I fear a Minister's word is worth but very little. Home & in bed by 1/2 p. 12.

436 DIARY, 20 MAY 1858

A very fine day but chilly and little Sun only. Busy about town & at the Post Office till 10. Then attended The Petty Trespass Act Committee and The Printing Committee 'till 12. Then in The Library for half an hour. Then dined – and went to The Leg. Council at 3 & the Ministers ans'd my question about The Hudson Bay Co's Charter & I brought up 3 Petitions. Afterwards Conducted McLean's Divorce Bill thro' the Council & examined The witnesses therein, & the Bill was ordered for a 3rd reading on tomorrow. Then moved the 2d reading of my bill to abolish the Property qualification of M.P.Ps. Spoke for more than an hour, & quoted Tuffnell's[361] [speech] & Ld Jno Russell. At 6 Debate adjourned till 3 tom'w. The Essex Election debated, & Rankins villainous Petition, signed by that fellow (Joe Mercer[362]) and other Scamps referred to a Select Committee & therefore taken out of the hands of *The House* as it ought to be. Spent an hour in the Saloon with Albert, W.P. Vidal, Stuart & others, and home & in bed by 11. As Cold as Nov'r!!

437 DIARY, 21 MAY 1858

A fine & bright, but still a Cold morng, & by no means Congenial for the time of year. Busy in the Leg. Council and at The Library all the morng & wrote some letters and sent off a great many Papers. Then about town on business &c: for an hour. After dinner went to The Leg. Council and debated my Bills for admitting English attorneys to practice here, and for abolishing M.P.Ps' prop-

---

361 Henry Tufnell, Whig member of the Imperial Parliament, was secretary to the treasury in Lord John Russell's government.

362 Joseph Mercer was a brother of Sheriff John Mercer, of Kent. He was reeve of the newly incorporated Town of Sandwich, 1858, and warden of Essex 1858–59. He died in a railway accident in 1862.

erty qualifications. A long debate, and both bills lost by very large Majorities. Somewhat annoyed at the Council's Illiberality. Spent an hour at E. Smith's, and at Seels's.[363] Then to the Rossin House[364] for an hour. At 9 got back to my Lodgings, and sat an hour with Mrs. Hetherington,[365] and then went to bed tired.

438 DIARY, 28 MAY 1858

A cold and comfortless day, with the wind from the East, & vegetation progresses very slowly. Busy, *Early*, with M.A. & Bell as the latter is leaving town for Home this morng. Called on Doctor *Beaumont*[366] to see Octy who is very weak & ill. His attack of Measles is very violent. Bell & Sep left at 11 a.m. by the Cars for Windsor. At 11 I attended a Select Committee at The Leg. Council in re S.S. McDonell's Petition &c. They refused its Prayer. M.A. all day with us, & now lodges here. Home to dinner at 1, and at 3 I went to the House & introduced the Windsor Assessment Bill. Spoke sharply to VanK. about a *register* Bill which he introduced. I fear I cannot agree much longer with The ministry in their *misconduct*. Home to Tea by 6. Octy some little better, thank God. Wrote to William & sent £10 towards house keeping. Went to bed at 11. Supped in Mrs. H[etherington]'s room.

439 DIARY, 5 JUNE 1858

A very fine day. Busily engaged at my table (in bed room) until 11 am in writing letters &c. Then met Mr. Atty Genl *McDonald* at The Speaker's room when he told me that the new Com[missio]n of the Peace for Essex was in progress, & that Becher would be sent up to The *Sault St Marie*. The House of Assembly sat 'till 4 p.m. upon the Essex controverted Election & examined witnesses, &c: &c: I wrote some letters there & sent off a good many Parliamentary Papers. Damp & showry [sic] towards Evening. Rec'd Comm'n for S.S. McDonell from Mr. Grant Reg'r in Ch[ancer]y. At The Atty Genl's Office in the Evg as to McCormick's & Leggatt's[367] Suits. Home to tea. Then spent the Evening at The Rossin House & also at Edwin Smith's with McLeod & Captn Grant[368] & others from Maidstone & Essex (a great many being down here), & home & in bed by 1 *am*!

---

363 John Henry Seels kept a saloon at 137 King Street West, Toronto.

364 The Rossin was a large Toronto hotel, at King and York Streets.

365 Maria Lapish Hetherington at this time operated a boarding house at 14 James Street, Toronto.

366 William Beaumont practised medicine on Wellington Street near York, Toronto.

367 This is probably Gordon Watts Leggatt, an Amherstburg lawyer.

368 Duncan Grant immigrated from Inverness to Petite Cote about 1830, and relocated to a farm in Maidstone Township in 1834.

440 Diary, 16 June 1858

Another fine morning but unusually Cool (if not cold) for the time of year! Busy all the morning at The Leg. C. and wrote several letters and mailed a good many Plmentary Papers. Home to dinner at 2. Called on Albert. Met Jno McLeod and the Atty General McDonald at The Ho: of Assy about The Essex New Comm'n of J.Ps. and finally settled it as to names &c, and "J.A." promised that S.S. McDonell shall be appointed County Atty in a few days. After dinner went to The L.C. and had an opportunity of saying a few sentences in favor of *Sir F.B. Head* & his former Government here.[369] Home to Tea, and went to The Theatre to Davidge's benefit. Saw "The Bottle Imp[?]" &c performed. Not much amused. Home & in bed by 12.

441 Diary, 23 July 1858

A very beautiful day & warm. Very busy all the morning at The Leg. Council, & sat upon 2 Select Committees, the Great Municipal Bill which we at last agreed upon. Called on J.S. Macdonald at The Rossin House. Then home to dinner at 1 and afterwards went to The Leg. Council and took part in the debate upon Mr. DeBlaquiere's Motion for an Address upon a federal Union of all The British N. American Colonies – which address we lost. The debate lasted until 9 pm; and I spoke severely against "Frenchmen ruling over us", &c &c, and ridiculed the material of which the 100th Regt was composed. At home & in bed by 11.

442 Report of Speech, 30 July 1858
[CPD]

HON. COL. PRINCE ... did not, he said, stand up to discuss politics. But he thought there ought to have been sufficient liberality among the members of the Council to have permitted him yesterday to pay that compliment to the members of the retiring Government which they so highly deserved. He thought he ought to have been permitted to have mentioned something of their virtues and short-comings. But he had been pronounced out of order ... The decision of Her Majesty had been acquiesced in by the country. She, with the advice of her Privy Council, had selected the Seat of Government, and he would say that the Ministry ought not to have resigned on such a vote. They ought to have treated it with contempt, and not resign to leave the business of the country. He did believe that the rage of public opinion concentrated on the ministry would serve only to illuminate and not consume them. (Cheers.)

---

369 In a debate on the transfer of some municipal debentures the phrase 'the principle of monarchy is honour' was quoted in calling for a vice-regal enquiry. Prince noted that the words had first been used by Sir F.B. Head, and took the occasion to deliver a eulogy.

443 DIARY, 7 AUGUST 1858

Another very hot and broiling day. Leg. C. met at 11; and Hon. Mr. Vankoughnet announced the new ministry, and I spoke in favor of them, as did Mr. DeBlaquiere and several other members. House adjourned at 1 till half past 3, and then met again, and The Governor General Came down at 4 and gave his assent to some Bills, and *we cheered him heartily* both on his arrival & departure. The "Grits" did not like it at all. I got home by 10, and went to bed. A very very hot night.

444 DIARY, 24 AUGUST 1858

A fine & warm day. Left London at 1/2 p 7 a.m., with a large Party, From Windsor, Sandwich & Elsewhere for St Thomas, where we arrived at 9, and at 12 held a meeting in The Town Hall to Elect 13 Directors of The New *N & D. Rway Co. Rankin & his Satellites* there, opposing Every thing, & behaved so ill, that they were all Ejected from the Room! McBeth M.P.P.[370] in The Chair. Directors chosen, & *I was Elected Solicitor to The Company*. I spoke at The Meeting in answer to Rankin & his Counsel, Mr. Eccles.[371] Atty Genl McDonald and all of us dined at St Thomas. Speeches made &c: &c: and we returned to London at 8 p.m.

445 DIARY, 25 AUGUST 1858

Another very warm day. Called on Attorney General McDonald, Morton,[372] Larwill & others in the morning. Then at 11 a.m. we embarked on The G.W.R. Cars, and I left them at Paris, and Larwill & I proceeded on to Buffalo, which place we reached safe & sound after an agreeable ride from Paris to Fort Erie over *The Buffalo & Brantford* Railway (a new & admirable road) at 5 pm. Put up at "The American" – a good Hotel. Then at 8 pm I attended (with Mr. Christie M.P.P.[373] Larwill & o'rs) a meeting of *2000 of The* Citizens, and addressed them at great length & was well rec'd. I urged the building of The International Bridge. Mr. Rogers and some few others spoke against it. Senator Wadworth & others for it. The audience was *most* orderly & respectful. Meeting adjourned at 10, & Larwill & I returned to The Hotel, and I was in bed by 11, & being fatigued soon fell asleep, well Satisfied with the Proceedings of yesterday and today.

---

370 George Macbeth, a landowner with railroading and other business interests, was elected to the Legislative Assembly for Elgin West in 1854.

371 Henry Eccles, Q.C., of Eccles, Carrall and Doyle, Toronto.

372 James Morton was a Kingston brewer, distiller, iron founder and locomotive builder.

373 David Christie represented Wentworth in the Assembly from 1852, and Brant East from 1854 until 1858, when he was elected to the Legislative Council from the Erie Division.

446 DIARY, 30 AUGUST 1858. *Toronto*

A damp, drizzling unpleasant day, and occasional heavy Showers toward Eveng. Went to The *Atty General's* by 10 as per his appointment, but, as usual, he never kept it, & I became very much annoyed at his treatment of me in more ways than one. I have lived long enough to know that the *word of a Minister is not worth one* farthing. They are full of deception & duplicity. Busy about town with Larwill, & at the Leg. C. room and wrote Several letters. In the Evening Saw Henry at The Rossin House & at 9 p.m. sent some Cheese by him to William. Afterwards spent an hour with Armour[374] & Tetu[375] drinking ale, & at home & in bed by 12.

447 DIARY, 26 NOVEMBER 1858

Another fine but a raw and Cold day and a hard & black frost. Very busy in & about town all day long, and at Alberts about Hartwick's[376] & other matters as Early as 9 a.m. Had an interview with *Attorney General Macdonald* at his *Lodgings* (he is very weak in health) when he behaved most kindly, and made me a faithful promise that I should have the *Northern Judgeship* next Spring. Nothing Could be more friendly than he was. Busy also at The Crown Land office, but I did not see Van K.[377] Spent an hour at Albert's. Back to my Lodgings by 10, & went to bed.

448 EXCERPT FROM REPORT OF CONFEDERATION
SPEECH, 11 FEBRUARY 1859
[CPD]

Hon. Col. PRINCE ... believed that it was but eight years since that he had taken the liberty to introduce into the other branch of the Legislature a petition to the House praying for an address to Her Majesty that she would be pleased to take measures to consolidate into one state the whole of the British Provinces of North America. That petition had not been received – only sixteen members of the House voting for it. But he had gone one little step further than presenting the petition. (Hear, hear, from Hon. Mr. Moore.[378]) Ah, his hon. friend might

---

374 Possibly this is Andrew H. Armour, a book dealer, stationer, binder, and printer on King Street West.

375 The reference is probably to Sabin Têtu, a clerk in the provincial secretary's office who boarded at the Rossin House.

376 John Hartwick, of Morpeth.

377 Vankoughnet had been appointed minister of crown lands 6 August 1858.

378 Philip Henry Moore, of Missisquoi County, Lower Canada, was appointed to the Legislative Council in 1841. He was a champion of the interests of the Eastern Townships, particularly in regard to obtaining recompense for Rebellion losses, and as to railroading. He ran as an independent Conservative in the federal election at Confederation, but was defeated.

cry "Hear, hear," but he (Col. Prince) defied him or any other member of the House, or any person, to put his finger on one single line that he had ever written, or one single word that he had ever uttered, recommending the annexation of Canada to the United States. But, however, he had said this – and he would, at the risk of being upbraided by mankind, still say – that the time was not far distant when this country would become so large, so prosperous, so independently, thoroughly British at heart, that, with the consent of the Sovereign of Great Britain, these Provinces will become an independent nation – united in kindly feeling with Britain, and like her in power, in wealth, in intelligence and in energy.

449 Diary, 24 February 1859

A slight frost, with a blowing wind, & air cold! What a change from yesterday! Busy at The L.C. Chamber & about town for an hour in the morning. Then lunched. Then to The House in the Evening, and moved several things in The Council. *Rec'd a letter from The Govr. General offering me the Northern Judgeship.* Called on Phillpotts,[379] & Albert & The Beaumonts, & Sat an hour at Albert's. Then spent 2 hours at Edwin Smiths & The House of Assembly & home and in bed by 12.

450 Report of Speech on Carrying Deadly Weapons, 4 March 1859
[CPD]

Hon. Col. PRINCE, as he had intimated yesterday, would to-day introduce a bill to make it penal for persons carryings deadly weapons ... The bowie knife was an importation from a country where that noble science in which he (Col. Prince) notwithstanding his age, delighted, was suppressed. Yes, where the noble science of self-defence was acknowledged, no such thing as the use of the knife was known. He was sorry to see the decline of this science in England, and the consequent introduction of the knife.

451 Diary, 31 March 1859

Rather a sharp Frost last night & this morng. Very busy in and about town as well as in my room and wrote several letters and sent off a great many papers by mail. Called at The Rossin House on Railway bus's with Mr. Smart[380] & others. After lunch went to The Leg: Council and passed my *"Deadly Weapon"* Bill, & it was sent down to the Leg: Assembly where it was rec'd with *acclamation*! & read a 1st & 2d time *without a division*. Home to dinner at 6, and did not go out all the Evening, but read a little & went to bed at 10.

---

379 George A. Philpotts was a Toronto lawyer.
380 W. Lynn Smart, of Woodstock, was secretary of the Niagara & Detroit Rivers Railway.

452 DIARY, 3 MAY 1859

A very fine day, but *Cool*. I feel a little better, but still very weak. This being the day for The Leg. Council to grant or withold The Bill of "*Supply*" I rose at 3 p.m. & dressed, and went to The L.C. against the advice of my wife, my Physicians, & even Mr. Vankoughnet & Sir E.P. Taché.[381] *Spoke & voted in favor of The Bill*, which we Carried by a Majority of only 4! I drank a bottle of Porter in The Speaker's room, & walked home by 9 & went to bed. This was my *last Speech in Parliament as a Legislative Councillor*, and (D.V.) never more will I return to it; for I am thoroughly sick of *public life* and as thoroughly disgusted with *Public men* – in whom I have failed to discover much Truth, honor, Sincerity, or Gratitude! Therefore, Farewell – a long Farewell to *all*!

453 DIARY, 25 MAY 1859. *Sault Ste Marie*

It *rained* and *thundered* & *lightened* again last night, but a fine, mild, & growing morng is this. Wrote to T.A. Hendrick Esq. Com'r of Land office at *Washington* about a farm for Sale near this place, on the Am'n side. At 9 crossed over in Mr. Wilson's large boat & met him, and we tramped until 2 p.m. over *rocks* and through *morasses* and up *hills* & down gullies looking at the land in rear of the Sault on our side, and was much disappointed in the Character of the Soil. There is very *little farming Land*, and they ask unreasonable prices for it. Dined with Wilson, & walked out again in the Evening through swamps &c: but saw not a lot that I could desire to purchase. Returned to Mr. Johnson's[382] in Wilson's Boat by 7 pm, very much fatigued by walking so much and through such desperately bad ground, swamps &c., &c. and after taking some whisky & water &c: went to bed at 9 pm. & soon fell asleep, although so much disappointed with the Land &c: as well as present appearances of The Sault &c. &c. I fear that farming there is out of the question for want of roads, servants &c., and I doubt, therefore, whether it will be worth my while to take the Judgeship. But I shall give much reflection to the Subject before I answer the Govt.

454 DIARY, 2–3 JULY 1859.
Georgian Bay, on board the PLOUGHBOY

We reached "Owen Sound" at 5 this morning, & Vankoughnet and most of us were up and admired the place much. Then at 7 (am) we proceeded on our voyage towards Killarney &c: as usual, en route for The Sault. The Sea a little rough, but not too much so. But, at about 3 p.m. and at a distance of about 15

---

381 Etienne Paschal Taché took his seat for L'Islet, as a Reformer, in 1841. He was appointed to the Legislative Council in 1848. He became a Liberal Conservative after the coalition of 1854, and was co-premier with Macdonald 1856–57. He was knighted in 1858.

382 George or James Johnson (Prince also spelled it Johnston) was a farmer and innkeeper, of Indian ancestry, on the American side.

miles from *Cabot's* head, and not less than 100 miles from Collingwood, the Iron crossbeam of our Engine broke in two, and the fine Steamer was left at the Mercy of the Sea & Waves! Nobody Could hold the smallest Command over her rudder or any other part of her! and there we were drifting gradually towards The Shore, which was one of the Most *dangerous and rocky* in the World! At 4 pm we had manned a boat and Sent her off to Owen Sound for aid, hoping to find The "*Canadian*" S.B. there. We kept on drifting all night Expecting to go ashore among the rocks & breakers Every hour. The *Ladies* behaved Cool and admirably, as indeed, did Every body Else on board. But nothing short of wreck & loss of life stared us in the face. We were miraculously saved by the following event. After drifting towards one of the most rocky, perpendicular and dangerous Shores on Lake Huron, and at *2 o'clock* this morng, just as we discovered rocks 100 feet high and within *20 yards* of our helpless vessel, the 2 Ankers (which had been out for 12 hours, *while we were drifting*) but which never got anchorage once because of the great depth of water, suddenly took hold of a *Ledge of the rock*, in about 30 fathoms, and close upon the shore, and they held the Boat firm! We remained *swinging* at anchor, not knowning but that she might part with her anchors Every minute, and then *Shipwreck* & loss of, probably, *Every Soul on board* (for *Swimming* in such a place would be useless & the swell & surf were very high). We remained there 'till 12, noon, when the swell and wind abated, and a boat was manned, and by degrees Every female and nearly all the passengers went ashore in a small bay about a Mile distant, intending to remain there 'till relief came. *I* never left the unfortunate "Ploughboy" once, as in Case of wreck I thought I co'd be useful, and no use on the *Land* where so many had gone. At 7 p.m. The Canadian hove in sight, and by 11 pm, all got on board, & left the rocks &c.

455 EXCERPT FROM PRINCE TO HENRY RONALDS
[*University of Western Ontario, D.B. Weldon Library, Robertson-Ronalds Papers*]

The Park Farm, July 23, 1859

I avail myself of this opportunity to mention to you that I have fully made up my mind *never* to Enter the Doors of Parliament again.

The trouble, & delays, and anxieties, which the importunities of People from *both sections* of the Province have imposed upon me, by their letters and personal interviews, are more than I can bear; and *I will be the slave of the People no longer*. Nor Can I afford the heavy expences attending it.

It is due to you, my dear Sir, (who took so much and such kind interest in my last Election as to *nominate* me), to announce my intentions to you, in order that you and my other friends may bestir yourselves, and decide upon some Gentleman of *liberal Conservative Principles* to take my place – which place I will *not* resign in favor of any "*Clear Grit*", although nothing shall induce me to appear in The Legislative Council again.

Every year *there* increases my troubles, & anxieties, and ruinous Expences;

and I am bound, at my time of Life, and with my Expensive family & Now limited means, to release myself from the Thraldom of being *"The People's"* Representative; and I have, at last, come to a *resolution* on the Subject which nothing shall induce me to revoke or Cancel.

You will much oblige me by submitting this letter to *Mr. Foott, Mr. Larwill,* and any other friends you please; and I shall be too happy to afford to any *liberal Conservative* who may be nominated by you all, any humble support in my power to afford him.

But I advise you and your friends to *lose no time in proceeding to the work.*

456 DIARY, 1 AUGUST 1859

Another beautiful day. Very busy in my office until 12 at noon. Then I attended the *Negro Celebration* of their Independence, which took place in one of my beautiful Groves & there were present not less than 12 or 1500 persons! I addressed them *twice* by their particular request from the Platform which contained 15 people. All went off peaceably & pleasantly. W.P. Vidal & Mr. Weller[383] & Judge Clarke[384] lunched with us, and many people Called. I went to bed at 10 *hot*. Mr. Dewar[385] called & sat for an hour.

457 DIARY, 17 AUGUST 1859

Another very broiling day. Hamilton is an Exceedingly pretty, but a very hot & a very dusty place. About the City a good deal in the Morning, and attended a meeting of The Directors of The Niagara & Detroit rivers Railway at 5 pm. I regret to say that our Prospects therein are *gloomy Enough*, as I fear Mr. Morton will not be able to Carry out his Contract. Honbles Messrs Foley[386] & Christie attended, and they are at this Royal Hotel with myself. Spent an hour in the Evening with Mr. McCuaig Superintendant of Fisheries in U.C. & drank some good ale with him & Mrs. McC. and his Son & dau'r-in-Law. Nice but very plain People. Then I sat for nearly an hour at the *"Anglo American"* Hotel, hoping to see Mr. Morton there, but was disappointed. The "Monument of injured innocence", Mr. Arthur Rankin there with his Henchman, McClennigan,[387] from Woodstock, "looking out for Squalls" I presume; and a Brace of precious Scoundrels they *do look*! Thank God, The *"Monument"* (*the biggest Rascal of the two*) will not be able to make any thing out of The N.& D.R.Rwy. Sat for an hour in The Bar-room with The Landlord and others, and went to bed at 11.

383 Henry Weller, probably W.H. Weller, a Cobourg lawyer, was a friend of Henry Prince.

384 No judge named Clarke has been found. The title might be an error, or a nickname. Possibly the reference is to G.M. Clark, a law partner of W.H. Weller of Cobourg.

385 The Reverend E.H. Dewar was rector of St John's Church, Sandwich, 1852–59.

386 M.H. Foley, Liberal member of the Assembly for Waterloo North, had served briefly as postmaster general and as a member of the Board of Railway Commissioners.

387 Alexander McClenaghan was publisher of the Woodstock *Times*.

458 DIARY, 23 SEPTEMBER 1859. *The Park Farm*

A dull damp day with occasional Showers. Within doors all day and I feel better than yesterday. Weaver's[388] newly brewed Beer does me good though it is only about 2 weeks old but mild & by no means strong. I was occupied all day in writing & in completing my securities to the Canada Loan Co. for £600! Sat up 'till past 11, & drank a good deal of the Weaver Beer, which gave me *life* & strengthened me. A very damp and wet night, and went to bed at 1/2 p 11 tired. M.A. in bed, but a good deal better thank God.

((Wrote the Atty General about my resignation being postponed &c. &c. till next year.))

459 DIARY, 2 MARCH 1860. *Quebec*

A very damp, rainy, slushy & unpleasant day. At 10 *Salter*[389] & *I* went to The Crown Land Department and had an Interview with Mr. *Vankoughnet*, the Commissioner, and a very satisfactory one it was. He promised Septimus employment at The *Sault St Marie* this year, in conjunction with Salter, & Pr[omise]d *Monck* the Kent agency of Crown lands, and that the Main Street at The "Soo" sho'd be made passable. I afterwards Called on *The Primroses*[390] (an affecting Interview!) and attended The Governor General when he rec'd our address. At 3 pm went to The House, & spoke twice. Back to my Lodgings by 6 p.m. & in bed by 11.

460 DIARY, 20 MARCH 1860

A mild morng and it rained, more or less, all day. I was Engaged writing till 12. Then Called on The Primroses, & sat half an hour with them. They could not go to The Leg. Council on account of the rain. After dinner I went there, & spoke at much length about my *Steam Boat Sail bill*, & *game bill*, and *Rate of Interest Bill*, which latter I withdrew. Home to dinner at 6, and it being a wet Evening, I did not stir out of Doors but went to bed at 1/2 p 9.

461 'COL. PRINCE'S JUDGESHIP'
[*Toronto* Globe, *20 March 1860*]

Mr. Brown incidentally introduced yesterday the subject of Colonel Prince's appointment to the judgeship of Algoma, pointing out the impropriety of the Government raising a member of the Upper House to a seat on the bench and

---

388 John Weaver was a Windsor innkeeper.
389 Albert Pellew Salter, of Sandwich, was a surveyor and land agent.
390 F.W. Primrose, of Quebec, was a bank solicitor and president of the St Andrew's Society. William Prince's fiancée, Louisa Primrose, had just died.

then withdrawing the nomination because they could not elect for his division a successor of their own political stripe. Mr. John A. Macdonald made the characteristic explanation that the office had been offered to Col. Prince and that he had refused it. We have not the least doubt that the ministry did offer the office to Col. Prince, that he accepted it, that he announced the fact to his constituents, that he made all his preparations for removing to the Sault Ste Marie, that he found an Oppositionist would be elected in his place and that he afterwards withdrew his acceptance and sent a refusal, at the instance and request of the administration. The Government no doubt will treat the acceptance as private and the refusal as alone fitted to meet the public eye. But they cannot get rid of the fact that Colonel Prince announced to his constituents that he was about to become judge of Algoma, and desired that they should nominate a successor. Nor will they be able to remove from the public mind the impression that the ministry retain the gallant colonel in his place in the Council, holding the judgeship vacant until they find it possible to elect a successor to their mind. If it is not so, why do they not fill up the office of judge in Algoma?

462 Diary, 28 March 1860

A fine morng. Spent a restless night, owing to the letters rec'd yesterday from the West about *Bullock's* defalcations, I being his surety, with others. Rose at 1/2 p 6, and wrote to Bank with money, and also wrote to Messrs Dougall as to renewing my note on pay'g $100 down. I am very *lowspirited* & unhappy, and am scarcely fit for any thing. Went to the House in the Evening, and had my Mast & Sail Bill read a third time and passed. In the Evening, at about 8 o'clock Mr. John Cameron M.P.P.[391] & I took a drive, outside St Louis Gate & spent an hour with an old friend. Walked back to our Lodgings by 10 & to bed. A cold night & a hard frost.

463 Diary, 23 April 1860

A most beautiful morning. Busy in writing at my desk until 10 a.m. Then to The House and wrote letters and Sent off some Papers, & had an interview with "*John A.*" (Atty Genl of U.C.) who *promised me that if I would remain for a few days after the Prorogation he would give me one Entire day to settle all Matters about The Judgeship and The "Soo"*. Took The Miss Primroses to The Leg. Council where they Saw the ceremony of The *Governor General assenting to 11 bills*. Dined at 6, and at 1/2 past 7 I went to The Cathedral & attended Service there (it being *St. George's* day) and bishop Mountain[392] preached. *The Choir*

---

391 John Cameron, Conservative member of the Assembly for Victoria from 1858, is referred to here. He should not be confused with John Hillyard Cameron.
392 George Jehosaphat Mountain was Anglican bishop of Quebec from 1837 until his death in 1863.

was very good. I then spent half an hour at The "City Restaurant", & home & in bed by 11.

464 DIARY, 26 APRIL 1860

Another beautiful day. Went to The House at 10, and made up & mailed several letters and Packets to Mrs. Partridge & divers other parties. After lunch, went to The House at 3 p.m. and remained there 'till 6, when the House adjourned till 1/2 p 7, when we again met & resumed. I introduced my bill for the division of Sandwich Township, and I spoke in support of *Newton's Patent* for manufacture of Paper from the fibres of wood.[393] Got back to my lodgings at 10 (after spending an hour in the Ass'y) & in bed by 11.

465 DIARY, 25 MAY 1860

A very beautiful day but very windy. At the House for half an hour in the morng. At 12 John McLeod & I had an hour's talk with Att'y Gen'l McDonald and Vankoughnet, and we "fixed" the Commission of The Peace for *Essex*, and I & "John A" went through my Items as to The *Algoma* Matter & things, & Promises were made to me by him which, I *hope*, may be fulfilled. At the House again in the afternoon and mailed a good many letters & Papers. Then about town for an hour & dined at 7. No appetite whatever so uneasy am I in Mind & so depressed in spirits, because I am so embarrassed in Circumstances. Read 'till 9 and then went to bed Miserable.

466 DIARY, 26 MAY 1860

Rose at 1/2 p 6 rather feverish, and after a somewhat restless night. Lowspirited as usual. Occupied in my room 'till 10. Then Mr. William Bell[394] Called, & drove me out to his place, and I paid visits to his brother David & wife, also to The *Sericoles*[?] (the latter not at home) & to Maingy,[395] & lunched at Wm Bell's. He drove me in, & called on The Att'y Gen'l McDonald, & rec'd *a letter appointing me Judge of Algoma*; and I am to see him again on Monday. Bell & I went to Ellison's[396] afterwards. Dined at 6, and did not go out afterwards. Talked with Isaac Buchan[397] 'till 10, & then to bed. Called at The Primroses' and Mr. P. is dangerously ill, & the family in much distress thereat. I fear he will not recover! He was out only 2 or 3 days ago!

---

393 William Edward Newton's application for a patent on an improved process to separate wood fibres was rejected in May 1860 on grounds that the applicant was not the inventor, and the process was already in use in Canada.
394 William Bell, with his brother David, operated Bell's Pottery on the outskirts of Quebec.
395 W.A. Maingy was a clerk to the Legislative Council.
396 G.W. Ellison & Co., photographers.
397 Prince probably intended to write Buchanan, not Buchan.

467 PRINCE TO JOHN A. MACDONALD. *Private*
[*PAC, M.G. 26, A1(d), Vol. 337, Pt. 1*]

Toronto, June 11, 1860

My dear Friend

I address you by the above appellation, because you have been, to me and mine, the *best friend* we Ever have had in Canada, after all my public services and Expenditure therein for *Seven & twenty years*! Your very kind letter of the 6th has duly come to hand, here, where business will, probably detain me until the middle of next week, and I purpose going up to the "Soo" by *next Thursday week's* "Ploughboy" – so that you may Expect, from me, a letter fully replying to yours as to the Courts, Justices of the Peace, &c. &c. within a fortnight *after my arrival there*; and depend upon it, I shall use *due discretion* in selecting the information you require. My thanks, again, for your Consideration towards *Charles*; and I do hope that you will make his Salary £150 a year, because he is clever and will do his duty well in various ways. On that you may depend; and the *Expence* of Settling him there will be very considerable. As regards old Carney,[398] I regret that friend *Patton*[399] sho'd *bore* you about him. But Surely, my dear friend, Patton's influence ought not to weigh against *John McLeod's* & Isaac Buchanan's, both of whom joined me in recommending *Mr. Thos. Wright*, than whom you Could not have a better Sheriff – and pray don't forget that *Patton's desire* is to get rid of Carney, *as a neighbour*, (for he was disliked at Barrie & O. Sound as he is at The "Soo"), and Patton, certainly, was not a staunch Supporter of you and yours *in times of difficulty* in the Session before last – aye, upon more than one occasion. Moreover, I don't think that old *Caliban* [struck out], (I beg his pardon I mean) *Carney* would take the Shrievalty at £200 a year; and I presume you could not give him more than you do The Registrar. However, I will write you more fully on this Subject when I have been at The "Soo" a few days.

I informed you, at our parting in Quebec, that I had written to S.S. McDonell about the W'n Division. I inclose his answer. Just shew it to our friend "*Van*"; and then burn it. I shall pay a visit tomorrow to our friend *McPherson*,[400] and press him upon the subject, and you shall know the result. God bless you my dear friend!

468 DIARY, 7 JULY 1860. *On board the* Ploughboy

Another very beautiful day with rather a fresh wind. We left "The *Bruce Mines*" at 6-1/2 this morning, and touched at The "*Wellington Mines*" (close by) at 7 and then on to The Sault St Marie, at which place we arrived (having

---

398 Richard Carney had located at Barrie by 1833. He was stipendiary magistrate of the Algoma District from its creation in 1858.

399 J. Patton was elected to the Legislative Council for the Saugeen Division in 1856.

400 David Lewis McPherson, a Conservative, succeeded J. Patton as the Legislative Council member for Saugeen in 1864. He had railroading and financial interests. He became speaker of the Senate in 1880 and was appointed to the cabinet in 1883. He was knighted the following year.

stopped at *Church's* Saw Mills, mouth of The River St Marie, to wood) at 1/2 p 12 pm, after a most beautiful & pleasant voyage without any obstacle since we left Collingwood on *Thursday Afternoon*. Went direct to *Mrs. Hetherington's*, whither Wilson, Salter, & others accompanied me, & spent a few hours. A *"feu de joie"* fired by half breeds & others by way of *Salute* to me, on my arrival. Quite complimentary. In the Evening Mr. & Mrs. Ley[401] arrived from ye Newcastle District. They purpose settling here, and have purchased largely, and will be a great acquisition to the place. She goes to England (Bath) to see her friends there, in a few days, and he goes out in the Spring to bring her back. They appear to be nice people. I am, thank God, better, and am, I hope, thank-ful for the safe & beautiful passage hither. Mrs. Hetherington's House is more comfortable than I expected to find it.

469 Diary, 10 July 1860

As cold & comfortless as yesterday although the Sun is brighter. Still the weather is unusually cold for the season. More like October than any other month!! Occupied at my desk all day long as usual in writing letters & among my papers. Wrote to The Att'y General as to sending up here a Clerk of The Peace and County Att'y o[the]rwise we cannot hold a Court of Quarter Sessions. *Bored, as usual, by a great many people calling upon me, & taking up my time*. I fear I shall be as much annoyed here by visitors & intruders as I was at Sandwich & Every Where Else!! The House crowded in the Evening (though poor Mrs. Hetherington is doing any thing but well); and I went to bed at 10 disgusted, disappointed, and very very lowspirited, but (thank God) my health is improving, & my appetite is much better than it was. In bed by 1/2 p 9.

470 Diary, 29 July 1860

A fine, warm, & growing day. No Church service here but I, as usual, am serving at my desk all day long in writing letters & preparing Papers to be sent off by The "Ploughboy" tomorrow morning, and a great many I had to attend to. Wrote to Albert, Octy, William, "John A" with Davidson's[402] letter to me & list of additional Kentish Magistrates. Also wrote a letter to The *"Globe"* (through Albert) as to The Essex Judgeship & stating that Joe Mercer was dismissed thro' my Instrumentality. The "Ploughboy" arrived at 10 this morng. Lots of people Called here but I would not see them. Read & wrote 'till 11 p.m. and then to bed.

471 Diary, 28 August 1860

A very fine day. Wrote to the remaining *J.P.'s* at *B. Mines, Killarney,* &

---

401 George Ley was formerly of Bewdley, Durham County.
402 John Davidson was a merchant at Bruce Mines.

Manitowaning as well as to Mr. Gibbard[403] at Collingwood to come & qualify. Then I walked down to The "*Grant*" Lot[404] & met *Campbell* as to my share of The Hay there, a part of which he housed in my cow shed. Back to Mrs. H's to dinner by 2 p.m. Professor Murray[405] and several other gentlemen Called & sat throughout the Evening, & drank, as usual, not a little grog. Messrs *Carney, Wilson, & Savage*[406] *& I myself* qualified as J.P.'s for Algoma, by taking the Oath of Office, in my room. I was Engaged in the afternoon in writing letters & among my papers, and I read 'till 1/2 past 11 pm, and then to bed.

472 PRINCE TO THE ELECTORS OF ESSEX AND KENT
[*Chatham* Planet, *22 October 1860*]

Sault Ste. Marie, October 15, 1860

For more than twenty years I have, at sacrifices the most ruinous in every point of view, faithfully and zealously represented you (and especially Essex) in the Legislature of this country.

....

In support of my industrious habits, I need only point to the Statute Book, wherein appear, as part of the existing law of this land, no less than sixty-two acts – all of my own creation – and not one of which has borrowed from the Imperial Statutes or from any foreign country; and no law of mine has ever been repealed, except at my own instance, to be re-enacted in a more enlarged and comprehensive form ...

Before we part, allow me to offer you a few words of advice upon the choice of my successor. I recommend you to select a man of *known* respectability and *honor* – known also for his liberal conservatism – for his good sound common sense – for his integrity, his industry, his honesty, and thorough independence of character – you have such among yourselves; and such a man will not deceive or betray you, come from where he may. Elect such a man far, far before any *party candidate*, and before any other candidate whose chief recommendations may be powers of language – professions of honor and honesty ... Next, I advise you, above all things, to set your faces against needy adventurers and speculators in *lands*, or *railways*, or *mines* – such candidates are not to be trusted ... Remember, you in Essex were partly sold just before the last election. You were within an ace of being wholly sold, and disposed of, and sacrificed altogether. But the treason failed, because the traitor's thirst for gold, and power, and his uncontrollable pride and vanity, and great 'smartness' had become insatiable, and he fell like Lucifer, and in his fall he crashed himself to atoms; and the long cherished Southern Railway which he so often and so solemnly, and so untruly told you he was prepared to give you, died with him. But I have since revived its spirit in a better garb and form; and if the baneful

---

403 William Gibbard was a surveyor.
404 'Call' Grant was the previous owner of the property bought by Prince east of the village.
405 Possibly the reference is to John Clark Murray, philosopher, who in 1862 was appointed to the faculty of Queen's University, Kingston.
406 Colonel John Savage arrived at Sault Ste Marie in 1859 as the first registrar of Algoma.

effects of his name can only be kept afar off, the enterprize may be revived in purity and truth, and your hopes may yet be realized.

473 DIARY, 20 NOVEMBER 1860

A beautiful day. Much occupied up to 10 a.m. Then at 11 Col. Savage and Salter & Wilson & Pilgrim[407] & Simpson,[408] & Pensioners Hughes[409] and Hynes[410] Called on me, and we proceeded to the Office of the late Stipendiary Magistrate (R[ichar]d Carney Esqre, our new Sheriff for this District) & *opened the first Court* (Quarter Sessions) Ever held in the District. Of Course I presided as *Chairman*, which I am, "Ex Officio", as *Judge* of the District. We did a Considerable amount of business, and all passed off well. But, I regret to say, that neither *Wilson*, nor Salter, nor Simpson accepted of Mr. Sheriff Carney's hospitality, because they *hate* him, and, as I think, unfairly & unjustly. He's a man of business & well informed, and, I think, quite equal to any of them, in point of information. After dinner I walked down to The Driver Lots[411] with Mrs. Hetherington & inspected them, and Mr. Ross's clearing work done for me. Back to tea, after receiving the Congratulations of many friends as to the mode in which I had conducted business as Chairman of the Quarter Sess. (our first Court). I read 'till 10 and then went to bed, but still lowspirited.

474 DIARY, 11 DECEMBER 1860

A fine & bright Morng but very Cold & the Sleighing is Capital. Rose at 8 notwithstanding my leg is so bad, & dressed, and several Magistrates Called upon me, and I proceeded to The Stone House[412] & opened the first Court of *General Quarter Sessions* for this district of *Algoma*. A Grand & a petty Jury empanelled, and I charged the *Grand* Jury at considerable length upon the Laws of U.C. in General, and upon their duties. The Charge appears to have given great satisfaction (see The Newspapers, the *"Windsor Herald"* & "Leader" & others where people here intend to publish it, they say). Also "Octy" opened *The District Court* in Septimus's absence. Col. Savage J.P. dined with me. Everything went off very well, & all seemed Satisfied and pleased; and delighted at the Judiciary having been established. The charge will be sent down to Government as recommended by The Grand Jury, and will also be published in a great many Newspapers. My leg is not so bad or so painful today as I expected it would be. I rode to the Court in Pim's[413] Cutter, and *walked*

---

407 Henry Pilgrim was appointed clerk of the Algoma District Court in 1858.
408 Wemyss (Wymess) M. Simpson was the Hudson's Bay Company factor at Sault Ste Marie.
409 Francis Jones Hughes arrived at Sault Ste Marie in 1856. He was chief constable.
410 Andrew Hynes arrived at Sault Ste Marie at the same time as F.J. Hughes and, like Hughes, was appointed constable in 1858.
411 Lots acquired by Prince from John Driver.
412 The stone Charles Oakes Ermatinger House was begun about 1814. The restored building serves today as a museum.
413 Irish-born David Pim was the postmaster.

back to Mrs. Hetherington's (about 300 yards) with Pim & Hughes. Read 'till 9, after dinner, and then went to bed, well pleased with the whole day's Proceedings. May my Judicial career prove Equally successful & agreeable until I, too, appear before & am disposed of by The Great Judge of all; and May He have mercy on me.

475 DIARY, 17 APRIL 1861

Another beautiful day, but a *hard frost*, and the Sun is bright & 'tis warmer out of doors than 'tis in the House. Lowspirited & very very unhappy, and a letter I got from M.A. defending the Conduct of that *ass* (W[illiam] P[rince]) and declining to come here to live makes me, of course, very desponding & very miserable. She appears to me to have become so *stubbornly wedded* to her own opinions as to be all-but senseless! Well, I fear the result will be *absolute ruin* to all of us! God grant it may be otherwise. After dinner Mrs. H. and I walked down to the Driver Lots. Joe Bedford & Michel[414] will finish their Job in removing the Loghouses tomorrow. Agreed to give Joe $6 to clear the little hill in the middle meadow of *Stone* fit to set Potatoes in. Walking slushy and bad, & very tiresome. We got back by 1/2 p. 5 somewhat fatigued. The Lots & The "Point" look *beautiful* even at this Season of the year. I was within doors all the Evening, and read 'till 10 as usual & then to bed, just as wretched and as miserable as yesterday, mainly through M.A.'s letter, refusing to come up here.

476 DIARY, 13 MAY 1861. *Bruce Mines*

The "Ploughboy" left at about 4 this morng. A damp, drizzling, & unpleasant day. Several persons called upon me, and at 11 a.m. I opened the Court, by a long address to the *Miners* and other parties assembled, upon the advantages of Division Courts, and as to the Civil & Criminal Law generally applicable to these remote Regions. I was listened to with great attention, and all the Magistrates attended, and Expressed themselves greatly satisfied & gratified with the Mode by which I expounded the Law, and the information *all* had derived from what I said in my address & remarks. This court was holden in a sort of *primitive* Saloon, fitted up for the purpose, & belonging to Mr. Cameron, Innkeeper, and was the *first Court of Law Ever held here*. There is something interesting about this; Is there not? *Octy* conducted several Suits well, as agent for the Pl[ain]t[iff]s. Then I proceeded to try Division Court Cases to dispose of and I tried [blank] in number, but they were all very troublesome to deal with. The Court sat 'till 6 pm. Then rain & wind, & got wet in returning to Cameron's. A most unpleasant and *unpropitious* day for such an occasion. I reserved only one Case for the next Court. Several persons called in the Evening, & I went to bed at 10, hoping to be able to leave tomorrow morng.

---

414 Michel and Joe Bedford were both labourers. They were brothers.

The "*Ploughboy*" returned from The "Soo" to The Bruce Mines at 1/2 p 6 p.m. in order to secure the future regularity of her Trips.

477 DIARY, 14 JUNE 1861. *Sault Ste Marie*

A most beautiful & steady rain began falling at about 4 this morng *and continued 'till 11 p.m.* It has done worlds of good to all the Crops of grass, oats &c. &c., being much wanted. Thanks be to God for it! I was busy in my room all the morning, and wrote to *Sheriff Carney* about some difficulties which I anticipated. *Mr. F. Williams*[415] arrived last Eveng, by The "City of Cleveland", from Chatham, and he called and sat for half an hour with me, & talked about friends below. Then at 6 pm *Windle Wigle* and 3 other men came here & took lodgings, hoping to get a subcontract on the Bruce Mine road which *young* Rankin[416] has the original contract for & which *old* Rankin advised Wigle to take a Subcontract for; but I fear he (W.) will find himself deceived and disappointed in the matter as Rankin is not to be trusted in word or deed, according to my opinion and that of others also. Wigle kept me up talking about that & other matters 'till 10 pm, and then I went to bed. No other persons Called today owing to the incessant & heavy rain which continued all day, and was then followed by a little Thunder & Lightning. Very growing weather.

478 DIARY, 22 JUNE 1861

A very beautiful, bright & cool day. Rose at 6 and was at my table in writing &c. After breakfast I took Mrs. *Stratton*[417] and Mrs. *Hetherington* out, on *Kelly's Dray* (with Kelly) to inspect Campbell's Lot, and Campbell accompanied us, and we got on very well, (Note: The first wheel carriage that Ever travelled that road!) and Mrs. Stratton was very much pleased with the Place and made up her mind to buy it at $300. We returned by 12 at noon, and found the "Ploughboy" at The Wharf, having brought up *Mr. Killaly* who came to inspect the progress of the new Court House & Gaol. He states that a great mistake has been made in The *Cellar*, and Basement parts, which Can Scarcely be remedied, and throws the fault upon the Contractor, Lavitt. I spent the whole Evening within doors, except taking a short walk to The Garden, and several persons Called, and sat for half an hour, and after reading my letters (8 or 10 in number) I went to bed. A fine night. Walked with Killaly & Lavitt to The New Gaol &c.

479 DIARY, 25 JUNE 1861

A very beautiful & very warm day, although the wind is high. The "*North Star*" did not arrive from above and Mrs. Stratton is, therefore, still here. I was

---

415 Francis Williams was a Chatham trader.
416 George Cameron Rankin was Arthur Rankin's son.
417 William Stratton was proprietor of the Windsor Saloon.

very busily engaged all the morning in writing letters to send by Mrs. Stratton to Windsor & o'r places as the "North Star" is expected every hour. I wrote a long letter to *M.A.* urging her compliance with Geo. Draper's[418] letter to secure the loan of £600 from The Trust & L[oan] Co. of Kingston. Also wrote to *Mr. Walker*[419] a long letter thanking him for the keg of Whisky he sent me last fall, and as to *Oats & Buck-wheat* & a *barrel* of Whisky which came the other day from Partridge and also as to the title to Partridge's lot which he bo't f'm Partridge. Also wrote to old *John Weaver* in ans'r to his letter, & agreeing to sell part of the Brewery upon any terms he & M.A. & Chas. agree to. Also wrote *Wade*[420] about the coming Election, & to send me The "Herald" regularly, & expressing my hope that O'Connor[421] would beat Rankin in the Coming Contest for Essex. I was a good deal engaged in my room all day, and was quite *sick at my stomach this morng*, as I used to be, but it passed off during the day. No boat arrived from above, so Mrs. Stratton did not go home. I read the newspapers 'till 1/2 p 9 pm, and then to bed lowspirited.

480 DIARY, 11 JULY 1861

A very fine & Cool morning like yesterday. I rose at 6, and wrote a little before breakfast. Drew a notice to owners of *breachy Cattle* & delivered it to Mr. Hynes to serve. After breakfast Mrs. Hetherington & I walked down to The New House & Burke was there pointing the Foundation &c. and *Sanderson* was moving the Log House, which he completed doing by the afternoon. Price for so doing $30.00. On my return I gave *Tait* a "blowing up" for having put the Joists so badly in the beams of the ground floor, & he shall do no more work as a Carpenter for me. Young Mr. Church from Sugar Island took a snack & a glass with me, and I directed him in *Gair's presence* as to going down for the Scantling & shingle boards for the roof of the House. The Grounds looked very well, & the grass gets on admirably & the Mowing will commence in about 2 weeks, if not in less time. Mr. Pim called & sat with me for an hour in the Eveng, and we took a "Horn" & congratulated each other upon the defeat of that *arch agitator* George Brown of Toronto. I read the Papers 'till 10 & then to bed, not lowspirited because Brown was defeated.

481 DIARY, 12 JULY 1861

A very fine & Comparatively Cool day. Busy in my room all the morning, & anxiously waiting to hear the results of The *Essex & Kent* Elections. How slow and uncertain is the arrival of *News* of all sorts in these distant & inhospitable

---

418 William George Draper, a Kingston lawyer, was a son of William Henry Draper.

419 Hiram Walker from 1858 was a distiller on the Canadian side of the Detroit River, above Windsor.

420 Robinson and Wade were printers and publishers of the Windsor *Herald* and the *Churchman's Friend*.

421 John O'Connor, formerly articled to Prince, was elected reeve of Windsor in 1859. Prince referred to him in 1852 as 'one-legged O'Connor'; he had lost a leg as a child, about 1834.

Regions! where I am doomed to pass the remainder of my days in nothing short of a species of "Expatriation"! But so has *Fate* ordained, & so must I submit, to its *destinies*, and to the Miseries entailed upon me by the life I led called "Public Life", and by that deceptive Syren, "*Popularity*", which I never sought, but which *haunted* me & overwhelmed me for 25 years, and eventually *ruined me*. Had I been a "*Party man*", or an "*agitator*" or an "*ass*", I might have grown rich under popular favor. But that which Elevated "Smart Men" (as Yankees & Canadians have it) has destroyed me, namely *Political Honesty*; as rare to discover as the *Philosopher's Stone*. Busy all the afternoon in hoeing Corn & Potatoes in Contin's (now Cameron's) field. *Very hot indeed*. A good deal interrupted of Course. Mr. *Church* called & so did Mr. *Ley*, & Each sat for an hour. Gave an Irishman half a Crown to finish hoeing the Potatoes. Wrote & read 'till 10 and then I went to bed lowspirited. A Cool night.

482 Diary, 28 September 1861

Another dull, damp, Cold & comfortless day. Much the same as yesterday & very unpleasant weather for the time of year. Busy all the morning at my Table, in writing. Also about the premises until One o'clock, when I dined and the "Ploughboy" having arrived soon after "Sep" walked up to the "*Soo*" for our letters &c. and I took my Gun and tried for *Ducks* towards Dennomee's. Saw 5 blue winged teal flying up the river but did not get a Shot at them. I killed in *Mr. Simpson's oat-field* 41 beautifully *fat "rice-buntings"* (commonly called "Blackbirds" in this country) at 6 shots from the "Bond" Gun, all on the *wing* but the *flocks large* & very *tame* comparatively speaking, & lodging upon & rising from the *oat* stubble), and also a *Golden Plover* (the first I shot at this Season, & wild & *poor*, & I saw 3 only) and a beautiful *Marsh Hawk*, while flying in pursuit of wounded blackbirds (very much to the *astonishment* of young Dennison to whom I gave 8 ricebuntings for his trouble in driving them round to me) and I returned home to tea by 6 p.m. Septimus & I terribly disappointed at not hearing from Albert or Octy, or The Crownland office or any body Else to our satisfaction in the smallest degree; and we went to bed dreadfully disappointed, disgusted & lowspirited. A cold & damp night, & a disgusting Fall so far.

((Septimus, Mrs. Hetherington & I decided upon giving the name of *Belle Vue Lodge* to the New Habitation.))

483 Diary, 30 October 1861

It rained hard all last night, and I am disturbed in my mind in consequence of the "blowing up" I, deservedly, gave that impudent *black nigger* Rascal, Henderson, the plasterer, for the tremendous *noises* he made at 10 last night in carrying on his work, which he ought to do by *Day light*. The imposing Scoundrel. I am very very lowspirited. At home all the morng & busy about the premises, and with Mr. Jos. Wilson who Called for my advice upon some Magisterial business in which *John Bell*[422] was Complainant. The weather cleared up at about 10 a.m. & is very dull & very mild yet. I was occupied with people all day (more or less) on business. Ryan[423] & Gair here and I settled a dispute between them as to Gair's & Sutton's[424] Copartnership, & Gair gave Ryan an order which I accepted (*see Gair's a/c with me*). Ryan very much admired this new House and the views &c. Every body who sees it does the same, and they had not the least idea it was so large and Commodious a House or so well arranged. I give all the credit to Mrs. Hetherington in that respect because she deserves it, and the plan was hers and hers only. I was at home all day, and after having read the papers and Criticisms upon the English bar, I went to bed at 9 p.m.

484 Diary, 7 August 1862

Heavy and most beautiful & acceptable rain all this morng, & showers off and on all day. Thank God for it. My Cough still very bad but I got an hour or two's sleep in the morng from 7 'till 9 and then rose but was very *weak* indeed. Pim came down he being about to start for Montreal to conclude a bargain with *Mr. Buchanan* for the Sale of his Premises here as a Warehouse for British goods &c. in this *Free Port*. I was too unwell to see him, & indeed was asleep, but *Sheriff Carney* afterwards wrote me a letter by Hynes, and I answered it, and Hynes showed it to *Pim*, my advice being to Pim to close at once with Buchanan's offer, & shew *no further Courtesy to the Govt* who left so many of our letters unanswered upon the subject of his property as the fittest place for our Court House & Gaol. *Pim left for Hamilton* by the City of Cleveland this day at 10 am to come to a final conclusion with Buchanan & Co. *Hynes* here nearly all day helping Mrs. H in cleaning her Carpets &c. I was in doors and in my bed nearly all day, and suffering a good deal from The Cough took *Ayer's* Cherry Pectoral and went to bed at 9 unhappy.

485 Diary, 17 August 1862

A dull morng & blowing fresh from the East. I rose early and was in my Office for an hour before breakfast. Wrote to *Colonel Denison*[425] thanking him for the Cow chains & Bull tether &c. &c. Mrs. Hetherington & I walked up to the Court House to attend divine service, but found that The Rev'd Mr. Chance[426]

---

422 John Bell was a fur trader, whom Prince described as 'that good old halfbreed.'
423 Thomas Ryan was a storekeeper at the American Soo.
424 Sutton was a housepainter from the American side.
425 In his diary Prince, several times in the 1860s, specifically mentions Colonel Richard L. Denison, of Dover Court, Toronto. References to his contemporary, Colonel George Taylor Denison, also of Toronto, have not been noted, however.
426 James Chance was an Anglican missionary to the Indians at Garden River.

did not come up, contrary to our Expectations, So we sat for a quarter of an hour with Sheriff Carney and then returned home & found Henry & Weller at home also. *Mr. Simpson & Captain Ironside*[427] rode down and dined with us and spent the Evening, and I drafted a long letter for Ironside to address to the Indian Department respecting the Sale of Great Manitoulin Island. Henry & Weller went over the River but returned to tea, and we went to bed at 1/2 p 9 pm, as they go off by the Ploughboy tomorrow morning, and intended rising Early on that account.

486 Diary, 5 December 1862

More snow, but not heavy. There is now about an average of 12 inches on the Earth. Martin[428] chopping roads to bring out our Cord wood from where it is stacked in the woods. I fear he is getting to be a *very idle* young fellow. Septimus returned home at 1 pm with Mr. Jos. Wilson, who dined with us, and we spent a couple of hours very (to me and I hope to him also) pleasantly & agreeably. Heavy snow fell for about 1 hour. It became Cold towards Evening, and at night froze very hard indeed, and was by far the Coldest night we have had. The Ram "Billy" very troublesome and I had to Cudgel him severely, but I think it will not alter his habits of butting us. Very annoying. We took tea at 6, and I read till past 9 and went to bed at 10. A very Cold night & hard frost. The Horse "*Bob*" escaped & was out all night.

((I gave *Mr. Wilson* a memorandum volunteering to serve as a full *Private* in any of the *Volunteer Corps* proposed to be raised in this District of Algom. notwithstanding the 35 Cap of the Con. S. of Canada, page 434 S. 7.))

487 Diary, 9 December 1862

Snow deep, and not a Cold day. Kelly brought down the Sleigh & racks. I attended *the Quarter Sessions*, and gave a long charge to The Grand Jury, who made a long & special *Presentment* as suggested by me respecting a Gaol and Court House here, and as to Petitioning Parliament for an Act to give certain Municipal Powers to the JPs. The G. Jury ignored the Bill ag'st Reuben Stuart for Larceny. Montreal Mining Co. vs. Walker, *Nonsuit*. Court rose at about 1/2 past 2 pm, and Septimus went up to Bampton's[429] to attend a meeting of the Volunteer Corps, and he remained in town all night. Mr. Hynes came down in the Evening & brought me my Q.C. Bag &c. and Sep's message as to his remaining in town all night. Lent him my *stick* to walk home with. We took tea at 6, and I read Pitt's life &c. till 1/2 p 9 & then to bed. Mild.

427 George Ironside, Junior, resident at Manitowaning, inherited his namesake father's Indian superintendency at Amherstburg before being transferred north in 1845. He was Wemyss Simpson's father-in-law.
428 Martin Goulding was an Irish-born servant.
429 Charles J. Bampton's inn at the Soo burned in 1864, but was replaced the following year. A Charles Bampton was listed as a Sandwich carpenter in the census of 1851.

488 DIARY, 13 DECEMBER 1862

It rained nearly all night & continues to do so, heavily, this morng, with a strong rain from the East. Bad time for the fresh Meats. I hope they will not become tainted. The Rain continued incessantly. I wrote a long letter to H.E. *The Governor General*[430] as to the absolute necessity of a *Gaol & Court House* here & detailing to him Cases which recently occurred here (*Sutton's*, &c. &c.) & which were over-looked for want of a Gaol to imprison offenders for their Offences in. It contained 2 sheets of Fool's Cap paper, & was accompanied by a Copy of the Grand Jury's Presentment on Tuesday last, & my comments therein, humbly craving H.E.'s favorable attention thereto. The *Ducks & Geese* out again all day enjoying themselves on the river. Septimus & I at home all day. In the Evening Mr. Jos. Wilson came down and sat for an hour or two & rode back in the dark at 9 pm. Read Pitt's life 'till 1/2 past 10 and then to bed.

489 DIARY, 31 MARCH 1863

About one inch of Snow fell last night, and the wind is strong from the west. Septimus busy again today in "fixing" The Hen House &c. I was at my table all day. Wrote to Sir *E.P. Taché* for Copy Board of Works report, & to be allowed to send him letters to frank occasionally. Also *the Provincial Secretary*[431] as to the days for holding the Division Courts at B. Mines, & for registers of Baptisms, Marriages &c. Also to *Mr. Forrest* of Scotland in reply to his letter as to fishing & shooting here, and offering him these Premises at £1500, St'g, 1/2 down & the o'r 1/2 in M't'ge & describing it, & *fishing & shooting* (not too favorably) & asking him to procure for me a steady old *Pointer* or Setter for Snipe & Cock. Also to John A. Macdonald with *Porteous'*[432] letter & *Forrest's*, and asking him to press Sanfield & The *Minister of Finance*[433] to include in The Estimates the Sum recommended by the Board of Works for building our Court House & Gaol and for a copy of the report of The Board of Works, and of Powell's report for names of the County Judges & their salaries fees &c. and my opinion about the S. Committee's report upon the Essex Contested Election &c. Also to *John Sanfield McDonald* to press Minister of Finance to Estimate in the Supply bill for our Court House & Gaol, and to send me *Report* of The Board of Works, & as to The *Murder* &c. committed at *Fort William*. Also to *John Webb*[434] in reply to his last with the 1/2 yearly a/c, and about the *Hoopers*[435] want of affection, and to address me to the Care of Hon'ble Mr. Gouvremont[436] if letters & Packets mailed from England by or

---

430 Sir Charles Stanley, Viscount Monck, was governor general 1861–68.
431 J.O. Bureau.
432 Porteous was an employee in a glassworks at Vaudreuil, Quebec.
433 William P. Howland.
434 John Webb, a cousin, living in Worcester, England, became Prince's agent following the death of Thomas Webb in 1859.
435 This could be any of various cousins and uncles in England.
436 Jean Baptiste Guevremont (Guévremont) was elected to the Legislative Council for Sorel, Quebec, in 1858.

before *1st May next*. Mr. Simpson called & lunched with us, and bro't me a letter from McIntyre[437] about a Murder lately committed there, & other offences at *Fort William*. I answered *Mr. McIntyre's* letter by advising that Every thing be allowed to remain *quiet* till the navigation opened so as not to arouse the Suspicions of the Indians or halfbreeds & then the Murderer probably wo'd not abscond, and that I & *Hughes & Hynes* will go up Early in the Spring, and arrange for the arrests of the Parties Concerned &c. &c. and would also arrange about the Division Court & other matters there. Hughes came down at 4 pm & sat for an hour and took my Mail to the Post Office. Pim recovering fast from his severe illness. Septimus attended Drill. I read 'till 1/2 p 9 & then to bed. A fine night.

490 DIARY, 22 JUNE 1863. *Lake Superior*

Rose at *2 o'clock* a.m. and Wilson, Hughes, Hynes and myself were lowered into the Ploughboy's *Life Boat* and towed up to *Fort William* where we arrived soon after *3 a.m.* and Mr. McIntyre, the Hudson Bay Company's agent at that Post got up and received us, and we breakfasted at about 8 a.m. The Scenery about the Post and (so called) "Fort" is very very beautiful & very bold, though confined. One Mountain of nearly pure Granite, covered with beautiful stunted but thickly foliaged Trees, stands upwards of *1000 feet* perpendicular above the pretty river which flows in front of the Post. Wilson & I were occupied from 9 'till 12 in taking down evidence against an Indian named Jacob Pishké for the Murder of one James Loutit in Nov. last, a brutal murder, and we issued a warrant, and left Hughes to follow him into the Country & apprehend him and bring him down to the "Soo". Also swore in 2 Constables for that part of the District. Re-embarked on board the Ploughboy at 2 p.m., and we proceeded on our homeward bound voyage. I turned into my Berth at 9 p.m.

491 DIARY, 19 JULY 1863. *Sault Ste Marie*

A beautiful morng, and we all rose Early and at 8 a.m. Septimus & Martin rowed Mr. Sallows[438] and Mr. Blain[439] down to Mr. S's church Below garden & river [Garden River], and they returned home at Six – pm –. I was occupied all the morng among my papers (there being no *service* here) and Mrs. H. took a short walk with me tho' still very weak. After dinner I walked up to town & called on Wilson for 5 minutes and from thence I walked up to The Hudson Bay Post and saw Simpson about the Petition to Gov't to appoint Alex'r McGregor Ironside to the office in the Indian Department held by his poor father, and I drafted the Petition there which Simpson approved of highly. Spent 20 minutes

---

[437] John McIntyre was a Hudson's Bay Company clerk at Fort William. He was appointed in 1855.

[438] The Reverend E. Sallows, Wesleyan Methodist, had previously served at Penetanguishene and Beausoleil Island.

[439] Blain was Albert Prince's law partner.

with poor Mrs. Ironside & Miss I. & Mrs. Simpson[440] and then walked home very much tormented by *my Corns*. Rain fell between the town & home & I got *wet through*. Glad of it, because the rain has done good, though we want more. At home all the Evening, and conversing with Blain & Sep, & Mrs. H., I think, improves a little. Went to bed at 10.

492 DIARY, 30 SEPTEMBER 1863

Another most lovely, bright, balm[y] & superior *Summer day*, & as warm as in July. Rose early. Wrote to *Albert* as to writ issued [at the suit of] *Hedley* vs. Richmond & Self & instructing him to appear & obtain for me all particulars of the Case, of which I am ignorant, and sending him *copy* of my letter to Nottle, & for him to comply with the requests in my 2 last letters & to send me money & the grain ordered, & to pay Dougall &c. & as to Reid's Trial with Inglis, & that I hope I need not attend it as a Witness. Also to *Colonel Lachlan* with Cheque for $42 (v Ledger) & that I would sell this property, if I could, & quit Canada for Ever & practice Law in the States, perhaps in Ohio or Illinois. Also to *Mrs. Masales*[441] in reply to her letter & sending her *something* & asking for *something* in return. Men busy in the Garden and among the Potatoes and finished the Potatoes there, and stowed away the Oats in the Jesse Cottage. Septimus went over the above 3 letters and mailed them for me. Kenosh[442] & I hunted for our lost tame ducks down to Hughes's place but did not find them. Read, and went to bed at 9.

493 DIARY, 21 OCTOBER 1863

Another *Gale* nearly all night & again this morng. Terrible weather, I fear, on the Upper Lake for Sailors. Septimus went up to Pim's to survey for him & he hopes to finish today. He mailed the above letters for me this morning at Pim's office. Much Engaged at my desk still in writing letters. Wrote to *Mr. Kirkpatrick*[443] of Kingston in reply to his of the 9th, and that I would send him the statement he wishes for Mr. Duckworth,[444] re Gardiner, and as to the state we were in from want of a Jail & Court House, & of Laws to compel Statute labor, and as to the Condition of our roads & Bridges, and as to the neglect by Parliament of our Petitions, and as to the Murderer & Robber *Pishké* being still at large about Fort William, & why, and as to The *Free Port* being utterly useless to Settlers, and sent a Message to *John A*, intending that he should know of our *Grievances* &c. &c. as set forth in my letter to *Kirkpatrick*. Also to

---

440 A sister of Mary Ironside and a daughter of George Ironside, Junior.
441 Mrs Masales (Prince also spelled the name Mesales) was the former Ellen Zimmerman. She was probably the wife of Eli Mosalis, a teacher in Louisville, Kent County.
442 Kenosh was an elderly hunter, of Indian ancestry.
443 Thomas Kirkpatrick was a lawyer and former mayor of Kingston.
444 Duckworth resided in Liverpool, England.

Octavius censuring him for not having sent up any thing by John Carney[445] for me & for not having pd. McPherson & Co's account and telling him to do so immediately out of the balance of Hughes's money in Albert's Hands & finding fault with items *extravagantly* charged on his (Octy's) a/c for clothing, board, &c. and censuring the clumsiness of the cash account sent in by Albert since he left this place, & asking for explanations about Rev'd Mr. Lewis a/c pd. ($37.55) & *Stovels* a/c pd. $50.68 & inclosing note to *Straford* to be taken care of & dropped into the PO at Toronto. Also answered *Lizzy's* letter to me of the 9th inst. declining to comply with her request of allowing the use of $1000 *Capital* of The *Trust Moneys* & fully explaining *why* and advising her to Consult Albert Thereon, and giving her good advice as to the management of her *children* & household &c. &c. Hughes Came down & Sat for an hour & smoked &c. & Jemmy McKay[446] brought down 5 Barrels of flour which I bought from *Smith of Collingwood* at $4.75 per bbl & Smith dined with me. I read "Trollope"[447] till 10 pm & then to bed.

494 DIARY, 14 JANUARY 1864

A fine day but a hard *white* Frost and the air keen & cold. A fine *Canadian* Winter's day nevertheless. After breakfast I walked up to town & met my brother Magistrates Wilson, Simpson, Ley & Davidson, & *Hynes & Hughes* also attended at the Court House & many other persons were present, when I read & discussed Sheriff *Carney's* letters in which he accused H. & H. of "insubordination", as he termed it, and of neglecting their duty as Police Constables. *The Sheriff did not attend, although I notified him of the meeting*. The Bench agreed that H & H. were undeserving of The Charges, & authorized me, as Chairman, to so Express their opinion to The *Att'y Gen'l for U.C.* Then I walked home & found that *The Sallows's* had left for their home about noon. In the Evening Mr. & Mrs. Chance & their children Called & Sat for half an hour on their way home, but Mrs. Hetherington & Sep had gone up to town. I went to bed at 9, by no means well & very lowspirited.

495 DIARY, 28 FEBRUARY 1864

A very severe black frost with a stiff breeze from the West. An Extremely cold morning, & freezing hard all day long. Septimus returned at 11 a.m. Church Called on his way up to Sunday School, on the other side, & proceeded on up to the Sault & will Call again tomorrow on his return. No service at our Town, but I understand that that *arch old Hypocrite*, Sheriff Carney, reads *prayers* and *the Scriptures* & a *Sermon* to the *weak ones* who go to listen to

---

445 John Carney, son of Richard Carney, was a storekeeper.
446 James McKay shortly hereafter returned to his home in Stormont County.
447 Anthony Trollope was an English novelist.

him. The malignant [obliterated in manuscript] & a pest to Society, (witness his conduct to Hughes & Hynes) and ought to be "cut" by all respectable people, and he attempts to mask his Evil deeds under the cloak of affected religion! At home all day, and quite alone! A great comfort and a great wonder! A cold & unpleasant day, & no inducement to stir out. Read a good deal, and went to bed at 9 p.m.

496 DIARY, 8 MARCH 1864

A beautiful day. Sep's drove me up to Town and I sat as Chairman of the Quarter Sessions, where a good deal of business was transacted, and *a Series of Resolutions* were moved by Captain Wilson against *"Old Nick"* who attended, and was so troublesome that I had to put him down occasionally and lecture him. Much discussion occurred both in Court & in Hamilton's[448] Office, when it was finally arranged that Sheriff Carney would withdraw all his charges made to Govt. ag'st Hynes & Hughes and that he should draw their Pay as usual, and thereupon Captain Wilson withdrew the Resolutions moved against him. Tried McKay & passed accounts, and the Court ended at 1/2 p 5 p.m. At Bampton's for 1/2 an hour. Got home to tea and in the Evening the Schoolmaster (Mr. Turner) & old Roderick McKenzie[449] came down & sat for an hour. *John Driver's* house all but burnt down. I went to bed at 10 rather tired.

497 DIARY, 12 MARCH 1864

A dull & windy morning, with slight Snow falling. Wrote a long, a very long letter *to Dupont*[450] about Indian matters, that the Indians were liable to serve on Juries and as Constables tho' not fineable but subject to Imprisonment; cannot be sued; subject to the Game law; advising them to give up hunting and attend to agriculture &c.; my own affection for hunting & shooting; that this Dist. may be considered as still unorganized, & why; & for him to send a Copy of my letter to the *Att'y Gen'l for U.C.* & to the *Comm'r of Crown lands*, & to keep a Copy for myself [himself?]; & pointing out *"Breakers ahead"*, so far as respects the Indians. After dinner Sep's drove Mrs. H up to Pim's where she met Mrs. Hughes, and talked matters over. They returned by 5 pm. Mr. Ley & Mr. Phipps[451] Called on their way up from Sugar Island & spent half an hour & took a Couple of horns each. After tea I read 'till 10 & then to bed. A fine night, but cold & freezing hard. I this day enter on my 69th year! God grant I may apply my heart more to religion & wisdom than heretofore.

---

448 John M. Hamilton, a lawyer, and clerk of the peace, married a daughter of Chief Justice Draper.
449 McKenzie was a market gardener, who came from Williams Township, Middlesex County.
450 Charles. L. Dupont was Indian superintendent in the Northern Superintendency, 1863–68.
451 James C. Phipps was a storekeeper.

498 PRINCE TO JOHN A. MACDONALD
[*PAC, M.G. 26, A1(d), Vol. 338, Pt. 2*]

Belle Vue Lodge, August 20, 1864

Your note of the 8th was very welcome, because you have not forgotten that there is such a person above ground.

You mention that you still give me my *Military* Title, and that you are one *or two letters in my debt*. As to the first, I pray you always to address me as "Colonel" Prince. In that Capacity *I* crushed the Invasions of the Province, on Dec'r 4th 1838, and did "the State some service"[452] (so say folk, and so will History say, when I am underneath the Sod;) but, can I add "Palmam qui meruit ferat"[453] or rather cannot I apply those lines of old Virgil to myself, "sic vos non vobis"&c: &c:?[454] – And, though no man respects law or legal knowledge more than I have ever done, and though I have practised Law for 42 years, in England & Canada, & tho' I have been a Queen's Counsel for 20 years, and though I am growing somewhat *bald*, (I suppose, by reason of so many Lawyers, and men styled Lawyers, having passed over my head) still, I have little reason to plume myself upon being a "Judge", for my learning, & my talents, (humble though they be), as well as my Experience, and energy, and industry, not in the least abated by years, are obscured *here*, and all-but "hid under a Bushel"! But I enlighten men, and all seem grateful for it. Thank God, I do my *Duty*.

With reference to the second, pardon me if I say that You are not only one or two letters in my debt, but one or, perhaps, two dozen. However, I am not so unreasonable, nor did I ever, expect an answer to all my letters – but I hope you will admit, if you received them, (*which I have always doubted*), that they were, for the Most part, upon matters of not inconsiderable public importance – Especially that on *Biron's*[455] Case which was a *New Case*, and upon which I was most anxious to obtain your opinion, but to no part of that letter did I Ever receive the honor or the pleasure of an answer. He was, however, *tried*, and I told the Jury that I thought the Evidence did not fully support the charges in the Indictment, and they *acquitted him*, but not without a great deal of Consideration and a long & tedious Trial, & a, by no means brief, Summing up from myself; and I think they did right. The Case was a Novel one – it affects this District Most materially; I felt Mortified, I confess, at not hearing from You as to your view of the applicability of the Statute to *Algoma*, and, even now, I venture to ask yr opinion upon that point, because I fear we shall have a Second edition of the language, from Manitoulin and other settlements of obstreperous Indians, under the undue influence of the Jesuits and others, ere the Summer has passed over.

And now, I have finished my Yarn. I think well of the Coalition, and I wish it

---

452 William Shakespeare, *Othello*, Act. v, Scene 2.
453 Let the deserving bear the palm.
454 *Sic vos non vobis mellificatis, apes*; bees, you make honey, but not for yourselves. (Probably wrongly ascribed to Virgil.)
455 This probably refers to Joachim Biron, a ferryman. Biron's father Charles, of Indian ancestry, was progenitor of a large family in the region.

Every success, and I hope the Country will profit by it, and I think the Country will. I believe that Mr. Brown will do his duty, and is *patriotic*, in the true Sense of the word, and [the Coalition] will not become impracticable, (as some folk surmise); and, as there is now a *strong* Ministry, I hope & believe This Country will prosper throughout; and I do believe it will. God grant it may be so.

I assure you that it has my best wishes for its success, and there is not a Member of it who is better fitted to "weather the Storm" than he whom I am now addressing, and for whom I Entertain more respect, & regard, & Esteem, than I do for any other Man in Canada.

God bless You, My dear Atty General, and May Every prosperity & happiness be with you! and believe me always to remain Yours Most truly, faithfully, & Sincerely,

John Prince

P.S. Let me advise you not to rely on Cold Water, & tea, & coffee *alone*, to sustain your not very robust & , sometimes, over-wrought frame & Constitution in yr present *arduous position*!

499 DIARY, 23 OCTOBER 1864

A beautiful sort of May day. Mrs. H. went up to attend the Methodist Church, but no Service there. Kate[456] went up to the R. Catholic Church, & did not return 'till 3 pm, thus leaving Mrs. H. to prepare dinner &c. &c. Mr. Phipps Came down & sat for half an hour & bro't me a letter from Col. Lachlan & some newspapers & also a letter from Septimus in pencil, from the wilderness! where he is still surveying, and inclosing a note to Mrs. Driver which I sent over to her. Went up to the D. Lots &c. and brought down the Cow and also the Sheep. At home all the Evening & a beautifully mild & damp Evening it was. Hughes bro't my mail down at about 7 pm, but few letters and those any thing but satisfactory. Much disgusted at old Sheriff Carney's having gone down to Quebec to injure Hynes & Hughes, in which, it seems, he has partially succeeded. Attacked with a slight pain just above my left hip. Read 'till 9 & then to bed.

500 DIARY, 22 NOVEMBER 1864

A very Cold morning & freezing hard. Anxious about writing & finishing my correspondence, but so numerous are my occupations that I am *worried* beyond all Conception. Shot 2 of our *beautiful wild Turkey Cocks*. It cut my heart to do so, but I can't afford to keep them. One I intended for a present to Mrs. Hamilton, & the other for this House. Wrote a long letter to *Att'y Gen'l John A. Macdonald* as to our Memorial to The Gov'r General upon the Act of last Session & for the op'n of the Law Officers, &c. Also *another* letter as to the vacant Vice Chancellorship of U.C. & shewing forth the neglect &c. &c. in

---

456 Catherine Pollard was a servant of Mrs Hetherington.

their not having *offered* it to me, & inclosing to him my letter to Cassells,[457] the [illegible]. Also wrote *Foott* thanking him for the Pea Fowls &c. &c. and for his care of them, and to let me know what I owed him, and that the money for the P. Fowls, & the Box, & cartage, & all, shall be Sent to him by *return of mail*. Still bothered with Brasseau's[458] & Driver's *starving Steers*. Septimus took up the above letters & mailed them with Pim, & he returned to tea. I read a little of Mrs. Hannah More's[459] life &c. 'till past 9 pm, & then to bed.

501 Diary, 13 December 1864

A fine day and not near so cold as it was yesterday. After breakfast I walked up to Court and Mrs. H'n & Sep's accompanied me. She spent the day at Pims. The General Quarter Sessions opened at 11 a.m., and continued 'till between 2 & 3 pm. I was compelled to be very Severe upon Sheriff Carney ("*Old Nick*" as he is called) in consequence of his impertinence and meddling in matters at Court which don't concern him, & also on account of the Exhorbitant [*sic*] charges sent in for his Journey to Quebec &c. &c., which charges the Court refused to allow or Sanction in any way. After Court I called on Mr. Borron & then accompanied Pim home where Mrs. H'n & I dined with them, and we got home by 5 pm. Pim accompanied us, & spent an hour & then walked back home. The Wild Turkeys came in & roosted in the Hen-House.

502 Diary, 20 March 1865

A very beautiful & mild April day. Air Soft & balmy. Walked along the road & about the lands & premises, & on the Snow and Ice opposite Grant's from 9 to 11, examining rails &c. &c. Home to dinner at 12. Young Dupont Called on his way to Garden River to measure Cordwood for Phipps. After dinner Sep's went up to town. I wrote by him a note to Mr. Brown (Superintendent of the Canal on the other Side) apologizing for not having returned his visit, & promising so to do on the opening of the River, the first chance that happens. The Reverend Mr. *Chance* Called at 2 p.m. and I told him a piece of my mind about his abusing the R. Catholic religion & the *Jesuits* from his Pulpit; and giving him (I hope) some good & *wholesome Advice*, by which (I also hope) he may profit as a Protestant Priest, and a good & worthy man, as he is, but somewhat *hasty* & indiscreet in the Pulpit occasionally, unnecessarily so, I think. After tea I read "Fox" 'till 1/2 p 9. Then to bed. A rainy night.

---

457 Robert C. Cassells was cashier and subsequently manager of the Bank of Upper Canada.
458 John Brasseau or Borasseau, who lived nearby, occasionally performed minor tasks for Prince at Belle Vue Lodge.
459 An English author, who died in 1833.

503 DIARY, 25 MARCH 1865

A hard frost last night & stiff breeze again this morning, but upon the whole a fine day. Busy among my papers as usual. Whenever shall I be relieved from correspondence? Wrote The *Hon'ble Mr. Chapais* of the Board of works strongly as to the necessity of our having our Court House & Jail without delay and that $8000 was voted for it, & as to the Indian woman being Confined therein charged with *Infanticide*, & sending him a Copy of the *advertisement* of the Sale of *these Prem'es* for a Court-House & Gaol, and the price &c., and stating that *Settlers had left* us & none would come here unless these buildings are Erected, & praying for Expedition being used in erecting the public Buildings. Also wrote a very long letter to *Mr. J.C. Taché* Deputy of Hon'ble *D'Arcy McGee*, Minister of Agriculture in reply to his Enquiries about last year's "Bluebook" (see Copy of my letter in pigeon Hole T). Shot a beautiful *old Raven* near our kitchen, as he came round foraging for Eggs, I suppose. Sun bright at noon. Greisor brought in 1 load of wood, & I pd. him $1, leaving me 30 cents in his debt. After dinner Septimus went up to town, & took my letters to Pim & Hamilton &c. &c. and returned to tea. Afterwards I read Fox's life 'till 10 pm and then to bed. A fine night.

504 DIARY, 13 MAY 1865

Quite a frost last night, with Ice 1/4 inch thick. Rose Early and among the Sheep & Lambs and about the Premises all day. Sep's went up to town preparing for his Journey tomorrow to Massasauga & God knows where on Mining Surveys for Wray.[460] At noon Mr. Sheriff Carney Came down with Mr. [blank] from the Board of Works to Consult me about our Court House & Gaol. A Canadian Consultation, (not a "*Senatus*" one), which seemed to me to amount to nothing, and my opinion is that sending the *innocent* looking young French official hither is a mere "*sham*", & that Gov't does not intend to build any Court House or Gaol here, after all the bluster, & blowing, & delay & correspondence about it. They dined with me, and the "*Young'un*" was much pleased with the place & Country. Of Course, all are, who are treated hospitably & kindly. Mrs. H. & I took a walk in the Evening among the Stock. Paid "Surveyor" Mayville[461] $8 and the men "Sandy" & Hugh $4 each. A lovely & *beautiful Evening*.

505 DIARY, 16 AUGUST 1865. *Below Bruce Mines*

We rose at 5 a.m. and struck our Tents and left our ground at 6. A fair breeze but not so good as yesterday. A pretty Island was our Camping ground last

---
460 Elsewhere Prince refers to Judge Wray, of Illinois.
461 Job Mayville lived adjacent to Prince.

night. Dew very strong, and Sun bright and a heavenly day it is. We proceeded on to a place Called *Thessalon Point* (a very pretty & romantic Point) running out from the Main Land & Thessalon River into the waters of Lake Huron, and there we breakfasted. The beach full of large quantities of Stones & pebbles & boulders. Left there at 10, and sailed & rowed on to Missasauga River where we were Met by a Band of Indians at 4 p.m. & Saluted by their firing their fowling pieces in honor of our arrival. I went out Duck-shooting for an hour in a Canoe, but saw only 3 or 4 birds, & could not get near them. The Whole Evening was spent in Mr. Dupont's paying the Indians their Annuities and in one of the *Bands Executing* a Cession of their Lands there which I & he witnessed. Turned in at 10 pm. A dark night.

506 Diary, 19 August 1865

A fine day. Dr. & Mrs. Layton[462] did not arrive, in their open boat, here from "Little Current" until Midnight. A fine day this is. Received great Civilities from The Duponts whose wife & sisters are very fine & amiable & genteel as well as handsome persons. Called on the old Indian Assiginac,[463] 96 yrs of age, and he returned my visit in the Evening, walking 3 or 400 yds over a rough road to do so. Also Called on Dr. & Mrs. Layton, and again in the Evening & spent half an hour very agreeably with Mrs. L. the Dr. not being very well. Also Called on The Rev'd Mr. Simons, & walked over the commons with Dupont. In the Evening we concluded the Cession of the Reserve at White Fish River, with the Band, at Dupont's Office, just at dark, and I assisted Dupont in hearing the Case against one George [blank] an Indian charged with stealing wood from Mr. Dods at L. Current which we dismissed. Engaged among our papers until 10 p.m. and, after a horn or so, I went to bed, tired.

507 Diary, 14 December 1865. *Sault Ste Marie*

Another *most Severe Frost*. Such Severe weather I never before Experienced Even in this "*New Siberia*" or in any other part of this dreadful Canada! Our Stock Geese have been away from home for 3 days, and I fear are on the broad waters or Ice and are frozen & dead. John Bennett and little William out all the morning looking for them! Oh what time is lost in this dreadful place, merely in keeping your property & things together! It is a Miserable place & Country, & *'tis impossible* to do any *good* in it. Young Norton Bennett came down. John Bennett & little William hunting our Geese, but could not get them home. *Ladouceur & Dales here*. The Geese on Sugar Island! At home all the Evening & I wrote a good many letters for Saturday's mail (see underneath) and after

---

462 Dr and Mrs Layton were from Manitowaning.
463 J.B. Assiginac was a chief and a former interpreter for the Indian Department at Manitowaning.

reading Siborne[464] 'till 10 p.m. went to bed. Snow falling. Wrote to Hon'ble *Mr. Chapais* B. Works recommending in our new Jail a *Treadmill* or something of the sort to keep Vagabonds at hard work. Also to *Mr. Fennings Taylor*[465] to give me all the time he can for my sketch of *myself & Dr. Dunlop*, & at least 'till Parliament meets and why I require so much delay, & as to how I am *bothered* here daily & hourly. Also to "*John A.*", Att'y Gen'l for U.C. (& inclosing my letter to Fennings Taylor as above) for permission to *draft a Bill* for the Government, bylaw of this District & to let me hear from him thereon forthwith, also as to reinstating Hynes to his pay of $1 per day and why, and as to the late Case of Murder & Robbery wherein Hynes gave us useful aid as a Policeman. Also to *Mr. Dupont* asking him to remit me the $24.60 and that an order on Phipps would answer my purpose, & inclosing to him my letter to Dr. Layton. Also wrote to *Dr. Layton* thanking him for the Chutney Sauce & asking for the *Receipt* for making it. Also to the Hon. *John Rose*[466] with Mr. Allen's letter to me about the London books (which memorandum he is to return to me) and a Memorandum of Ins[truc]tions to Enquire at The Customs House in Montreal &c., and to write me thereon, and as to "Fenianism" in these Parts.

508 DIARY, 1 JANUARY 1866

A fine day. Rose Early and walked up to Morning Service at the Court-room which was performed by The Rev'd. Mr. Carry.[467] Then occupied in admitting a Man to bail, who was Sent up from the Bruce Mines charged with stabbing another. Simpson & Col. Savage took the recognizances. Then I attended *The Township Meeting* at Bampton's Saloon (the first meeting of the kind Ever held there), and I addressed the voters upon several points & questions. Great & *good* order was observed, but the great majority of those present were afraid of being heavily taxed (all a bug-bear) and they declined Electing any township officers, and then I left the meeting which dispersed, and so nothing was done. I walked home by 5 pm and after tea read till 10, & then to bed.

509 DIARY, 30 JANUARY 1866

A dull morning & the earth Covered with deep snow. A sad accident befel [sic] me. The Horse "Charly", a shying brute, broke his rope halter or rather Cord & got loose in the Stable. I went in to tie the 2 ends together, i.e. the End of that part left tied fast to the Manger & that End also hanging from his head. Having partly finished the knot, I put my thumb in to open the tie a little more,

---

464 William Siborne, an English historian, was author of *The Waterloo Campaign, 1815*.
465 John Fennings Taylor, clerk to the Legislative Council, was the editor, 1867–68, of *Portraits of British Americans*.
466 Sir John Rose was a cabinet member from 1857 until 1861, and again in 1868–69.
467 Irish-born John Carry was ordained in 1850, and served in various Church of England parishes in Canada East and West. In 1860 he published a book of sermons.

when the Brute jumped & jerked back as if shot in the Eyes, jamming my thumb in the "knot", & there I was *fixed*, as in a vise! and completely broke the bone between the 2 joints, & there I remained, until the rope broke by his *main force*! I ran into the house for my penknife, and I Cut *the thumb off with my Pen-knife*! Mrs. H. went thro' the deep snow & met Hick[468] & sent for Dr. Kelly[469] who was here in less than an hour, & *sawed off the bone Splinters* &c. & dressed the wound, and left me to return tomorrow morning. *I Suffered much Pain.*

510 DIARY, 27 FEBRUARY 1866

A very fine & beautiful day and the Sun bright. Dr. Kelly came down & dressed my wound. *Swinburne*[470] called & took a horn or two. Also Mrs. S. drove with him. *Coulson*[471] also took a horn, and gave me a sad account of Septimus' last *drinking bout* & his Del. tremens' attack. *Towers*[472] called on his way up from Mr. Chance's with a servant girl. My stump not quite so painful as it was (thank God). Busy among my papers & Memoires. Mrs. H. went over the river & bro't me some coarse meal &c. Wrote to *Mr. Fennings Taylor* with my *own* long Memoires and also with those of *Dr. & Capt'n Dunlop* for his *Series*, and also with 4 newspapers to be returned to me, & requesting him to let Mine be published at full length &c. &c. and I wo'd pay for the *Extras*, also to tell Mr. Notman[473] to save 12 extra Copies for me. Also wrote to his uncle *Mr. J.F. Taylor* Clk of the Leg. Council with the above packet, & with letters from me to the Ministers mentioned below, & giving him instructions. Very busy all day. After tea I read till 9 & went to bed at 10. "Stump" rather painful.

511 DIARY, 14 MARCH 1866

Another very fine day tho' a fall of Snow of about 2 inches took place early & ceased at 10 a.m. Mild & fine. Very busy at my desk in writing letters for the mail tomorrow. Dined at 2. Then Mrs. H. accompanied me up to town, and I attended the adjourned Court of General Quarter Sessions & passed the accounts &c. &c. &c. Called at Bampton's with the Magistrates from the Bruce Mines. Mrs. H. spent a Couple of hours with Mrs. Pim and Mrs. Butchert. Mrs. H. & I walked home to tea by 6 pm. Rev'd. Mr. Chance Called & took refreshments on his way home. Wrote a long letter to *Mr. Galt*, Minister of

---

468 This probably refers to an employee of George Ley, named Hicks.
469 Dr Kelly, of the Royal College, Dublin, arrived at Sault Ste Marie late in 1863, and was recommended by Prince as coroner at that time.
470 Swinburne was a merchant, apparently in partnership with James Phipps.
471 An innkeeper.
472 This is probably T.A.P. Towers, a storekeeper.
473 Scottish-born William Notman was the leading photographer in Montreal. He was co-publisher, with Fennings Taylor, of *Portraits of British Americans*.

finance,[474] (private) asking him to frank my letter. Also a very long letter to *him* fully as to the uselessness of the *Free Port* here, and the Mischief it did and no good to poor Settlers, and the Prices *Shopkeeper[s]* asked for Pork &c. & as to their paying the poor Settler in Store pay (but, not in Pork & Flour) & that they (the Shopkeepers) were the only persons benefitted, & pressing the abolition of it, & that the Provincial Revenue has lost $80,000 by it since 1st Established, & suggesting that Government Stores, for goods yielding a moderate profit should be Erected on this frontier, as formerly they were at Trafalgar in U.C. After tea read 'till 10, & then to bed. A fine night.

512 DIARY, 4 MAY 1866

A fine day but cold & raw with a cold wind from the NWest, as usual. Feel a little better than I did yesterday, but not in good spirits, tho' the arrival of *The "Algoma"* (the first boat up) cheered me a little. We all hailed her as she *passed our House*, & she *blew* out a response to us. There is *something* in seeing *once more* an *old friend* after so long & so dreary a winter of nr. 6 mos. Still, I remain lowspirited, & I presume I shall continue so 'till death. Hughes brought my Mail down at 12 noon, and dined here, & I gave him my long letter *to Bella* to mail for me by The "Algoma" which left for Collingwood at 2 p.m. today thereby affording us only 2 hours to answer our letters. Mr. *Sheriff Carney* called & Sat an hour with me and we talked over divers matters of business. I like him much better than I used to do; & I think more of his *honesty* &c. than I formerly did, and he certainly is intelligent and Courteous. Dr. *Kelly* also called, & examined Mrs. H's sore finger and advised a poultice. It inconveniences her very much. I read, and then went to bed at 9 very lowspirited.

513 DIARY, 22 MAY 1866

A fine & bright but comfortless day with wind rising again from the West, & cold weather. Nothing grows in the Gardens &c. &c. Warm weather badly wanted. Busy among the Stock & premises and also in endeavouring to complete the full Ins[truc]tions for our New Act for this District, but constantly interrupted thereat. Then wrote to Mrs. *Farmer*,[475] Korah, with *Rhubarb seed & instructions*. After dinner Mrs. Hetherington [went] up to town with the 2 children[476] and got them some shoes &c. &c. Miss Newton also went *about*

---

474 Sir Alexander Tilloch Galt, who represented Sherbrooke in the Legislative Assembly, was the leading English-speaking member from Lower Canada. He was a strong supporter of Confederation, and played a major role in formulating the British North America Act.

475 The Farmers lived on the Goulais Bay road.

476 William and Sarah Arroll, orphans, arrived at Belle Vue lodge from Toronto in the care of Mrs Hetherington, 2 November 1865.

nothing & did nothing as usual. How very useless she is. A half gale of wind all day from the west. I was busily occupied at my table for hours in rummaging over the Old Statutes of U.C. & preparing "instructions" for a new bill for this District as asked to do by *The Att'y General* of U.C. Very busy all day &, as usual, lowspirited, and went to bed at 1/2 p 9 p.m. in the same state of mind.

514 DIARY, 24 MAY 1866

A fine & mild morning, without wind. The only springlike day we have had for a long time. The wind however rose into a good breeze at 9 am, and it became Colder afterwards. Busily engaged at my table until 1 pm in drawing my "*observations*" (for the Attorney General) upon my "*Suggestions*", the former Containing 7 pages and the latter 9, all full of law & requiring time labour & attention to complete. What the result will be or what thanks I shall receive from *any body* for all my trouble about the matter, perhaps "Nil", but the old Proverb "*Ex Nihilo nihil fit*"[477] can't apply in this instance. At 11 a.m. Mrs. H. took little William & Sarah up to town to see the Volunteers & artillery salute The Queen's Birthday, and they returned at 4 pm, much pleased, Captain Wilson being the "*hero" of the day*, and a good fellow he is. No Mistake. We dined at 4 pm. At home all day of Course. Found a *Guinea Fowl's nest with 9 eggs*. The 1st common Chick hatched. About the house & premises all day and read 'till past 9 and then to bed. A very fine night.

515 DIARY, 31 MAY 1866

A fine & bright but a dry, chilly, & by no means a growing day. Warm rain & warm weather wanted so late is the Spring this year. Very cold last night with a sharp hoar frost & hard. Wrote *Hamilton* why I co'd not attend today in him vs. Bogue, but wo'd see him tomorrow in town. Very busy all the morning (& indeed all day) as usual about the Stock & premises. The 1st stone of The Court-House & Gaol laid, and I sent little Henry[478] & Sarah up to see the Ceremony and with letters & the $12.50 for Mr. Carry. Wrote a long letter to *Mr. C. Lamorandiere*[479] & to Captain *Thebo*[480] (*by Wilson*) advising as to the prospect of Killarney being surveyed and laid out as a village, & as to Jos. Wilson recommending its being done forthwith, & I inclosed my letter in mine to Wilson. Arranged for going out to the Lafleur Lot with Mrs. H. tomorrow. Bothered all day long with useless Stock &c. &c. and went to bed, as usual, *quite Miserable*! My Memory is fast (very fast) failing me, and I begin to be

477 Nothing is created from nothing.
478 This is probably a slip. The orphan William Arroll seems to have been intended here.
479 Charles De Lamorandière was a justice of the peace at Killarney.
480 Solomon Thomas Thebo had been known to Prince since the 1830s as a resident of Sandwich, where he was a clerk in 1851. By 1860 he resided at Killarney.

tired of *life* (or rather of my *Existence*) in this damnable & detestable part of the world, & poor & *Good* Mrs. Hetherington *killed with work*!

516 DIARY, 9 JUNE 1866

A warm (tho' windy) and beautifully growing morning. No weather Can be finer for the growing crops. Not very well & much embarrassed with the Stock &c. and as to the threats of *Fenians* coming here *en masse*. *Church here* for 15 minutes about his accounts and I gave him a thorough "*blowing up*" as, I think, he wished to impose upon me as to the lumber delivered here for these Cursed premises. After luncheon I walked up to town and transacted some business and drew and Executed the Deed from myself to Mrs. Hetherington of the 80 acres in Korah which I bought of D. McNab, and which fronts her 200 a. bought by her from poor old Doherty.[481] It is due to her in return for the use of her *furniture* &c. by me, and her great & kind attentions to my comfort & convenience. Called on Hamilton & conferred with him upon the Coming Gen'l Qu'r Sessions business &c. &c. Also on several other persons. William Carney called, & I lent him our Cornish Rifle. Occupied in the town some time & encouraged the *People* by precept & example as to the anticipated Invasion by The Fenian Rascals, & went to bed at 10 quite unhappy because I can find no peace of mind or rest of body, like *1838*!!

517 DIARY, 17 JUNE 1866

A wet, damp, & blowing, and uncomfortable day. No peace of Mind. I clearly see that as long as "*This Canada*" remains an appendage of the British Crown, there will never be peace or rest or quietude of mind or Body within it Especially on the Frontiers of more than a Thousand Miles. The thousands of Ruffians, especially *Irish* ruffians, who form a great portion of the U. States population and the Majority, far the Majority of the higher & middle & poorer classes of American Citizens *hate* us and *Every thing British* and wars and rumours of wars & raids & tumults will from time to time be waged among us until a decided separation takes place between England & us here, and we are an independent Nation, of ourselves. Received 2 Peafowls (yearlings) from Mr. Douglas, Chatham,[482] & fine birds they are. At my desk nearly all day, & wrote several letters which are entered as of tomorrow (which entries, post, see). Jameson[483] & his wife Called and spent half an hour and Mrs. J. advised Mrs. H'n as to her sore leg. Mrs. H. still suffering much. At 10 I laid down for the night on the Settee, thinking it by no means unlikely that Fenians would cross over.

481 Edward Doherty had died by 26 February 1865.
482 William Douglass was a Chatham lawyer in the 1860s.
483 Jameson was a carpenter, employed by Church.

518   JOHN A. MACDONALD TO THE HON. GEORGE S.
BOULTON
[*PAC, M.G. 26, A1(e), Vol. 512*]

Ottawa, July 13, 1866

I have your note about Col. Prince's Bill. I shall endeavour to put it into shape, but as he sent it to me it is one of the most incomprehensible documents you ever saw.

519   DIARY, 12 SEPTEMBER 1866

A dull, damp, uncomfortable day with frequent Showers so as to prevent any thing in the shape of Harvest work, and my peas want cutting, and some of the oats too. After 9 a.m. I walked up to Court and signed my name to a great number of accounts allowed by the JPs, and I rec'd the *presentment* of The Grand Jury, and addressed them at some considerable length thanking them &c. &c. and speaking somewhat harshly against the Government & the Attorney General "*John A.*" for not having introduced the Bill I drew, at his request, for Establishing a sort of limited Municipal Council in this District. My address greatly approved of by all who heard it, and indications of applause began which I, at once, stopped & censured. After passing a great many accounts, I walked home, wet, and got home by 4 p.m. and remained busy among the Stock &c. and read a little after tea, and went to bed between 8 & 9 pm completely tired in mind & body, so bothered am I by Every body!

520   DIARY, 27 SEPTEMBER 1866

A very bright, & beautiful & quiet day (no wind or hurricanes as heretofore) and what few crops of Spring wheat &c. as are now *out* will, please God, ripen, if we have a few days of this weather. A carpenter from *Damp*[484] Came to do some job work at the house & about the premises. Joe Biron called. So did an U.S. soldier (who seemed & acted as a *respectable* man) and he took a "*horn*" with me, and was intelligent and very well-behaved. Talked to him a good deal about the *U.S. & British Services.* Weather lovely, throughout the day! Damp's Mechanic dined with Mrs. H. and the children. I was *bothered* all day among the sheep (in the afternoon) with Toussaint Sayer.[485] News reached us of the stoppage of the Bank of Upper Canada, which will, it's feared, Cause much distress throughout the Country. A sad affair, I fear, & I also fear it is one that will not *Embarass me a little*, for I apprehend they have some hundreds of Dollars in their hands in respect of which my divers Cheques have *not been presented*.

484 John Damp was a contractor, who in 1862 had worked on the Simcoe County Jail at Barrie.
485 Sayer, a man of French and Indian extraction, might have been previously employed by Septimus Prince.

521 DIARY, 14 NOVEMBER 1866

An unpleasant, windy, chilling & wet day. I am any thing but well, distracted in mind with farming & Servants, & little or no chance of being able to get in our Potatoes from the field, so deluged are we with rains. Moreover, I am unwell, my appetite being *entirely gone*! and I feel weak & my memory has failed of late in a Most extraordinary manner. At 2 pm *Rankin [&] Dupont* Came down in Wilson's boat and dined here and left at 5, and seemed to Enjoy themselves a good deal, but I was very lowspirited and feel far from well, & unable to entertain them with any pleasant Conversation. Wilson too busy to come down & dine with them. Rankin very kind, & we parted good friends. He reminded me a good deal of *former times*. Sold McKoy a fat Ewe for $6, & he pd. me, down, for her. A strange payment in this Country. I went to bed at 8, & a bad cold coming on I fear.

522 DIARY, 19 DECEMBER 1866

A splendid day for the time of year. My mind somewhat (and only *somewhat*) *more tranquil* than yesterday but still I am very miserable. Wrote a letter to *Jos.Wilson* enquiring as to why the Patent had not issued for the *160 acres nr. the Kilroy*[486] *40 acres* (see Copy) & Censuring Gov't as men of bus[ines]s. But what's the use of writing? The whole machinery of Gov't wants *oil*, & vigour & intellect. Drones!! They are a lazy & a rusty set, "Drones" & mere "*Noodles*", like most Colonial Governments. They want (as all Provincial Gov'ts do), *Energy & knowledge*. No such animal as a "*Statesman*" amongst the *Mean degraded Crew*. None such ever ruled a Colony. They are chiefly composed of slightly educated Adventurers, and *advertising*, pettifogging attorneys. Such is, and such has been my opinion of Canadian "*Statesmen*" (God save the mark!) and Canadian Governments during the 33 years I have been Cursed & ruined by living in their most damnable & most detestable Country, and *stung* all the time by their base and accursed Ingratitude towards *me* who have *done so much for them*. God damn them all, say I! Read, in a melancholy mood, as usual, 'till 9 and then to bed miserable & despondent, as usual, and, as usual, Cursing (sincerely) all & Every thing in "*This Canada*".

523 DIARY, 11 JUNE 1867

Sharpe[487] & little William rowed me up to town, and at 11 am I presided as Chairman of the General Quarter Sessions. Got thro' the business stronger & better than I expected, & a heavy Sessions it was. *Good Mrs. Hetherington* came up & saw me home safely. Prisoners to be sentenced tomorrow. Bothered

---

486 This is probably Thomas Kilroy, who lived near Root River.
487 The Sharpes, Stephen, Joe, and their father, were residents of Korah Township.

very much by the "Heathens" in this accursed "Soo", and parts adjacent. But, in the accursed soil must rest & rot my miserable remains, & on that solitary Island opposite, for I will not allow my dust to mingle with the human race, whom I *hate*!!

524 DIARY, 1 JULY 1867

A most beautiful day. Confederation of B.N. America began to take effect. Lunched at 12. The[n] old Sharpe rowed Mrs. H. & me over the river (little William with us) & we disembarked nr. Johnson's on the *opposite* side, & she & I walked up to the Saut [*sic*], and Called upon old *Mrs. Gally*[488] & saw her *poultry* &c. and also on the Ryans &c. & spent an hour at each place. I am very unwell & breathe with difficulty. I fear my heart & lungs are affected. We got home by 5 pm, not stopping at the "Soo" on our side at all, where a dinner to the *Volunteers* is going on, & the *Confederation* day celebrated with flags innumerable, & firing Guns &c. I went to bed at 8 pm tired & disgusted!

525 DIARY, 8 JULY 1867

Yesterday I wrote to *Henry & Charles* about Septimus' bad Conduct, & as to his having gone down to Toronto with Stratton on Thursday last, as an *Inebriate*! Very busy all day tho' unwell. Wrote to *Josh. Coatsworth*[489] that Henry had given up running for Algoma. Also to *Hon. Ferguson Blair*[490] for 3 mo's leave of Absence for Septimus. Also to *J. Pollard*, Toronto, that Mrs. H'n was going down next week, and as to their returning with her. Also *Rowsell*[491] as to mistake in this last Almanac. Mr. Cumberland,[492] the Candidate for Algoma arrived but I did not attend his meeting. Very busy & very low spirited, and went to bed at 1/2 p 10 pm as I rather expected Mr. Cumberland to sleep here but he came not.

526 DIARY, 9 JULY 1867

Another beautiful day. Went down with Captain Jos. Wilson with his crew and boat to Garden River where I superintended a Surrender by the Indians there

---

488 Mrs Gally was the wife of a sergeant posted at the American Soo.

489 Coatsworth was the postmaster, a justice of the peace, and clerk of the Division Court at Bruce Mines.

490 Adam Johnston Fergusson Blair, a Reformer and a son of Adam Fergusson, began his parliamentary career in 1849, representing Waterloo and, subsequently, Wellington South. He was elected to the Legislative Council, for the Brock Division, in 1860. He was president of the Privy Council in the first Dominion government, until his death on 30 December 1867.

491 Henry Rowsell was a Toronto printer, stationer, and publisher. He provided the volumes in which Prince kept several years of his diary.

492 Frederic William Cumberland was a Toronto architect and engineer. He was also managing director of the Northern Railway.

of a *Mill site* to Father Kohler and the Jesuits. Quite a large meeting, & 5 R.C. Priests there. The Rev'd *Mr. Chance* (of the Anglican Church) was also there, and I gave him a thorough good Scolding for his improper & impertinent conduct at G. River this day. Beautiful weather and we had a pleasant row home & got to Belle Vue Lodge by 6 p.m. Went to bed at 9 tired.

527 DIARY, 12 AUGUST 1867

A very fine day. Much distressed at having heard of poor Septimus's death, a letter from Octavius viâ U. States. Walked up to town with Mrs. H'n & saw Jos. Wilson and others on business. Also saw Wilson about offering the Clerkship of the District Court to Pilgrim. Called at Wilson's. Paid Turner a sum. Walked home. Took leave of Mr. & Mrs. Down[493] and went to bed Early, distressed & lowspirited, greatly affected by poor Sep's almost sudden death! & so is poor Mrs. H'n & Old Kate also.

528 PRINCE TO JOHN A. MACDONALD
[*PAC, M.G. 26, A1(d), Vol. 340*]

Belle Vue Lodge, August 29, 1867

It seems that the office lately filled by Judge Harrison of Toronto (now deceased, & an upright & Excellent Judge he was)[494] still remains vacant. I had hoped that it would have been offered to me. My hopes were grounded thus, that I am the Senior Queen's Counsel in Upper Canada (my Patent dating from 1821,[495] in Ld. Sydenham's time), that I have assiduously & Successfully practised Law in England & in this country ever since Hilary Term, in the Year of Grace, *1821*, when I was admitted in Westminster Hall – that I have been an active Member of the U.C. Bar ever Since 1838, and by no means an inactive Member of Parliament for more than 20 years, as the Statute Book of my adopted Country abundantly proves, in Conjunction with The Journals of both Houses. And yet, *here* do I remain – the least of all the Canadian Judges, both as to Rank and Salary, and, certainly, Exercising that Tact & management to keep matters straight & the Laws respected by a strangely heterogeneous Community; and I have laboured in my vocation, with admitted success, for Seven Years and upwards *without one single holiday*, or absence from my duty for one single hour! I forbear to dwell upon or boast of my having *crushed*, in my Military Capacity, the attempts of "*Patriots*", rebels, and Sympathizers,

493 Samuel Down was a Wesleyan Methodist clergyman, who served Chatham and Sarnia before going to Bruce mines.

494 Samuel Bealey Harrison, judge of the York County Court from 1848, combined public service and political careers, serving first as private secretary to Sir George Arthur, then provincial secretary and a commissioner of public works under Sydenham. He represented Kingston in the Legislature from 1841, and Kent, briefly, in 1844–45. In 1845 he was made a judge of the Surrogate Court.

495 Prince must have intended 1841.

who sought to crush all loyal Subjects of Her Majesty in 1837 and 1838, or upon the mode in which I did crush it, or upon the (comparatively speaking) ruinous expences I incurred during my Command of my regiment on that Western Frontier. The History of my Life will tell the Tale when I am under ground; and a comparison between the rewarded & neglected, and the relative duties of both sets, will be accurately displayed to the world.

So much for my feelings, so far. But I feel that I have been grievously neglected by Canada. Now, as to *this Judgeship* – You cannot, Sir, have forgotten that, at yr own request, but, I confess upon my own suggestion, I submitted to you the full heads of a Bill absolutely necessary for the welfare & good Government of this District. I was assured by two Members of Parliament – your friends & supporters – that you Entertained a favorable opinion of my scheme, *and that you would introduce the Measure and that it should become a Law*. I have never been honored Even with an acknowledgement from you of the Pains I took in that matter! Have I offended you? If I have, pray tell me *how*, that I may repair or Explain how it is that I am deserving of your neglect. I beseech you to write to me, and tell me *how it is* that I am considered deserving of Such silent Contumely. I pray you to relieve my mind. No man hath a higher regard for you than I have (I am sure you ought to know it); and I *do* hope that you will, at least, frame a Bill for the coming New Parliament, to do justice to the People *and to me*, as the Judge of this Most important District.

529 PRINCE TO THE HON. ALEXANDER CAMPBELL[496]
[*PAC, M.G. 26, A1(a), Vol. 59*]

Belle Vue Lodge, March 28, 1868

A few days ago I addressed a letter to your Colleague, The *Secretary of State for Canada*,[497] informing him that I have good grounds for believing that, on the opening of The Navigation, a Set of Brigands, & Ruffians, & others from *the Mines above this place* – fellows who are about to be discharged because the Copper mines do not "pay" – will invade us, and plunder us of Every thing moveable, and not only us but Every body Else in the District whose personal property they can consume, or carry away &c. They are represented to me to number, at least, *five hundred*; and against such a force any resistance by us would be utterly useless – for we have neither *Men*, nor arms, nor ammunition wherewith to prevent their outrages.

On my return home from holding a Division Court at The Bruce Mines, (a Journey of about *100 miles* over *Ice and Water*, & fraught *with actual danger Every minute*), I have received additional Evidence, from the principal Saloon-keeper here, that such an invasion is actually intended and likely to be carried

---

496 Sir Alexander Campbell, a law partner of John A. Macdonald, was elected to the Legislative Council for Cataraqui, in 1858. He was made a commissioner of crown lands in 1864, and was appointed to the Canadian Senate in 1867.

497 Sir Hector Louis Langevin.

out. The rascals profess to be *Fenians*; and that they mean to "*take*" *this District*, and to hold it until reinforced by a large Band of fellows from below; and my informant assures me that he has been told all this by *one of the U. States Soldiers* who is one of the force in the opposite Fort, and who is a professed Fenian, and who states to my informant that many, if not most, of his Comrades would join in the Invasion. *I believe the Statement to be correct*, and I suggested to the Secretary that Government may send up to *Marquette*, & other places above this where the fellows are at present, one or two clever men who can proceed, *by rail*, to Marquette, and return to Ottawa with the information procured; and then, if necessary, to send us aid. A *gun-boat* would be of infinite Service to us; for my last named informant collected from the Soldier that their plan was to compel certain Schooners to bring them down to *Point aux Pins* (about 10 miles above this) where they intend landing, and then march, before daylight, upon this place. That is intended to be their plan, but their landing could be prevented by a Gunboat, I think.

You will pardon the brevity & hastiness of my letter, because I have only A few Minutes to send this over to be mailed on the other side. I write by the U. States Mail, lest the one by our mail should be delayed or Miscarry, and because (when I wrote the latter) I had not rec'd the Saloon keeper's information.

I think the Navigation will *open Early* in these regions, because the immense mass of Snow (3–6 & Even 10 feet deep in many places) is fast disappearing, and the ice getting rotten. Such a dreadful winter was never before known in *this horrid country*! and I hope never to live to see such another!!

530 DIARY, 4 APRIL 1868

A very hard frost and a Cold day. Walked up to town to hold my division Court. "Lilly" (Rebecca)[498] accompanied me & took her lesson. Held Court at 11 and gave Judgment for defendant in *Turner* vs. *Pim* much to the surprize and dis-satisfaction of Plt. to whom I was obliged to address some *severe remarks* on account of his obstinate & ignorant pertinacity. Also had Mr. *C. Bampton* in the office (room) of Mr. Hamilton, after the Court rose, and gave him a thoroughly severe lecture as to his proclivities to *Feniansim*, which I believe exist, but which he denies. Conferred with the JPs & others, & *Pilgrim*, as to sending up a *Spy* to the Mines above, but they seemed *indifferent about it*. Walked home by 3 pm & read 'till 10, and then to bed. A cold night.

531 DIARY, 16 APRIL 1868

A rapid thaw & no frost, but heavy rain fell, and a heavy Gale of wind from the South continues to break up the Ice in all parts above & below, and a great deal flows down the River, and it continued a most unpleasant day throughout. I

---

498 Rebecca Lapish was Mrs Hetherington's niece.

was busily engaged in sorting my boxes of papers and letters up-stairs, but found little or nothing of those most interesting as to my life in *"this horrid Canada"* in 1837, 1838 & 1839, when, *like a fool*, I endangered my life so often in its defence and in support of Monarchy! I suppose all such papers were used up or lost or destroyed at The Park Farm after I left it in 1860 to come to this dreadful place. In bed by 11 pm.

532 Diary, 5 August 1868

Another foggy, warm, dry, heated & unpleasant morning. Busy at home & among the live Stock & about the premises all day. Walked up to town, & *inspected our new Gaol & Court House* with Sheriff Carney & Damp and the Gov't Inspector (the 2 latter came down and paid me a visit in the Evening), and *Mrs. Simpson* and one of her daughters also came down and called on Mrs. Hetherington & Rebecca, & saw the Garden & seemed to admire Every thing. I went to bed at 9 much *tired*.

533 Excerpt from John A. Macdonald to Prince.
Private
[PAC, M.G. 26, A1(e), Vol. 515]

Ottawa, July 16, 1869

I was not aware that you had any idea of being transferred from your present position until I received your note, which arrived too late. I shall see what can be done hereafter.

By the way if you would write Hervey Price, the Judge of the County of Welland, asking him if he would exchange, I think it likely that he would do so. This must, however, come from yourself and not from any inspiration from me.

534 Prince to John A. Macdonald
[PAC, M.G. 26, A1(d), Vol. 342]

Belle Vue Lodge, July 24, 1869

I thank you very much for your kind letter. I have lived, as Judge here, for nine years. I preferred this wild part of U.C. to any other, because I was *told*, (by some who knew better but who were desirous of getting me hither), that *Deer & other large Game* were abundant; whereas I believe it to be the *only part of North America where they do not exist!* I have, therefore, had no *Enjoyment of life since I came here.* On that account I wish to leave, though the Sacrifice to me by doing so will entail a loss to me of *many thousands of Dollars* by disposing of my *real Estate* in this District. My great desire is to spend the remainder of my days *where Game abounds*, even if it be without *the pale of much Civilization.* May I then solicit your favorable & due consideration toward my being appointed Chief Judge, or Recorder, (or whatever the title may be) of the newly acquired *North West Territory*? I think I should be very happy there, and should be able *to organize a good Judiciary in that New Country*; and this Judgeship would be a most welcome appointment to any friend of yours, who may obtain advantages *here* (Especially as to *Healthiness*) which Cannot be found below.

Pray do me the favor to turn in yr. mind, with favor to me, what I have suggested; & *when Convenient*, do oblige me with yr. opinion of my proposal.

I have been very much shocked at what has appeared in the papers Concerning Mr. Riffenstein.[499] What a misfortune it is that some men know not when they are well off, & cannot be Contented with good fortune!

As regards your Suggestion of an Exchange with Mr. H.P., I could not be happy in *the Midst of a large Community & much Civilization*.

535 EXCERPT FROM PRINCE TO JOHN A. MACDONALD
 [*PAC, M.G. 26, a1(d), Vol. 342*]

Belle Vue Lodge, August 3, 1870

My own health is far from what it was, Even a year ago. But I have too much "pluck" to give up the Ship until she "founders". I have steered her, tolerably well, for 50 years (being now in my 74th year), and I am as vigorous as Ever in mind, and as tough in body as Ever, tho' not *quite* so active in the field; and my motto is, "No Surrender", until the last Summons comes.

536 EXCERPT FROM JOHN A. MACDONALD TO JOHN SANDFIELD MACDONALD. *Confidential*
 [*PAC, M.G. 26, A1(e), Vol. 517*]

Ottawa, November 29, 1870

I note what you say about Algoma, & think that you are quite right in the course you propose to take. Our legislation with respect to Algoma was althogether experimental. It was represented to us that that Country would not be settled until it had Judicial Institutions & Tribunals which would protect life and property. The experiment has now been fully tried and has not resulted in an influx of settlers. While on this subject I will say that I endeavoured to secure the resignation of our old friend Prince through his son. I did not mention my object which was to provide for Walter McCrea[500] and make a vacancy for Frank Smith.[501] You mentioned to me when I saw you last, that you contem-

---

499 George C. Reiffenstein, chief clerk in the Receiver General's Department, was charged with misappropriating public monies.
500 Walter McCrea was a Chatham lawyer and a member of the Legislative council who for a brief period owned a Liberal Chatham newspaper.
501 Sir Frank Smith was appointed to the Senate in 1871.

plated making the change, and had Prince consented I intended to have written you on the subject to ask you to promise to appoint Walter McCrea the Stipendiary Magistrate.

537 'DEATH OF JUDGE PRINCE'
[*Toronto* Evening Globe, *6 December 1870*]

We regret to learn that on the 30th Nov. Judge Prince, of Algoma, died suddenly at his residence in Sault Ste. Marie. He had been ailing during the summer, but was somewhat better when death suddenly struck him while alone in his room. Col. Prince was for many years a leader of the Western circuit at the bar of Upper Canada, and a member of Parliament for the county of Essex, of which he was a resident. He became celebrated during the rebellion of 1837 by the promptitude with which he acted against the sympathizers, and his summary execution of several of them. He was a man of fine presence, a beautiful speaker when in his prime, and had he been a more consistent politician would have made a greater mark in the history of the country. He was appointed Judge on the setting off of Algoma as a judicial district, and has been widely and favourably known through the great county over which he has borne almost unlimited sway. His family is large; among them are Mr. Albert Prince, Q.C.; and Capt. Prince, Chief of Police in this city.[502]

[502] William Stratton Prince was appointed in 1859.

BIBLIOGRAPHY
AND
INDEX

BIBLIOGRAPHY

MANUSCRIPTS

ONTARIO

Archives of Ontario, Toronto
  A.N. Buell Papers
  RG 1, Crown Lands Papers
  Western District Records: Court of General Quarter Sessions of the Peace, minutes. (Microform in Hiram Walker Historical Museum, Windsor.)
  Miscellaneous manuscripts

Fort Malden National Historic Park, Amherstburg
  Miscellaneous manuscripts

Hiram Walker Historical Museum, Windsor
  Documents Relative to Colonel the Honourable John Prince, 1837–1838. ND. (Bound photostats and transcripts of documents, mostly or all in the Public Archives of Canada)
  20–135(78), George F. Macdonald Papers: 'Military.' (Microform; original loaned to Archives of Ontario)
  20–275, John Prince Papers: diary. (Microform; original loaned to Archives of Ontario)
  20–248, Western District Records: Court of General Quarter Sessions of the Peace, various series. (Microform: original loaned to Archives of Ontario)

Metropolitan Toronto Central Library
  William Allan Papers
  Robert Baldwin Papers
  Boulton Papers
  James Hamilton Papers
  Henry Rudyerd diary; in Boulton Papers

St John's Church, Sandwich (Windsor)
  Parish register. 1833 et seqq.

University of Western Ontario, D.B. Weldon Library, London
  Robertson-Ronalds Papers

Canada

Public Archives of Canada, Ottawa
  MG 24, Nineteenth Century Pre-Confederation Papers
  MG 26, Papers of the Prime Ministers
  RG 1, Records of the Executive Council, Canada
  RG 5, Records of the Civil and Provincial Secretaries' Offices, Canada West
  RG 7, Governor General's Office Records
  RG 9, Records of the Department of Militia and Defence

England

Gloucester City Library
  St Mary's Church, Cheltenham: parish register. 1824. (Transcript)

County Record Office, Gloucester
  Land tax assessments: Cheltenham, north side, 1826–30; Cheltenham, south side, 1824; Winchcombe parish, Lower Kiftsgate hundred, hamlet of Coates, 1829–30

Record Office, Hereford
  Land tax assessments: Lugwardine (civil) parish, Radlow hundred, 1808–25
  Lugg Bridge Mills: abstract of title, 1797–1825
  Lugwardine Parish Church: account book. 1818

PUBLISHED PRIMARY SOURCES

DOUGHTY, SIR ARTHUR G., ed. *The Elgin-Grey Papers, 1846–1852.* 4 volumes. Ottawa: King's Printer, 1937.
GIBBS, ELIZABETH, ed. Debates of the Legislative Assembly of United Canada. Vol. IV. part 1, 1844–45 Montreal: 1973.
Gray's Inn, London (England). *Admission Register.* 1831.
Indian Treaties and Surrenders. 3 volumes. Ottawa: King's Printer, 1912. Republished Toronto: Coles Publishing Company, 1971.
NISH, ELIZABETH, ed., Debates of the Legislative Assembly of United Canada. Vol. I, 1841. Montreal: 1970; Vol. III, 1843, Montreal: 1972.
The Register of Electors ... for the Western Division of the County of Gloucester ... Dursley (England): 1832.
SANDERSON, CHARLES E., ed. *The Arthur Papers.* 3 volumes. Toronto Public Library and University of Toronto Press, 1943–57.
Upper Canada, House of Assembly. *Journals.* 1836 et seqq.

NEWSPAPERS AND PERIODICALS

Ontario

Chatham *Chronicle*
Chatham *Planet*
Hamilton *Spectator, and Journal of Commerce*
Sandwich *Canada Advertiser*
Sandwich *Canadian Emigrant and Western District Advertiser*
Sandwich (after 5 February 1857, Sandwich and Amherstburg) *Maple Leaf*
Sandwich *Western Express*
Sandwich *Western Herald and Farmers Magazine*
Toronto *British Colonist*
Toronto *Christian Guardian*
Toronto *Constitution*
Toronto *Correspondent and Advocate*
Toronto *Daily Leader*
Toronto *Globe*
Toronto *Weekly Messenger* (later, *Mackenzie's Toronto Weekly Messenger*)
Windsor *Herald*
WILSON, THOMAS B., ed. *The Ontario Register*. Quarterly. Lambertville, New York, 1968–71.

Canada

Canada Parliamentary Debates. Canadian Library Association Microfilming Project, n.d.
Montreal *Gazette*
Montreal *Mirror of Parliament*
Montreal *Transcript and Commercial Advertiser*
Quebec *Morning Chronicle and Commercial and Shipping Gazette*

England

Cheltenham *Chronicle*
Cheltenham *Journal*
Hereford *Journal*
Hereford *Times*
London *Observer*
London *Times*

United States

Detroit *Daily Advertiser*

BIBLIOGRAPHY
DIRECTORIES

Ontario

County of Essex Gazetteer and General and Business Directory for 1866–7. Woodstock: Sutherland & Co., 1866.

County of Kent Gazetteer and General and Business Directory for 1864–5. Ingersoll: Sutherland & Co., 1864.

WALTER, GEORGE. *The City of Toronto and the Home District Commercial Directory ... for 1837.* Toronto: 1837.

FOTHERGILL, CHARLES, ed. *The Toronto Almanac and Royal Calendar of Upper Canada for the Year 1839.* Toronto: 1839.

LEWIS, FRANCIS. *The Toronto Directory and Street Guide for 1843–4.* Toronto: 1843.

BROWN, GEORGE. *Brown's Toronto City and Home District Directory, 1846–47.* Toronto: 1846.

BROWN, W.R. *Brown's Toronto General Directory, 1856.* Toronto: 1856.

CAVERHILL, W.C.P. *Caverhill's Toronto City Directory for 1859–60.* Toronto: 1859.

Canada

MACKAY, ROBERT W.S. *The Canada Directory ...* Montreal: 1851.

LOVELL, JOHN. *The Canada Directory ...* Montreal: 1857.

Mitchell's Canada Gazetteer and Business Directory for 1864–65. Toronto: 1864.

Lovell's Canadian Dominion Directory for 1871. Montreal: 1871.

Gazetteer and Directory of the Great Western Railway and Branches ... Toronto: 1874.

England

Williams's New Guide to Cheltenham. 1824

New Historical Directory of Cheltenham and its Vicinity. Cheltenham: S.Y. Griffith & Co., 1826.

HILL, S., AND TEESDALE COCKELL, eds. *Clarke's New Law List.* London: 1803–40.

United States

MACCABE, JULIUS P. BOLIVAR. *Directory of the City of Detroit ...* Detroit: 1837. Reproduced Detroit: R.L. Polk & Co., 1937.

SELECTED SECONDARY SOURCES

Commemorative Biographical Record of the County of Essex, Ontario. Toronto: J.H. Beers & Co., 1905.

Commemorative Biographical Record of the County of Kent. Toronto: J.H. Beers & Co., 1904.

CAPP, EDWARD H. *The Story of Baw-a-ting, Being the Annals of Sault Sainte Marie.* Sault Ste Marie, Ontario: 1907.

CARELESS, J.M.S. *The Union of the Canadas; the Growth of Canadian Institutions, 1841–1847.* McClelland and Stewart Limited, 1967.

CLEARY, FRANCIS. 'The Battle of Windsor,' in Essex Historical Society, *Papers & Addresses*, vol. 2, ca. 1915.

CORNELL, PAUL G. *The Alignment of Political Groups in Canada, 1841–1867.* Toronto: University of Toronto Press, [ca. 1962].

CRAIG, GERALD M. *Upper Canada; the Formative Years, 1784–1841.* McClelland and Stewart Limited, 1963.

COTÉ, J.O. *Political Appointments and Elections in the Province of Canada From 1841 to 1865.* 2nd ed., 1866, republished with *Appendix From 1st January, 1866, to 30th June, 1867* and *Index*. Ottawa: N. Omer Coté, 1918.

ERMATINGER, C.O. *The Talbot Regime.* St Thomas: 1904.

EVANS, HERBERT A., and FREDERICK L. GRIGGS. *Highways and Byways in Oxford and the Cotswolds.* London, England: 1905.

FARMER, SILAS. *The History of Detroit and Michigan.* Detroit: Silas Farmer & Co., 1884.

GRAHAM, W.H. *The Tiger of Canada West.* Toronto and Vancouver: 1962.

GUILLET, EDWIN C. *The Lives and Times of the Patriots.* Toronto: University of Toronto Press, 1938 and 1963.

――― *Pioneer Inns and Taverns.* 5 volumes and appendix. Toronto: Ontario Publishing Co. Ltd., 1958.

HAMIL, FRED COYNE. *The Valley of the Lower Thames, 1640 to 1850.* Toronto: University of Toronto Press, 1951.

HINSPERGER, AILEEN [COLLINS]. *Stories of the Past; 300 Years of Soo History.* Sault Ste Marie, Ontario: Sault Star Commercial Printing, 1967.

HODGETTS, J.E. *Pioneer Public Service.* Toronto: University of Toronto Press, 1955.

MARTYN, J.P. 'The Patriot Invasion of Pelee Island,' in *Ontario History*, vol. LVI, no. 3, September, 1964.

MORTON, W.L. *The Critical Years; the Union of British North America, 1857–1873.* McClelland and Stewart Limited, 1964.

NEAL, FREDERICK. *The Township of Sandwich (Past and Present).* Windsor: Record Printing Co., 1909.

NOTMAN, W., and FENNINGS TAYLOR. *Portraits of British Americans, With Biographical Sketches.* 2 volumes. Montreal: William Notman, 1865 and 1867.

PALMER, GENERAL FRIEND. *Early Days in Detroit.* Detroit: 1906.

PRINCE, ALAN CHARLES. *Narrative of Col. The Honourable John Prince, Delivered before the Essex Historical Society May 28, 1923.* Photocopy in Hiram Walker Historical Museum, Windsor.

Public Archives of Canada, Manuscript Division. *Preliminary Inventory, Record Group 9, Department of Militia and Defence, 1776–1922.* Ottawa: n.d.

——— *Preliminary Inventory, Record Group 10, Indian Affairs.* Ottawa: 1951.

——— *Preliminary Inventory, Record Group 19, Department of Finance.* Ottawa: 1954.

Records of the Municipal Council of the Western District, the United Counties of Essex, Kent and Lambton, the United Counties of Essex and Lambton, and the Essex County Council ... Amherstburg: The Echo Printing Company, 1923.

Report[s] of the Pioneer Society of the State of Michigan (from 1889, *Reports and Collections of the Michigan Pioneer and Historical Society*). 40 volumes, plus indices. Lansing, Michigan: [1877]–1907.

SCADDING, HENRY. *Toronto of Old.* Toronto: 1878.

SHORTT, ADAM, and ARTHUR G. DOUGHTY. *Canada and its Provinces.* 23 volumes. Toronto: Publishers' Association of Canada Ltd., 1913–17.

STEWART, CHARLES H., comp. *The Service of British Regiments in Canada and North America.* 2nd edition. Ottawa: Department of National Defence Library, 1964.

WOODS, R.S. *Harrison Hall and its Associations.* Chatham: Planet Book and Job Dept., 1896.

Woolhope Club (England). *Transactions.* 1924.

INDEX

Adamson, Rev. W.A. 150n
Africa 148
Airey, Lieut. Dionysius 30n
Airey, Lieut. Col. Richard xxvii, 27n, 33
Algoma, 195
Algoma District xlvi, lii, liii, liv, lv, lvi, lix, 170, 171, 172, 175, 182, 188, 195, 196, 198, 200, 202, 205, 206
Algoma District Court. *See* Courts
Algoma District Court of Quarter Sessions. *See* Courts
Algoma District Division Court. *See* Courts
Algoma District Surrogate Court. *See* Courts
Alien bill xxiv, 13, 14–15, 49
Allan, William 117n
Allen, Mr 193
American Hotel, Buffalo. *See* Inns
Amherstburg xxv, xxxiv, xli, li, 15, 17, 21, 27, 28, 43, 64, 65, 87, 140
Amherstburg and St Thomas Railroad. *See* Railroads: Southern
Anderdon Township xxv, 58, 87, 106
Anderson, Mrs A. *See* Inns – Toronto: Half Way
Anderson, Charles E. xxvii, 27n, 33, 34
Anderson's (Half Way House), Toronto. *See* Inns
Anderton, William 39n, 104
Anglo American Hotel, Hamilton. *See* Inns
Anne. See Patriot War
Annexation xli, xliii, xlv, 106, 110–11, 115, 128
Argo 105n
Armour,– 165n
Army
– British: 85th Regt. (King's Shropshire Light Infantry) xxviii, 33n; 15th Regt. (East Yorkshire) 16; 34th Regt. (Border) 29, 33n; 43rd Regt. (Oxfordshire and Buckinghamshire Light Infantry) 44; 71st Regt. (Highland Light Infantry) 69n, 131, 157; 100th Regt. (The Prince Regent's County of Dublin) 163
Arroll, Sarah 195n, 196
Arroll, William 192, 195n, 196n, 199, 200
Arthur, Sir George xxvii, xxix, 22n, 27, 28, 38, 39, 131
Askew, Mr 48

Askew, Isaac 145n
Askin, Charles 42n
Askin, James 42n
Assiginac, J.B. 192n
Assumption Church xxix
Athenæum Hotel, Toronto. *See* Inns
Aylwin, Thomas C. xxxvii, 51n, 80n, 86, 87, 88, 89

Babcock and Gardiner 29
Baby, Charles xxx, xxxi, xliv, xlv, 6n, 32, 33, 44, 45, 47, 54, 112, 126
Baby, François (Francis) 30n, 34, 39, 105
Baby, Jean Baptiste xxxi
Baby, William Duperon xxxiii, xli, xlvii, xlviii, 62n, 65, 66, 105, 106, 116n, 142, 143
Baby, Mrs William Duperon 73, 143
Badgley, William 86n, 90, 94
Baily, George 146
Baldwin, Robert xxxi, xxxii, xxxiii, xxxiv, xxxvii, xxxviii, xl, xlii, 54n, 55, 56, 59, 65, 68, 75, 83, 88, 94, 98n, 101, 108, 109, 113
Bampton, Charles J. lix, 203. *See also* Inns: Sault Ste Marie
Bampton, William 139n
Bampton's saloon, Sault Ste Marie. *See* Inns
Banking bill 15
Banks: Western District xxiv, 10, 11; British North America xxiv, 11, 48; Upper Canada xxiv, 171, 198; City (Montreal) 82, 90
Banwell, Henry xlvii, 141n
Baptiste Creek 134
Barrett 129
Barrie 173
Barstow, Samuel 91n
Bath, England 174
Battle of Windsor. *See* Patriot War
Battle of Windsor (paper) 28–31, 36, 39
Baxter 39
Bear Creek 52
Beaumont, Dr William 162n, 166
Becher, Miss 154
Becher, H.C.R. 129n, 135, 143, 162
Becher, Mrs H.C.R. 154, 160
Bedford, Joseph 177n
Bedford, Michel 177n
Beeman, Mrs 66. *See also* Inns – Sandwich: Prince Albert

INDEX

Beeman, Elam 59n, 91. *See also* Inns – Sandwich: Prince Albert
Beeman's (Prince Albert) Sandwich. *See* Inns
Bell, David 172n
Bell, John 181n
Bell, William 172n
Belle River 43, 44
Belle Vue Lodge lvi, lvii, lviiin, lix, 179, 180–1, 201
Bennett, Mr (Patriot prisoner) 29
Bennett, John 192
Bennett, Norton 192
Berkeley, Mr xx
Berkeley, William Fitzhardinge xix
'Bertie' (modern Fort Erie) 95n, 96, 114
Bethnal Green, London, England xx
Biddle House, Detroit. *See* Inns
Biron, Joachim (Joe, 'Swachart') 188n, 198
Biscoe (Briscoe), Captain Vincent 37n
Bissell, Mr 146n
Blackburn, Mrs Thornton 42, 73
Blacks xliii, xlix, l, liii, 16, 117, 147, 156–7, 169
Blain, D. 184n, 185
Blair, Adam Johnston Fergusson. *See* Fergusson Blair
Bogue 196
Bois Blanc Island, Detroit River li, 17, 18, 19
Boismier, Edward 148n
Bondy, Gabrielle xlix
Bonsecours Market, Montreal 101
Borasseau, John. *See* Brasseau
Boron, E.B. *See* Borron
Borron (Boron), E.B. 190
Boston 81
Bosworth, Thomas Holmes xix
Botsford, David 25n
Boulton, Miss 154
Boulton, Mrs D'Arcy 11n
Boulton, George S. 12n, 198
Boulton, Mrs Henry 150, 154. *See also* Rudyerd, Charlotte
Boulton, Henry John 145n, 146
Boulton, William Henry 77n
Bower, Dr Martin 82n, 98
Brady, General Hugh 26n
Brantford 81
Brasseau (Borasseau), John 190n
Brewster, Miss 129n
Briscoe, Captain Vincent. *See* Biscoe
British American Bank (British North American Bank). *See* Banks
British Army. *See* Army: British
British North American Bank. *See* Banks
British North American Mining Company. *See* Mines

Broderick, Captain 29, 30, 34
Brougham, Lord xxix, 38n
Brougham, Henry Peter. *See* Brougham, Lord
Brown (at Windsor) 83
Brown, Mr (Sault Ste Marie, Michigan) 190
Brown, George xxxix, xl, xlii, xliii, xlvi, xlviii, li, liii, lvii, 97n, 98, 99, 100, 103, 121, 124n, 131, 132, 142, 170, 179, 189
Bruce, James. *See* Elgin, Earl of
Bruce Mines lv, lvi, lviiin, 173, 174, 178, 183, 193, 194, 202. *See also* Mines
Brush, Edmund A. 15n
Buchanan, Isaac 148n, 172n, 173, 181
Buell, Andrew Norton 130n
Buffalo 26, 77, 126, 164
Buffalo and Brantford Railway. *See* Railroads
Bullock, George xli, liv, 43, 91n, 105, 171
Bullock, Colonel Richard xxvii, xxxiii, 53n, 60, 142n
Bullock's tavern, Amherstburg. *See* Inns
Bureau, J.O. 183n
Burke, Patrick 179
Butchert, Mrs 194
Butterfield Island lviiin

Cabot Head 168
Cahoon, Benjamin P. 7n, 35
Caldwell, Francis xxx, 7n, 44, 45
Caldwell, Captain John 17
Cambray, Cheltenham, England xix
Cameron 180
Cameron, Alexander. *See* Inns: Bruce Mines
Cameron, Alexander (Toronto?) 130n
Cameron, Lieut. Allen 32n
Cameron, John 171n
Cameron, John Hillyard xxxviii, xxxix, 87n, 92, 93
Cameron, Malcolm xxxv, xxxvi, xxxvii, xxxviii, xxxix, xl, xlvi, 35n, 74, 79, 80, 81, 83, 84, 87, 92, 93, 97, 104, 118, 119n, 128, 131
Cameron's inn, Bruce Mines. *See* Inns
Campbell 175, 178
Campbell, Captain 23
Campbell, Sir Alexander 202n
Canada Advertiser. *See* Newspapers: Sandwich
Canada Gazette. *See* Newspapers: Kingston
Canada Loan Company 170
Canada Oak. *See* Newspapers – Sandwich: *Oak*
Canadian 168
Canadian Emigrant. *See* Newspapers: Sandwich
Canosh. *See* Kenosh
Canton. *See* Contin

INDEX 217

Carney, John 186n
Carney, Richard lv, lvii, 173n, 175, 176, 178, 181, 182, 186, 187, 189, 190, 191, 195, 204
Carney, William 197
Caron, Francis (François) xlii, 116n
Caron, René Edouard xxxvi, 78n
Carroll, Mr 89n
Carroll, Peter xxxix
Carry, Rev. John 193n, 196
Cartier, Sir George Etienne liii, 83n
Cartwright, John Solomon 12n, 13
Cary, Joseph 62n
Cassells, Robert C. 190n
Castle, C.H. 90n
Cataract 126
Cathcart, Lord xxxv, 76n, 78
Cathcart, Lady 76n
Cathcart, Charles Murray. *See* Cathcart, Lord
Cauchon, Joseph Edouard 104n
Cayley, William lii, 94n, 160
Chalmers, George 79n
Chambly 69n
Chance, Rev. James 181n, 186, 190, 194, 201
Chancery, Court of. *See* Courts
Chapais, Jean Charles 191, 193
Chappu, Benjamin. *See* Inns: Petite Cote
Chappu's tavern, Petite Cote. *See* Inns
Charles, Mr 35
Chatham xxxii, xxxv, xxxvi, xlii, xlix, 27, 56, 72, 84, 92, 93, 104, 121, 123, 136, 145, 146, 147, 149, 178
Chatham *Planet. See* Newspapers
Chauveau, P.J.O. 132n
Cheeseman, Lieut. Benjamin 28
Cheltenham, England xix, xx, xxi
Chenail Ecarté 148n
Chewett, Alexander xxxiv, xxxv, xxxvi, 30n, 42, 59, 61, 66, 71, 73
Chewett, Sarah (Mrs Alexander) xxxv, xxxvi, xxxix, 42, 59, 61, 73, 74, 81, 82
Chicago lix
Chichester, Colonel Sir Charles 69n
Child(s), Mr 86n
Christie, David 164n, 169
Christie, Robert 47n, 68, 94, 104, 136
Church. See Newspapers: Toronto
Church, Mr 174, 179, 180, 197
City Bank, Montreal. *See* Banks
City of Cleveland. 178, 181
City Restaurant, Quebec. *See* Inns
Clarke, Judge 169n
Clarke, Ann and Susan 23
Cleeve Hill, Cheltenham, England xix
Clergy reserves xxviii, xxix, xliii, 9–10, 12–13, 40, 87, 120, 123, 130

Clinton, Henry Pelham Fiennes Pelham. *See* Newcastle, Duke of
Coatsworth, Joshua 200n
Colborne, Sir John. *See* Seaton, Lord
Colborne Furnace 7n, 44
Colchester Township xxvi, 43, 87
Coldbath Fields, London, England. *See* Courthouses and Jails
Colley, Mr 106n
Collingwood 168, 174, 175, 186, 195
Colonist. *See* Newspapers: Toronto
Colonnade (The), Cheltenham, England xix, xx
Colston, Mr. *See* Coulson
Commercial Herald. See Newspapers: Toronto
Commercial Hotel, Chatham. *See* Inns
Conciliation, Court of. *See* Courts
Confederation liii, lix, 163, 165–6, 200
Conté. *See* Contin
Conteau. *See* Contin
Contin (Canton, Conté, Conteau, Conton) 180
Conton. *See* Contin
Cornish, Dr William King 72n
Coulson (Colston), Mr 194n
Court, Mr 97
Courthouses and Jails
– Chatham 148, 150
– Detroit 18
– London, England: Coldbath Fields xx, xxii; Fleet Prison xx
– Sandwich xxiii, 16, 33, 35, 56, 59, 91, 105, 117, 136, 139, 140, 158
– Sault Ste Marie lvi, 178, 181, 182, 183, 185, 186, 191, 193, 196, 204
Courts: Chancery (Equity) xxiv, li, 8n, 11, 12n, 40, 110, 136, 154, 162; Western District Quarter Sessions xxiv, xxviii, 14, 31, 32, 38; Inquiry (military) xxviii, 32, 36, 38; Western District xxviii, xxxiv; Algoma District liv, 176, 201; Algoma District Quarter Sessions lv, 174, 176, 182, 187, 190, 194, 197, 199; Algoma District Surrogate lv; Algoma District Division lv, lvi, 177, 183, 184, 202, 203; King's Bench 25; London District 103; Conciliation 112, 119
Cowan, James M. 83
Cowan, John xxxvi, 31n, 34, 79
Crawford, Mr 90
Crimea xlv, 135, 136, 138
Cronyn, Mr and Mrs 131n
Crooks, James 37n
Cross, Dr T. 148n
Crow, Mr 129n
Cumberland, Frederic William 200n
Customs bill 71

Cuthbertson, James xxxvii, 90n
Cuvillier, Augustin xxx, 45n, 46

Daily Advertiser. See Newspapers: Detroit
Dale, John. *See* Dales
Dales (Dale), John 192
Daly, Sir Dominick 59n, 62, 66, 82, 91, 94, 102
Daly's Hotel, Montreal. *See* Inns
Damp, John 198n, 204
Davidge 163
Davidson, John 174n, 186
De Blaquière, Peter Boyle 152n, 153, 163, 164
Deedes, Major H. 33n
De Lamorandière, Charles 196n
Delmage, John F. 150n
Denison, Colonel Richard L. 181n
Dennison, Mr (Patriot prisoner) 29
Dennison, Mr (Sault Ste Marie) 180
Dennomee (Denommée, Dennomée) 180
Dennomée. *See* Dennomee
Denommée. *See* Dennomee
Derby, Earl of 68n
de Rottenburg, Colonel G.F. 138n
Detroit xxii, xxvi, xxvii, xxviii, xlv, 15, 17, 18, 19, 28, 35, 77, 82, 90, 117, 118, 128, 129, 137, 140, 141
Detroit *Daily Advertiser. See* Newspapers
Detroit frontier xxv, xxvin, xliii, 16, 26
Detroit River xxi, xxv, xliii, l, li, 71, 80, 140, 155n; bridge 1, 140, 150; tunnel 140
Detroit Street, Sandwich xxii, xliv
Dewar, Rev. E.H. 169n
De Witt, J. 111n
Dewson, Dr A.K. 11n
Deykes, Mr 47n
Dibble, Colonel Orville B. 129n
Dissolution of Parliament bill xxiv, 8, 13
Dixie, W.A. 73n
Dixie, Mrs W.A. 146n
Dobson, Cyrus. *See* Inns – Sandwich: Western
Dobson's (Western Hotel), Sandwich. *See* Inns
Dods, Mr 192
Dods, John 39
Doherty, Edward 197n
Dolly's Chop House, Montreal. *See* Inns
Donegana, Giuseppe. *See* Inns: Montreal
Donegana's Hotel, Montreal. *See* Inns
Dorion, Sir Antoine Aimé liii
'Double Shuffle' liii
Dougall, James xlviii, xlix, 16n, 28, 29, 131, 146, 147, 148, 149, 150, 171, 185
Douglass, William 197n
Down (Dunn), Rev. and Mrs Samuel, 201n

Draper, William Henry xxxi, xxxii, xxxvi, 51n, 59, 60, 70, 71, 76, 78, 79, 85, 149
Draper, William George 179n
Drew, John 39
Driver, Mrs 189
Driver, John 176n, 177, 187, 189, 190
Drummond, Lewis Thomas 128n
Dryden, John 5
Duck, George 132n
Duckworth, Mr 185n
Dundas xxxiv
Dunlop, Dr William ('Tiger') xxin, 72, 82, 89, 90, 193, 194
Dunn, Mr 33
Dunn, Rev. and Mrs Samuel. *See* Down
Dupont, Charles L. 187n, 190, 192, 193, 199; family, 192
D'Urbain, Lieut. General Sir Benjamin 104
Durham, Lord xxviii
Dynes, Ralph 97

Eberle, John 20n
Eccles, Henry 164n
Elections
– For Legislative Assembly: 1848 xxxix, xl, 97; 1854, xlv–xlvi, 131–2; 1857 li, lii, 158–9, 161, 162; 1861, lvi, 179, 183
– Municipal: 1850 xli, xlvii, 106n. *See also* Prince, John – Political: Elections
'Elector' (pseudonym) xlix
Elgin, Earl of 85n, 91, 104, 105, 108, 113, 119, 130
Elgin County 129
Elgin Mines. *See* Mines
Eliot, Charles xxii, xxiii, xxiv, xxviii, xxxii, 3n, 4, 5, 6, 7, 14, 16, 29, 31, 32, 34, 57, 73, 74
Elliott, Mr 66
Elliott, William xxv, xxviii, xxx, 14n, 23, 29, 31, 32, 33, 44, 76, 91
Elliott's Point 19
Ellison, G.W. 172n
Emerald 126
Emery 140, 141n
England, Colonel 69n
English Church. *See* St John's Church, Sandwich
Enquiry, court of (military). *See* Courts
Equity, Court of. *See* Courts: Chancery
Ermatinger House 176n
Essex County xxvi, xxviii, xxix, xxx, xxxi, xxxiii, xxxvii, xxxviii, xl, xlii, xlv, xlvi, xlviii, xlix, l, lii, liv, lvi, 5, 13, 44, 49, 58, 61, 62, 63, 64, 65, 67, 79, 80, 83, 86, 91, 96, 97, 105, 108, 114, 115, 116, 123, 126, 132, 134, 139, 142, 144, 151, 156, 157,

INDEX 219

159, 160, 161, 162, 163, 172, 174, 175, 179, 183, 206; separation from Kent 113
'Essex Elector' (pseudonym) 146
Essex Militia. *See* Militia

'Fair Play' (pseudonym) 136
Farmer, Mrs 195n
Fenianism lvi, lvii, lix, 193, 197, 203
Fergusson, Adam 36n
Fergusson Blair, Adam Johnston 200n
Ferry (The) 19n, 25, 27, 28, 32, 42, 43, 83. *See also* Windsor
Fighting Island 17. *See also* Patriot War
Fisher, Mr 43
Fitzgibbon, Colonel 22
Fitzherbert, Maria Anne ix
Fleet Prison, London, England. *See* Courthouses and Jails
Flint, Billa 96n
Foley, M.H. 169n
Foott, George Wade xxxix, 27n, 59, 61, 74, 148, 150, 169, 190
Foott, Jane 74
Foott, Wade 83n
Forrest, Mr 183
Forsith, Marion 105
Forsyth, Mr 35
Forsyth, Major Robert A. 82n
Fort Erie (formerly Waterloo) 164. *See also* 'Bertie'
Fort Erie Rapids 14. *See also* 'Bertie'
Fort Gratiot 18n
Fort Malden xxv, xxvii, 19, 21, 26, 28, 29, 32. *See also* Amherstburg; Malden Township
Fort William lv, lvii, 183, 184, 185
Fox 135
Fox, Charles James 61, 191
Fox, Michael 143n
Fraser, Colonel 27
Free Mason's Arms, Sandwich. *See* Inns
French, Major H.I. 33n

Gair (Gear, Grear), John 179, 181
Gally, Mrs 200n
Galt, Sir Alexander Tilloch 194–5, 195n
Garden River lvii, 184, 190, 200, 201
Game legislation xxxii, xxxiv, xliv, li, liv, 1, 15, 56, 69, 71, 124, 155, 170, 187
Gardiner, Samuel 7n, 16, 32, 37, 39n, 66, 118, 138, 185
Garrison, Toronto 10, 11, 13
Gaspé 68
Gatfield, William 23n, 32, 104
Gazette. *See* Newspapers: Kingston
Gear, John. *See* Gair

'George' (Indian) 192
George III 10
George IV ix
Gibbard, William 175n
Gibraltar, Michigan 17
Girty, Prideaux 6n, 20, 21, 27, 37, 66
Glasgow, Captain 20n
Glengarry County 75n
Globe. *See* Newspapers: Toronto
Gordon, Alexander 131n
Gordon, James 150n
Gosfield Township xxvi, 1, 44, 64
Goulding, Martin 182n, 184
Gould's Hotel, Montreal. *See* Inns
Gowan, Ogle Robert 81n, 87, 88n
Grand Trunk Railroad. *See* Railroads
Grant, Alexander 162
Grant, 'Call' 175n, 190
Grant, Captain Duncan 162n
Grant, Henry C. xxxi, 53n
Grant's Point lv
Gray's Inn, London, England xx
Grear, John. *See* Gair
Great Southern Railroad. *See* Railroads: Southern
Great Western Railroad. *See* Railroads
Greisor, Frederick 191
Grenville, Baron 95
Grey, Sir George 137n
Grundy, Captain 73n, 81, 82
Guelph and Sarnia Railroad. *See* Railroads
Guevremont (Guévremont), Jean Baptiste 183n
Guévremont, Jean Baptiste. *See* Guevremont
Guischard, Dr Daniel 135n, 147
Gunn, Mr 118n
Gzowsky, Casimir 98n

Hagerman, Christopher xxiv, 8n, 12, 13, 22, 27
Haggerty, James 20n
Haldimand County 112, 125, 127
Half Way House, Toronto. *See* Inns
Hall, William 27n. *See also* Inns: Sandwich
Hall, William Gaspé 35n
Hall's tavern, Sandwich. *See* Inns
Hamilton xxiv, 10, 81, 101, 129, 169, 181
Hamilton, J.R. 47n
Hamilton, Colonel James 16
Hamilton, John M. 187n, 191, 196, 197, 203
Hamilton, Mrs John M. 189
Hamilton *Spectator*. *See* Newspapers
Hands, Mrs William 73n
Harrington, Mr 112
Harris, Robert W. 148n
Harrison, Samuel Bealey 201n

Hartwick, John 165n
Hastings County 96
Hastings, Howland 37n
Hawkens, Mrs Honor (Honour) 6n. *See also* Inns: Sandwich
Hawkens's Tavern, Sandwich. *See* Inns
Head, Sir Edmund Walker xlvi, xlviii, liii, 137n, 138
Head, Sir Francis Bond xxiii, lii, 10n, 21, 50, 60, 101, 163
Hedley 185
Hen Island lviiin
Henderson, Mr 180
Hendrick, T.A. 167
Hennell, William. *See* Inns: Sandwich
Hennell's inn, Sandwich. *See* Inns
'Henry.' *See* Arroll, William
Hepburn, William 12n
Herald. See Newspapers: Montreal; Windsor
Hetherington, Maria L. liv, lvi, 174, 175, 176, 177, 178, 179, 180, 181, 184, 185, 186, 187, 189, 190, 191, 194, 195, 196, 197, 198, 199, 200, 201, 204. *See also* Inns: Sault Ste Marie; Toronto
Hetherington's boarding house, Sault Ste Marie. *See* Inns
Hetherington's boarding house, Toronto. *See* Inns
Hereford, England xix, xxix
Hewlett Road, Cheltenham, England xix
Hicks 194n
Higginson, Captain J.M. 64n, 66
Hincks, Francis xxxix, xl, xliii, 88n, 97, 100, 101, 120, 121, 128, 134
Hog Island (modern Belle Isle) 30, 32
Holland, Mrs Edward 61n
Hooper, Rev. Thomas lviii
Hooper family 183n
Horton, Mr (attorney) 103
Hotels. *See* Inns
House of Correction, Coldbath Fields, London, England. *See* Courthouses and Jails
Howard, John Henry xx
Howe, Joseph 113n
Howland, William P. 183n
Hudson's Bay Company lii, 161, 184
'Hugh' (workman) 191
Hughes, Mrs 187
Hughes, Francis Jones lvii, 176n, 177, 184, 185, 186, 187, 189, 195
Humber River xxviii
Hume, Dr John James 26, 29
Hunt, Frank 118n
Hunt, Mrs Frank 118n, 129, 138n. *See also* Prince, Mrs Albert
Hunter, Richard 55n, 157

Huron Church Line xliv
Huron Church Reserve xliv, xlv, 126
Huron Copper Bay Company. *See* Mines
Huron County xlvii, 125, 137
Huron Reserve xxv, 14, 15
Hutton, John 43. *See also* Inns – Windsor: Windsor Castle
Hutton's (Windsor Castle), Windsor. *See* Inns
Hyde, George 108n, 131
Hynes, Andrew lvii, 176n, 179, 181, 182, 184, 186, 187, 189, 193

Illinois 185
Independence Manifesto. *See* Prince, John: Political
Independent. See Newspapers: Toronto
India xxi, li, 157, 158
Indian affairs xxv, xxxiv, xliii, xliv, lvi, lvii, 14, 15, 30, 51, 126, 182, 184, 187, 188, 192, 200
Inglis 185
Inglis, Russell. *See* Inns – Toronto: Wellington
Innes, Miss 65
Inns
– Amherstburg: Bullock's 43n; Laliberté's 28; Middleton's 21
– Belle River: Markham's 42
– Bruce Mines: Cameron's 177
– Buffalo: American 164
– Chatham: Mason's Commerical 145, 149
– Cheltenham: Plough xx
– Detroit: Biddle 129n; National 128
– Gosfield Township: Henry Leighton's 43; Robinson's 44
– Hamilton: Anglo American 169; Royal 169; Weekes's 81
– Maidstone Township: Shaffer's 42, 43
– Mersea Township: Leonard Wigle's 43, 44
– Montreal: Daly's 82n, 86, 90 (*see also* Rasco's); Dolly's Chop House xxxix, 76n, 81, 100, 101, 104; Donegana's 90, 94, 101, 104; Gould's Mansion House 69n, 71, 76, 78, 81; Orr's 73; Ottawa (Lavine's) 101; Rasco's 68n, 71, 76 (*see also* Daly's); Mrs Steele's 90, 103; Têtu's 81n, 86
– Morpeth: Morpeth (Sheldon's) 132n
– Petite Cote: Chappu's 42
– Port Sarnia: McAvoy's 131
– Quebec: City 172; Lamb's 124n
– Sandwich: Free Mason's Arms (Laughton's) 106, 108; Hall's 27, 42, 53; Mrs Hawkens's 6, 7, 14, 23, 33; Hennell's 135n, 143, 145, 158; Jessop's 45; Mears's 39n, 66; Parent's 117n; Prince Albert (Beeman's) 59n, 66, 91; Teakle's 116,

143; Western (Dobson's) 144
- Sault Ste Marie: Bampton's 182n, 187, 193, 194; Mrs Hetherington's 177
- Toronto: Athenæum 111; Half Way (Mrs Anderson's) 160n; Mrs Hetherington's 162n; Lamb's 151; Montgomery's li–lii; North American 7, 8; Ontario 15, 22, 25n, 35, 39, 40; Rossin 162n, 163, 165, 166; Seels's 162n; Smith's 154n, 162, 166; Swords's 154n; Wellington (Inglis's) 143n, 151, 152
- Windsor: Mason's 91; Windsor Castle (Hutton's) 43, 131
Inquiry, court of (military). See Courts
Ironside, Alexander McGregor 184
Ironside, George, Sr 30n
Ironside, George, Jr lvii, 182n
Ironside, Mrs George, Jr 185
Ironside, Mary 185n

Jackson, Sir Richard Downes 53n
Jackson, Sir William 128n
Jails. See Courthouses and Jails
James, Samuel 31
Jameson, Mr and Mrs 197n
Janisse 82
Jersey Villa, Cheltenham, England xix, xx
Jessop, George 16n. See also Inns: Sandwich
Jessop's tavern, Sandwich. See Inns
Jobin, A. 90n
Johnson, Dr David D. 6n
Johnson (Johnston), George or James (Sault Ste Marie, Michigan) 167n, 200
Johnson, William 30n
Johnson, Rev. William 23n, 31, 66
Johnson, Mrs William xxxvi
Johnston, George or James (Sault Ste Marie, Michigan). See Johnson
Johnston, James (Carleton County) 68n, 72, 81
Jones, Jonas 23n, 24

Kanosh. See Kenosh
Keating, John W. 51n, 90, 123
Kell, Frederick Polhill xx
Kelly, Dr 194n, 195
Kelly, Thomas 178, 182
Kennedy, Mr 35
Kenosh (Kanosh, Canosh) lvii, 185n
Kent 72
Kent County xxix, xxxvii, xxxviii, xxxix, xlii, xlviii, xlix, l, liv, lvi, 52, 79, 84, 92, 93, 97, 98, 99, 105, 109, 111, 115, 124, 132, 134, 144, 145, 147, 149, 151, 160, 170, 174, 175, 179; separation from Essex and Lambton 113

Kent, Provisional District of. See Western District; division bill
Killaly, Hamilton Hartley 99n, 178
Killarney 167, 174
Kilroy, Thomas 199n
King's Bench, Court of. See Courts
Kingston xxxi, 47, 57, 58, 91, 109, 179, 185
Kinzie, John H. 82n
Kirkpatrick, Thomas 185n
Kohler, Father Augustin 201
Korah Township 195, 197

Lachine 103
Lachlan, Robert xxxiii, 14n, 20, 43, 62, 63, 64, 65, 66, 119, 185, 189
Ladouceur 192
Lafleur 196
LaFontaine, Sir Louis Hippolyte xxxii, xxxiii, xxxvi, xxxviii, xl, 60n, 65, 67, 79, 83, 100n, 101, 102, 110n
Lake Erie xxxviii, xliv, xlix, l, 26, 77, 134, 148
Lake Huron xxxv, l. lv, 151, 168, 192
Lake Ontario 126
Lake St Clair xlix, l, 42, 148
Lake Superior xxxv, xliv, 80, 122
Laliberté, Jean Baptiste xxxiii, 28n, 58n, 59, 60, 61
Laliberté's tavern, Amherstburg. See Inns
Lalonge 135
Lamb, William. See Melbourne, Viscount
Lambs' Hotel, Quebec. See Inns
Lamb's Hotel, Toronto. See Inns
Lambton, John George. See Durham, Lord
Lambton County xlvi, xlviii; separation from Essex, xlv; separation from Kent 113
Lanark County xxxv, 74, 78, 79, 87
Langevin, Sir Hector Louis 202n
Langlois, Dominique 6n, 7, 117
Lansing, Colonel E.A. 139n
Lanton ('colored man') 156
Lapish, Rebecca ('Lilly') 203n, 204
Larwill Edwin xlix, 152n, 164, 165, 169
Laughton, John B. 106n. See also Inns – Sandwich: Free Mason's Arms
Laughton's (Free Mason's Arms), Sandwich. See Inns
Lavallée, Benjamin 6n, 66
Lavine. See Inns – Montreal: Ottawa
Lavine's (Ottawa tavern), Montreal. See Inns
Lavitt (Levitt) 178
Law Society of Upper Canada xxvi
Layton, Dr and Mrs 192n, 193
Leader. See Newspapers: Toronto
Leeds County 88
Leggatt, Gordon Watts 162n

INDEX

Leighton, Henry 43n
Leighton's inn, Gosfield Township. *See* Inns
Lennox and Addington, United Counties of 13
Leslie, Captain G. 27n, 32
Leslie, James 108n, 109
Lewis, Rev. 186
Lewiston 126
Levitt. *See* Lavitt
Ley, George 174n, 180, 186
Liquor legislation 118, 125–6
Lisle ('the colored man') 147
Litchfield, E.C. 83n
Little Current 192
London and Gore Railroad. *See* Railroads
London District 98, 103, 108
London District Court. *See* Courts
London, England xx, xxi, xxiii, 68
London, Ontario xxxii, xxxiv, 60, 73, 98, 135, 164; fire 72
London *Western Globe*. *See* Newspapers – Toronto: *Globe*
Loutit, James 184
Love, Sir James Frederick 131n
Lugg Bridge Mills, Herefordshire, England xix
Lugwardine, Herefordshire, England xix

Macaulay, Sir James Buchanan 134n
McAvoy's Hotel, Port Sarnia. *See* Inns
Macbeth, George 164n
McClenaghan, Alexander 169n
McCormick 162
McCrea, Walter 205n, 206
McCuaig family 169
Macdonald, Donald Alexander 83n
Macdonald, John Alexander xlviii, li, lii, liii, liv, lv, lvi, lvii, lx, 86n, 91, 92n, 133, 142, 143, 158, 161, 162, 163, 164, 165, 171, 172, 173, 174, 183, 185, 188, 189, 193, 198, 201, 204, 205
Macdonald, John Sandfield xliv, 75n, 112n, 118n, 130, 163, 183, 205
Macdonell, Bishop Alexander 20n
MacDonell, Father Angus 16n, 20
Macdonell, Lieut. Colonel D. 86n, 115n, 138, 139
Macdonell, S.S. 114n, 147, 162, 163, 173
McEwen, John 159n
McFarland, D. 95n, 96
McGee, Thomas D'Arcy 191
Macintosh, Captain Donald 150n
McIntyre, John 184n
McKay (McKee, McKoy), James 186n, 187, 199
McKee, James. *See* McKay
McKee, Thomas 140, 141n

McKee's Marsh 15, 82
McKee's Point 42
McKenzie, Roderick 187n
Mackenzie, William Lyon xxv, xl, xlii, xliii, xliv, xlvi, 102n, 112, 114, 119, 121, 125, 127, 133, 134
McKoy, James. *See* McKay
McLean, Archibald 7n, 8
McLean, John 161
McLeod, John xlix, li, 158n, 159, 162, 163, 172, 173
McLeod, Mrs John 160
McMullin, Dr Patrick 26n, 41, 43, 44, 54, 66
MacNab, Sir Allan Napier xxxiv, xxxviii, xl, xlii, xliii, xliv, liv, 8n, 12, 14, 16, 23, 46, 68, 86n, 89, 94, 97, 101, 111, 120, 121, 127, 136
McNab, Donald 197
McPherson, David Lewis 173n
McPherson & Co. 186
Macomb 18
Maidstone Cross 144n
Maidstone Township 162
Maingy, W.A. 172n
Maisonville, Oliver 117
Maitland, Lieut. Colonel John 20n, 21
Malden Township 16, 17, 43, 58, 59, 62. *See also* Amherstburg; Fort Malden
Malloch, E. 102n
Manitoulin Island lvi, lvii, 157, 182, 188
Manitowaning lv, 175
Mansion House. *See* Inns: Montreal
Maple Leaf. *See* Newspapers: Sandwich
Markham, Harrison. *See* Inns: Belle River
Markham's tavern, Belle River. *See* Inns
Marquette 203
Marryat, Captain Frederick xxv, 15
'Martin' (Indian) 31
Masales, Ellen. *See* Mosalis
Mason, Stevens T. 16n, 17, 18, 19
Mason's Commercial Hotel, Chatham. *See* Inns
Mason's Tavern, Windsor. *See* Inns
Massasauga. *See* Mississagi
Maule, Fox. *See* Panmure, Lord
Mayville, Job 191n
Mears, John xxviii, xliv. *See also* Inns: Sandwich
Mears, Mrs John (Hannah) *See* Inns: Sandwich
Mears's inn, Sandwich. *See* Inns
Mears's Orchard 126
Melbourne, Viscount 95
Menzies 141
Mercer 82
Mercer, John xlix, 146, 148, 150
Mercer, Joseph 161n, 174

INDEX

Mercer, Robert xxxi, 23n, 27, 31
Meredith, Edmund Allen 90n
Merritt, William Hamilton 36n, 109n
Mersea Township xxvi, 43, 44
Mesales, Ellen. *See* Mosalis
Metcalfe, Lord xxxii, xxxiii, xxxiv, xxxv, 58n, 60, 64n, 65, 68, 70, 72, 74, 88
Metcalfe, Sir Charles Theophilus. *See* Metcalfe, Lord
Michigan xlix, 19, 24, 25, 139
Middleton, John 21n
Middleton's inn, Amherstburg. *See* Inns
Militia
– Essex County 16; 3rd Regt. xxvi, xxxi, xxxiii, xlvii, 28, 37n, 51, 53, 83; 2nd Regt. xxviii, 29, 45; 1st Regt. 37n, 39n
– Ninth Military District xlvii, 138, 141
Miller, Sergeant 37
Millington, Mary Ann. *See* Prince, Mary Ann
Mills, Mr 20n
Mines: British North American Mining Company xxxvi, xxxvii, xxxviii, xxxix, 82, 90, 94, 100; Bruce xxxvii, 90; Montreal Mining Company xxxvii, 86, 182; Huron Copper Bay Company xxxviii, 90; Elgin 90; Wellington 173. *See also* Bruce Mines
Mississagi 191
Mississagi River lvii, 192
Moffatt, George 37n, 70, 86, 101
Monck, Viscount 183n
Monck, Richard 148n, 150, 170
Monklands 104n
Monroe, Michigan 18
Montgomery, John xlii, 112n. *See also* Inns: Toronto
Montgomery's tavern, Toronto. *See* Inns
Montreal xxxii, xxxv, xxxvi, xxxix, 56, 58, 66, 67, 79, 94, 103, 109, 181, 193
Montreal City Bank. *See* Banks
Montreal *Herald*. *See* Newspapers
Montreal Mining Company. *See* Mines
Montreuil, Luc (Luke, St Luc, St Luke) 91n
Moore, Philip Henry 165n
More, Hannah 190n
Morin, Augustin-Norbert xxxiv, xliii, 67n, 68, 69, 94, 132n, 133
Morin, Pierre Hector xxxiii, 67n
Moring (?), Mr 35
Morning Chronicle. *See* Newspapers: Quebec
Morpeth 146
Morpeth Hotel, Morpeth. *See* Inns
Morris, James 104n
Morrow, Mr 35
Morton, James 164n, 169
Mosalis (Masales, Mesales, Thesales), Ellen 185n

Mountain, Bishop George Jehosaphat 171n
Moy 35n
Moynahan, Denis (Dennis) xlvi, 133, 159
Munday, Colonel G.C. 133, 135
Municipal corporation bill 50
Murney, Edmund 40n, 69, 156
Murray, Professor 175n
Murray, Amelia 134n

National Hotel, Detroit. *See* Inns
Neebish Island lviiin
Nelson, Horatio (Horace) 37n, 106
New South Wales 48
Newcastle, Duke of 130n, 133, 135
Newcastle District 174
Newfoundland fishery 1
Newspapers
– Amherstburg xxxiv
– Chatham: *Planet* xlviii, 146, 147
– Detroit: *Daily Advertiser* 31
– Hamilton: *Spectator* xxxviii
– Kingston: *Canada Gazette* 96, 110
– London: *Western Globe*. *See* Toronto: *Globe*
– Montreal: *Herald* 48
– Quebec: *Morning Chronicle* 136
– Sandwich: *Canada Advertiser* xliv; *Canada Oak* (*see* Oak); *Canadian Emigrant* 3, 4, 5, 31n; *Maple Leaf* xlviii, xlix; *Oak* 114, 141; *Western Express* xxxiii, 66; *Western Herald* xxviii, xxx, xxxi, 51, 52; *Western Mercury* 136n; *Western Standard* 93
– Toronto: *Church* xxxviii, 92, 93; *Colonist* l, 157; *Commercial Herald* 41; *Globe* xxxvii, liv, 103n, 174; *Independent* 106; *Leader* 176; *United Empire* xliv; *Weekly Messenger* lii
– Windsor: *Herald* xlviii, lv, 136, 140, 142, 146, 176, 179
Newton, Mariane ('Munny') 106n, 195
Newton, William Edward 172n
New York City xlvii
Niagara and Detroit Rivers Rail Road Company. *See* Railroads
Niagara Falls xlvii, 7
Niagara River: bridge liii, 164
Ninth Military District. *See* Militia
Norfolk County 12, 96
Normanby, Lord xxix, 38n
North American Hotel, Toronto. *See* Inns
North Star 178, 179
Northwest Territory 205
Northwood, Mr 120
Notman, William 194n
Nottle 185

224 INDEX

Oak. See Newspapers: Sandwich
O'Connell, Daniel 78
O'Connor, John 179n
Ogdensburg 126
O'Hara, Colonel 78n
Ohio 156, 185
Ontario House, Toronto. See Inns
O'Reilly, Miles 140n
Orford Township 146
Orr's Hotel, Montreal. See Inns
Osgoode Hall, Toronto 112
Ottawa lvi, 151, 203
Ottawa Tavern, Montreal. See Inns
Ouellette, Antoine 83n
Owen Sound 167, 168, 173
Oxford County xxxix, xl, 97, 100

Palmerston, Lord 158n
Panmure, Lord 136n, 137, 157, 158
Papineau, D.B. 88n, 90n
Parent, Joseph B. 132n
Paris, Ontario 164
Parent, Fabien. See Inns: Sandwich
Parent's inn, Sandwich. See Inns
Park, Thomas 114n
Park Farm (The) xxiin, xxv, xxviii, xl, xlv, xlvi, xlvii, xlviii, li, liv, 14, 39, 43, 58, 66, 73, 81, 91, 128, 160, 204
Parry, 'Cam' 105n, 121
Partridge, Maria 82
Partridge, Thomas 103
Partridge, William 134, 179
Partridge, Mrs William 82n, 172.
  See also Woods, Mrs
Patrick, Alfred 40
Patriot War: schooner Anne incident xxv, xxvi, 17–19, 37, 136; battle of Fighting Island xxv, 20; battle of Pelee Island xxv, xxvi, xxvii, 20, 23, 24, 136; battle of Windsor xxvi–xxviii, xxx, xxxi, lvii, 26, 27, 28–31, 36, 39, 50, 136
Patronage l, lii, liv, 155–6, 160, 170, 172
Patton, J. 173n
Pelee Island, battle of. See Patriot War
Pennefather, Richard Theodore 146
Penner, John 73n, 90, 97
Perry, Ebenezer 150n
Petite Cote 3, 4, 17, 42, 134
Philpotts, George A. 166n
Phipps, Constantine Henry.
  See Normanby, Lord
Phipps, James C. 187n, 189, 190, 193
Pickering 15
Pigeon Bay pier l, 150
Pilgrim, Henry 176n, 201, 203
Pim, David 176n, 177, 179, 181, 184, 185, 187, 190, 191, 203

Pim, Mrs David 194
Pinder, Captain 12, 13
Pishké, Jacob 184, 185
Pitt, William 95, 182, 183
Planet. See Newspapers: Chatham
Plough Inn, Cheltenham, England. See Inns
Ploughboy liii, 168, 173, 174, 177, 178, 180, 182, 184
Point Pelee Island. See Patriot War: battle of Pelee Island
Pointe aux Pins, Algoma District 203
Pointe aux Pins, Kent County. See Rondeau
Pollard, Catherine 189n, 201
Pollard, J. 200
Pontiac, Michigan 19
Port Sarnia xxiv, 79. See also Sarnia
Porteous 183n
Powell 183
Price, James Hervey 68n, 101, 204, 205
Primrose family 170n, 171, 172
Prince, Albert xix, xxii, xlv, xlvi, xlvii, xlix, lvi, 10, 11, 43, 72, 73, 82, 113, 129, 131, 132, 135, 138, 141, 158, 160, 161, 163, 165, 166, 174, 180, 185, 186, 206
Prince, Mrs Albert ('Lizzy') 160, 186.
  See also Hunt, Mrs Frank
Prince, Arabella Delancy xx, xxii, 42, 54, 55, 59, 82, 112, 137, 140, 141, 150, 154, 162, 195
Prince, Charles xx, xxii, 8, 131, 141, 160, 173, 179, 200
Prince, George xxii, xxiii
Prince, Henry xxi, xxii, 8, 11, 74, 82, 105, 106, 131, 140, 141, 154, 160, 165, 182, 200
Prince, John
– Personal: birth xix; parentage xix; law practice at Westerham xix; marriage xix; career at Cheltenham xix–xx; joins Gray's Inn xx; supports Whig candidates (1832) xx; abandons father xx–xxi; removal to Sandwich xxi; suicidal tendency xxi, xxiii, xxxvi, xlv, 82, 84, 106, 141; father's death xxii, establishes Park Farm xxii; clash with Charles Eliot xxii–xxiii, 3–6; death of son, George xxiii; fear of assassination xxviii, 38; death of mother xxix, xxx; libel action against Henry Grant xxxi, 51–4; seeks Western District judgeship xxxii, 56–7; disillusionment with Canada xxxii, xxxviii, xlii, xlv, lv, 40, 42, 55, 112, 126, 137, 143, 192, 197, 199, 203, 204; marital difficulties xxxv, xxxvi, xxxix, xliv, xlv, xlvii, 74, 81–2, 129, 141, 177; volunteers for military service xxxv, xlv, xlvi, li, lvi, 78, 130–1, 133, 135, 136–7, 137–8, 157, 158, 182; reclusiveness xxxvii, xl, 89, 130, 200, 205; enmity towards Arthur Rankin xxxvii, xliii,

xlvi, xlix, liv, lvi, 117, 139; libel action against Arthur Rankin xxxvii, 73; libel action against George Brown xxxix-xl, 99-100, 103; ejects W.L. Mackenzie from Parliamentary Library xl, 102n; racial attitude xliii, l, 117, 156-7, 180; seeks Lambton County judgeship xlv, xlvi; applies to be superintendent general of Indian affairs xlv, xlvi; seeks Algoma District judgeship xlvi, xlvii, li, lii, liii, 136, 160, 161, 165, 166, 167; intemperance xlvii, 96, 103, 137; seeks Huron County judgeship xlvii, 137; seeks command of Ninth Military District xlvii, 138-9; seeks solicitorship of Great Western Railway xlvii, 140; removal to Sault Ste Marie liv; builds Belle Vue Lodge lv-lvi; desires to practise law in the United States lvii, 185; seeks vice chancellorship of Upper Canada lvii, 189-90; seeks York County judgeship lvii, 201-2; seeks judgeship of the Northwest Territories lvii, 204-5; rejects Welland County judgeship lvii, 204; reconciliation with Arthur Rankin lvii, 199; amputates his thumb 193-4; death of son, Septimus lvii, 201; marooned lvii-lviiin; autobiography lviii, 193, 194; last days lix-lx, 206

– Legal: barrister xx, xxvi, 25; magistrate (1833) xxii; chairman of Western District Court of Quarter Sessions xxiv, xxviii, 14, 31, 38-9; boundary line commissioner xxix; queen's counsel xxxi, xlii, xlv, xlvi, xlviii, 51, 54-5, 60, 61, 71, 108-9, 113, 143, 188, 201; magistrate (1843) xxxi, 54; commissioner of bankruptcy for the Western District xxxii, xxxiii, xxxiv, 59, 66, 69; solicitor for Southern Railroad li; judge of Algoma District liv, 170-1, 172, 176, 202; chairman of Algoma Court of Quarter Sessions lv, 176, 186, 187, 199; judge of Algoma Surrogate Court lv

– Business: milling xxi, xxii; brewing xxii, xxiv, 5, 23, 41, 44, 107, 179; ferrying xxii, xxiv; railroading xxiii, xxiv, xxxv, xxxvi, xxxvii, xlii, xliii, xlv, xlvi, xlvii, xlix, l, li, liii, liv, 7, 10, 11, 14, 23, 75, 76-8, 80-1, 88, 89, 95-6, 97, 101, 111, 118, 120-1, 140, 148, 155, 164, 166, 169; mining xxxv, xxxvi, xxxvii, xxxviii, xxxix, 73, 75, 76, 78, 80, 81, 82, 86, 88-9, 90, 94, 100, 139; fishing xxxviii, 90-2, 134; canal building xlix, 148, 151

– Political: election as member of Legislative Assembly: (1836) xxiii, 6-7; (1841) xxix-xxx, 41-5; (1844) xxxiii, 58-67; (1847) xxxviii, 91; (1851) xlii-xliii, 115-17 major interests: clergy reserves xxiii, xxviii, xxix, xliii, 9-10, 12-13, 37, 40, 130; union of Upper and Lower Canada xxviii, xxix, xxx, xl, 37, 40, 101; rebellion losses xxviii, xxix, xl-xli, xliii, 37, 40, 70, 100, 101-2; Independence Manifesto xli, xlii, 106-8, 109, 115, 120
other interests: (1836) xxiii, 8; (1837) xxiv, 10-15; (1839) xxviii, 35; (1840) 40; (1841) xxxi, 49, 50; (1842) xxxii; (1843) xxxii, 56; (1844) 68; (1845) xxxiv, 69-71; (1846) 79; (1847) xxxviii, 84, 88; (1851) 113; (1852) xliii, 118, 120; (1853) xliv, 122-3, 124, 125-6; (1857) l, li, 155; (1858) li, 160-3; (1859) liii, liv, 166-7; (1860) liv, 170, 171, 172; (1866) 197, 198
allegiances: supports Reformers: (1836) xxiii-xxiv, (1852) xliii; supports Tories: (1837) xxiv, (1848) xxxviii, 93, (1854) xlv; independent: (1841) xxx, (1844) xxxiv, 61, 68, (1847) xxxviii, (1848) 92, (1849) xl, (1853) xliv
election as member of the Legislative Council: (1856) xlviii, xlix, 144-50
summarizes his legislative contribution lv, 175

– Military: tenders resignation of command of 3rd Regt. of Essex Militia xxxi, xxxiii, 53, 83. *See also* Patriot War; Prince, John – Personal (volunteers for military service)

– Speeches: (1836) 8-9, 9, 10; (1841) 46-7, 47, 48, 49; (1843) 57-8; (1845) 70-1; (1846) 74-5, 75, 80; (1847) 85-6, 87, 87-8, 88; (1849) 99-100, 101-2; (1850) 109-10, 110-11, 111; (1851) 112, 113, 114; (1852) 119, 120; (1853) 124, 125-6, 126-7, 128; (1856) 148-9; (1857) 151, 151-2, 153, 154, 155, 156-7; (1858) 163; (1859) 165-6, 166

Prince, Mary xxix, xxx
Prince, Mary Ann xix, xxii, xxvi, xxxv, xxxvi, xxxix, xlv, xlvi, xlvii, 11n, 12, 13, 19, 23, 25, 40, 74, 76, 78, 81, 82, 97, 98, 129, 130, 131, 140, 141, 162, 170, 177, 179
Prince, Octavius xxx, lv, 91n, 143, 150, 151, 154, 160, 162, 174, 176, 177, 180, 186, 201
Prince, Richard xix, xx
Prince, Septimus Rudyerd xxvi, lv, lvii, 23, 162, 170, 176, 180, 182, 183, 184, 185, 186, 187, 189, 190, 191, 194, 200, 201
Prince, William Stratton xix, xxii, 8, 10, 11, 16, 23, 55, 59, 68, 69, 112, 113, 130, 131, 138, 157, 160, 162, 165, 174, 177, 206n
Prince Albert tavern, Sandwich. *See* Inns
Prince and Kell xx
Prince Edward County 70
Prince, Kell and Howard xx
Prince's wharf xxii, xxiv, 5

Prisons. *See* Courthouses and Jails
Probett, Stephen T. 72n
Provincial union. *See* Union of Upper and Lower Canada

Quebec l, 56, 80, 86, 89, 103, 119, 120, 124, 126, 131, 173, 189, 190
Quebec *Morning Chronicle. See* Newspapers

Raglan, Lord 130
Railroads: Niagara and Detroit Rivers xxiii, xxiv, xxxv, xxxvii, xlii, xliii, xlvii, liii, 14, 23, 77, 80, 81, 88, 89, 95, 148, 164, 169; London and Gore xxiv, 77; Great Western xxiv, xxxv, xxxvii, xlii, xliii, xlv, xlvi, xlvii, 10, 11, 77, 80, 81, 89. 95, 97, 114, 118, 120, 121, 129, 134, 140, 164; Southern xlvii, xlix, l, li, 139, 140, 148, 175; Grand Trunk l, 154, 155; Toronto and Guelph 120; Guelph and Sarnia 121; Buffalo and Brantford 164
Rankin, Arthur xxxvii, xli, xlii, xliii, xliv, xlvi, xlvii, xlviii, xlix, li, lii, liii, liv, lv, lvi, lvii, 73n, 90, 105, 106, 115, 117, 132, 135, 136, 139, 140, 141, 144, 145, 146, 147, 148, 150, 154, 158, 159, 161, 164, 169, 178, 179, 199
Rankin, George Cameron 178n
Rasco's Hotel, Montreal. *See* Inns
Read, Mr 43
Rebellion losses xxviii, xxix, xl, xliii, 37, 40, 70, 100n, 101–2
Rees, Dr William 160n
Reid 185
Reid, Colonel (or Major) H. 26n
Reiffenstein, George C. 205n
Rendt 39
Restaurants. *See* Inns
Reynolds, Colonel 17
Richardson, Charles 12n, 13
Richardson, Henry 27n
Richmond. *See* Ferry (The); Windsor
Richmond,– 185
Ridgetown 132
Ridout, G.P. 120n
Ritchie, Rev. William xxxvi, 66n, 74, 81
Ritchie, Mrs William 74
Robinson 60
Robinson, James. *See* Inns: Gosfield Township
Robinson, Sir John Beverley 23n, 125
Robinson's tavern, Gosfield Township. *See* Inns
Roblin, John Philip 70n, 71
Rogers, Mr 164
Rolph, Dr John 9n, 10, 133
Ronalds, Henry 148n, 150, 168
Rondeau xxxviii, xliv, xlvi, l, 84n, 90, 91, 133–4, 151; lighthouse 151

Rose, Sir John 193n
Ross, Mr 176
Ross, John xlv, 128n, 130, 160
Rossin House, Toronto. *See* Inns
Rouge River 82
Rowan, Sir William 104n
Rowsell, Henry 200n
Royal Hotel, Hamilton. *See* Inns
Rudyerd, Charlotte ('Tatty') 26n. *See also* Boulton, Mrs Henry
Rudyerd, Henry xxvi, 8n, 11, 12, 13, 14, 15, 16, 17, 20, 21, 25, 26, 27, 32, 39, 43, 82
Rudyerd, Mrs Henry 11, 12, 13, 25, 26, 82
Russell, Dr 105n
Russell, Lord John 137n, 138, 161
Ryan, Thomas 181n, 200

Sabbath Desecration (Profanation) bill xxxiv, xliii, 69–70, 71–2, 119
St Clair, Chatham and Rondeau Ship Canal xlix
St George's Church, Bloomsbury, London, England xix
St John's Church, Sandwich xxiin
St Joseph's Island lviiin
St Lawrence Hall, Toronto 112
St Lawrence River 99, 107, 152
St Mary's River 128, 174, 190
St Maurice 151
St Thomas 14, 164
Sallow, Rev. E. *See* Sallows
Sallows (Sallow, Sellers, Sollars, Sollers), Rev. E. 184n, 186
Salt Island lviiin
Salter, A.P. 170n, 174, 176
Sanderson, Robert 179
Sandwich, town of (now part of Windsor) xxi, xxii, xxiii, xxvi, xxxi, xxxii, xxxiv, xxxv, xxxvi, xl, xliii, xlvii, xlix, l, liii, 6, 7, 14, 16, 17, 20, 23, 25, 26, 27, 28, 29, 31, 32, 33, 34, 35, 41, 45, 50, 51, 54, 55, 56, 59, 60, 62, 66, 72, 76, 93, 104, 114, 116, 127, 128, 132, 143, 144, 147, 149, 150, 152, 154, 156, 158, 164, 174
Sandwich *Canada Advertiser. See* Newspapers
Sandwich *Canada Oak. See* Newspapers – Sandwich: *Oak*
Sandwich *Canadian Emigrant. See* Newspapers
Sandwich East Township liv, 172
Sandwich Ferry. *See* Ferry (The); Windsor
Sandwich *Maple Leaf. See* Newspapers
Sandwich *Oak. See* Newspapers
Sandwich Township xli, xlvii, xlix, liv, 172
Sandwich West Township liv, 172
Sandwich *Western Express. See* Newspapers
Sandwich *Western Herald. See* Newspapers

Sandwich *Western Mercury*. *See* Newspapers
Sandwich *Western Standard*. *See* Newspapers
'Sandy' (workman) 191
'Sarah' (orphan). *See* Arroll, Sarah
Sarnia 10. *See also* Port Sarnia
Sault Ste Marie, Michigan 128
Sault Ste Marie, Ontario xlv, xlvi, xlvii, li, liii, liv, lv, lvi, lvii, lix, 122, 123, 128, 162, 167, 170, 171, 173, 178, 180, 184, 186, 200, 206
Savage, Colonel John 175n, 176, 193
Sayer, Toussaint 198n
Schweiger, Lieut. Augustus William 51
Scott, William 140n, 150
Seat of Government xxxii, xl, l, lii, liii, 56, 58, 103, 109, 152–3, 163
Seaton, Lord xxi, xxiv, 131n
Secret ballot bill xxxi, 49
Seels, John Henry. *See* Inns: Toronto
Seels's saloon, Toronto. *See* Inns
Seigneuries xli, 111
Sellers, Rev. E. *See* Sallows
Sericole (?) 172
Shade, Absalom 36n
Shaffer, Jacob 42n. *See also* Inns: Maidstone Township
Shaffer's inn, Maidstone Township. *See* Inns
Sharpe, Mr 199n, 200
Sheldon, John B. 146n
Sheldon, William. *See* Inns – Morpeth: Morpeth
Sheldon's (Morpeth Hotel), Morpeth. *See* Inns
Shelwich Court, Gloucestershire, England xix
Sherwood, Henry xl, 22n, 25, 70, 71, 77, 101n, 103
Siborne, William 193n
Sicotte, L.V. 130n
Simcoe County xxviii, xxx
Simons, Rev. 192
Simpson, Miss 204
Simpson, John 155n
Simpson, Wemyss (Wymess) M. 176n, 180, 182, 184, 186, 193
Simpson, Mrs Wemyss (Wymess) 185n, 204
Sivewright, Mrs 160n
Sloan, John 58n, 60
Small, James 49n
Smart, W. Lynn 166n
Smith (Collingwood) 186
Smith, Mr (Sault Ste Marie) 128n
Smith, Charles 37n
Smith, Edwin. *See* Inns: Toronto
Smith, Sir Frank 205n
Smith, Henry 58n, 125
Smith, James 88n
Smith's restaurant, Toronto. *See* Inns
Smooth Rock 59

Sollars, Rev. E. *See* Sallows
Sollers, Rev. E. *See* Sallows
Sombra Township 131
Somerset, Fitzroy James Henry. *See* Raglan, Lord
Somerville, Mr 97
Southern Railroad. *See* Railroads
Sparke, Captain 28n
Spectator. *See* Newspapers: Hamilton
Spencer, 'Captain' Patrick xxv, 21n
Splitlog, Thomas xxv
Springwells 17, 26
Stamborough, Orin and Russell. *See* Stanborough
Stanborough (Stamborough), Orin and Russell xxii, 4
Stanley, Lord. *See* Derby, Earl of
Steele, Mrs 90n. *See also* Inns: Montreal
Steele's inn, Montreal. *See* Inns
Steers, Thomas 66n
Stephenson, Robert 128n
Stevens, Enoch 146n
Stevens, Susan xxii, 116n
Stevens, William xxii, xxviii, xlvii
Stewart, Andrew 22
Stone House. *See* Ermatinger House
Storks, H.R. 158
Stovel(s) 186
Straford, Joseph Cooper xix
Straford and Prince xix, xx
Stratton, William 178n, 200
Stratton, Mrs William 178n, 179
Stuart 161
Stuart, Sir James 40n, 88, 124
Stuart, Reuben 182
Sugar Island, Detroit River 18, 29
Sugar Island, St Mary's River lviiin, 179, 187, 192
Sutherland, 'General' Thomas J. xxv, 19, 21, 22
Sutton 181n, 183
Sutton, A.B. 138n
Swinburne, Mr and Mrs 194n
Swords' Hotel, Toronto. *See* Inns
Sydenham, Lord xxix, xxx, 39n, 46, 48, 51, 201
Sydenham River. *See* Bear Creek

Taché, Lieut. Colonel Sir E.P. 86n, 167n, 183
Taché, Joseph Charles 130, 191
Tait, Mr 179
Talbot, Captain 44n
Talbot Street 146n
Taverns. *See* Inns
Taylor, John Fennings lviii, 193n, 194
Teakle, George 23n, 116. *See also* Inns: Sandwich

Teakle, Thomas 23n
Teakle's Inn, Sandwich. *See* Inns
Temperance. *See* Liquor legislation
Temple, Henry John. *See* Palmerston, Lord
Têtu, Sabin 165n
Têtu's Hotel, Montreal. *See* Inns
Tewkesbury, England xx
Thalberg, Sigismond 154n
Thames River: bridge xxiv, 14, 84;
  lighthouse xxiv; canal 148
Thebo, Solomon T. 196n
Theller, Edward Alexander 21n, 22
Thesales, Ellen. *See* Mosalis
Thessalon Point 192
Thessalon River 192
Thomson, Charles Poulett.
  See Sydenham, Lord
Thunder Bay xxxvii
Tofflemire, James 22
Tor Bay, England xxi
Toronto xxiii, xxviii, l, liv, lix, lx, 7, 21, 22,
  25, 26, 35, 40, 66, 92, 101, 103, 129, 179,
  186, 200, 201
Toronto and Guelph Railroad. *See* Railroads
Toronto *Church*. *See* Newspapers
Toronto *Colonist*. *See* Newspapers
Toronto *Commercial Herald*. *See* Newspapers
Toronto *Globe*. *See* Newspapers
Toronto *Independent*. *See* Newspapers
Toronto *Leader*. *See* Newspapers
Toronto *United Empire*. *See* Newspapers
Toronto *Weekly Messenger*. *See* Newspapers
Torrance, Mr 120
Towers, T.A.P. 194n
Townsend, Colonel or Major H.D.
  See Townshend
Townsend, W.A. xxxvi, 82
Townshend (Townshend), Colonel or Major
  H.D. 20n
Tracey, Mr xx
Trafalgar Township 195
Trollope, Anthony 186n
Tufnell, Henry 161n
Turner, Mr 187, 201, 203
Turner, Robert John xxxi
Two Creeks 148

Union of Upper and Lower Canada xxviii,
  xxix, xxx, xl, 37, 40, 46-7, 101
United 17
United Empire. *See* Newspapers: Toronto
Upper Canada, Bank of. *See* Banks
Upper Canada Rebellion. *See* Patriot War

Van Diemen's Land 19n, 68
Vankoughnet, P.M.M.S. lii, 154n, 160, 164,
  165n, 167, 170, 172, 173

Vansittart, John George xxxix, xl, 97n, 99,
  100, 101
Vidal, Captain Richard E. 76n
Vidal, William P. 54n, 73, 112, 131, 161, 169
Villaire, Vitus 66n
Vincent House, Cheltenham, England xx
Virgil 188n
Vollans, George 158n

Waddell, John 132n, 160
Wade, William 179n
Wadworth, Senator 164
Walker 182
Walker, Hiram 179n
Wall, Joseph 38n
Ward, Major 81
Ward, Joseph 140, 141n
Washington, D.C. 109, 167
Waterloo (modern Fort Erie). *See* 'Bertie'
Waterloo County 121
Watson, Mr 63
Watson, John G. 52
Weaver, John 170n, 179
Webb, John 183n
Webb, Thomas xxi, 113n
Weekes's Hotel, Hamilton. *See* Inns
Weekly Messenger. *See* Newspapers: Toronto
Welland County 95, 204
Weller, Henry 169n, 182
Wellesley, Arthur. *See* Wellington, Duke of
Wellington, Duke of 127
Wellington Hotel, Toronto. *See* Inns
Wellington Mines. *See* Mines
Westaway, William 16n
Westerham, Kent, England xix
Western District xxi, xxii, xxiii, xxiv, xxvi,
  xxvii, xxviii, xxix, xxxi, xxxii, xxxiv,
  xxxvi, xxxvii, 10, 22, 27, 37, 41, 56, 67, 74,
  84, 88, 110, 111; division bill xxxvii, 84, 88
Western District Agricultural Society 14n
Western District Bank. *See* Banks
Western District Council 79
Western District Court. *See* Courts
Western District Court of Quarter Sessions.
  See Courts
Western District Grammar School 116n
Western Division xlviii, l, lii, liv, lv, 144,
  146, 150, 151-2, 159, 173
Western Express. *See* Newspapers: Sandwich
Western Globe. *See* Newspapers – Toronto:
  Globe
Western Herald. *See* Newspapers: Sandwich
Western Hotel, Sandwich. *See* Inns
Western Mercury. *See* Newspapers: Sandwich
Western Standard. *See* Newspapers: Sandwich
Westminster Hall, London, England xix, 201
Westwood, Gloucestershire, England xx, xxii

Wetherall, Sir G.A. 131n
White 121
Whitefish River lvii, 192
Whiting, W.L. 16n
Wiggins, Charles xxxi, 52n, 53, 54
Wigle, Leonard. *See* Inns: Mersea Township
Wigle, Wendel 143n, 178
Wigle's inn, Mersea Township. *See* Inns
Wildfowl. *See* Game legislation
Wilkinson, James H. 126n
Wilkinson, John A. xxxi, l, 14n, 53, 154, 156
'William' (orphan). *See* Arroll, William
Williams, Francis 178n
Wilson, John 103n, 143
Wilson, Joseph xlvi, 128n, 167, 174, 175, 176, 181, 182, 183, 184, 186, 187, 196, 199, 200, 201
Wilson, Thomas 47n, 48, 49
Windmills (The) 30n, 34
Windsor xxii, xxviii, xliii, l, 26, 27, 28, 30, 32, 34, 35, 36, 50, 72, 91, 97, 117, 118, 128, 129, 131, 134, 137, 139, 144, 145, 146, 147, 149, 156, 162, 164, 179. *See also* Ferry (The)

Windsor, battle of. *See* Patriot War
Windsor Castle, Windsor. *See* Inns
Windsor *Herald. See* Newspapers
Wingfield, Rowland xxxiii, 58n, 59, 60, 62, 63, 64, 65, 66
Wood, William R. xxviii, xli, 32
Woodbridge, Thomas l, 117n, 139, 145, 154, 156
Woods, Mr 66
Woods, Mrs 59. *See also* Partridge, Mrs William
Woods, Joseph 52n, 70, 84
Woods, R.S. 90n, 111
Woodstock 169
Wray, Judge 191n
Wright 39
Wright, Miss 65
Wright, Thomas 37n, 173

Yonge Street lii, 37
Young, Colonel Plomer 86n

Zimmerman, Samuel 132n

www.ingramcontent.com/pod-product-compliance
Lightning Source LLC
Chambersburg PA
CBHW051401070526
44584CB00023B/3241